Reading/Writing Canada

Short Fiction and Nonfiction

Half of the author's royalties will be donated to PEN Canada,
a centre of International PEN, the worldwide literary and
human rights association.

$\mathcal{PEN}$ CANADA
for FREEDOM of EXPRESSION
www.pencanada.ca

W. W. Norton & Company, Inc., also publishes

THE NORTON INTRODUCTION TO LITERATURE

THE NORTON INTRODUCTION TO LITERATURE, SHORTER

THE NORTON READER

THE NORTON READER, SHORTER

THE SEAGULL READER: LITERATURE

Reading/Writing Canada

Short Fiction and Nonfiction

Judith Maclean Miller

Renison College, University of Waterloo

W. W. Norton & Company • New York • London

W. W. Norton & Company has been independent since its founding in 1923, when William Warder Norton and Mary D. Herter Norton first published lectures delivered at the People's Institute, the adult education division of New York City's Cooper Union. The Nortons soon expanded their program beyond the Institute, publishing books by celebrated academics from America and abroad. By mid-century, the two major pillars of Norton's publishing program—trade books and college texts—were firmly established. In the 1950s, the Norton family transferred control of the company to its employees, and today—with a staff of four hundred and a comparable number of trade, college, and professional titles published each year—W. W. Norton & Company stands as the largest and oldest publishing house owned wholly by its employees.

Since this page cannot legibly accommodate all the copyright notices, pages 435–38 constitute an extension of the copyright page.

The text of this book is composed in Adobe Garamond
with the display set in Bernhard Modern.
Designed by Chris Welch.
Composition by PennSet, Inc.
Manufacturing by R. R. Donnelley & Sons—Haddon, Bloomsburg Division.
Production Manager: Benjamin Paul Reynolds.

ISBN 0-393-92595-1

W. W. Norton & Company, Inc., 500 Fifth Avenue, New York, N.Y. 10110–0017
www.wwnorton.com
W. W. Norton & Company Ltd., Castle House, 75/76 Wells Street,
London W1T 3QT

1 2 3 4 5 6 7 8 9 0

*

Contents

*

Acknowledgments

I am deeply grateful to each writer whose work is represented here, for all the pleasures of their courage, skill and imagination. Would that there were room for as many more.

I thank Peter Simon, Robert Bellinger and Evan Leatherwood of Norton for their good humour, patience and guidance; Julia Bauer at University of Waterloo's Graphic Services for her careful attention to detail; Lois Clifford in Renison College's library for her quiet good sense and efficiency; Marcia Stentz of the Manitoba Archives for her thoroughness and inventive problem-solving; Kirsten Smith of the Parliamentary Bureau of CanWest Global for her curiosity and her helpfulness.

Katharine Ings copy-edited this book with careful, insightful attention. Thank, you, Katharine.

I have learned a great deal from all the many University of Waterloo students in my Canadian literature courses, with their questions and insightful answers. Thank you all for many wonderful hours.

My colleagues at Renison College have always provided generous companionship, for which I am deeply grateful.

And Hugh Miller has been there through it all. *Mille fois merci!*

Asking the Questions

This collection gathers short nonfiction and short fiction from the wide store of Canadian literature. Reading these pieces alone is one kind of pleasure. Sharing them with other people is another. Sometimes, though, it is hard to know how to share a reading experience.

Asking questions is a good place to start. As we ask questions like the following, we take the first steps toward sharing a reading, in conversation or in writing. They become a kind of toolbox.

What is nonfiction?

Nonfiction has much in common with letter-writing. It could be said that all nonfiction is a kind of "open letter" written by someone to someone about something. Nonfiction conveys information or asks a question or records an impression—all the many reasons we might write a letter. There are degrees of public and private in nonfiction just as there are in letters. A strong speaking voice, usually close to the writer's voice, remains a constant. A nonfiction writer is always aware of audience.

What kinds of nonfiction do people write?

Nonfiction has many **sub-genres**. Only some are represented in this collection.

The **essay** is the most familiar. An essay presents information for a reader to share, simply because it is interesting, or in an attempt to persuade, instruct, or entertain.

A writer may create a highly **personal essay**, close to a journal or diary entry, about a personal experience. The essay may be written to record the experience, or perhaps to reflect on it, in a search for wider understanding or personal growth.

Occasionally, parts of a **journal** are shared directly or adapted to be more public.

Letters can become significant documents. A letter written to a single individual or to a group of people may reach a much wider readership—either as a historical document or a piece of biography.

Travel writing is a popular kind of nonfiction, where a writer shares an experience of an unusual, perhaps exotic—or new—place.

The **documentary** account is closely related to the traveler's. The writer urges the reader to trust this telling because it comes from first-hand experience ("I was there and I saw it"). Documentary writing has been especially influential in Canadian literature. It runs through fiction and nonfiction as a strong impulse. The first Europeans in Canada wrote to send reports to supporting religious or business organizations, and the habit has endured.

Creative nonfiction has become a useful term for nonfiction which relies heavily on the methods of fiction—characterization or dialogue, for instance—rather than straight expository prose.

Autobiography comes from three Greek words: self, life, writing. It is written about one's own life, trying to make sense of it all, maybe, or offering hard-won wisdom. More recently, the term **life-writing** has been used to include fiction as well as nonfiction accounts of a life, usually the writer's, distinct from **biography**, which is written about someone else.

What do I watch for when I read nonfiction?

In nonfiction, **voice** is a key issue. The tones of a voice may seek to persuade, inform, or entertain. It may have some other purpose—declared or masked. The voice may be personal, even intimate, or it may be carefully objective. Its effects may be to draw a reader in close or to create a distance. It may be persuasive—or not. The voice may be a clue to **audience**: expert or novice, specific or general, familiar or strange.

The **theme** or main idea of nonfiction is often its central purpose. Such themes may be immediately apparent, or they may emerge later, even at the end. Less central but related **sub-themes** can support or challenge the central one.

The **language** of any piece of writing is always engaging, whether it is formal, informal, slang, neutral, ardent, lyrical, objective, subjective, familiar, or exotic. Often, several different kinds of language work together, shifting moods, tones and the way a reader reacts. Language also determines what kind of audience can receive the work.

What is fiction?

In **fiction**, a narrator, or storyteller—not the author—presents characters, setting and events, allowing a reader to watch what happens. The reader, then, is somewhat distant, a kind of observer watching from outside the story. Often, a writer creates a story for personal satisfaction or pleasure. The reader is not as central for the fiction writer as for the nonfiction writer.

What kinds of short fiction do people write?

Like nonfiction, **short fiction** also has a number of **subgenres**. Shifts and changes in forms of story-telling have been linked to periods of time, even of literary history. In all the cultures which make up Canada, oral forms like **teaching tales**, **folktales**, **sagas**, **fables**, **anecdotes** and **trickster tales** are ways of sharing stories. Ghosts of these forms appear in this collection. Contemporary writers often use these forms, adapted to suit their purposes. Each is described in the Glossary at the back of this book.

The **short story** is fairly new, as literary forms go, created in the nineteenth century by writers like Guy de Maupassant in France, Anton Chekhov in Russia, Edgar Allan Poe in the United States. It is carefully constructed, less wandering or diffuse than the older oral forms and intended for reading. Often it was used to make a moral point or teach a lesson, a leftover from the earlier oral traditions. Nineteenth-century **Victorians** were sometimes suspicious about fiction. It was, after all, not true. In nineteenth-century Canada, poetry was highly regarded. Its tones and rhythms often influence stories.

In the first half of the twentieth century, **Modernist** writers rejected the idea that a story needed a moral message. They valued art for art's sake, so they experimented with ways to create a story. The traditional pattern of an introduction followed by a rising action toward some end or conclusion gave way to other forms, often based in the new science of psychiatry. These Modernist writers were interested in character, in people's actions and in their ways of expression. The reader may be invited to be a psychiatrist, watching and trying to understand people's motivations and actions.

The later part of the twentieth century in Canada saw a move away from Modernist realism into forms that writers prefer to call **short fiction**. These **Postmodernist** writers extended the experiments of the earlier twentieth century. The reader of these works is invited to be an artist, to help create the story. The ancient oral influences come into these stories, as do nonfiction strategies from letters, journals, documentaries, and newspaper reports.

What do I watch for in short fiction?

When we read short fiction, the first thing we notice is the **narrator**, the story-teller who relates a story. In nonfiction, the author speaks directly to the reader. In fiction, the speaking voice is that of a created character. Usually, it has little connection to the author. The narrator's position in relation to the story is highly significant. The narrator may be **limited** by experience or by being too close to characters or events. A narrator may be **omniscient**, all-knowing, distanced from what is being told and not involved in it. For all sorts of reasons, the person telling a story may be **reliable** or **unreliable**. **Characters** in a story always intrigue us because they carry the action, the ideas. They are not always set up in opposition to one another, but their interactions matter. We learn about them through what they say, what they do, what they value, and through what other characters, including the narrator, think about them. When, as readers, we describe a character, we construct a **character sketch**. Attention to how the character is presented becomes an examination of processes of **characterization**.

The **setting** of a story may be real or imagined. It may be crucially important—or backdrop. It might be urban or rural, small town or wilderness, domestic or public, interior or exterior. Often settings are multifaceted, multiple, playing off one another. Setting also relates to time. A story may be set close to the author's own era. It may be set back—or forward. Time may be very important to a story, or incidental.

The way time moves in a story is closely connected to **plot**, which is the arrangement of events. A sequence of events may appear in chronological order, in flashback or in flash forward. They may seem deliberately connected, or unconnected, until a reader builds the links. Describing the **plot line** is a way of tracing these patterns and their effects.

The **theme** or **sub-themes**, the main and supporting ideas which make their way into fiction are not as directly presented as those of nonfiction. They tend to arise indirectly, as they connect to a character, the narrator or a reader.

In fiction, the **language** is likely to be close to the way a narrator and the characters think and speak. It is a way of creating character. Degrees of formality and informality affect our ideas about a character's background, age, time period, gender, class, race, and attitudes. The language of descriptive passages sets tone or mood. Quickly exchanged dialogue can make a story move fast. Long reflective passages may slow it down. Writers use language deliberately to create effects—or just for the sheer pleasure of working with it, pushing to see what it can do, what the echoes of a word are.

Structure, or the overall shape of short fiction, has been highlighted as writers move away from expected or usual forms of storywriting. A story may follow a logic which is associative, rather than move in a straight line from event to event or idea to idea. A piece of a story may be put in as it occurs to a narrator—or a character—or the author. It may look like collage, where some thread holds together fragments which might at first seem unrelated. Carefully placed gaps or spaces invite a reader in.

Imagery is a term which is used to speak about the pictures created within a reader's mind. Usually it contributes to the setting or the atmosphere, the mood of a story.

Symbolism in a story presents concrete objects which take on abstract significance, contributing to character development or to the themes and ideas of a story.

Do I know who the author is?

Ideas about the author have shifted over time. We used to see authors as powerful—the authority—who provided us with a piece of writing (a text). We thought about it, maybe argued with it, but we received it. More recently, we have shifted to the word "writer." Now, we are invited to engage in a piece of writing, to help create it. The reader and the writer meet in a text, in its open spaces. We co-create it.

The time when someone was writing may influence the structure of a piece and its assumptions. The place where a writer works may offer hints about whether a piece is real or imaginary. An early work may be different from something written later in a career.

For a number of different reasons, then, it can be worth knowing something about a writer. Some people insist that is not necessary, even irrelevant. All that matters, they say, is the work.

Do I know who the reader is?

Roles for the reader have shifted. The word comes from an old Anglo-Saxon word, meaning "to be advised." A reader picked up a text to be taught, to learn something. Now, as readers, we expect to work, to engage in making the text—nonfiction or fiction. Our learning is active rather than passive.

We also understand that all readers *experience* a text differently. There is no single reader or reading. That multiplicity is one of the reasons why sharing a text can be so satisfying. The writer sets up certain parameters but then each reader, with unique life and reading history, moves differently within those limits.

It can be a good idea to think hard about who we are as readers, what values and attitudes affect our reading, what we bring with us to a text. Our cultural assumptions, for instance, hover close to us and may be hard to see.

The moods we bring to a text can radically affect the way we experience it. There are rewards in setting these aside, even for the short time of reading. Respect for a work matters. It may take effort to "suspend disbelief," to enter into the place a writer has created and to appreciate it on its own terms, but it is worth the effort, like learning to listen to a new friend.

The term **implied reader** is often used to refer to the reader a writer might have had in mind. The characteristics of such a reader show up in the assumptions made about what a reader knows.

The **actual reader** may be close to an implied reader—or dramatically different. Language, values, assumptions, and experiences change over time.

That space between the actual reader and the implied reader can be fun to explore.

xvi   ✱   I N T R O D U C T I O N

Do I know when this piece was written?

Like forms, styles of writing change from one era to another. There are fashions in the way words are used.

In Canada, eighteenth-century **neo-Classical** writers valued clear observation and recording, usually writing nonfiction. They were discovering science and wanted their readers to use it too.

The **Romantic** writers of the first part of the nineteenth century thought writing should include emotional response and wanted to share that response with a reader. They saw the natural world as linked to the divine or the mystical. They wrote to celebrate it, valuing imagination and poetic expression.

Victorian writers of the second half of the nineteenth century wanted literature to teach a lesson, to have a message. They were reticent about sexuality, in particular. The new and rising middle class turned to literature as a way of understanding their world. Writers were concerned about rising industrialization and urbanization. They wanted to alert their readers to those dangers, through fiction as well as nonfiction.

Modernists writing in the first half of the twentieth century did not want to make moral points. They wanted to create art and to present life realistically. They wanted readers to share the pleasure of a piece of created art. They were delighted by the possibilities of psychological and sexual exploration. Paperback books and rising literacy made their work accessible.

Postmodernist writers from about 1965 on in Canada became especially aware of language and how it works. They see themselves as challenging prevailing orthodoxies of all kinds: in literature, public life, and private life. They often draw on forms from previous times and from the multiple cultures of Canada.

These attitudes tend to linger from century to century, affecting our expectations as readers. Often readers are more at home with one style and set of attitudes than another. Taste is personal. In the end, it is powerful—and valid—in determining our reactions. Appreciation for a writer's methods, though, does not have to depend on taste.

Do I know where this piece was written?

The place where we sit affects what we see. Some effort to look at a text through the writer's perspective can be informative as well as respectful. It is one of the imaginative acts expected of a reader.

A writer's or reader's stance can be useful to think about too. We all have positions on issues we confront and people we meet—in life or in writing. They affect the way we experience a text.

Do I know why this piece was written?

Questions about why are tricky—and they are ones we love to ask. They usually lead into speculative answers. Why did this character make this decision? Why did this writer make this argument? Anyone asking such questions has to study a text closely for answers. Otherwise, attention can move away from the work being considered. (And sometimes that's okay too.)

We can, usefully, look hard at why we respond as we do to a piece of writing. Our reactions can be manipulated by voices and by arrangements of details or events. We can respond the way we do because of something in ourselves. The intersection between a writer's strategies and a reader's biography can be complex.

Notice that these questions, asked in relation to nonfiction or fiction, are grounded in the five linked questions which have guided journalists for years. They are a good place to start reading and writing.

What kind of piece am I reading? What elements construct it? What is their effect? What themes come into it?

Who is speaking in this piece? Who are the characters? Who is the writer? Who is the implied reader? Who am I, reading?

When was this text written? When do the events within it happen? Are they close to the writer's time—or mine? When am I reading it?

Where was this piece written? Where is it set? Has the writer ever been there? Have I? Where am I?

Why is it constructed the way it is? Why do the characters act as they do? Why do I react the way I do to this text?

Factual information to help answer these questions is included in each headnote in this collection.

Nonfiction and fiction braid in and out around one another. It can be hard to tell where one begins and the other ends. An author may play with the differences or may use the strategies of one within the other. An early documentary writer may tell a story to illustrate a point. A contemporary fiction writer may use a documentary piece within a story to explore where truth is to be found.

Similarly, reading and writing are wonderfully intricate. Place itself can become a kind of writer, tattooing a person with mosquito bites or frost bite, blistering a foot on a city street. In turn, a person reading a place or a situation writes it, as nonfiction, fiction, or a blend of the two. Then the reader picks up what has been written, participates in the creation of the text, and goes on to write the experience of reading it, for yet another reader.

*

Approaching the Stories

Each piece in this collection stands alone. They have been arranged alphabetically by author, to make them easy to locate. Placing the pieces in various relations to one another, though, can make for lively comparative reading. Following are some suggested groupings of authors, whose stories play off one another, creating possibilities for quiet reflection, discussion, or written responses. Readers will likely see other possible groupings.

By topic

As readers, we engage with the ideas or topics (themes) of a piece of writing, meeting new concepts, having old assumptions challenged, acquiring insight into how authors and characters see issues, values, or human interaction. These are presented directly in nonfiction, less directly in fiction. Some themes recur across the works of these authors. There are also many more, and often one reader will notice or enjoy a theme which is of less interest to another reader.

Art: David Arnason, Norman Bethune, Ann Copeland, Northrop Frye, Linda Hutcheon, Eric McCormack, Rohinton Mistry, Alice Munro, P. K. Page, Catherine Richards, Leon Rooke, Jane Urquhart, Aritha van Herk.

Coming of Age: Michael Crummey, George Elliott, Jacques Ferron, Alistair MacLeod, Diane Schoemperlen, David Thompson.

Cross-Cultural Encounter: Shauna Singh Baldwin, Sharon Butala, Roch Carrier, Ann Copeland, Thomas Haliburton, Claire Harris,

Hudson's Bay Company Officials, Linda Hutcheon, J. B. Joe, Thomas King, Rohinton Mistry, Duncan Campbell Scott, David Suzuki, David Thompson, Aritha van Herk.

The Environment: Sandra Birdsell, Sharon Butala, Roch Carrier, George Elliott, Harold Horwood, Isabel Huggan, J. B. Joe, P. K. Page, Catherine Richards, Duncan Campbell Scott, David Suzuki, David Thompson.

Family: Ernest Buckler, Morley Callaghan, Roch Carrier, Wayson Choy, Michael Crummey, George Elliott, Jacques Ferron, Timothy Findley, Hugh Garner, Anne Hébert, Harold Horwood, Alistair MacLeod, Eric McCormack, Rohinton Mistry, P. K. Page, Diane Schoemperlen, Duncan Campbell Scott, W. D. Valgardson.

Immigration: Shauna Singh Baldwin, Sharon Butala, Anne Hébert, Hudson's Bay Company Officials, Eric McCormack (*Introduction*), Rohinton Mistry, Susanna Moodie, David Suzuki, David Thompson, W. D. Valgardson.

Stereotypes: David Arnason, Shauna Singh Baldwin, Ernest Buckler, Ann Copeland, George Elliott, Stephen Leacock, Rohinton Mistry, Susanna Moodie, Alice Munro, P. K. Page, Leon Rooke, W. D. Valgardson.

Travel: Norman Bethune, Ann Copeland, Hugh Garner, Thomas Haliburton, Claire Harris, Hudson's Bay Company Officials, Isabel Huggan, J. B. Joe, Eric McCormack (*Introduction*), Susanna Moodie, Diane Schoemperlen, David Thompson, Jane Urquhart, W. D. Valgardson, Aritha van Herk.

Women and Men: David Arnason, Morley Callaghan, Michael Crummey, Jacques Ferron, Timothy Findley, Claire Harris, Annabel Lyon, Alice Munro, Sinclair Ross, Stephen Scobie, Jane Urquhart, W. D. Valgardson.

Work: David Arnason, Shauna Singh Baldwin, Norman Bethune, Ernest Buckler, Sharon Butala, Roch Carrier, Ann Copeland, Timothy Findley, Northrop Frye, Thomas Haliburton, Hudson's Bay Company Officials, Linda Hutcheon, Alice Munro, Sinclair Ross, David Thompson.

By place

A sampling of pieces by the place where they are set provides a sense of some Canadian geography, physical as well as social and cultural. The dynamic between writer and place is intriguing. Writers may create places, but it is just as true that places create writers.

Atlantic Canada (Newfoundland, Prince Edward Island, Nova Scotia, New Brunswick): Ernest Buckler, Ann Copeland, Michael Crummey, Thomas Haliburton, Harold Horwood, Alistair MacLeod.

Quebec: Shauna Singh Baldwin, Roch Carrier, Jacques Ferron, Anne Hébert, Stephen Leacock, Duncan Campbell Scott.

Ontario: Morley Callaghan, George Elliott, Timothy Findley, Thomas King, Rohinton Mistry, Alice Munro.

The Prairie Provinces (Manitoba, Saskatchewan, Alberta): Sandra Birdsell, Sharon Butala, Catherine Edwards, Sinclair Ross, Diane Schoemperlen, W. D. Valgardson.

British Columbia: Wayson Choy, J. B. Joe, Annabel Lyon, P. K. Page, Stephen Scobie, Audrey Thomas.

The North: Anne Hébert, David Thompson, Aritha van Herk.

By genre

Traditional boundaries between fiction and nonfiction blur in this collection. Some authors use the techniques usually associated with fiction to enliven nonfiction. Fiction writers include pieces from newspapers or journals. The following, though, could be labeled "nonfiction."

Hudson's Bay Company Officials, *Letter to Captain Leonard Edgcombe*, 1688
David Thompson, *I Join the Hudson's Bay Company*, 1789
Susanna Moodie, *A Journey to the Woods*, 1852
Norman Bethune, *An Apology for Not Writing Letters*, 1937
Northrop Frye, *Canadian and Colonial Painting*, 1940
Anne Hébert, *Québec: the Proud Province*, 1967
Stephen Scobie, *Intertext, Love, Post, West*, 1990
Linda Hutcheon, *The Particular Meets the Universal*, 1990
Aritha van Herk, *In Visible Ink*, 1991
Harold Horwood, *Of Frogs and Fairy Godmothers*, 1996
Wayson Choy, *The Ten Thousand Things*, 1997
Sandra Birdsell, *Why I Live Where I Live*, 1997
David Suzuki, *Introduction to* The Sacred Balance, 1997
Sharon Butala, *The Spirit of the Land*, 2000
Catherine Richards, *Excitable Tissues and Virtual Worlds: Art, Science and Technology*, 2002
Isabel Huggan, *Snow*, 2003

By elements of a text

Characterization

The people in any piece of writing always interest us. How do we get to know them? After all, we meet them only as letters, words and sentences on a page. Some authors, like the following, have a particular interest in character. Their ways of presenting people cover a wide range.

Ernest Buckler, Wayson Choy, Ann Copeland, Timothy Findley, Hugh Garner, Claire Harris, Thomas King, Annabel Lyon, Alistair MacLeod, Rohinton Mistry, Alice Munro, Sinclair Ross, W. D. Valgardson.

Narrator

Some writers draw attention to the storyteller, playing with degrees of objectivity or distance. Others create shadowy, almost invisible narrators.

David Arnason, Shauna Singh Baldwin, Wayson Choy, Thomas Haliburton, Linda Kenyon, Stephen Leacock, Alistair MacLeod, Eric McCormack, Alice Munro, Audrey Thomas.

Voice

Who speaks—and how? The following authors have all given particular attention to these questions.

Margaret Atwood, Ernest Buckler, Ann Copeland, Claire Harris, Anne Hébert, Linda Hutcheon, J. B. Joe, Linda Kenyon, Thomas King, Eric McCormack, Duncan Campbell Scott, Aritha van Herk.

Setting

The following writers have all seen physical setting as more than a casual backdrop. In one way or another, setting affects the people, the ideas, or the events.

Domestic: Shauna Singh Baldwin, Michael Crummey, Timothy Findley, Alistair MacLeod, Alice Munro, P. K. Page, Sinclair Ross, W. D. Valgardson.

Urban: Shauna Singh Baldwin, Sandra Birdsell, Morley Callaghan, Wayson Choy, Ann Copeland, Timothy Findley, Hugh Garner, J. B. Joe, Stephen Leacock, Annabel Lyon, Rohinton Mistry.

Small Town: Michael Crummey, George Elliott, Eric McCormack, Alice Munro, Duncan Campbell Scott.

Rural: Ernest Buckler, Sharon Butala, Roch Carrier, Ann Copeland, Thomas Haliburton, Harold Horwood, Sinclair Ross.

Wilderness: Michael Crummey, J. B. Joe, Susanna Moodie, David Thompson, Aritha van Herk.

Plot/Structure

We think of plot as almost essential to a story; we expect to follow a series of events to see where they are leading, but plot has become a complex issue in contemporary fiction. Many of the writers in this book resist the idea of simple plot lines. Insight, into people or ideas, may matter more than events—or argument—so the overall shape of a piece of writing interests most authors, in fiction or in nonfiction.

The text may follow a timeline, in chronological order. It might move around in time. There could be any of several organizing principles, such as logic, association, collage, allusion, image patterns, intertextuality, or fragments of story-telling and reporting. Each of the following authors has developed a somewhat unorthodox structure.

Margaret Atwood, Timothy Findley, Claire Harris, Anne Hébert, Linda Hutcheon, Linda Kenyon, Thomas King, Eric McCormack, Alice Munro, P. K. Page, Diane Schoemperlen, Stephen Scobie, Audrey Thomas, Aritha van Herk.

Oral Story-Telling Influences

Although the short story is a relatively new form in literature, having been born in the nineteenth century, telling stories is as old as humanity. Influences from those ways of telling stories before they were written down make their way into contemporary writing. Some authors enjoy highlighting those influences.

Margaret Atwood, Roch Carrier, Wayson Choy, Jacques Ferron, Claire Harris, J. B. Joe, Thomas King, Alistair MacLeod, Diane Schoemperlen, Aritha van Herk.

Reading/Writing Canada

Short Fiction and Nonfiction

David Arnason
b. 1940

*Arnason always says that he was born in Gimli, Manitoba, in
what was once the Republic of New Iceland, established in 1875.
After doctoral studies at the University of New Brunswick, Arnason
returned to Winnipeg to teach Canadian literature and creative
writing at the University of Manitoba, where he chaired the Department of English for several years.*

*In difficult circumstances in nineteenth-century northern Mani-
toba, Arnason's ancestors valued books and stories. Even though
they often could not read, they would wrap a single book carefully
in cloth or build a special shelf for it. Arnason shares that respect for
the written word as something set apart from the everyday. In his
own books of fiction, non-fiction, and poetry, such as* The Happiest Man in the World and Other Stories *(1989),* The Pagan Wall
(1992), and The Demon Lover *(2002), Arnason resists realism. A
story, he believes, has its own ways of being, its own logic.*

In this story from The Circus Performers Bar *(1984), the
narrator is a writer. He may or may not be like Arnason, but he
certainly seems to share Arnason's ideas about fiction. The narrator
puts together a piece which is as much about writing as it is about
three characters and a river. He offers the reader a choice: to be a
writer like him, or to be one of the characters in the story.*

*Watch how I do this, he invites. Help me do it. Sometimes he
scolds. If you think these characters are not realistic, he says, then
"why don't you just run out to the grocery store and buy a loaf of
bread? The grocer will give you your change without even looking
at you. That's what happens in real life, and if that's what you're after, why are you reading a book?" This piece quickly becomes parody, making fun of the usual "romance novel" or the usual manual
about how to write a story. It also laughs at the writer himself.
Sometimes, he drinks too much. He is not too bad at beginnings,
but he is not very good at endings. Underneath all this, he writes a
love story.*

A Girl's Story

You've wondered what it would be like to be a character in a story, to sort of slip out of your ordinary self and into some other character. Well, I'm offering you the opportunity. I've been trying to think of a heroine for this story, and frankly, it hasn't been going too well. A writer's life isn't easy, especially if, like me, he's got a tendency sometimes to drink a little bit too much. Yesterday, I went for a beer with Dennis and Ken (they're real-life friends of mine) and we stayed a little longer than we should have. Then I came home and quickly mixed a drink and starting drinking it so my wife would think the liquor on my breath came from the drink I was drinking and not from the drinks I had had earlier. I wasn't going to tell her about those drinks. Anyway, Wayne dropped over in the evening and I had some more drinks, and this morning my head isn't working very well.

To be absolutely frank about it, I always have trouble getting characters, even when I'm stone cold sober. I can think of plots; plots are really easy. If you can't think of one, you just pick up a book, and sure enough, there's a plot. You just move a few things around and nobody knows you stole the idea. Characters are the problem. It doesn't matter how good the plot is if your characters are dull. You can steal characters too, and put them into different plots. I've done that. I stole Eustacia Vye from Hardy and gave her another name. The problem was that she turned out a lot sulkier than I remembered and the plot I put her in was a light comedy. Now nobody wants to publish the story. I'm still sending it out, though. If you send a story to enough publishers, no matter how bad it is, somebody will ultimately publish it.

For this story I need a beautiful girl. You probably don't think you're beautiful enough, but I can fix that. I can do all kinds of re-touching once I've got the basic material, and if I miss anything, Karl (he's my editor) will find it. So I'm going to make you fairly tall, about five-foot eight and a quarter in your stocking feet. I'm going to give you long blonde hair because long blonde hair is sexy and virtuous. Black hair can be sexy too, but it doesn't go with virtue. I've got to deal with a whole literary tradition where black-haired women are basically evil. If I were feeling better I might be able to do it in an ironic way, then black hair would be okay, but I don't think I'm up to it this morning. If you're going to use irony, then you've got to be really careful about tone. I could make you a redhead, but redheads have a way of turning out pixie-ish, and that would wreck my plot.

So you've got long blonde hair and you're this tall slender girl with amazingly blue eyes. Your face is narrow and your nose is straight and thin. I could have turned up the nose a little, but that would have made you cute, and I really need a beautiful girl. I'm going to put a tiny black mole on your cheek. It's traditional. If you want your character to be really beautiful there has to be some minor defect.

Now, I'm going to sit you on the bank of a river. I'm not much for setting. I've read so many things where you get great long descriptions of the setting, and mostly it's just boring. When my last book came out, one of the reviewers suggested that the reason I don't do settings is that I'm not very good at them. That's just silly. I'm writing a different kind of story, not that old realist stuff. If you think I can't do setting, just watch.

There's a curl in the river just below the old dam where the water seems to make a broad sweep. That flatness is deceptive, though. Under the innocent sheen of the mirroring surface, the current is treacherous. The water swirls, stabs, takes sharp angles and dangerous vectors. The trees that lean from the bank shimmer with the multi-hued greenness of elm, oak, maple and aspen. The leaves turn in the gentle breeze, showing their paler green undersides. The undergrowth, too, is thick and green, hiding the poison ivy, the poison sumac and the thorns. On a patch of grass that slopes gently to the water, the only clear part of the bank on that side of the river, a girl sits, a girl with long blonde hair. She has slipped a ring from her finger and seems to be holding it toward the light.

You see? I could do a lot more of that, but you wouldn't like it. I slipped a lot of details in there and provided all those hints about strange and dangerous things under the surface. That's called foreshadowing. I put in the ring at the end there so that you'd wonder what was going to happen. That's to create suspense. You're supposed to ask yourself what the ring means. Obviously it has something to do with love, rings always do, and since she's taken it off, obviously something has gone wrong in the love relationship. Now I just have to hold off answering that question for as long as I can, and I've got my story. I've got a friend who's also a writer who says never tell the buggers anything until they absolutely have to know.

I'm going to have trouble with the feminists about this story. I can see that already. I've got that river that's calm on the surface and boiling underneath, and I've got those trees that are gentle and beautiful with poisonous and dangerous undergrowth. Obviously, the girl is going to be like that, calm on the surface but passionate underneath. The feminists are going to say that I'm perpetuating stereotypes, that by giving the impression the girl is full of hidden passion I'm encouraging rapists. That's crazy. I'm just using a literary convention. Most of the world's great books are about the conflict between reason and passion. If you take that away, what's left to write about?

So I've got you sitting on the riverbank, twirling your ring. I forgot the birds. The trees are full of singing birds. There are meadowlarks and vireos and even Blackburnian warblers. I know a lot about birds but I'm not going to put in too many. You've got to be careful not to overdo things. In a minute I'm going to enter your mind and reveal what you're thinking. I'm going to do this in the third person. Using the first person is sometimes more effective, but I'm always afraid to do a female character in the first person. It seems wrong to me, like putting on a woman's dress.

Your name is Linda. I had to be careful not to give you a biblical name like Judith or Rachel. I don't want any symbolism in this story. Symbolism makes me sick, especially biblical symbolism. You always end up with some crazy moral argument that you don't believe and none of the readers believe. Then you lose control of your characters, because they've got to be like the biblical characters. You've got this terrific episode you'd like to use, but you can't because Rachel or Judith or whoever wouldn't do it. I think of stories with a lot of symbolism in them as sticky.

Here goes.

Linda held the ring up toward the light. The diamond flashed rainbow colours. It was a small diamond, and Linda reflected that it was probably a perfect symbol of her relationship with Gregg.

Everything Gregg did was on a small scale. He was careful with his money and just as careful with his emotions. In one week they would have a small wedding and then move into a small apartment. She supposed that she ought to be happy. Gregg was very handsome, and she did love him. Why did it seem that she was walking into a trap?

That sounds kind of distant, but it's supposed to be distant. I'm using indirect quotation because the reader has just met Linda, and we don't want to get too intimate right away. Besides, I've got to get a lot of explaining done quickly, and if you can do it with the character's thoughts, then that's best.

Linda twirled the ring again, then with a suddenness that surprised her, she stood up and threw it into the river. She was immediately struck by a feeling of panic. For a moment she almost decided to dive into the river to try to recover it. Then, suddenly, she felt free. It was now impossible to marry Gregg. He would not forgive her for throwing the ring away. Gregg would say he'd had enough of her theatrics for one lifetime. He always accused her of being a romantic. She'd never had the courage to admit that he was correct, and that she intended to continue being a romantic. She was sitting alone by the river in a long blue dress because it was a romantic pose. Anyway, she thought a little wryly, you're only likely to find romance if you look for it in romantic places and dress for the occasion.

Suddenly, she heard a rustling in the bush, the sound of someone coming down the narrow path from the road above.

I had to do that, you see. I'd used up all the potential in the relationship with Gregg, and the plot would have started to flag if I hadn't introduced a new character. The man who is coming down the path is tall and athletic with wavy brown hair. He has dark brown eyes that crinkle when he smiles, and he looks kind. His skin is tanned, as if he spends a lot of time outdoors, and he moves gracefully. He is smoking a pipe. I don't want to give too many details. I'm not absolutely sure what features women find attractive in men these days, but what I've described seems safe enough. I got all of it from stories written by women, and I assume they must know. I could give him a chiselled jaw, but that's about as far as I'll go.

The man stepped into the clearing. He carried an old-fashioned wicker fishing creel and a telescoped fishing rod. Linda remained sitting on the grass, her blue dress spread out around her. The man noticed her and apologized.

"I'm sorry, I always come here to fish on Saturday afternoons and I've never encountered anyone here before." His voice was low with something of an amused tone in it.

"Don't worry," Linda replied. "I'll only be here for a little while. Go ahead and fish. I won't make any noise." In some way she couldn't understand, the man looked familiar to her. She felt she knew him. She thought she might have seen him on television or in a movie, but of course she knew that movie and television stars do not spend every Saturday afternoon fishing on the banks of small, muddy rivers.

"You can make all the noise you want," he told her. "The fish in this river are almost entirely deaf. Besides, I don't care if I catch any. I only like the act of fishing. If I catch them, then I have to take them home and clean them. Then I've got to cook them and eat them. I don't even like fish that much, and the fish you catch here all taste of mud."

"Why do you bother fishing then?" Linda asked him. "Why don't you just come and sit on the riverbank?"

"It's not that easy," he told her. "A beautiful girl in a blue dress may go and sit on a riverbank any time she wants. But a man can only sit on a riverbank if he has a very good reason. Because I fish, I am a man with a hobby. After a hard week of work, I deserve some relaxation. But if I just came and sat on the riverbank, I would be a romantic fool. People would make fun of me. They would think I was irresponsible, and before long I would be a failure." As he spoke, he attached a lure to his line, untelescoped his fishing pole and cast his line into the water.

You may object that this would not have happened in real life, that the conversation would have been awkward, that Linda would have been a bit frightened by the man. Well, why don't you just run out to the grocery store and buy a bottle of milk and a loaf of bread? The grocer will give you your change without even looking at you. That's what happens in real life, and if that's what you're after, why are you reading a book?

I'm sorry. I shouldn't have got upset. But it's not easy you know.

Dialogue is about the hardest stuff to write. You've got all those "he saids" and "she saids" and "he replieds." And you've got to remember the quotation marks and whether the comma is inside or outside the quotation marks. Sometimes you can leave out the "he saids" and the "she saids" but then the reader gets confused and can't figure out who's talking. Hemingway is bad for that. Sometimes you can read an entire chapter without figuring out who is on what side.

Anyway, something must have been in the air that afternoon. Linda felt free and open.

Did I mention that it was warm and the sun was shining?

She chattered away, telling the stranger all about her life, what she had done when she was a little girl, the time her dad had taken the whole family to Hawaii and she got such a bad sunburn that she was peeling in February, how she was a better water skier than Gregg and how mad he got when she beat him at tennis. The man, whose name was Michael (you can use biblical names for men as long as you avoid Joshua or Isaac), told her he was a doctor, but had always wanted to be a cowboy. He told her about the time he skinned his knee when he fell off his bicycle and had to spend two weeks in the hospital because of infection. In short, they did what people who are falling in love always do. They unfolded their brightest and happiest memories and gave them to each other as gifts.

Then Michael took a bottle of wine and a Klik[1] sandwich out of his wicker creel and invited Linda to join him in a picnic. He had forgotten his corkscrew and he had to push the cork down into the bottle with his filletting knife. They drank wine and laughed and spat out little pieces of cork. Michael reeled in his line, and to his amazement discovered a diamond ring on his hook. Linda didn't dare tell him where the ring had come from. Then Michael took Linda's hand, and slipped the ring onto her finger. In a comic-solemn voice, he asked her to marry him. With the same kind of comic solemnity, she agreed. Then they kissed, a first gentle kiss with their lips barely brushing and without touching each other.

Now I've got to bring this to some kind of ending. You think writers know how stories end before they write them, but that's not

---

1. Cheap pressed, tinned meat.

true. We're wracked with confusion and guilt about how things are going to end. And just as you're playing the role of Linda in this story, Michael is my alter ego. He even looks a little like me and he smokes the same kind of pipe. We all want this to end happily. If I were going to be realistic about this, I suppose I'd have to let them make love. Then, shaken with guilt and horror, Linda would go back and marry Gregg, and the doctor would go back to his practice. But I'm not going to do that. In the story from which I stole the plot, Michael turned out not to be a doctor at all, but a returned soldier who had always been in love with Linda. She recognized him as they kissed, because they had kissed as children, and even though they had grown up and changed, she recognized the flavour of wintergreen on his breath. That's no good. It brings in too many unexplained facts at the last minute.

I'm going to end it right here at the moment of the kiss. You can do what you want with the rest of it, except you can't make him a returned soldier, and you can't have them make love then separate forever. I've eliminated those options. In fact, I think I'll eliminate all options. This is where the story ends, at the moment of the kiss. It goes on and on forever while cities burn, nations rise and fall, galaxies are born and die, and the universe snuffs out the stars one by one. It goes on, the story, the brush of a kiss.

1984

Margaret Atwood
b. 1939

Atwood may be Canada's best-known writer, at home and throughout the English-speaking world, which has awarded her its highest literary honors. Her writing is rooted in both her experience and her imagining. It rings true. Among her best-selling, prize-winning novels are The Edible Woman *(1969),* The Handmaid's Tale *(1985),* Alias Grace *(1996), and* The Blind Assassin *(The Booker Prize, 2000).*

Atwood has no patience with the idea that people—especially women—especially her—are supposed to be "nice" or motherly or nurturing. Her writing often has sharp edges, challenging assumptions, turning them upside down, inside out, to see what is really going on in there. A strong sense of social justice runs through all her work. Atwood's social satires can be very funny, particularly when they are read aloud. They have strong performance elements of voice, situation, imagery, and unexpected attitudes. They rest on cleverness and wit. No one could call them sweet or sentimental.

*One evening, beginning a prestigious university lecture, Atwood opened her briefcase in a dignified way, apparently to take out her notes. Slowly and deliberately, she pulled out a long, dark, very masculine sock and held it up to look at it. "Oh," she said. "I wonder how **that** got in there."*

Atwood knows exactly how to understate or sidestep, so that her audience or reader is left filling in the gap. Every person at the lecture smiled, chuckled, frowned, or laughed, constructing a fantasy to explain that sock. Her writing works the same way—invites the reader in to create a piece which will be highly literary, rich with intertextuality: with references to literary works, fairy tales, and current fashions. And she undercuts these references in mischievous, enlightening ways. Novels, poems, short stories, lectures, essays— Atwood writes them all, blurring genres. Sometimes, as with the following piece from Good Bones *(1992), it can be hard to decide which is which.*

Unpopular Gals

1.

Everyone gets a turn, and now it's mine. Or so they used to tell us in kindergarten. It's not really true. Some get more turns than others, and I've never had a turn, not one! I hardly know how to say *I*, or *mine;* I've been *she, her, that one,* for so long.

I haven't even been given a name; I was always just *the ugly sister;* put the stress on *ugly.* The one the other mothers looked at, then looked away from and shook their heads gently. Their voices lowered or ceased altogether when I came into the room, in my pretty dresses, my face leaden and scowling. They tried to think of something to say that would redeem the situation—*Well, she's certainly strong*—but they knew it was useless. So did I.

You think I didn't hate their pity, their forced kindness? And knowing that no matter what I did, how virtuous I was, or hardworking, I would never be beautiful. Not like her, the one who merely had to sit there to be adored. You wonder why I stabbed the blue eyes of my dolls with pins and pulled their hair out until they were bald? Life isn't fair. Why should I be?

As for the prince, you think I didn't love him? I loved him more than she did; I loved him more than anything. Enough to cut off my foot. Enough to murder. Of course I disguised myself in heavy veils, to take her place at the altar. Of course I threw her out the window and pulled the sheets up over my head and pretended to be her. Who wouldn't, in my position?

But all my love ever came to was a bad end. Red-hot shoes, barrels studded with nails. That's what it feels like, unrequited love.

She had a baby, too. I was never allowed.

Everything you've ever wanted, I wanted also.

2.

A libel action, that's what I'm thinking. Put an end to this nonsense. Just because I'm old and live alone and can't see very well, they accuse me of all sorts of things. Cooking and eating children, well, can you imagine? What a fantasy, and even if I did eat just a few, whose fault was it? Those children were left in the forest by their parents, who fully intended them to die. Waste not, want not, has always been my motto.

Anyway, the way I see it, they were an offering. I used to be given grown-ups, men and women both, stuffed full of seasonal goodies and handed over to me at seed-time and harvest. The symbolism was a little crude perhaps, and the events themselves were—some might say—lacking in taste, but folks' hearts were in the right place. In return, I made things germinate and grow and swell and ripen.

Then I got hidden away, stuck into the attic, shrunken and parched and covered up in fusty draperies. Hell, I used to have breasts! Not just two of them. Lots. Ever wonder why a third tit was the crucial test, once, for women like me? Or why I'm so often shown with a garden? A wonderful garden, in which mouth-watering things grow. Mulberries. Magic cabbages. Rapunzel, whatever that is. And all those pregnant women trying to clamber over the wall, by the light of the moon, to munch up my fecundity, without giving anything in return. Theft, you'd call it, if you were at all open-minded.

That was never the rule in the old days. Life was a gift then, not something to be stolen. It was my gift. By earth and sea I bestowed it, and the people gave me thanks.

3.

It's true, there are never any evil stepfathers. Only a bunch of lily-livered widowers, who let me get away with murder vis-à-vis their daughters. Where are they when I'm making those girls drudge in the kitchen, or sending them out into the blizzard in their paper dresses? Working late at the office. Passing the buck. Men! But if you think they knew nothing about it, you're crazy.

The thing about those good daughters is, they're so *good.* Obedient and passive. Snivelling, I might add. No get-up-and-go. What would become of them if it weren't for me? Nothing, that's what. All they'd ever do is the housework, which seems to feature largely in these stories. They'd marry some peasant, have seventeen kids, and get "A dutiful wife" engraved on their tombstones, if any. Big deal.

I stir things up, I get things moving. "Go play in the traffic," I say to them. "Put on this paper dress and look for strawberries in the snow." It's perverse, but it works. All they have to do is smile and say hello and do a little more housework, for some gnomes or nice ladies or whatever, and bingo, they get the king's son and the palace, and no more dishpan hands.

Whereas all I get is the blame.

God knows all about it. No Devil, no Fall, no Redemption. Grade Two arithmetic.

You can wipe your feet on me, twist my motives around all you like, you can dump millstones on my head and drown me in the river, but you can't get me out of the story. I'm the plot, babe, and don't ever forget it.

1992

Shauna Singh Baldwin
b. 1962

Born in Montreal, Baldwin grew up in India and completed an M.B.A. at Marquette University, Milwaukee, Wisconsin. She is an information technology consultant whose clients are banks and data processing companies. From 1991 to 1994, she was an independent radio producer. Her novel, What the Body Remembers *(1999), won the Saturday Night-CBC Literary Prize.* The Tiger Claw *(2004) was short-listed for the prestigious Giller Prize.*

Baldwin is interested in what happens when people move from one culture to another, learning other customs, religions, value systems. Even well-meaning people can make thoughtless comments. There are not many interpreters as one culture meets another. Time, she suggests, may be the best teacher.

This story comes from English Lessons and Other Stories *(1996). Some of the citizens of Montreal in 1962 are wary of a man with long hair, in a turban. They have no idea what it means to observe the Sikh religious tradition. Cut your hair, they suggest, and you can have the job. The turbans become the central image of the story, showing us how much this man and his wife love each other. She realizes that their lives will change in this strange northern city, but that might not be altogether bad.*

Twenty-seven years later, in 1989, the Commissioner of the Royal Canadian Mounted Police recommended that the turban be permitted as part of the uniform of the red-clad Mounties. It was, even then, a controversial suggestion, but it was approved by the federal government in 1990. The young woman telling this story was right. Canadians did eventually learn to respect what it means to wear a turban.

Montreal 1962

In the dark at night you came close and your voice was a whisper though there is no one here to wake. "They said I could have the job if I take off my turban[1] and cut my hair short." You did not have to say it. I saw it in your face as you took off your new coat and galoshes. I heard their voices in my head as I looked at the small white envelopes I have left in the drawer, each full of one more day's precious dollars—the last of your savings and my dowry. Mentally, I converted dollars to rupees and thought how many people in India each envelope could feed for a month.

This was not how they described emigrating to Canada. I still remember them saying to you, "You're a well-qualified man. We need professional people." And they talked about freedom and opportunity for those lucky enough to already speak English. No one said then, "You must be reborn white-skinned—and clean-shaven to show it—to survive." Just a few months ago, they called us exotic new Canadians, new blood to build a new country.

Today I took one of my wedding saris to the neighbourhood dry-cleaner and a woman with no eyebrows held it like a dishrag as she asked me, "Is it a bed sheet?"

"No," I said.

"Curtains?"

"No."

I took the silk back to our basement apartment, tied my hair in a tight bun, washed the heavy folds in the metal bathtub, and hung it, gold threads glinting, on a drip-dry hanger.

When I had finished, I spread a bed sheet on the floor of the bathroom, filled my arms with the turbans you'd worn last week and knelt there surrounded by the empty soft hollows of scarlet, navy, earth brown, copper, saffron, mauve and bright parrot green. As I waited for the bathtub to fill with warm soapy water, I unravelled each turban, each precise spiral you had wound round your head, and soon the room was full of soft streams of muslin that had protected your long black hair.

---

1. Fabric holding the long hair which is one of the 5 essential symbols of Sikhism, a religion founded in sixteenth-century India.

I placed each turban in turn on the bubbly surface and watched them grow dark and heavy, sinking slowly, softly into the warmth. When there were no more left beside me, I leaned close and reached in, working each one in a rhythm bone-deep, as my mother and hers must have done before me, that their men might face the world proud. I drained the tub and new colours swelled—deep red, dark black mud, rust, orange, soft purple and jade green.

I filled the enamel sink with clean water and starch and lifted them as someday I will lift children. When the milky bowl had fed them, my hands massaged them free of alien red-blue water. I placed them carefully in a basin and took them out into our grey two rooms to dry.

I placed a chair by the window and climbed on it to tie the four corners of each turban length to the heavy curtain rod. Each one in turn, I drew out three yards till it was folded completely in two. I grasped it firmly at its sides and swung my hands inward. The turban furrowed before me. I arced my hands outward and it became a canopy. Again inward, again outward, hands close, hands apart, as though I was back in Delhi on a flat roof under a hot sun or perhaps near a green field of wheat stretching far to the banks of the Beas.

As the water left the turbans, I began to see the room through muslin screens. The pallid walls, the radiator you try every day to turn up hotter for me, the small windows, unnaturally high. When the turbans were lighter, I set the dining chairs with their halfmoon backs in a row in the middle of the well-worn carpet and I draped the turbans over their tops the way Gidda dancers wear their chunnis[2] pinned tight in the centre parting of their hair. Then I sat on the carpet before them, willing them: dance for me—dance for us. The chairs stood as stiff and wooden as ignorant Canadians, though I know maple is softer than chinar.[3]

Soon the bands of cloth regained all their colour, filling the room with sheer lightness. Their splendour arched upwards, insisting upon notice, refusing the drabness, refusing obscurity, wielding the curtain rod like the strut of a defending champion.

---

2. Veils. Gidda dancers: traditional Indian folk-dancers.

3. The "royal tree" in Kashmir.

From the windows over my head came the sounds of a Montreal afternoon, and the sure step of purposeful feet on the sidewalk. Somewhere on a street named in English where the workers speak joual[4] I imagined your turban making its way in the crowds, bringing you home to me.

Once again I climbed on a chair and I let your turbans loose. One by one, I held them to me, folding in their defiance, hushing their unruly indignation, gentling them into temporary submission. Finally, I faced them as they sat before me.

Then I chose my favourite, the red one you wear less and less, and I took it to the bedroom. I unfurled the gauzy scarlet on our bed and it seemed as though I'd poured a pool of the sainted blood of all the Sikh martyrs there. So I took a corner and tied it to the doorknob just as you do in the mornings instead of waking me to help you. I took the diagonal corner to the very far end of the room just as you do, and rolled the scarlet inward as best I could within the cramped four walls. I had to untie it from the doorknob again to roll the other half, as I used to every day for my father, then my brother and now you. Soon the scarlet rope lay ready.

I placed it before the mirror and began to tie it as a Sardar[5] would, one end clenched between my teeth to anchor it, arms raised to sweep it up to the forehead down to the nape of the neck, around again, this time higher. I wound it swiftly, deftly, till it jutted haughtily forward, adding four inches to my stature. Only when I had pinned the free end to the peak did I let the end clenched between my teeth fall. I took the saliva-darkened cord, pulled it back where my hair bun rested low, and tucked it up over the turban, just as you do.

In the mirror I saw my father as he must have looked as a boy, my teenage brother as I remember him, you as you face Canada, myself as I need to be.

The face beneath the jaunty turban began to smile.

I raised my hands to my turban's roundness, eased it from my head and brought it before me, setting it down lightly before the mirror. It asked nothing now but that I be worthy of it.

---

4. Colloquial French of Montreal.   5. Title of respect for a high-ranking leader.

And so, my love, I will not let you cut your strong rope of hair and go without a turban into this land of strangers. The knot my father tied between my chunni and your turban is still strong between us, and it shall not fail you now. My hands will tie a turban every day upon your head and work so we can keep it there. One day our children will say, "My father came to this country with very little but his turban and my mother learned to work because no one would hire him."

Then we will have taught Canadians what it takes to wear a turban.

1999

Norman Bethune
1890–1939

Bethune was flamboyant, energetic, creative, defiant, charming, heroic, and almost always in trouble with somebody, usually the authorities. He was born in Gravenhurst, a small Ontario town, but his restlessness took him to many places—like Montreal, which he loved and where he was a prominent, popular surgeon.

Bethune operated on himself to prove a point about lung surgery for patients with tuberculosis. His dangerous act deeply offended his medical colleagues. Once, when he disappeared from the Royal Victoria Hospital, concerned staff wondered if they should try to find him. An eavesdropping older doctor asked gruffly, "Tell me, is there also a nurse missing?" It seems there was, so they concluded that "Beth" would eventually reappear.

Civil authorities became very angry with Bethune when he insisted that tuberculosis was a problem of poverty, poor diet, and rickety housing, rather than a medical issue. It did not help that he was right. Bethune ached to commit himself to grand causes.

During the Spanish Civil War in the 1930s, he took blood transfusions to soldiers at the battlefront, saving many lives. When war with Japan was ravishing China, Bethune took medicines to soldiers in those battle zones. He died there from an infection in a small cut on his hand, inflicted during surgery done without protective gloves. Chairman Mao Tse Tung's article about Bethune's courage, in The Little Red Book, *made him a hero across the People's Republic of China.*

In addition to professional articles and speeches for various causes, Bethune wrote poetry and long public letters. He also painted, often doing ironic self-portraits, like the one of himself, bright yellow, suffering with jaundice. These articles, and some paintings, are collected in The Politics of Passion *(1998), edited by Larry Hannant. The following letter-become-essay, written from the battlefields of Spain in 1937, demonstrates Bethune's passion for language, art, truth and hard work.*

An Apology for Not Writing Letters

To my friends in Canada:
This is an attempt at an explanation why I, who think of you so often, with love and affection, have not written—or so briefly—since my arrival in Spain.

I had thought to say simply (that is, shortly)—I have been too busy; I am a man of action; I have no time to write. Yet as I look at these words, I see they are false. They simply aren't true. In fact, I have had plenty of time to write you, that is if I had cared to write, but, in truth, I did not care. Now why is this? Why have I not written to those of you who, I know, without illusion, would like to hear from me? Why is it I can not put down one word after another on paper and make a letter out of them?

I will try and be truthful. It is difficult to be truthful, isn't it?

First of all, I don't feel like writing. I don't feel the necessity of communication. I don't feel strongly the necessity of a re-construction of experience—my actions and the action of others—into the form of art which a letter should take. As an artist, unless that re-construction take a satisfactory form which is truthful, simple and moving, I will not, nay, I can not, write at all. I feel that unless I can re-construct those remembrances of action into reality for you, I will not attempt it. To me, a letter, is an important thing—

words are important things. At present, I don't feel any necessity to communicate these experiences. They are in me, have changed me, but I don't want to talk about them. I don't want to talk about them yet.

Besides, I am afraid to write you. I am afraid of the banality of words, of the vocal, the verbal, of the literary re-construction. I am afraid they won't be true.

Only by a shared physical experience—tactile, visual or auditory—may an approximately similar emotion be felt by two people without the aid of art. Only through art, can the truth of a non-shared experience be transmitted. To share with you what I have seen, what I have experienced in the past six months, is impossible without art. Without art, experience becomes, on the one hand, the denuded, bare bones of fact—a static, still-life—the how-many-ness of things; or, on the other hand, the swollen, exaggerated shapes of fantastically coloured romanticism. And I will do neither. I refuse to write either way. Both are false—the first by its poverty, the second by its excess.

So I despair of my ability to transpose the reality of experience into the reality of the written word. Art should be the legitimate and recognizable child of experience. I am afraid of a changeling. I am afraid it would have none of the unmistakable, inherited characteristics of its original, true, parental reality.

I can not write you, my friends, because this art of letters is a second, a repeated form of action. And one form of action at a time is enough. I can not do both—but successively, with an interval of a year, or ten years. Perhaps I can do both. I don't know. I don't think it matters very much.

I think that art has no excuse, no reason for existence except through the re-creation—by a dialectical process—of a new form of reality, for the old experience—transmitted through a man's sensorium—changed and illuminated by his conscious and unconscious mind. Exact reproduction is useless—that way lies death. The process of change from the old to the new is not a flat circular movement—a turn and return on itself, but helical[1] and ascending.

The process of creative art is the negation of the negation. First

1. Shaped like a helix: a spiral.

there is the change, that is, the negation, of the original, the positive reality; then the second change (or negation), which is a re-affirmation, a re-birth, through art, of the original experience, to the new positive, the new form of reality.

Let us take an example from painting—a moving object such as a tree swaying in the wind, a child at play, a bird in flight—any form of action, seen and perceived. This is the positive, the thesis. Reduced from the dynamic positive in time and space to a static form, by representation, (in this case, by paint on canvas) it becomes the negation of action, the denial of action. This is the antithesis. Then by the miracle of creative art, this static thing, (of necessity static, owing, to the medium employed) is vivified, transformed into movement again, into life again, but into a new life, becomes positive again, becomes the negation of the negation, the synthesis—the union of life and death, of action and non-action, the emergence of the new from the old, but retaining the old within the new.

Now the same thing applies to the literary art, the plastic arts, music, the dance or what not—any art form. And unless that fresh emergent form, with its core of the old, is a new thing, a dynamic thing, a quick and living thing, it is not art. It arouses no response except intellectual appreciation, the facile response to familiar, recognizable objects, or admiration for technical skill.

And because I can't write you, my friends, as I should like to write you, because my words are poor, anaemic and hobbling things, I have not written. Yes, I could write, but I am ashamed to write—like this:

"We were heavily shelled today. It was very uncomfortable. Fifty people were killed in the streets. The weather is lovely now although the winter has been hard. I am well. I think of you often. Yes, it is true I love you. Good bye."

I put them down and look at these words with horror and disgust. I wish I could describe to you how much I dislike these words. "Uncomfortable"—good god! what a word to describe the paralysing fear that seizes one when a shell bursts with a great roar and crash near by; "killed," for those poor huddled bodies of rags and blood, lying in such strange shapes, face down on the cobble-stones, or with sightless eyes upturned to a cruel and indifferent sky; "lovely" when the sun falls on our numbed faces like a benediction;

"well" when to be alive is well enough; "think" for that cry rising from our hearts day by day for remembered ones; "love" for this ache of separation.

So you see, it's no good.

Forgive me if I talk more about art. It must seem to you that I know either a great deal about it or nothing at all. I really know very little about it. I think it is very mysterious, very strange. But it seems to me to be a natural product of the subconscious mind of man, of all men, in some degree. Arising into the realm of deliberate thought, its life is imperilled. A theory of art reminds me of a medieval chart of the then-known world—curious, fantastic and wonderfully untrue. A theory of art is an attempt of the rational mind to impose its discipline and its order on the seeming chaos and seeming disorder of the emotional subconscious. If this is attempted—and it has frequently been attempted, a certain form of art, ordered and neat, arises. By its subjection to the conscious mind, to the deliberate directional thought of the artist and his theory, it lives for a while and then languishes and dies. It can not survive its separation from the great breeding ground of the unconscious. The mind (that alien in the attic) by its dictatorship, destroys the very thing it has discovered.

Most great artists of the world have been—thank Heaven—"stupid" in the worldly sense. They didn't think too much, they simply painted. Driven on by an irresistible internal compulsion, they painted as they did, as they must paint.

A great artist lets himself go. He is natural. He swims easily in the stream of his own temperament. He listens to himself. He respects himself. He has a deeper fund of strength to draw from than that arising from rational and logical knowledge. Yet how beautifully the dialectical process comes in again,—modified by thought, his primitive unconsciousness, conditioned by experience, reacts to reality and produces new forms of that reality. These particular forms of art arise, satisfy for their time, decay and die. But, by their appearance, they modify and influence succeeding art forms. They also modify and influence the very reality which produced them. Art itself never dies. Art itself is a great ever blooming tree, timeless, indestructible and immortal. The particular art forms of a generation are the flowers of that immortal tree. They are the expressions of their particular time but they are the products also of all the preceding time.

The artist needs, among other things, leisure, immense quietness, privacy and aloneness. The environment in which he has his being, are those dark, sunless, yet strangely illuminated depths of the world's subconscious,—the warm, pulsating yet quiet depths of the other-world.

He comes up into the light of every-day, like a great leviathan[2] of the deep, breaking the smooth surface of accepted things, gay, serious, sportive and destructive. In the bright banal glare of day, he enjoys the purification of violence, the catharsis[3] of action. His appetite for life is enormous. He enters eagerly into the life of man, of all men. He becomes all men in himself. He views the world with an all-embracing eye which looks upwards, outwards, inwards and downwards,—understanding, critical, tender and severe. Then he plunges back once more, back into the depths of that other-world,—strange, mysterious, secret and alone. And there, in those depths, he gives birth to the children of his being—new forms, new colours, new sounds, new movements, reminiscent of the known, yet not the known; alike and yet unlike; strange yet familiar; calm, profound and sure.

The function of the artist is to disturb. His duty is to arouse the sleeper, to shake the complacent pillars of the world. He reminds the world of its dark ancestry, shows the world its present, and points the way to its new birth. He is at once the product and the preceptor[4] of his time. After his passage we are troubled and made unsure of our too-easily accepted realities. He makes uneasy the static, the set and the still. In a world terrified of change, he preaches revolution—the principle of life. He is an agitator, a disturber of the peace—quick, impatient, positive, restless and disquieting. He is the creative spirit of life working in the soul of man.

But enough. Perhaps the true reason I can not write is that I'm too tired—another 150 miles on the road today, and what roads!

Our first job is to defeat fascism[5]—the enemy of the creative artist. After that we can write about it.

---

2. A sea-monster.   4. Teacher.
3. Cleansing.   5. One-party authoritarian government.

Good bye. I do think of you with love and affection. Forgive me when I do not write.

Salud[6]
Norman Bethune

1937, 1998

Sandra Birdsell
b. 1942

Born in Hariota, Manitoba, Birdsell grew up in Morris, a small town not far from Winnipeg. She lived longest in Winnipeg, but also in several other cities across Canada, often as a university writer-in-residence. She now lives in Regina, Saskatchewan.

Birdsell has written short stories, screenplays, stageplays, novels, and one children's book: The Town that Floated Away *(1997). In 1993, she was awarded the Marian Engel Award, from the Writers' Development Trust, for major contribution to literature. Birdsell's short story collections include* Night Travellers *(1982),* Ladies of the House *(1984), and* The Two-Headed Calf *(1997). Her novels are* The Missing Child *(1989),* The Chrome Suite *(1992), and* The Russlander *(2001).*

The following selection is non-fiction, a personal essay written for an anthology called Writing Home *(1997). It has the same tones as Birdsell's fiction, which might be described as "magic realist." Unexplainable things happen in an odd world haunted by ghosts of the prehistoric Lake Agassiz, which used to cover the area of Manitoba where Birdsell grew up. Hardly anyone knows that lake was there, thousands of years ago, but it lurks in Birdsell's writing, which often includes water or flood imagery. Lake Agassiz is never actually identified in this essay, but all the same, it is there in the background.*

In this piece Birdsell reveals her sense of the macabre, as well as her willingness to accept new experiences or unusual people. Her

---

6. Health (Spanish).

deep sense of connection to her own place comes through clearly as she tries to answer the question about why she lives where she does. Inviting the reader to watch this process, Birdsell includes her false starts, the parts we usually edit out. She recognizes that they move steadily toward an answer, even as they tell us what the answer is not. Writing a personal essay for publication, Birdsell allows us to see how her mind and her imagination work.

Why I Live Where I Live

I live in the Red River Valley. I grew up in a small prairie town, moved on, and lived in several others. You know the type: one grain elevator, railroad tracks, abandoned train station, general store, and a curling rink with eight sheets of artificial ice. The kind of place about which people say that if you blink when you drive by, you'll miss it. Now I live in Winnipeg, and I suppose some may say the same comment applies. But these are just tourists skimming across the valley in their boats or trolling with empty hooks. Valley, they say. Where are the hills?

True, one must travel far to find them—but they're here. Comforting little brown humps on the shoreline. Why do I continue to live here in Winnipeg in the Red River Valley? It's God in a CBC[1] T-shirt, calling to make me think.

I've contemplated moving to Vancouver, where they tell me that the difference between Vancouver and Toronto is that in Toronto people dress up in bizarre costumes and pretend they're crazy, while in Vancouver they really are crazy. I don't mind the crazy people in Vancouver. They're like wildflowers on the side of a mountain, pretty to look at from a distance but never meant to be picked and taken home. But I find when I'm in Vancouver that after three days I no longer see the mountains. All I want to do is find a quiet place, huddle down in the sand, and stare at the ocean. And the same thing happens to me when I'm on the east coast. Why do I live here?

---

1. Canadian Broadcasting Corporation, a public radio and TV network.

I ask a friend. Grasshoppers and crickets sing from either side of the dirt road. It's not quite a full moon but bright enough for long shadows. Perfect night to play Dracula. It's my turn to wear the cape. The question eats at me, interferes with the game. On the horizon Winnipeg shimmers pink and still. You live here, he says, because you're short. You're close to the ground and if a big wind should come along you'd be safe. And yet you feel tall. Naw, that's not it, my daughter says.

It's Sunday, and the question rankles as I make my weekly trip through the forest where thick dark trees wrestle the granite boulders for soil. I push the speed limit to get to the lake before all the others, and finally I find my spot, huddle down into the sand, and stare out across the water. I think: Why do I live here? The answer comes to me. It's because when I live in the Red River Valley, I'm living at the bottom of a lake.

When you live at the bottom of a lake you get cracks in your basement walls, especially in River Heights, where they can afford cracks and underpinning and new basements. I like the cracks. The wind whistles through them, loosens the lids on my peach preserves, makes the syrup ferment, and the mice get tipsy. In the potato bin, sprouts grow on wrinkled skin, translucent, cool sprouts. They climb up the basement walls, push their way through air vents and up the windows in my kitchen. I don't have to bother about hanging curtains.

And time is different here. The days piled on top of lake sediments shift after a good storm so that yesterday slips out from beneath today. Or even last Friday with all its voices will bob up from the bottom and it's possible to lose track of tomorrow. You can just say to hell with tomorrow and go out and play Dracula.

When you live here at the bottom of a lake you can't pin your ancestors down with granite monuments. They slide out of their graves. They work themselves across the underground on their backs using their heels as leverage, they inch their way back into town until they rest beneath the network of dusty roads, and they lie there on their backs and read stories to you from old newspapers.

Now, this is something tourists can never discover as they roar across the valley in their powerboats, churning up the water with their blink-and-you'll-miss-it view of my place. Sometimes a brave one will leap from the boat, come down, and move in next door. I've seen it happen. They become weak and listless, like flies trapped inside a house at the end of summer. And you'll see them walking along the highway in scuba gear muttering to themselves or rowing across the lake in search of a hill. I'll admit, sometimes it's nice to surface, to take off the cape and put on my respectable prairie jacket and boots and do a walking tour of Halifax, sniff a wild mountain flower in Vancouver, get a stiff neck looking up at all those skyscrapers in Toronto, or a three-day party headache in Montreal. But inevitably my eyes grow tired, glazed, and like a sleepwalker I awake to find myself crouched down beside an ocean, a lake, a river, and I know it's time to get back there—to get down in the basement and breathe the wind in the cracks of my walls where, nestled up against the foundation of my house, is the pelvic bone of an ancestor.

1997

Ernest Buckler
1908–1984

For years, reporters called Buckler "the shy oyster." He said that a writer works the same way an oyster does. When something gets under his skin, he works and works at it until it turns into a jewel: a pearl for the oyster, a story for the writer. The "shy" label stuck because, having agreed to be interviewed by a Canadian Broadcasting Corporation reporter, Buckler saw her arriving and hid in a cornfield until she left. Was he was hiding from a reporter—or from a woman? Whatever his reason, he protected his reclusive life in rural Nova Scotia.

Buckler chose to return to the family farm in Nova Scotia after he finished his studies at Dalhousie University in Halifax and at the University of Toronto. He spent a short time working in an actuarial office in Toronto, but he felt smothered in the big city.

Out of his quiet farming life and close observations of people around him, Buckler wrote The Mountain and the Valley *(1961), a novel about David, a writer-as-a-young-boy. For many years, it was more highly valued in the United States than it was in Canada. When it was published, some Canadians were scandalized by the sex behind the barn. Others did not see how it could be taken seriously as a novel. It was just about ordinary life in a familiar rural community and a little boy who seemed to talk too much. It has since become a Canadian classic. Among Buckler's other books are* The Cruelest Month *(1963), a novel;* Ox Bells and Fireflies *(1968), non-fiction sketches; and* Window on the Sea *(1973), prose responses to photographs by Hans Weber. Marta Dvorak edited* Thanks for Listening: Stories and Short Fictions *(2004).*

In the following story from The Rebellion of Young David and Other Stories *(1975), Buckler investigates the dilemmas of people like his neighbours who are sensitive and caring, whose feelings run deep—and unspoken. It is not that they distrust words—they value them extraordinarily highly. A spoken word is a bond. Words, for them, are not to be spoken glibly—or often.*

Penny in the Dust

My sister and I were walking through the old sun-still fields the evening before my father's funeral, recalling this memory or that—trying, after the fashion of families who gather again in the place where they were born, to identify ourselves with the strange children we must have been.

"Do you remember the afternoon we thought you were lost?" my sister said. I did. That was as long ago as the day I was seven, but I'd had occasion to remember it only yesterday.

"We searched everywhere," she said. "Up in the meeting-house, back in the blueberry barrens—we even looked in the well. I think it's the only time I ever saw Father really upset. He didn't even stop to take the oxen off the wagon tongue when they told him. He raced right through the chopping where Tom Reeve was burning brush, looking for you—right through the flames almost; they couldn't do a thing with him. And you up in your bed, sound asleep!"

"It was all over losing a penny or something, wasn't it?" she went on, when I didn't answer. It was. She laughed indulgently. "You were a crazy kid, weren't you."

I was. But there was more to it than that. I had never seen a shining new penny before that day. I'd thought they were all black. This one was bright as gold. And my father had given it to me.

You would have to understand about my father, and that is the hard thing to tell. If I say that he worked all day long but never once had I seen him hurry, that would make him sound like a stupid man. If I say that he never held me on his knee when I was a child and that I never heard him laugh out loud in his life, it would make him sound humourless and severe. If I said that whenever I'd be reeling off some of my fanciful plans and he'd come into the kitchen and I'd stop short, you'd think that he was distant and that in some kind of way I was afraid of him. None of that would be true.

There's no way you can tell it to make it sound like anything more than an inarticulate man a little at sea with an imaginative child. You'll have to take my word for it that there was more to it than that. It was as if his sure-footed way in the fields forsook him the moment he came near the door of my child's world and that he could never intrude on it without feeling awkward and conscious of trespass; and that I, sensing that but not understanding it, felt at the sound of his solid step outside, the child-world's foolish fragility. He would fix the small spot where I planted beans and other quick-sprouting seeds before he prepared the big garden, even if the spring was late; but he wouldn't ask me how many rows I wanted and if he made three rows and I wanted four, I couldn't ask him to change them. If I walked behind the load of hay, longing to ride, and he walked ahead of the oxen, I couldn't ask him to put me up and he wouldn't make any move to do so until he saw me trying to grasp the binder.

He, my father, had just given me a new penny, bright as gold.

He'd taken it from his pocket several times, pretending to examine the date on it, waiting for me to notice it. He couldn't offer me *anything* until I had shown some sign that the gift would be welcome.

"You can have it if you want it, Pete," he said at last.

"Oh, thanks," I said. Nothing more. I couldn't expose any of my eagerness either.

I started with it, to the store. For a penny you could buy the magic cylinder of "Long Tom" popcorn with Heaven knows what glittering bauble inside. But the more I thought of my bright penny disappearing forever into the black drawstring pouch the store-keeper kept his money in, the slower my steps lagged as the store came nearer and nearer. I sat down in the road.

It was that time of magic suspension in an August afternoon. The lifting smells of leaves and cut clover hung still in the sun. The sun drowsed, like a kitten curled up on my shoulder. The deep flour-fine dust in the road puffed about my bare ankles, warm and soft as sleep. The sound of the cowbells came sharp and hollow from the cool swamp.

I began to play with the penny, putting off the decision. I would close my eyes and bury it deep in the sand; and then, with my eyes still closed, get up and walk around, and then come back to search for it. Tantalizing myself, each time, with the excitement of discovering afresh its bright shining edge. I did that again and again. Alas, once too often.

It was almost dark when their excited talking in the room awakened me. It was Mother who had found me. I suppose when it came dusk she thought of me in my bed other nights, and I suppose she looked there without any reasonable hope but only as you look in every place where the thing that is lost has ever lain before. And now suddenly she was crying because when she opened the door there, miraculously, I was.

"Peter!" she cried, ignoring the obvious in her sudden relief, "*where* have you been?"

"I lost my penny," I said.

"You lost your penny . . . ? But what made you come up here and hide?"

If Father hadn't been there, I might have told her the whole story. But when I looked up at Father, standing there like the shape of everything sound and straight, it was like daylight shredding the memory of a silly dream. How could I bear the shame of repeating before him the childish visions I had built in my head in the magic August afternoon when almost anything could be made to seem real, as I buried the penny and dug it up again? How could I explain that pit-of-the-stomach sickness which struck through the whole day when I had to believe, at last, that it was really gone? How could I explain that I wasn't really hiding from *them*? How, with the words and the understanding I had then, that this was the only possible place to run from that awful feeling of loss?

"I lost my penny," I said again. I looked at Father and turned my face into the pillow. "I want to go to sleep."

"Peter," Mother said. "It's almost nine o'clock. You haven't had a bite of supper. Do you know you almost scared the *life* out of us?"

"You better get some supper," Father said. It was the only time he had spoken.

I never dreamed that he would mention the thing again. But the next morning when we had the hay forks in our hands, ready to toss out the clover, he seemed to postpone the moment of actually leaving for the field. He stuck his fork in the ground and brought in another pail of water, though the kettle was chock full. He took out the shingle nail that held a broken yoke strap together and put it back in exactly the same hole. He went into the shed to see if the pigs had cleaned up all their breakfast.

And then he said abruptly: "Ain't you got no idea where you lost your penny?"

"Yes," I said, "I know just about."

"Let's see if we can't find it," he said.

We walked down the road together, stiff with awareness. He didn't hold my hand.

"It's right here somewhere," I said. "I was playin' with it, in the dust."

He looked at me, but he didn't ask me what game anyone could possibly play with a penny in the dust.

I might have known he would find it. He could tap the alder bark with his jackknife just exactly hard enough so it wouldn't split but so it would twist free from the notched wood, to make a whistle. His great fingers could trace loose the hopeless snarl of a fishing line that I could only succeed in tangling tighter and tighter. If I broke the handle of my wheelbarrow ragged beyond sight of any possible repair, he could take it and bring it back to me so you could hardly see the splice if you weren't looking for it.

He got down on his knees and drew his fingers carefully through the dust, like a harrow; not clawing it frantically into heaps as I had done, covering even as I uncovered. He found the penny almost at once.

He held it in his hand, as if the moment of passing it to me were a deadline for something he dreaded to say, but must. Something that could not be put off any longer, if it were to be spoken at all.

"Pete," he said, "you needn'ta hid. I wouldn'ta beat you."

Beat me? Oh, Father! You didn't think that was the reason . . . ? I felt almost sick. I felt as if I had struck *him*.

I had to tell him the truth then. Because only the truth, no matter how ridiculous it was, would have the unmistakable sound truth has, to scatter that awful idea out of his head.

"I wasn't hidin', Father," I said, "honest. I was. . . . I was buryin' my penny and makin' out I was diggin' up treasure. I was makin' out I was findin' gold. I didn't know what to *do* when I lost it, I just didn't know where to *go*. . . ." His head was bent forward, like mere listening. I had to make it truer still.

"I made out it was gold," I said desperately, "and I—I was makin' out I bought you a mowin' machine so's you could get your work done early every day so's you and I could go in to town in the big automobile I made out I bought you—and everyone'd turn around and look at us drivin' down the streets. . . ." His head was perfectly still, as if he were only waiting with patience for me to finish. "*Laugh*in' and *talk*in'," I said. Louder, smiling intensely, com*pell*ing him, by the absolute conviction of some true particular, to believe me.

He looked up then: It was the only time I had ever seen tears in his eyes. It was the only time in my seven years that he had ever put his arm around me.

I wondered, though, why he hesitated, and then put the penny back in his own pocket.

Yesterday I knew. I never found any fortune and we never had a car to ride in together. But I think he knew what that would be like, just the same. I found the penny again yesterday, when we were getting out his good suit—in an upper vest pocket where no one ever carries change. It was still shining. He must have kept it polished.

I left it there.

1948, 1975

Sharon Butala

b. 1940

Butala grew up in Saskatoon, Saskatchewan, and considered herself a city person until she married Peter Butala and moved to a ranch in southwest Saskatchewan. She is well known as a novelist of that world, fascinated by the people she found herself among, by the difficulty of their lives on isolated ranches. She was especially struck by the women, who work inside their homes and also outside, often in harsh conditions of dust or snow.

More and more, Butala became interested in the land itself, in the aboriginal history of the area, and in the vulnerability of the fragile grasslands. The Perfection of the Morning *(1994),* Coyote's Morning Cry *(1995) and* Wild Stone Heart *(2000), from which this essay is taken, form a non-fiction trilogy, as Butala writes herself into an understanding of this prairie landscape.*

These works record a spiritual struggle, with Butala trying to link herself to forces around her which she does not fully understand. She is brave in recording the difficult-to-express sense of herself as intruder on this land which was taken from aboriginal people. They lived on it for thousands of years before white settlers did, and surely, she thinks, they understand it better. They can help her find her way into its secrets.

"I cannot pretend not to know what I know," she says, wondering how her readers will respond to accounts of her growing spiritual connection to the land. She feels responsible for it and wants to be fair to its original inhabitants. Butala concludes sadly that she is European in culture, not native, much as she loves this place. She works at finding ways to protect the grasslands, to return them to what they were before they were grazed over by cattle.

The Spirit of the Land

Almost thirty years ago now, when I was teaching a class of teenagers with learning difficulties in the Saskatoon school system, I attended a teachers' conference. Although I had no Amerindian children in my classes and there were at the time perhaps only two in the entire inner-city school where I worked, I chose to attend a session given by two Amerindian male lecturers on, I thought, the needs of Amerindian children in the classroom. There were only perhaps fifteen to twenty people in the audience, all women, I think, and all elementary school teachers. I recall the two leaders of the session each speaking quietly for a while and showing some slides, although I can't remember of what. I think they called for questions. Hands went up.

A woman in her late thirties or early forties and nicely dressed spoke first. She asked what we might do, specifically what *she* might do, to help these children. The two male lecturers glanced briefly at each other, their faces revealing nothing at all—I remember thinking that this was deliberate, that they were hiding emotion—and then simply went on talking, ignoring her question. It was as if she hadn't spoken at all. She didn't ask another question, I'm not sure that anyone else did either, and the session ended very soon after that.

For nearly thirty years I pondered that incident, trying to understand it, and mostly failing. Why would you ignore such a question, I asked myself? Because it was a stupid question? Because it was unanswerable without a basis of understanding or information that plainly wasn't there, so that the lecturers found it most polite to simply pretend it hadn't happened? And what was it that the woman who asked the question—and me, too, and everybody else in the audience—failed to know? Or was it simply (as I'm sure I thought at the time) that they were men and we were women and they had no respect for us to start with? But although I was and continue to be always on the alert for such built-in contempt of the feminine, I did not really think it was operative in that instance.

I think I see now the built-in racism in the well-intentioned question, the implication that Amerindian children needed something different, something more. And perhaps that is all that the two lecturers were reacting to. But it seemed to me there was more than that to it, although I was never able to be clear about what it was, beyond thinking that the question itself indicated a failure to see the world in any terms but those of a middle-class person whose cultural roots were in Europe.

A year or two ago I was working in my kitchen and had the radio tuned to our beloved CBC.[1] A tape was being played of an incident at a teachers' conference, once again in Saskatoon, and an Amerindian woman was on the stage. Apparently the lecture she'd given had just ended, and the floor was open for questions. The sound of the question coming from the floor, a woman again, was muffled and distant but clear enough that I knew she was asking the same question the woman had asked in the session I'd attended thirty years earlier. "What can I do to help Amerindian children in my classroom?" The speaker shot back, her voice cracking with anger, "*You can admit that you're the problem!*" In an instant she got a grip on herself and added some qualifying remark that marginally took the sting out of her accusation, but I doubt very much that anybody in that audience, which sounded as if it were large, was much fooled by it. She was very angry, again I thought, at what she saw as the unconscious racism in the question, so angry that for an instant she couldn't hide it.

Standing in my kitchen more than two hundred miles away, I was more or less stunned by her open rage, especially coming from an Amerindian woman, something I'd never heard before, by the sudden memory of the almost identical incident, and by the fact that they had occurred thirty years apart. Plainly, I wasn't going to be able to forget this; I was going to have to give it a lot of thought, because I knew it meant something important, that somehow all of this was material for a book I hoped to write, once I could figure out what it was about and how to write it. My hands were wet with dishwater, but I wiped them fast on my jeans and grabbed a pencil and made an illegible note on a pad by the phone of the speaker's name and the date and what she had said. Then time passed and I lost the note.

If the school system in Saskatchewan, the public schools in the cities now full of Amerindian children, and also the large Amerindian community in our cities have changed a great deal in the intervening thirty years between the two incidents, it was plain, too, that the sensibilities and even the information base of the rest of us in Saskatchewan hadn't changed nearly enough. Now I knew this, as I hadn't thirty years earlier; I was even beginning at last to realize— aside from the unconscious racist basis of the two questions of

---

1. Canadian Broadcasting Corporation, a public radio and TV network.

which I was also guilty—what else was missing from the understanding of the two questioners.

I was beginning to comprehend this, finally, through my more
than twenty years here, as I like to say, living in the landscape. For
the most part I was being taught it by the landscape, by Nature itself, and specifically by my experiences in the field. But sadly I was
not learning it from long conversations with Amerindian people. As
I've said, there are virtually no Amerindian people in southwest
Saskatchewan except for the one reserve north of here. They were
driven out in the 1880s by the starvation policy of Lieutenant-
Governor Dewdney (1881–1888) after the buffalo were gone and
many of the leaders refused to "take treaty" because they understood
all too well what this would mean to their people. (I am told that
the Nakota people, now of Carry the Kettle Reserve, were force-
marched three hundred miles east of here to their reserve, although
the "force-marched" interpretation depends on whom one is talking
to—Amerindian or non-Amerindian.) It is also instructive to learn
that leaders of the Blackfoot nation, plus the Plains Cree and Lakota
people, wished to have all of southwest Saskatchewan for contigu-
ous reserves, making an Indian homeland, a situation the people
in power couldn't contemplate since they saw the massing of
Amerindian people as far too dangerous.

I'd been given a few hints of understanding from books. My first
clue was the day that I realized that those eloquent and moving
speeches of the old leaders, now the ancestors, were not metaphoric
at all, as all we Europeans chose to understand them, but actual.
Though we saw such speeches as childish and faintly silly, if also
eloquent, I knew now that *they meant every word they said.* We just
could not comprehend this.

Over and over again I've thought back to my childhood in a village on the banks of the Saskatchewan River where the many
Amerindian and Métis[2] children were often shunned and taunted
by non-native children. I had been taught that *if they were inferior to
us* (this part was unspoken) we must nonetheless never show it in
any way and must never verbally abuse anyone who was different

2. People of mixed French and Amerindian descent.

from us, no matter who, but especially not the dark-skinned children in our village. If our parents had taught us that we must never say such things, they didn't say we couldn't think them, and the society around us had no such compunctions.

I have carried around with me since I was six years old the shame of something that happened one hot summer day when we girls had been playing in two separate groups. We had become angry with each other and quarrelled as children do, and I broke the rule I'd been raised with. I said to another little girl, "Why is your skin so dark!" as an accusation, as the final, clinching line of our conflict. I was saying, in fact: You're only an Indian, and I am not, so of course you lose. How I have since despised myself for that and wished to find some way to make up for it.

Since that incident as a six-year-old, which I've carried around with me like a stone in my heart, I've had very few dealings with Amerindian people. I was a student in the days when Amerindian children went to residential, not public, schools, and I was a schoolteacher in the days before a significant number of Amerindian people had moved into the cities to live, sending their children to the public schools. When I taught at the university, the few Amerindian professors taught in their own departments of Native Studies or Indian Education with nearly all Amerindian students, and our paths never crossed. It wasn't until I came to southwest Saskatchewan to live, into the one area of the province where nearly all Amerindian people had been driven out a century earlier, that I began to think about them, that I found I could not forget them, that I began to study what I could find about them and their history, that I began at last, although still very rarely, to meet them.

My interest grew, my desire to know more kept expanding and nagging at me. I would probably not have been able to say, when this first began to happen, why it was, but thinking back, I see that my insatiable desire *to know* about them grew out of the experiences I was beginning to have on the land, out of the land, from the land. I wanted to know what all the stone circles were for, what they meant, and how the people who created them might have understood the land I was so slowly and so minimally coming to know: the plants, the animals, the seasonal variations of both. How did it *look* to them? What did it *mean* to them? What did they know? How did they know it? How did they understand Spirit? How did they know about Spirit? And on and on.

I slowly came to know that much that was being published by people with cultural roots primarily in Europe about Amerindian belief systems was false, that there was much charlatanism out there in response to our rising interest in Amerindian ways and beliefs. Also, that much of it was dangerous and sometimes despicable in its theft of what was left to a conquered people. I wanted to peel all of that back to find the truths. I had only two resources to help me do this: books and the land itself.

When my husband and I finally concluded the arrangements to turn the Butala ranch into the Old Man On His Back Prairie and Heritage Preserve, an evening celebration was to be held in the local community hall. The people of the nearby reserve were invited to stage their own celebration during the day as a blessing on the new preserve. They chose a site and planned to build a sweat lodge and hold a sweat bath and to follow this with a feast and a round dance. Because it was our doing and our land, they invited Peter and me to take part in their ceremonies, especially to join the sweat-bath ceremony.

About this last I had strong misgivings. I have suffered from varying degrees of claustrophobia since my labour when my son was born, and in the last ten or so years I have developed a pretty severe asthma-like reaction to cigarette smoke if I inhale it directly, and I am generally very sensitive now to air that isn't fresh. As well as these physical conditions, I've had enough experiences of the supernatural, as this book will testify, to be afraid of them. But I changed in the back of somebody's van into a pair of shorts and a sleeveless low blouse, and when people began to move into the sweat lodge and beckoned to me, I went, trying not to show how scared I was.

Nor did I know anything practical about this ritual. I didn't know that once you go into the lodge and seal it up, you don't stay there forever, that there is in fact a set sequence of songs and prayers to be gone through in each of (at least, in this case) four separate sessions, each of which lasts perhaps twenty minutes to half an hour. In between each sequence the passage is opened and everyone

goes outside and gets fresh air and rests before the sweat goes on.
No one had in any way prepared me for this by even telling me this
simple fact. As I was walking in, the woman entering beside me told
me I needed a towel and a blanket, and I had to go back and get
them. We women sat on one side and the men on the other. I watched
the people filing in, was surprised at how very many there were, and
saw to my growing horror that a number of the men were carrying
lit cigarettes that they hadn't finished smoking. More and more people came in and sat down, and I began to worry that there would be
no fresh air to breathe at all, worse, that it would be full of cigarette
smoke and I would have an asthma attack and choke and die on
the spot. I was so scared that I almost jumped up and ran out as the
keeper of the door began to replace the canvas and hides to seal us
in. Something held me back, and it wasn't common sense, but a
kind of clumsy attempt at courtesy.

When the heat began to rise and I felt I couldn't breathe, I was
close to panic, but an older woman seated beside me whispered in
my ear to lie down and put my face in the grass and it would be easier to breathe when it got really hot. I reached behind and tried to
squeeze my fingers between the earth and the canvas and blankets
covering the willow frame. I thought if I could even feel the air outside, I'd be able to stand the heat and lack of oxygen—a part of me
knew my real problem was simple fear—but the coverings were
stretched so tightly that I couldn't push my fingers between them
and the earth.

I was too afraid to stop fighting the physical occasion, the steam,
the sensation I had of not being able to breathe. I couldn't bring
myself simply to go with what was happening, not wanting to lose
myself in the experience for fear of what might happen. I *knew* what
might happen: spirits, voices, visions. I suppose I was really afraid of
losing control. So I held on and squirmed and threw myself around
in a panic, and the kind, good woman next to me whispered, "Do
you want to go out?" And I thought, You mean I can go out if I
want to? I'd thought I was stuck there until I died or went insane.
"Yes," I said. "Please!"

She hesitated for a minute, but then she called out in Cree, and
voices went around the men's side in Cree, calling to each other, and

the shaking of rattles or leafy branches or whatever it was died away, and the singing; and then people called to the man seated outside the entrance, and he called back, then began to open the canvas, and finally I could escape and I did. The voices behind me started up again with their chanting, and then I realized I had done something shameful.

I walked away, so upset by what I had done that I couldn't really grasp it, couldn't really understand it, just had this sensation of some appalling cloud hovering around me that would soon descend and crush me. That there would be no escape from it, that I had done this myself. I went across the field, past the mothers rocking babies, and other women who hadn't gone in and were waiting for the sweat to end, and down into a deep coulee[3] behind them. I kept walking. I was gone perhaps a half-hour, the whole time the realization of what I'd done growing bigger and bigger, not gaining in clarity, no mitigating circumstances appearing to me, and when I finally started back to the camp, I met one of the women coming to look for me.

I said to her that I had just realized that I was going to have to live with what I'd done for the rest of my life. She must have replied, but I can't remember anything she said. I remember also that I said to her that maybe after all, instead of there being anything special about me with regard to her people, I was just another one of those people fascinated by Indian people and their beliefs. She said little, but the fact she'd come looking for me and walked back with me, never saying a word of chastisement or showing the slightest anger or even disdain, was the only comfort I've been able to take from the whole episode. (In fact, later she asked me if I'd be interested in being a volunteer at Okimaw Ohci Healing Lodge on the Nekaneet reserve, an institution for federally sentenced aboriginal women run on native spirituality principles.)

When I got back to the camp, everybody had left the sweat and was recovering in preparation for the next round. Seeing this, I said to the elder who'd invited us that if I'd known it would be over in a few minutes, I would have been able to stick it out to the end. I said that I had known for days I was going to have to do this, and I'd

---

3. On the prairies, a dry creek bed.

been afraid, but felt that I had to. The elder watched me closely, then asked me, "Do you want to go again?" All the people around us were rising now and re-entering the lodge. I hesitated for an instant, but then I said, "No!" shaking my head vigorously. Even as I said this, I knew I was wrong, but I did it anyway. I thought that perhaps some day I'd be able to, but never then. I no longer know, if I ever did, what it was I was resisting at that moment, and it has even crossed my mind to wonder if my refusal was merely self-punishment for the way I'd shamed myself and damaged the ceremony for others.

At the celebratory supper that night in the hall I tried to go around to every table where the people of the reserve sat—thinking back, I don't believe there was any mixing of locals with the Amerindian people—and say to them who I was and that I was glad they had come. At a table of men I tried to explain why I had run out of the sweat lodge, and they laughed, and one of them caught my hand and teased me, but one of them turned his body away from me, his face set, wouldn't look at me or speak to me, and I was ashamed and remorseful and wanted to explain to him and ask him to forgive me.

That shaming episode taught me something else. Fascinated by and admiring of it as I am, I find I don't really want to *live* in the traditional Plains Amerindian world as some non-aboriginal people I've met or read about have done, giving up everything they'd been raised in, from material goods to Christianity and their own culture's value system. Despite being very critical of it, I'm not completely alienated from the world I was raised in. I think, also, that it's too late for that.

I'm a hybrid. I've been taught European culture as the only kind of culture that counts, and I've cherished it and wished very much, to have more of it than my birthplace and position in life will allow me. Of all things in life I love books best, and writing, and then the other arts, especially painting. But because I'm third-generation Canadian and westerner on one side and, on the other, Canadian since 1650 and westerner since 1911, and because I've lived in the countryside for the last twenty-four years (and also for my first six years), I've absorbed this North American Great Plains landscape into my blood and bones, and I know things about it now that make me intensely admiring of what I've come to understand about the system of thought of Plains Amerindian people. But I can't—I don't wish—to shake off my absorption in European culture. It's a dilemma I'm not the first Western North American writer to point out. It's clear to me, though, that our "two solitudes" have to come to some kind of an accord, some kind of livable recognition of each other's rights and wisdom.

I have begun to have an idea of the continents of the world—I've been only in North America, Europe, and, briefly, Africa—as each being a complete, self-enclosing, and unique world. By this I mean not just the climatic systems or the geographical or the biological worlds, but especially the world of the spiritual. I remember thinking when I was in Africa in 1995 that I understood why the colonizers referred to Africa by the now-hated phrase, "the dark continent," but that it had nothing to do with the skin colour of its many diverse peoples, or even of the soil, which also is greatly varied, or of the differing spiritual systems of its many cultures. It had instead to do with some indefinable richness that hovered in the air, indescribable—at least for one there hardly a month—that was an essence not to be pinpointed or amenable to scientific investigation. Even now, trying mentally to compare this *thing* I perceived faintly, on the edge of my awareness when I was there, to the aura or ambience of this continent I know so well, I feel a great difference, not an aura I can easily describe, though, but of equal beauty and power.

To carry this idea through logically, I try to think of what I felt when travelling in Europe and I get no sense at all of an *essence*, as if that continent is far too varied, its cultures so profoundly involved in art and literature and treasures of history—unless that is its essence—that sniffing the air for a measure of its true nature, I come away with nothing.

Surprised in Addis Ababa[4] to see stunted goats and cattle wandering in and out of the thick stream of traffic on the main thoroughfare of this city of then three million, I asked an African with us, who lived in South Africa, if this was typical of African cities. He

4. The capital of Ethiopia, Africa.

glanced around, then said, "Yes, in the sense of the closeness to nature." No one would ever say that of European cities, and North
America, I think, occupies a middle position in this scale.

Every continent has evolved its own variety of spiritual life,
eroded to varying degrees by the advent of missionaries and travellers from elsewhere bringing the ideas of their own continents to
places where they may very well not fit at all. Or it may be not that
the variety of spiritual life evolved but, as I see it, that it was a *given*,
along with the varieties of trees and soil and insects and animals,
and each set of indigenous peoples slowly discovered it or grew up
with it as it grew up.

Vine Deloria, Jr., an influential Lakota writer and historian, says,
in *God Is Red*, that this was a new continent; a new continent needs
new understanding, that is, new gods, new systems of spirituality,
that Christianity might have worked in Europe, but it did not—
does not—work for this continent. (Surely the ongoing destruction
of Nature is evidence of this.)

Further, the Amerindian people already had the system that belonged to—that fitted, that came out of—this continent, if only
Europeans had listened to them. I think that the Amerindians arrived at their beliefs and the accompanying rituals through their at-
tentiveness to and their compliance with the land. For this bond,
there is, there can be, no substitute.

This, I think, with all its implications, is finally what we stole
from Amerindian people when we stole their land. Because we did
not believe what they told us about their understanding of the natural world, and because we stole their children so that they would
never again be able fully to believe what their old people told them
about the world, and no longer knew who they were, we came near
to destroying them, too.

The famous case of the Gitskan and Wet'suwet'en fighting for
their hereditary lands in British Columbia must surely have helped
more people to understand the Amerindian point of view. The
hereditary chiefs, Gisday Wa and Delgam Uukw, presented their
case to the Supreme Court in a written (and later published) brief
called *In the Spirit of the Land: Statement of the Gitskan and Wet'-
suwet'en Hereditary Chiefs in the Supreme Court of British Columbia,
1987–1990*:

For us, the ownership of territory is a marriage of the Chief and the land. Each Chief had an ancestor who encountered and acknowledged the life of the land. From such encounters come power. The land, the plants, the animals and the people all have spirit—they all must be shown respect. That is the basis of our law. . . . When the chief directs his house properly and the laws are followed, then that original power can be recreated.

My power [Delgam Uukw] is carried in my House's histories, songs, dances and crests. It is recreated at the Feast when the histories are told, songs and dances performed and crests displayed. With the wealth that comes from respectful use of the territory, the House feeds the name of the Chief in the Feast Hall. In this way, the law, the Chief, the territory and the Feast become one.

The Gitskan and Wet'suwet'en speak of "the life of the land," and reiterate, as so do many Amerindian societies, that the land, the plants, the animals, and the people have spirit and must be shown respect.

Take away the land from people who are a part of the land and not only do you take away their ability to support themselves, you take away their spiritual base, for without the land all else in the culture loses its basis, its sense, its natural rhythms, its coherence, its entire life-giving and spirit-nourishing *raison d'être*.[5] Not to mention the damage done to a people from centuries-old mourning and grief, from endless poverty, from constant, endemic injustice, humiliations, and disenfranchisement of nearly every kind. Take away land from *us* and we may be impoverished, but we still have our schools, churches, governments, and hierarchy of relationships. We may lose status, but our belief systems, which create our culture and sustain us within it, remain intact.

One day, walking in the field, I crossed a hill I had often crossed and noticed for the first time that I could remember, although how I could have missed it I don't know, that on this one low hill there were—I counted them in disbelief and some rising emotion that took me by surprise—four burial cairns. How great the deaths must

5. Reason for being (French).

have been here, I thought, and spontaneous tears of grief and shock at so many deaths sprang to my eyes.

All those years I'd walked that field and seen the cairns, and not seen them, and then rediscovered them, and lost them again, only to see them once more, and I had felt no emotion other than surprise and sometimes pleasure at finding them, as if I were particularly perspicacious[6] and vigilant and deserving.

Now what I felt was what I should have felt all along, if I had believed the bones of those beneath the cairns were once living and walking and breathing human beings: that they were *people*. *People* had died here, and those who loved them had buried them in sorrow. I wept for a moment, and my grieving was for once genuine. I felt ashamed that I had not felt this before, that I'd been so proud of myself, so possessive of what was not mine at all, of a place where I walked only on the sufferance of the ancestral spirits guarding it, and only because those to whom this field and those graves rightly belonged had been rendered powerless to stop me.

The eminent American writer Gary Snyder, in *The Practice of the Wild*, in an essay called "The Place, the Region, and the Commons," says this:

> Sometime in the mid-seventies at a conference of Native American leaders and activists in Bozeman, Montana, I heard a Crow elder say something similar: "You know, I think if people stay somewhere long enough—even white people—the spirits will begin to speak to them. It's the power of the spirits coming up from the land. The spirits and the old powers aren't lost, they just need people to be around long enough and the spirits will begin to influence them."

To understand the profound meaning of land—to walk on it with the respect, born of real understanding, of the traditional Amerindian, to see it as sacred—is to be terrified, shattered, humbled, and, in the end, joyous. It is to come home at last.

2000

---

6. Understanding.

Morley Callaghan
1903–1990

For many years Callaghan was Canada's premier short story writer and a widely read novelist. Born in Toronto, and very much of that city, Callaghan lived in Paris during the thirties, as part of the Lost Generation, with other writers such as James Joyce, Ernest Hemingway and F. Scott Fitzgerald. He returned to Toronto, to his own place. That Summer in Paris *(1963) by Callaghan,* Memoirs of Montparnasse *(1970) by John Glassco, and* A Moveable Feast *(1964) by Ernest Hemingway make a lively trilogy of memoirs.*

A devout Roman Catholic, Callaghan wrote fiction which has been compared to medieval morality plays. There is always a moral issue, personal in his early fiction, social in his later work. Among his well-known novels are Such Is My Beloved *(1934),* More Joy in Heaven *(1937), and* The Loved and the Lost *(1951). His short stories were gathered into* Morley Callaghan's Stories *(1959), which included this story, first published in 1934. This version is from* The Complete Stories *(2003).*

In a time when readers still valued the romantic, decorated fiction of Victorian writers, Callaghan was criticized for his plain, straightforward style, described by reviewers as blunt and ugly. His fiction was written at arm's length, without his presence in it, and he was among the first to explore life in the urban environment. It took a while for readers to get used to him, as seems to happen with the beginning of all literary movements. In the 1920s and 1930s, Callaghan introduced Canadians to early modernist fiction.

This story is typical of his work, as it does not judge who was right and who was wrong. Who knew what? Callaghan leaves much unsaid in this story, by Bob as well as by Sheila. The understanding between Bob and the men in her family infuriates Sheila. She may not recognize—or want—the protection it gives her.

One Spring Night

They had been to an eleven o'clock movie. Afterward, as they sat very late in the restaurant, Sheila was listening to Bob Davis, showing by the quiet gladness that kept coming into her face the enjoyment she felt in being with him. She was the young sister of his friend, Jack Staples. Every time Bob had been at their apartment, she had come into the room, they had laughed and joked with her, they had teased her about the way she wore her clothes, and she had always smiled and answered them in a slow, measured way.

Bob took her out a few times when he felt like having a girl to talk to who knew him and liked him. And tonight he was leaning back good-humouredly, telling her one thing and then another with the wise self-assurance he usually had when with her; but gradually, as he watched her, he found himself talking more slowly, his voice grew serious and much softer, and then finally he leaned across the table toward her as though he had just discovered that her neck was full and soft with her spring coat thrown open, and that her face under her little black straw hat tilted back on her head had a new, eager beauty. Her warm, smiling softness was so close to him that he smiled a bit shyly.

"What are you looking at, Bob?" she said.

"What is there about you that seems different tonight?" he said, and they both began to laugh lightly, as if sharing the same secret.

When they were outside, walking along arm in arm and liking the new spring night air, Sheila said quickly, "It's awfully nice out tonight. Let's keep walking a while, Bob," and she held his arm as though very sure of him.

"All right," he said. "We'll walk till we get so tired we'll have to sit on the curb. It's nearly two o'clock, but it doesn't seem to matter much, does it?"

Every step he took with Sheila leaning on his arm in this new way, and with him feeling now that she was a woman he hardly knew, made the excitement grow in him, and yet he was uneasy. He was much taller than Sheila and he kept looking down at her, and she always smiled back with frank gladness. Then he couldn't help squeezing her arm tight, and he started to talk recklessly about any-thing that came into his head, swinging his free arm and putting passionate eloquence into the simplest words. She was listening as she used to listen when he talked with her brother and father in the evenings, only now she wanted him to see how much she liked hav-ing him tonight all for herself. Almost pleading, she said, "Are you having a good time, Bob? Don't you like the streets at night, when there's hardly anybody on them?"

They stopped and looked along the wide avenue and up the towering, slanting faces of the buildings to the patches of night sky. Holding out her small, gloved hand in his palm, he patted it with his other hand, and they both laughed as though he had done something foolish but charming. The whole city was quieter now, the streets flowed away from them without direction, but there was always the hum underneath the silence like something restless and stirring and really touching them, as the soft, spring night air of the streets touched them, and at a store door he pulled her into the shadow and kissed her warmly, and when she didn't resist he kept on kissing her. Then they walked on again happily. He didn't care what he talked about; he talked about the advertising agency where he had gone to work the year before, and what he planned to do when he got more money, and each word had a feeling of reckless elation behind it.

For a long time they walked on aimlessly like this before he noticed that she was limping. Her face kept on turning up to him, and she laughed often, but she was really limping badly. "What's the matter, Sheila? What's the matter with your foot?" he said.

"It's my heel," she said, lifting her foot off the ground. "My shoe has been rubbing against it." She tried to laugh. "It's all right, Bob," she said, and she tried to walk on without limping.

"You can't walk like that, Sheila."

"Maybe if we just took it off for a minute, Bob, it would be all right," she said as though asking a favor of him.

"I'll take it off for you," he said, and he knelt down on one knee while she lifted her foot and balanced herself with her arm on his shoulder. He drew off the shoe gently.

"Oh, the air feels so nice and cool on my heel," she said. No one was coming along the street. For a long time he remained kneeling, caressing her ankle gently and looking up with his face full of concern. "Try and put it on now, Bob," she said. But when he pushed the shoe over the heel, she said, "Good heavens, it seems tighter than ever." She limped along for a few steps. "Maybe we should never have taken it off. There's a blister there," she said.

"It was crazy to keep on walking like this," he said. "I'll call a taxi

as soon as one comes along." They were standing by the curb, with
her leaning heavily on his arm, and he was feeling protective and
considerate, for with her heel hurting her, she seemed more like the
young girl he had known. "Look how late it is. It's nearly four
o'clock," he said. "Your father will be wild."

"It's terribly late," she said.

"It's my fault. I'll tell him it was all my fault."

For a while she didn't raise her head. When she did look up at
him, he thought she was frightened. "What will they say when I go
home at this hour, Bob?"

"It'll be all right. I'll go right in with you," he said.

"Wouldn't it be better . . . Don't you think it would be all right if
I stayed the night with Alice—with my girl friend?"

She was so hesitant that it worried him, and he said emphatically,
"It's nearly morning now, and anyway, your father knows you're
with me."

"Where'll we say we've been till this hour, Bob?"

"Just walking."

"Maybe he won't believe it. Maybe he's sure by this time I'm staying with Alice. If there was some place I could go . . ." While she
waited for him to answer, all that had been growing in her for such
a long time was showing in the softness of her dark, sure eyes.

A half-ashamed feeling came over him and he began thinking of
himself at the apartment, talking with Jack and the old man, and
with Sheila coming in and listening with her face full of seriousness.
"Why should you think there'll be trouble?" he said. "Your father
will probably be in bed."

"I guess he will," she said quickly. "I'm silly. I ought to know
that. There was nothing . . . I must have sounded silly." She began
to fumble for words, and then her confusion was so deep that she
could not speak.

"I'm surprised you don't know your father better than that," he
said rapidly, as though offended. He was anxious to make it an argument between them over her father. He wanted to believe this
himself, so he tried to think only of the nights when her father, with
his white head and moustache, had talked in his good-humoured
way about the old days and the old eating-places, but every one of
these conversations, every one of these nights that came into his

thoughts, had Sheila there, too, listening and watching. Then it got so that he could remember nothing of those times but her intense young face, which kept rising before him, although he had never been aware that he had paid much attention to her. So he said desperately, "There's the friendliest feeling in the world between your people and me. Leave it to me. We'll go back to the corner, where we can see a taxi."

They began to walk slowly to the corner, with her still limping though he held her arm firmly. He began to talk with a soft persuasiveness, eager to have her respond readily, but she only said, "I don't know what's the matter. I feel tired or something." When they were standing on the street corner, she began to cry a little.

"Poor little Sheila," he said. Then she said angrily, "Why 'poor little Sheila?' There's nothing the matter with me. I'm just tired." And they both kept looking up and down the street for a taxi.

Then one came, they got in, and he sat with his arm along the back of the seat, just touching her shoulder. He dared not tighten his arm around her, though never before had he wanted so much to be gentle with anyone; but with the street lights sometimes flashing on her face and showing the bewildered whiteness that was in it, he was scared to disturb her.

As soon as they opened the apartment door and lit the lights in the living room, they heard her father come shuffling from his bedroom. His white moustache was working up and down furiously as he kept wetting his lips, and his hair, which was always combed nicely, was mussed over his head because he had been lying down. "Where have you been till this hour, Sheila?" he said. "I kept getting up all the time. Where have you been?"

"Just walking with Bob," she said. "I'm dead tired, Dad. We lost all track of time." She spoke very calmly and then she smiled, and Bob saw how well she knew that her father loved her. Her father's face was full of concern while he peered at her, and she only smiled openly, showing no worry and saying, "Poor Daddy, I never dreamed you'd get up. I hope Jack is still sleeping."

"Jack said if you were with Bob, you were all right," Mr. Staples said. Glancing at Bob, he added curtly, "She's only eighteen, you know. I thought you had more sense."

"I guess we were fools to walk for hours like that, Mr. Staples,"

Bob said. "Sheila's got a big blister on her foot." Bob shook his head as if he couldn't understand why he had been so stupid.

Mr. Staples looked a long time at Sheila, and then he looked shrewdly at Bob; they were both tired and worried, and they were standing close together. Mr. Staples cleared his throat two or three times and said, "What on earth got into the pair of you?" Then he grinned suddenly and said, "Isn't it extraordinary what young people do? I'm so wide-awake now I can't sleep, I was making myself a cup of coffee. Won't you both sit down and have a cup with me? Bob?"

"I'd love to," Bob said heartily.

"You go ahead. I won't have any coffee. It would keep me awake," Sheila said.

"The water's just getting hot," Mr. Staples said. "It will be ready in a minute." Still chuckling and shaking his head, for he was glad Sheila had come in, he said, "I kept telling myself she was all right if she was with you, Bob." Bob and Mr. Staples grinned broadly at each other. But when her father spoke like this, Sheila raised her head, and Bob thought that he saw her smile at him. He wanted to smile, too, but he couldn't look at her and had to turn away uneasily. And when he did turn to her again, it was almost pleadingly, for he was thinking, "I did the only thing there was to do. It was the right thing, so why should I feel ashamed now?" and yet he kept on remembering how she had cried a little on the street corner. He longed to think of something to say that might make her smile agreeably—some gentle, simple, friendly remark that would make her feel close to him—but he could only go on remembering how yielding she had been.

Her father was saying cheerfully, "I'll go and get the coffee now."

"I don't think I'd better stay," Bob said.

"It'll only take a few minutes," Mr. Staples said.

"I don't think I'll wait," Bob said, but Mr, Staples, smiling and shaking his head, went into the kitchen to get the coffee. Bob kept watching Sheila, who was supporting her head with her hand and frowning a little. There was some of the peacefulness in her face now that had been there days ago, only there was also a new, full softness; she was very quiet, maybe feeling again the way he had kissed her, and then she frowned as though puzzled, as though she was listening and overhearing herself say timidly, "If there was some place I could go . . ."

Growing more and more uneasy, Bob said, "It turned out all right, don't you see, Sheila?"

"What?" she said.

"There was no trouble about coming home," he said.

As she watched him without speaking, she was not at all like a young girl. Her eyes were shining. All the feeling of the whole night was surging through her; she could hardly hold all the mixed-up feeling that was stirring her, and then her face grew warm with shame and she said savagely, "Why don't you go? Why do you want to sit there talking, talking, talking?"

"I don't know," he said.

"Go on. Please go. Please," she said,

"All right, I'll go," he muttered, and he got up clumsily, his face hot with humiliation.

In the cold, early-morning light, with heavy trucks rumbling on the street, he felt tense and nervous. He could hardly remember anything that had happened. He wanted to reach out and hold that swift, ardent, yielding joy that had been so close to him. For a while he could not think at all. And then he felt a slow unfolding coming in him again, making him quick with wonder.

1934, 2003

Roch Carrier
b. 1937

Carrier was born in Sainte-Justine-de-Dorchester, a village in the southeastern part of the province of Quebec. A sophisticated writer, educated in Montreal and at the Sorbonne in Paris, with a long list of literary credits and prizes, Carrier has almost folk hero status in Quebec and in the rest of Canada for his many novels and plays about the people he has lived among.

This story comes from a collection called Les enfants du bon-homme dans la lune (The Children of the Man in the Moon). *That title seems exactly right for these whimsical, sometimes nostal-*

*gic stories about people who lived close to the land and to one an-
other, isolated from urban beliefs, suspicious of them.*

In English, that collection of stories is The Hockey Sweater and
Other Stories *(1979). It is a much more prosaic title, but on a new
Canadian $5 bill, in tiny print, in French and then in English, are
the opening lines of the title story:*

> *The winters of my childhood were long, long seasons. We lived in
> three places—the school, the church and the skating rink—but
> our real life was on the skating rink.*

*Most school children in Canada have read that story, or have seen
the National Film Board's animated adaptation of it.*

*These are the stories of small boys wandering their world, trying
to figure out why girls have bumps, why some people speak another
language (English), or where God lives. The story which follows is
the final one in the collection, where the narrator has left that
world for another one, which values science and learning above experience and folkways. He discovers that this other learning comes
at a cost. Ancient skills can be lost in the acquiring of newer, more
measurable ones. That loss can have far-reaching effects.*

A Secret Lost in the Water

After I started going to school my father scarcely talked any
more. I was very intoxicated by the new game of spelling;
my father had little skill for it (it was my mother who wrote
our letters) and was convinced I was no longer interested in hearing
him tell of his adventures during the long weeks when he was far
away from the house.

One day, however, he said to me:

"The time's come to show you something."

He asked me to follow him. I walked behind him, not talking, as
we had got in the habit of doing. He stopped in the field before a
clump of leafy bushes.

"Those are called alders," he said.

"I know."

"You have to learn how to choose," my father pointed out.

I didn't understand. He touched each branch of the bush, one at a time, with religious care.

"You have to choose one that's very fine, a perfect one, like this."

I looked; it seemed exactly like the others.

My father opened his pocket knife and cut the branch he'd selected with pious care. He stripped off the leaves and showed me the branch, which formed a perfect Y.

"You see," he said, "the branch has two arms. Now take one in each hand. And squeeze them."

I did as he asked and took in each hand one fork of the Y, which was thinner than a pencil.

"Close your eyes," my father ordered, "and squeeze a little harder . . . Don't open your eyes! Do you feel anything?"

"The branch is moving!" I exclaimed, astonished.

Beneath my clenched fingers the alder was wriggling like a small, frightened snake. My father saw that I was about to drop it.

"Hang on to it!"

"The branch is squirming," I repeated. "And I hear something that sounds like a river!"

"Open your eyes," my father ordered.

I was stunned, as though he'd awakened me while I was dreaming.

"What does it mean?" I asked my father.

"It means that underneath us, right here, there's a little freshwater spring. If we dig, we could drink from it. I've just taught you how to find a spring. It's something my own father taught me. It isn't something you learn in school. And it isn't useless: a man can get along without writing and arithmetic, but he can never get along without water."

Much later, I discovered that my father was famous in the region because of what the people called his "gift:" before digging a well they always consulted him; they would watch him prospecting the fields or the hills, eyes closed, hands clenched on the fork of an alder bough. Wherever my father stopped, they marked the ground; there they would dig; and from there water would gush forth.

Years passed; I went to other schools, saw other countries, I had children, I wrote some books and my poor father is lying in the earth where so many times he had found fresh water.

One day someone began to make a film about my village and its inhabitants, from whom I've stolen so many of the stories that I tell. With the film crew we went to see a farmer to capture the image of a sad man: his children didn't want to receive the inheritance he'd spent his whole life preparing for them—the finest farm in the area. While the technicians were getting cameras and microphones ready the farmer put his arm around my shoulders, saying:

"I knew your father well."

"Ah! I know. Everybody in the village knows each other . . . No one feels like an outsider."

"You know what's under your feet?"

"Hell?" I asked, laughing.

"Under your feet there's a well. Before I dug I called in specialists from the Department of Agriculture; they did research, they analyzed shovelfuls of dirt; and they made a report where they said there wasn't any water on my land. With the family, the animals, the crops, I need water. When I saw that those specialists hadn't found any I thought of your father and I asked him to come over. He didn't want to; I think he was pretty fed up with me because I'd asked those specialists instead of him. But finally he came; he went and cut off a little branch, then he walked around for a while with his eyes shut; he stopped, he listened to something we couldn't hear and then he said to me: 'Dig right here, there's enough water to get your whole flock drunk and drown your specialists besides.' We dug and found water. Fine water that's never heard of pollution."

The film people were ready; they called to me to take my place.

"I'm gonna show you something," said the farmer, keeping me back. "You wait right here."

He disappeared into a shack which he must have used to store things, then came back with a branch which he held out to me.

"I never throw nothing away; I kept the alder branch your father cut to find my water. I don't understand, it hasn't dried out."

Moved as I touched the branch, kept out of I don't know what sense of piety—and which really wasn't dry—I had the feeling that my father was watching me over my shoulder; I closed my eyes and, standing above the spring my father had discovered, I waited for the branch to writhe, I hoped the sound of gushing water would rise to my ears.

The alder stayed motionless in my hands and the water beneath the earth refused to sing.

Somewhere along the roads I'd taken since the village of my childhood I had forgotten my father's knowledge.

"Don't feel sorry," said the man, thinking no doubt of his farm and his childhood; "nowadays fathers can't pass on anything to the next generation."

And he took the alder branch from my hands.

1979

Wayson Choy
b. 1939

Born in Vancouver in what he refers to as "Old Chinatown," Choy has spent his adult life in Toronto, writing and teaching at Humber College. He has always been fascinated by the stories he heard around him as a boy and by the secrets of his community. He tells his students to turn off the television and listen to their families before their stories are all lost. Choy has always especially valued the story-telling voice which connects people to one another.

For many years, Choy rejected his Chinese heritage. He wanted to be "Canadian." He had always thought that his own family was ordinary and that no one would be interested in them. That attitude changed when he decided to write The Jade Peony *(1995), his first novel about his childhood community. This best-selling and highly influential novel won the prestigious Trillium Award. Its sequel is* All That Matters *(2004). Because of these books, Choy has become an informal spokesperson for Canada's Chinese-speaking communities.*

This personal essay, from the anthology Writing Home *(1997), opens out into the history of Vancouver's Chinese community. It might also be described as creative nonfiction, because it includes strategies usually associated with fiction, such as imagery, dialogue, and character development. Indirectly, we learn a good deal about Choy, as he makes himself the narrator of this account, telling the story of a startling discovery about his life, which continues in his non-fiction book,* Paper Shadows *(1999), winner of the Edna Staebler Award for Creative Non-Fiction. Choy is the subject of a documentary film,* Wayson Choy: Unfolding the Butterfly.

The Ten Thousand Things

"I saw your mother last week."

The stranger's voice on the phone surprised me. She spoke firmly, clearly, with the accents of Vancouver's Old Chinatown: "I saw your *mah-ma* on the streetcar."

Not possible. Mother died nineteen years ago.

Nineteen years ago I had sat on a St. Paul's hospital bed beside her skeletal frame, while the last cells of her lungs clogged up. She lay gasping for breath: the result of decades of smoking. I stroked her forehead, and with my other hand I clasped her thin motionless fingers. Around two in the morning, half asleep and weary, I closed my eyes to catnap. Suddenly, the last striving for breath shook her thin body. I snapped awake, conscious again of the smell of acetone, of death burning away her body. The silence deepened; the room chilled. The mother I had known all my life was gone.

Nineteen years later, in response to a lively radio interview about my first novel, a woman left a mysterious message, URGENT WAYSON CHOY CALL THIS NUMBER.

Back at my hotel room, message in hand, I dialled the number and heard an older woman's voice tell me she had seen my mother on the streetcar. She insisted.

"You must be mistaken," I said, confident that this woman, her voice charged with nervous energy, would recognize her error and sign off.

"No, no, not your mother," the voice persisted. "I mean your *real* mother."

"My first crazy," I remember thinking. *The Jade Peony* had been launched just two days before at the Vancouver Writers' Festival, and already I had a crazy. "Watch out for the crazies!" my agent had, half-whimsically, warned me. The crazies had declared open season upon another of her clients, a young woman who had written frankly of sexual matters. I was flattered, hardly believing that my novel about Vancouver's Old Chinatown could provoke such perverse attention. Surely, my caller was simply mistaken.

"I saw your *real* mother," the voice insisted, repeating the word "real" as if it were an incantation.

My *real* mother? I looked down at the polished desk, absently studied the Hotel Vancouver room-service menu. My real mother was dead; I had been there to witness her going. I had come home that same morning nineteen years ago and seen her flowered apron carefully draped over the kitchen chair, folded precisely, as it had been every day of my life. I remember taking the apron, quickly hiding it from my father's eyes as he, in his pyjamas, shuffled on his cane into the kitchen. Seeing the apron missing from the chair, he asked, "She's—?" but could not finish the question. He stood staring at the back of the chair. He leaned his frail eighty-plus years against me. Speechless, I led him back to his bed.

The voice on the hotel phone chattered on, spilling out details and relationships, talking of Pender *Gai*[1] and noting how my brand-new book talked of the "secrets of Chinatown." I suddenly caught my family name pronounced distinctively and correctly, *Tuey*. Then my grandfather's, my mother's, and my father's formal Chinese names, rarely heard, sang into my consciousness over the earpiece.

"Yes, yes," the voice went on, "those are your family names?"

"Yes, they are," I answered, "but who are you?"

"Call me Hazel," she said.

Months later, Hazel turned up to be interviewed; we had tea, some dumplings, and bowls of *jook*.[2] In 1939, when she herself was in her teens, Hazel had taken care of a baby named *Way Sun*. Her family home had been a kind of short-term foster home for in-transit Chinatown children. It was 1939, the year of the Royal Visit, and Hazel's own mother had desperately wanted to see the King and Queen parade down Hastings and Granville streets.

"That's why I remember your name," Hazel said. She proved to be a friendly, talkative woman in her late sixties, wisps of grey hair floating about her. "Unusual name, *Way Sun*. Your new mother worried that you wouldn't have a birth certificate."

"But I have one," I insisted.

"That was because *my* mother was a midwife," Hazel said. "My mother told the government clerk you born at home." She sipped from her teacup and laughed. "What do they know? What do they

---

1. Street (pron. "guy").   2. Rice gruel.

care?" Her eyes sparkled with memory. "Those old days! Here was a
China baby, just a few weeks old! They maybe think, things done
differently in Chinatown! Anyway, nobody care about one more
China baby! Everybody worry about the war."

A few months before Hazel and I met, I had cornered my two
aunts, to whom I had dedicated my book. Was I adopted, I wanted
to know, as Hazel had told me? My two aunts looked at each other.
In an interview with me, the reporter from *Maclean's* magazine had
noted that "a caller" had left me perplexed about my birth. Surely
Aunt Freda and Aunt Mary knew the truth.

I had written a novel about the secrets of Chinatown, and in the
kaleidoscope of my life, one single phone call had altered the picture significantly, shifted all the pieces: my life held secrets, too.
This real-life drama beginning to unfold, this eerie echo of the life
of one of my fictional characters, seemed absurd. Suddenly, nothing
of my family, of home, seemed solid and specific. Nothing in my
past seemed to be what it had always been.

During the Depression and the War years, the trading and selling of
children, especially the giving and taking of male children, were not
uncommon practices either of Old China or of the Old Chinatowns
of North America. Canada's 1923 Exclusion Act and similar racist
laws passed earlier in the United States all forbade the immigration
of Chinese women and children. Thus, there were only limited
numbers of Chinese families in North America. Chinatowns became social and sexual pressure cookers; bachelor-men dominated
the population. Children were being born, wanted and unwanted.
Scandals and suicides multiplied. Family joys were balanced by family suffering.

In the hothouse climate of Vancouver's Chinatown in the 1920s,
'30s, and mid-'40s, children were born and kept mainly within their
own families, or family tongs;[3] however, a secret few were sold,
traded, or given away to fill a childless couple's empty nest, or to
balance a family that lacked a first-born son to carry on their kin-
ship name; family pride and Confucian tradition[4] demanded a son

---

3. Associations, often secret.　　4. Philosophical system named for Con-
fucius (551–479 B.C.E.)

to inherit the family artefacts. And so, I must have been sold, traded, or given away to balance my adoptive parents' empty nest. I was to be the only child, a son, heir to the family name and worldly goods.

My adopted parents had both died, believing that I would never discover that they were not my birth parents, that my memory of home had been fraudulent in a sense, lovingly fraudulent. Now the truth was trickling out. The ground shifted under me. Was it true? Was I adopted?

At the airport restaurant where we spoke, my two aunts looked sheepishly at each other, and then, eyes full of loving concern, they turned to look at me. I said nothing. At last, Freda confessed, "Yes, yes, you are adopted." Mary quickly added, "So what? To me, you're just as much a part of our family."

"You're even better than that!" Freda laughed. "You were chosen. We just got born into the damn family!"

I didn't laugh. Hearing them confirm Hazel's claim made me pause: all those years that I had taken "home" for granted. . . . A long drawn-out sigh escaped from me: I had become an orphan three weeks before my fifty-seventh birthday. I glanced at the date registered on my watch.

"Tomorrow is April Fool's Day," I finally said, voice maudlin. Then, barely able to contain ourselves, we all three burst out laughing.

"Life has no beginning . . . nor ending." The man whom I thought was my father had said this to me three days before he died. "Good things go on being good," he said, sighing that long sigh that I had learned from him. "Bad things go on being bad."

Unlike the woman whom I had thought was my mother, the man whom I'd taken for my father was not afraid to talk of other mysteries and losses, of life past, and even of his own eventual dying that summer's end at St. Paul's Hospital.

In this hospital, throughout the '30s, the nuns had lobbied the city fathers and the health authorities to admit the people of Chinatown into its ill-lit, mildewed basement. In this hospital, the Chinese and other undesirables—"Resident Aliens"—were to be nursed back to health or to die there, at least in the care of God's holy servants. *His* father died there, in the basement; and in September of 1982, the man I had known as *my* father ended his life, at eighty-five, of a stomach cancer he accepted as the last indignity.

He stayed, not in the basement, but in a sixth-floor bed that looked over the West End, in a newly built wing of St. Paul's, in a room that was flooded with morning light, free of dampness and mildew. His eyes had grown too cloudy to see anything but light. I rubbed his back with mineral oil, his skin like a baby's. He barely smiled. He had been happy to greet my friend Marie, who had flown in from Toronto to be with both of us. That last evening, with Marie's gentle encouragement, he accepted from me a spoonful of fruit salad. He took into his dry mouth a seedless grape, but would not swallow.

The next morning at eight o'clock, when he died, a torrential rainstorm lashed the city. Marie, so beloved of my father, touched my father's stiff hands and brought them together. As his only son, I kissed his still-warm forehead and marvelled at life and death.

I did not know then that he was not my *real* father; I only knew that this old man—whose outward frailty betrayed the tough spirit within—was the man I had loved as my father all my life. There was no other.

Since hearing from Hazel, I have thought often of the Chinese phrase "the ten thousand things," whose number symbolically suggests how countless are the ways of living and dying, how much of love and life cannot be fathomed. And I have thought of the Cantonese opera.

"My Aunt Helena says that your father was a member of one of the opera companies," Hazel told me, much later, in her young-again, excited voice.

On my behalf, Hazel had been earnestly digging up as much information from the Elders as she could. She had already learned that the person she thought was my *real* mother, the old woman she saw on the streetcar, was not my real mother after all. She, it turns out, had died decades ago. And, yes, the man who fathered me was a member of one of the opera companies. Alas, there was no more information; at least, no more was revealed by the Elders. Not even Mrs. Lee, a best friend of my adoptive parents, would admit she knew anything. So much you can know, and no more.

For the past two years, long before Hazel's first telephone call sent her seismic quake through my world, I had been, ironically, researching the Cantonese Opera, especially the touring Chinese opera companies that had thrived all through the '30s and '40s from Canton to Hong Kong, from San Francisco to Seattle to Vancouver, the semi-professional companies that formed "the Bamboo Circuit." My second novel, the one I'm writing now, is centred around the Vancouver opera companies of Old Chinatown.

Since childhood, I had been enthralled with the high drama and acrobatics of Chinese opera. The woman who was known to me as my mother had taken me to see the operas and then, afterwards, to visit Shanghai Alley and the smoky backstage of the opera company. There, among jewelled headpieces, gleaming costumes, and prop curtains, she played mah-jong[5] with members of the troop, while I was being spoiled by sweetmeats or left alone to play with costumed opera dolls with fierce warrior faces. Alone, I became a prince and a warrior, my parents the Emperor and Empress. All the adventures of the world were possible, and I the hero of them all. Finally, I remember the laughter and sing-song voices, the *clack-click* of the bamboo and ivory game tiles, lulling me to sleep.

Even today I recall, as a child, dreaming of the fabled opera costumes, how they swirled to glittering life, how I flew acrobatically through the air between spinning red banners and clouds of yellow silk and heard the roar and clanging of drums and cymbals. And how I fought off demons and ghosts to great applause. Were those dreams in my blood?

"The way things were in those old days," Hazel said, pushing back a strand of her salt-and-pepper hair, "best to let the old stories rest. Your father belonged to the opera company, that's what my Aunt Helena says."

For the past two summers, I had pored over the tinted cast and production photos of the opera companies in Vancouver. For intense seconds, without realizing it, I must have caught a smile, a glimpse of a hairline as familiar as my own; I must have seen eyes looking back through the photographer's plates, eyes like my own: I might have seen, staring back at me, the man who surely was my fa-

---

5. A game for four, played with 144 tiles.

ther. I cannot help myself: I imagine the man who fathered me, dressed in imperial splendour, sword in hand; he is flying above me, majestic and detached. If I were seventeen, and not fifty-seven, would I weep to know that this man abandoned me?

"Best to let the stories rest," Hazel repeated.

And so I do. I let the stories rest, though not quite. My writer's mind races on, unstoppable. I had always thought of my family, my home, in such a solid, no-nonsense, no-mystery manner, how could I possibly think that the untold stories would never be told?

I think of myself as the child I was, playing with the fierce-faced dolls among the backstage wooden swords and stretched drums of the opera company. I see myself, five years old, being watched and wondered at by a tall figure behind me, a figure who slips away if I turn my head towards him. Was that the man who fathered me? And perhaps a woman—the birth mother—raises her hand at the mah-jong table and smiles at me, briefly noting how blessed my life now seems. How lucky I am, to share the fate of the man and woman I came to know as Mother and Father, decent and good people, who, all my life, loved me as their own.

I marvel that the ten thousand things should raise questions I never thought to ask, should weave abiding mystery into my life. How did most of us come to think of parents and family and home, as if there were no mysteries, really? How did most of us contrive for decades to speak neither of the unknown nor of the knowable? And how, with the blessing of a community that knew when to keep silent and when—at last—to speak up, I am come home again, like a child, opened up again to dreams and possibility.

At home, I turn on my computer to begin tapping out the second novel; in the middle of a sentence—like this one, in fact—I laugh aloud. I had been writing fiction about life in Chinatown; Chinatown, all these years, had been writing me.

1997

Ann Copeland
b. 1932

Copeland has had a somewhat complicated life. She spent thirteen years as an Ursuline nun, she has been married for many years, she has raised two sons. When she moved from Chicago to New Brunswick, she discovered that she could not find work teaching, so she decided to write fiction. Copeland says that she began to teach herself to write, in a small corner inside a United Church chapel, partly to try to find a thread to hold together all the discontinuities of her life. At Peace (1979) was her first of several short story collections. Another, The Golden Thread *(1989), was nominated for a Governor General's Award.*

Copeland also wanted to explore links between religious and secular life, without relying on religious language or symbolism. She watches the implications of language and how people use it. She also believes that a fiction writer creates worlds to dramatize human questions, to challenge a reader's moral imagination.

Copeland's varied experiences and purposes come together in this story, taken from The Back Room *(1979), which presents people— who think they understand one another—trying to talk. The narrator knows that she is watching two different styles of language, values and being—which never connect. Urban business discourse and a rural artist's discourse simply do not match. Ann Copeland's time as an Ursuline nun may have helped her to understand the observer, the narrator who watches this disconnect, without judging it. She knows both these very different worlds, both these languages, but she cannot find a way to help these two women talk to one another.*

The Bear's Paw

From the beginning I had the feeling Honey might blow it, with her nose for a bargain and her hunger to win. She *is* shrewd though, and I've often underestimated her before. So, despite my doubts, I took her along to see Minnie. I'd already placed my bet on who would win.

The day was bleak in a way that spells Maritime non-spring to me. Slate sky, nipping marsh wind, a chill to eat the heart out of any foolhardy crocus. Of these there were none, though we'd left plenty behind in Connecticut. Just miles and miles of evergreens here saving the landscape from total desolateness; and just as many miles of stripped maples, dead grey, and grey dead snow chunking and rutting here and there. Too cold to melt. Spring thaw is a joke here: it comes in May. *Late* May.

The road was even nastier than its border. Sprinkled with potholes—not slight bumps but deep wide holes that throttled the car and us inside, shaking our guts.

"Good God, Marion! This isn't what those gorgeous brochures promised! All those sailboats skimming along on blue ocean! Fresh lobster cheap. Charming rural countryside. Who'd want to live here? Don't they know winter's over?"

"No such thing as spring here, Honey. I warned you. They move right into summer. A gorgeous summer, too. No humidity. While we're boiling in Westchester barely able to drag ourselves around, they're enjoying clear fresh sunny weather here."

"I'll believe that when I see it, if I ever do. But this whole scene strikes me as the last word in dismal. What do they *do* here? Broken-down houses, collapsing barns. My God, it looks poor!"

She stared at rows of small pastel-coloured houses as we pulled into the village. Then she ground out her cigarette and pulled tight the lapels of her London Fog.

"Should've told me I needed my fur coat!"

"Hold on, Honey. We'll be back in civilization tomorrow. Do you really want to see Minnie or not? I wrote we *might* come, but it's easy enough to write again from the other end in a few days and say I'm sorry we didn't make it. What do you say?"

"Oh sure, sure." She turned toward me with that swift shift of mood that can devastate her customers. "I'd kick myself if I had this chance for a bargain and passed it up. You know that!"

Her father was a pawnbroker. She specializes in tag sales. Doesn't sound like much but she's made a bundle and continues to. One man's trash is another man's treasure. In her case that's true. She can sniff out a bargain miles away. If you could watch her scan the local *Bargain News* you'd see what I mean. A real pro. All business. If you need space, she'll rent you a place for your sale. If you've leftovers that didn't go, she'll buy them. She spends her Saturdays travelling around from neighbourhood to neighbourhood in Westchester County dickering, snapping up bargains. Fascinating to watch. She'll approach a housewife who has cleaned out her attic and inquire innocently about an item. Then she'll explain she's really shopping for a friend and offer a sum substantially below the price. She'll hang around long enough to size up the competition, go around the corner and call on the phone to say she's just talked her friend into going a dollar or two higher. In the end she gets her item, usually without making an enemy. Later—resells it for twice the price. She knows her goods.

It seemed pointless to remind her we were light-years away from New York, in every sense. After all, she'd been driving through that landscape with me for two days. So—on to Minnie's.

Her house is unobtrusive: grey clapboard with a small evergreen on either side of the cement steps leading up to the enclosed front porch. As we turned down Everett Street I saw the light on the porch and knew she'd be sitting there, sewing. Planning. Dreaming up designs. I honoured a twinge at the sight of that light: two summers since I'd seen Minnie. The usual Christmas cards, the occasional note. When I'd written that we would be coming through off season and might stop, I was prodded into it by Honey.

"Where did you *ever* find it, Marion?" she raved at the sight of the quilt Minnie sent my daughter Cathy for her birthday. The scent of a bargain was in the air. She knew I'd never pay the Bergdorf[1] price—up to $500 these days.

"An old friend of ours, Honey. An ancient lady who lives in Nova Scotia. She spends her time quilting . . . does all her own work. Cathy fell in love with Minnie's quilts years ago. And this arrived for her fifteenth birthday."

"Well, what're we waiting for? *Let's go to Nova Scotia!*" Said in jest then but remembered later when the chance came to do just that. So here we were.

I hadn't minded having her along. Honey's good company. But we both knew that underneath all her good humour there was the

1. Bergdorf Goodman is a luxury clothing store on Fifth Avenue in New York City.

hope of a kill. If she could snare one of these patchwork wonders for, say $50, she'd carry it back to Westchester crowing. To say nothing of what she'd do if she could work out some steady arrangement. I could feel her wheels turning.

One ding-a-ling of the bell and the chair inside squeaked. She was there. Predictably.

"Damn weather!" groaned Honey as she stamped her feet on the porch to warm her toes. "Perfect weather for quilts!"

The plastic curtain behind the door-window moved slightly. Then the latch jiggled.

I always forget just how tiny Minnie is until I am confronted by that frail body and have to look down into those deep-set grey eyes and wispy hair.

"Marion! Come in, come in!"

The fingers that grasped my arm were strong and urgent, drawing me in from the cold. With a quick eye toward Honey she indicated the door was to be shut tight.

"How *are* you, Marion! I've been hoping you'd get here. Sit down, sit down." She glanced about apologetically. Her porch was, as always, a mess. No chairs cleared, the card-table beside her chair heaped with tiny squares of coloured cloth, papers, magazines, needles, thread, scissors. "You'll have to clear a spot, I'm afraid. But take off your coats, sit down, sit down."

Honey was pulling off her pigskins finger by finger, bargain antennae already quivering.

"I've brought a friend who came up with me for the company, Minnie. We've checked out the damage at the cottage and are on our way back home, but she didn't want to pass up the chance to meet you." Beware, Minnie. "This is Honey Sterling."

"How do you do, Minnie? I've heard *so much* about you from Marion."

Her best meet-the-potential-client manner. Not purely insincere mind you, just shrewdly calculated beneath a layer of real charm.

Minnie was easing back into her chair now, counting on us to clear our spaces, hang coats on the corner coat-tree, find a spot to sit and talk. While she got on with her work.

I could remember that from before. From always. Sit and talk. In such a formula rested the most agreeable way of passing the time for

Minnie. Sit and talk. That meant sitting there while she sorted her pieces, snipped expertly, stitched a bit—working steadily away on one of the quilt-tops she always had going. *You* sat and talked. She sat and talked and worked. As if needle and thread, colour and design could catch the passing moment and fix it in place forever. One felt the possibility of timelessness on Minnie's porch: the tiny bent figure shaping her design, intent, while you sat there and chatted companionably in the pool of sunny warmth and clutter, wondering, perhaps, what sleeping body that quilt would warm long after Minnie's thread had been snipped.

She worked with unflagging enthusiasm—not so much for what she had just produced (though she loved appreciation and wanted to show her work) as for the pattern she'd begun to dream about: Daisy, Tulip, Ship of Dreams, Grandmother's Garden. Some new design was always working inside her ageing head, pushing toward life through fingers that had knotted and swollen but refused yet to stop. You sensed a controlled urgency behind Minnie's steady output: when the needle stopped, she would.

"How did you find the cottage, Marion? Was the damage really that bad?"

"Not as bad as Jack made out in his note, Minnie." Jack is the fisherman who lives there year round and watches out for the place till we get up there summers. Honey was eyeing the bright pieces of cotton. Revving up for the kill. "But there was no way to be sure except to drive up and see. Luckily Honey could come along. Bill couldn't manage any time off and we didn't want to let it go any longer."

"And you, Mrs. Sterling." Minnie had picked up her needle, was threading it as she spoke, then let her hand rest a moment on the blue-and-white print housedress that covered her shallow lap. I couldn't imagine thighs under there: just bones. She seemed to have shrunk even since I'd last seen her. "How do you like our spring?"

I watched Honey mentally select the suitable response. Medium: not too harsh. Negative enough to honour the obvious; positive enough not to insult anyone locked into this world.

"Well, to tell the truth Minnie—do you mind if I call you Minnie, for I've always heard of you that way, you know—it's a bit cold for my tastes!" She glanced about. "You certainly seem to have a few projects going here!"

The offensive was on.

Minnie stalks her prey, too. But not in any way Honey would recognize.

"Well, now, Marion may have told you this is what keeps me going." Minnie reached a knotted hand toward a pile of white squares with designs appliquéed on each piece. She tucked her needle in a pincushion and started to go through the patterns. "I'll show you what I'm working on now, if I can find the sample . . . let's see . . . Double Irish Chain, Drunkard's Path, Nine Patch. . . ."

As she leafed through the old patterns murmuring the litany of titles, that other world we'd so recently left—the world of monogramed bath towels, designer clothes, decorator décor and manicured lawns—seemed to fade like a suggestion of spring on the April marsh. We were back in maritime Canada, all right, O Canada—land of summer vistas and winter withdrawal. The only maple leaves around in this season were red on white, flying over the post office and the elementary school.

What did Honey feel sitting there in her red wool slacks and calf-skin boots soaking up the warmth before we headed out again? Her diamonds gleamed in the sun.

"Here it is! The Bear's Paw!" She pulled forth a yellowing square of cotton on which a design was appliquéed: four tiny triangles for a claw, one square for the centre. "This is old. My mother's work." She held the pattern over for each of us to examine: yellow centre, soft purple (*mauve* she called it) claws. "I'm working on one of these right now, in prints. Almost all the squares are done."

I knew what Honey would think of these colours. Dull. Too pale. Faded. *They just didn't go, Marion. Whoever heard of yellow and— what did she call it?—mauve. No life!* Honey has that way about her. Very dismissive.

"But do you have any that are *finished*, Minnie?" Then, an after-thought. "This *is* lovely, of course."

You goofed, Honey. Royally. Time, friend. It takes time.

Minnie's sharp eyes stared at her for the shade of an instant before she turned back to me.

"And will you be back up this summer, Marion?"

Honey seemed oblivious. No telling. She's good at disguises. She'd picked up a pile of finished squares and was flipping through them, examining colours.

"Late July, it looks like. Eddie is off to camp but Cathy still can't imagine doing anything else with her summers except coming up here. She was thrilled with the quilt you sent, Minnie. She'd always wanted to ask you for one but was too shy."

"Good. I'm glad she likes it. Thought she would."

Unemphatic, but pleased. She had heard from Cathy, I knew. Cathy had joined in the annual visit to Minnie Glover's house ever since our accidental meeting ten years ago at the United Church Summer Bazaar where she sat quietly by her display of quilts and quilt-tops. Something in the quality of her dedication to her craft arrested me. Her prices even then were ridiculously low—if you could ever get her to quote a price. But I felt it then, and on each return visit since then: this whole business was a matter of heart with her. Nothing could induce her to part with one of these treasures unless she saw it would be valued. And that had little to do with dollars and cents. On the other hand, it might have everything to do with it. You could insult her if you offered too little. She knew the amount of time and labour that went into every quilt. A tricky woman to do business with.

I once watched her parry an eager-beaver from Ontario.

TOURIST: "Your work is *love-ly*! And such *de-tail*! Such colour!"
MINNIE: "Thank you. I'm glad you like it." Continuing to stitch.
TOURIST: "I would just love to bring home one of these to show my friends. They'd all be so jealous! You say you've been doing this for years?" Trying not to sound patronizing.
MINNIE: "About 70. My mother—"
TOURIST: "And can you tell me any of the prices? I don't see any marked. . . ."
MINNIE: "Well now, that depends. . . ."

And so it went on and on. The tourist eventually left without her quilt, having offered too little in every sense. Later on Minnie donated it to the Dominion Day Raffle.

Far be it from me to catechize Honey on the perils of bargaining.

Minnie was watching Honey.

"Would you have any *completed* quilt-tops or quilts for sale, Minnie? I just *love* them!"

What made her voice sound a trifle too eager, her crimson nails a shade too bright?

"A few," said Minnie hesitantly, as if wondering whether to drag them out. This was, I knew, just so much manner. They were ready, all of them, stacked neatly in the corner. She was just waiting to be asked.

"Would you show them to us?" Honey leaned forward ingratiatingly.

One point for you, Honey.

"I'll help you, Minnie." I forestalled her, got to the corner first, lifted the plastic garbage-bag and the carton beneath and carried them into the small living-room. "We can spread them out in here." How many times had Cathy and I been through this ritual!

Minnie moved her fragile bones into the living-room and Honey followed, settling herself quickly in the vinyl chair beside the upright—taking in, no doubt, the dog-eared hymn-book propped on the piano.

Minnie lowered herself onto the chesterfield,[2] a long low affair with prickly upholstery and a granny Afghan folded over the back.

I set the bag and carton near her.

"If you'd like to see this—it's my Lovers' Knot," she said, grasping the other two ends while I spread it out on the floor. "My mother's variation on the pattern." Assuming we'd know the original. "I still have all her patterns. They're old, very old. Mother quilted from the time she was a little girl, as I did, and I'm 84, so . . ." Unhurrying.

"Perfectly lovely," murmured Honey in a tone I knew so well. She looked back toward the stack expectantly. Then she picked up one corner of the quilt before her to examine the stitching closely. "A real find! I like the design ever so much . . . but I might rather have an original. And I'm not partial to pink, really."

Minnie seemed not to hear. She was already pulling out another to spread over the Lovers' Knot.

2. A couch or sofa.

"Dresden Plate," she explained.

It lay softly resplendent before us: plates delicately patterned in green, yellow and maroon paisley and spread in seven even rows, each plate a swirl of colour outlined in black feather-stitching.

"Gorgeous colours in this one," said Honey approvingly. "The turquoise is a bit sharp in the centre, but still it is lovely. Is the feather-stitching your own?"

Minnie caught her breath. No reply.

Strike two.

"This one, you see," she stared down at the quilt—"is for my grandchild." She has no grandchild. Her only child died at two. Her husband passed out of the picture long before we ever met her. "She's little now and this doesn't mean too much. But later . . . it may."

She started to refold it with me.

"And what will you do with it in the meantime?" asked Honey curiously.

"Hide it for the day," replied Minnie evenly. "And do you have any children?"

"None of my own, Minnie. But a dear little niece who right now has a Bloomingdale's[3] quilt on her bed. I'd like to bring her a real handmade one."

One after another the wonders were displayed: two patchworks, one Aunt Lizzie's Star, one Drunkard's Path, one Maltese Cross. She explained the patterns to us in a way that assumed we already knew them and wanted only to hear it all again. I'd noticed that before about Minnie, about other Maritimers of her vintage: the assumption that things had always been like this, would always be like this. They had a way of making the world beyond the limits of their established habits a mirage, a fantasy. The Christmas ornaments were still around Minnie's small living-room. She was like the village itself: Christmas decorations up until late May, when summer at last became a sure bet.

"Do you know the work of the Mountain Artisans, Minnie?" asked Honey as we folded the Drunkard's Path away.

Minnie looked up inquiringly.

---

3. A fashionable eastside department store in Manhattan.

"Very beautiful," said Honey. "Their colours tend to be a bit brighter, but that" she conceded thoughtfully, "is a matter of taste, of course. My little niece Deirdre's quilt is a copy of their work."

No mention of the price they command on Madison Avenue.

"Would you care to see the one I'm working on now?"

Honey was beginning to simmer. How she loathes delay, being put off! There comes a moment when you can almost see her gathering her energies for the kill.

"Are you working on it right now, you mean?"

Stalling. Translate: what use is it to me? You're winding up for a strike, Honey.

"We'd love to, Minnie." This much I could do for Honey's cause. . . .

"The Bear's Paw," said Minnie as she slowly pulled herself to the sun-porch and came back carrying a small pile of squares. Honey and I hastily folded away the riot of colour that had piled up on the floor. "I showed you the original pattern before. . . . My but cotton's gone sky-high here." She settled back down on the chesterfield. "Is it that way in the States? It's over a dollar a yard here now. Almost up to two. I can remember when we used to pay 38¢ a yard, years ago. And it gets harder and harder to find it with no stuffing. It's a good thing I've lots of leftovers, enough to keep me going a good long time." She waved toward the sun-porch with its clutter.

Honey's foot was tapping lightly. I could feel her longing for a cigarette.

"Now, Minnie, I really would like to buy one of your *completed* quilts. Can you tell me what you charge?"

Strike-out?

Minnie was bent over laying four squares on the floor.

"I've never done one in prints before," she said as she set down the finished paws, one by one. "When they're arranged like this we call it a block. I've completed enough for all but three blocks. Can't decide on the colour of the sashing. Guess I'll be able to tell when I spread them all out complete."

Honey was stifling a yawn.

"Here, I'll show you another block."

Was Minnie beginning to enjoy herself? What possessed her, I wondered frantically, as we bent down to spread out more blocks and stare at the possibilities of the Bear's Paw. I could feel Honey's eyes wandering back to the pile of folded quilts, trying still, no doubt, to size up her options. Plotting her next move.

"It'll be lovely," she breathed, leaning forward to do her duty by the design spread out on the floor, trying to suppress her irritation. "You never seem to run out of ideas, Minnie. Now could you give us a price on one of your quilts? Or even a quilt-top? I do have a superb seamstress back in Rowayton and I'm sure she could quilt it for me, if need be."

I've never been able to figure out exactly why the efficient approach doesn't work here. It's as if the more oil you apply to the machinery of getting business done, the more you gum up the works. It can be maddening in the extreme. My sympathies had begun to shift a bit. I could feel sorry for Honey now. *Don't say another word,* I thought. *You'll be sorry. You can't hurry them.*

"It would depend," said Minnie inscrutably, deliberately. "The bats are up to $5 now. It seems incredible to me. We used to get them for under a dollar." She smiled pleasantly.

"Yes, yes," said Honey half-attentively. I could almost feel the dryness in her mouth. "Well, Minnie, what would the whole thing, one whole quilt put together say, be worth?"

Minnie looked at her steadily, holding between her swollen thumbs the pieces of the Bear's Paw.

"Then too," she continued imperturbably and politely, "I try to get my quilting thread on sale but don't always succeed. Generally when she sees it on sale at the 1¢ store my neighbour will bring some in."

3.45 PM. I'd promised Honey we'd be over the border before nightfall. Unlikely. Things always took longer around here than you expected. A world out of time.

"Was there one you were particularly interested in?" She looked directly at Honey.

"I'd really settle for any one," Honey answered—lamely, I thought. Perhaps she was beginning to suspect. "I suppose if I had my pick it would be the Dresden Plate even though that's not exactly my shade of blue. But I know that one's out. The Maltese Cross is interesting, too . . . but how about the Drunkard's Path?"

The quilts were all folded up now and stacked back in the carton and garbage-bag. In my own mind they had blurred into a composite thing of beauty—soft, faded, sadly beautiful somehow. How could Honey possibly remember one from the other?

She was standing up, gripping her tooled-leather shoulder bag purposefully, shifting her weight.

"The Drunkard's Path," repeated Minnie thoughtfully, looking up at her. "I like that one, too. Would you want to see it again?"

"No, no!" almost groaned Honey, straining to sound polite. She lit a cigarette.

"It is an interesting quilt. I'm glad you like it. The local Kinsmen's Club wants it for their Dominion Day Raffle. I still don't know if I'll part with it." She looked faintly embarrassed.

"Well then," said Honey as she looked about hopelessly for an ashtray, then tried to look casual as Minnie handed one up to her, "I can't take the Lovers' Knot. It wouldn't go in her bedroom. Patchworks can be found at home in good imitation. Your Aunt Lizzie's Star I like a lot but you say it's for a niece."

Quickly she crushed out the cigarette and began pulling on her gloves.

Inscrutable Minnie. Was she hurt? Triumphant? Disappointed? That she could use the money I was certain.

We managed to get ourselves quickly out to the sun-porch. I kissed her goodbye.

"It's too bad, really. I've done less this winter than I'd planned," said she apologetically as she opened the front door to a blast of cold. "But I'm always planning ahead."

We'll stop for a drink, I thought. O Lord, where?

"Perhaps you could come back at the end of the summer," she went on, seemingly unaware of the draught. "Or Marion could come back for you."

We knew it was courtesy. Old-world courtesy. With an edge. In the depths of the old lady's eyes I seemed to catch a gleam that said she knew she'd won.

"If you come back in late summer," she said, "the Bear's Paw should be finished. . . . And good luck on your way home now. The prediction's pretty good for tonight, I believe." She surveyed the sky with knowing eyes. Honey was shivering. "But there are storm-warnings out for tomorrow. So be careful."

Tomorrow.

Already the forsythia was gleaming golden on the Henry Hudson Parkway.[4] Back to that. Dogwood soon. The sky might be grey but there would be some sure sign of spring down there. None, absolutely none here.

The small figure stood watching from behind her storm-door until our car finally gasped to a start and jerked away.

"Good God!" snapped Honey. "Why didn't you warn me? It was like trying to do business with a sphinx. Let's get out of here! All that endless stuff about the price of cotton, bats, quilting thread! Who cares? How can you do business that way? It was hopeless. If the money meant so damn much to her why didn't she set me a good stiff price? Instead, we were to sit around watching every goddamn bear's paw being pieced, assembled and blended! I could feel it about to happen! Doesn't she have any sense of the value of time?"

A tiny yellow flame licked up from her lighter to meet the impatient cigarette. I turned on the heater.

Ahead of us the horizon was purple-blue shading into turquoise. Beyond that, a faint bank of pink faded off into grey, dead blank grey, the grey of winter enduring, distant summer buried far beneath the other side of that pale border.

Not even a mirage as yet.

Only a dream.

1979

Michael Crummey

b. 1965

> Born in Buchan, Newfoundland, Crummey grew up there and in Wabush, Labrador. He is a Newfoundlander through and through. He knows a great deal about people, especially people within families. And he has a strong sense of belonging within a history, as well as an ear for the music and grace of language.
>
> Crummey has published poetry, short stories, and a novel, River

---

4. A main westside thoroughfare in New York City, along Riverside Park.

Thieves *(2002). This story comes from the collection* Flesh and Blood *(1998). Crummey says he hopes that this "writing thing" works out for him, because he is not very good at anything else. Certainly, so far his writing has been well received, warmly appreciated. It is grounded in Newfoundland, but goes beyond place, engaging with people and their complex relationships.*

Crummey says his friends complain that he is not very observant, that he does not notice things or observe details about the people around him. But in his fiction, as in this story, significant understanding can open from a small fact—like a pair of boots in the wrong place.

Much of Crummey's writing starts from father-son interactions. Some part of a father is always a stranger, he suggests. That may be the part that fascinates Crummey, the part that he tries to reach imaginatively because he cannot know it through fact or even experience.

Serendipity

When my father was assigned a home by the Company and moved out of the bunkhouse, we carried our belongings by cart and boat from Twillingate across New World Island and down to Lewisporte where we caught the train for Black Rock.[1] Fourteen hours in the single passenger car at the end of a line of empty ore boxes and most of that time in darkness, the clatter of the rails carrying us deeper into the island's interior, into the unfamiliar shape of another life. I woke up just after first light as the train leaned into the half-mile turn of Tin Can Curve. Out the window I could see a rusty orange petticoat of abandoned scrap metal poking through the white shawl of snow at the foot of the rail bed. Twenty minutes later we crossed a trestle and chuffed into town. My father met us at the red warehouse that served as a train station, his lean face dwarfed by a fur hat, his grin lop-sided, like a boat taking on water.

I'd never been away from Durrells before. Everything in this new

1. Places in Newfoundland.

place looked the same to my eyes. Streets as neat as garden furrows with rows of identical four unit buildings painted white or green or brown planted on either side. For the first three weeks after we arrived, my mother tied a kerchief to the door handle so my sister and I would be able to find our house in the line of uniform, indistinguishable quads.

Even my father got confused on one occasion, coming home from a card game at the bunkhouse. He'd been drinking and turned onto the street below ours, mistaking the third door in the second building for his own. Only a small lamp over the stove lighted the kitchen, the details of furniture and decoration were draped in darkness. He took off his shoes in the porch, hung his coat neatly on the wall and was about to have a seat at the kitchen table when Mrs. Neary walked in from the living room. "Can I get you a cup of tea?" she asked him.

He was too embarrassed to admit he'd made a mistake. "That would be grand, Missus," he said. "I wouldn't say no to a raisin bun if you had one to spare."

"Carl," Mrs. Neary shouted up at the ceiling. "We've got company."

For years afterwards, my father dropped in on Mr. and Mrs. Neary for tea on Saturday evenings. My father and Mr. Neary hunted together, played long raucous poker games at the kitchen table with my Uncle Gerry.

My mother said that was just like him, to find his best friend that way—everything that ever happened to my father was a happy accident. She said it with just a hint of bitterness in her voice, enough that I could taste it, like a squeeze of lemon in a glass of milk.

When I turned thirteen, my father began taking me with him to check his rabbit slips on the other side of Company property. We'd set out before dawn, following the Mucky Ditch that carried mine tailings across the bog, the squelch of footsteps in wet ground the only sound between us. When we reached the tree line we struck off for the trails through the woods. My father grinned across at me in a way that he hoped was reassuring, but I didn't understand why he invited me along or wanted me with him. Every winter he took twice as many brace of rabbit in the slips as Mr. Neary, for no reason but chance as far as anyone could see. Of ten hands of poker, my father won eight, sometimes nine. Mr. Neary swore never to play another game on more occasions than I could count. "That man," he announced often and loudly, "has a horseshoe up his arse."

My father smiled his lop-sided grin as he shuffled the cards. "One more before you go?" he asked.

It's hard not to feel ambivalent about someone that lucky, and that casual about his good fortune. "How can you love a man," I once overheard my mother confide to Mrs. Neary, "that you never feel sorry for?"

I wouldn't have gone into the woods with my father at all if my mother hadn't encouraged me, and it was mostly for her sake that I paid attention when he showed me how to tie the slips, and how to use boughs to narrow the run where the slip was set. He explained how a night of frost set them running to keep warm. He tied the paws of the dead rabbits together with twine. "Not that lucky for these little buggers," he said lightly. I carried them over my shoulder, the bodies stiff as cordwood against my back.

Around noon we stopped to boil water for tea. "You've got a good head for the woods," my father told me one Saturday. I suppose he was trying to soften me up a little. The enthusiasm in his voice suggested he'd just discovered something I had been hiding out of modesty. "Why don't you see if you can find us a bit of dry stuff for the fire."

I tramped off into the bush, annoyed with his irrepressible good humour, with his transparent praise. He had no right, I thought, and as I moved further into the spruce I decided not to go back, to keep walking. I wanted him to panic, to feel his world coming apart as he crashed through the woods yelling my name. I wanted him to feel the sadness my mother felt, the same sick regret. I kept my head down, not bothering to check my trail, working deeper into the green maze of forest. When I stopped to catch my breath I closed my eyes, turning three times in a circle before looking up. A light snow had started falling, stray flakes filtering through the branches of the spruce like aimless stars. I had no idea where I had come from, or where I was going. I was completely, perfectly lost.

Before he moved to Black Rock, my father worked as a fisherman in Crow Head on Twillingate Island. The year he turned eighteen he courted a girl who lived with her parents down the Arm in Durrells. Every night of the week he'd walk the six miles in from Crow Head to have tea and shortbread cookies with Eliza. Then he'd walk home again, arriving after one in the morning, crawling into bed for a few brief hours before heading out on the water by six.

During the winter he walked both ways in total darkness, often in miserable weather. On a particularly blustery evening in February Eliza's family tried to convince him to spend the night, but my father politely declined. His mother was expecting him at home, and the bit of blowing snow wasn't bad enough to keep him in. The old man tapped the weather glass beside the front door. "She's dropping fast, you'd best be going if you're going."

There were no roads through Twillingate in those days. The paths quickly disappeared under snow. Wind pummelled the treeless shoreline, visibility dropped to zero. My father walked for half an hour before he decided to turn around and spend the night. An hour later he had no idea where he was. His hands and feet were numb, his eyelashes were freezing together. He hunkered below a hummock to catch his breath out of the wind. He leaned against the face of the small hill and fell backwards through the door of a root cellar. There was a bin of dark-skinned potatoes, shelves of onions, parsnip, cabbage. He was near a house. He stared through the snow looking for a sign of life in the white-out, and then marched toward what he thought might be a light in a window. My mother answered his knock at the door. "Can I get you a cup of tea?" she asked him as he unwrapped himself from his frozen winter clothes.

My grandmother went into the pantry, digging out a plateful of buns, cheese, and crackers. "Sarah," she called to my mother, "get a few blankets upstairs, we'll set him up on the daybed for tonight."

The storm went on unabated for four days. On the fifth day, my father left my mother's house to walk back to Crow Head. On the way he met his father, who had set out to look for him as soon as the weather eased up.

"Well," my grandfather said, "you're all right then."

My father grabbed both his arms through the bulk of his winter coat. "I'm getting married," he said.

My grandfather turned and they began walking back home

through the thigh-deep snow. "It's about time," he said finally. "We were starting to wonder about you two."

Eliza's uncle was the merchant in Twillingate and after my parents married he made it impossible for my father to make a living as a fisherman. According to the merchant's tally at the season's end, my father's catch of salted cod didn't even cover the cost of supplies and equipment taken on credit in the spring. It was unfair and petty, but there was no recourse. My mother's oldest brother, Gerry, was working underground in Black Rock at the time and he had a word with his foreman who spoke with the Company manager. When my father left in November to start work in the mine I was already lodged in my mother's belly, undiscovered, like a pocket of ore buried in granite.

For the first eleven years of my life I saw my father only at Christmas, when he had enough time off to make the three day trip to Twillingate by train and boat. He stayed with us from Christmas Eve until Boxing Day, then began the return trip in order to be back at work on New Year's Day. I looked forward to his appearance with the same mix of anticipation and anxiety my sister reserved for Santa Claus. As if I suspected he wasn't quite real, that this year my mother would sit me down and explain he was simply a story made up for children. He arrived in the middle of the night, the pockets of his winter coat heavy with oranges and blocks of hard taffy. He sat us on his knee, our small faces disfigured by interrupted sleep and shy, helpless excitement as he bribed us with nickels to kiss the unfamiliar wool and oil smell of his cheek. Then he disappeared for another year.

As I grew older my simple disappointment with this arrangement soured. I began to suspect that he chose to live away from us, chose to visit only three days a year. It made no difference how often he explained that the Company had yet again refused his application for a house, or how lucky he was even to have a job. The promise of moving us to Black Rock was like a gift my father was constantly saving for, but could never quite afford. I had been waiting for so long that I stopped expecting it would ever happen, had stopped wanting it altogether.

Like her children, my mother became more and more accustomed to the idea of life without him. During the summers she tended the garden with my grandmother, helped her brothers cut the meadow grass for hay in the fall. She sewed and mended and knit through the winter; she taught me my sums by the light of a kerosene lamp in the evenings. For eleven years she lived alone, married to a man she knew only through occasional letters, a brief annual visit. It should have been no surprise to anyone, least of all my mother, that she was no longer in love when he finally sent for us to join him in Black Rock.

It was a Christmas tradition at the house in Durrells, before we left for Black Rock, that the story of how my parents met and became engaged would be recounted by the people present during the storm. It was an informal telling, a story thrown out piecemeal, with everyone describing their own particular role or viewpoint on this detail or that, as if they were discussing a movie they had seen together years before. My father got lost and fell backwards into the root cellar, my mother opened the door to a hill of clothes covered in snow. My mother's youngest brother caught them furtively holding hands as they sat together on the second day. Uncle Gerry slams an open palm on the table, making the glasses of whiskey and syrup jump. Nothing at all would have happened between them if he had been at home at the time, he announces, and what was my grandmother thinking to allow such a thing in the first place?

My grandmother lifts a hand from her lap-full of crochet cotton to dismiss her son's feigned outrage. "When Sarah came to my bed that night to say he'd proposed I thought, What odds about it? You lot are all alike under the clothes anyway. Go ahead and marry him if you want to, I told her. One man is as good as another."

Everyone laughs at this, my mother included. I am too young to think there could be anything prophetic in my grandmother's words.

My father says, "It was fate is what it was. It was in the stars." He digs in his pocket for a coin. "Come over my darling," he says to my mother, "and kiss me."

"You men," my grandmother says, "you're all alike."

Whatever her feelings about leaving Durrells might have been, my mother was determined to make the best of our new life in Black

Rock. She thought that pretending to be a family long enough would make it real for all of us. She hoped that would be the case. She insisted we see my father off to work before each shift, turning our faces up to receive a ritual peck on the cheek. We took the Company bus out to the lake on weekends, summer and winter, sitting on a blanket on the sand or skating across to Beothuk Island. We went to matinee shows at the theatre, standing with the rest of the audience to whistle and slap the seats of our folding chairs when, inevitably, the film broke and Smitty had to splice it together before continuing. In all of these activities my mother's selfless, brittle enthusiasm was a delicate and beautiful thing, like blown glass. I travelled cautiously in the wake of that beauty, as if she was the last star in the night sky.

My sister, on the other hand, cheerfully took root. She joined the Brownie troop, the school glee club, played hop-scotch and Cut-the-butter with half a dozen other children on our street. She sat in my father's arms as he played poker with Mr. Neary and my uncle, sleeping soundly through the laughter and cigarette smoke and the cursing while I sulked in my room, refusing to be placated by my mother's trays of shortbread cookies, by the second-hand pair of skates my father left on a nail in the porch. "I don't know what we're going to do with that one," my mother said whenever I retreated up the stairs.

"Don't worry," my father reassured her. "He's just missing Twillingate. He'll come around. It'll all work out in the end." More than anything else, it was that blind faith in his luck that infuriated me. It hardened my resolve to show him how wrong he was about the world.

The further I walked through the bush, the more dense it became. Branches scraped my face and hands, but I hardly noticed. I was elated. I felt like shouting, but didn't want to give myself away. I kept moving, putting as much distance between myself and my father as possible, stumbling deeper into the forest like a man walking into a river, his pockets full of stones. I pictured my father scrambling through the woods behind me, calling helplessly.

Minutes later I broke through a web of alders into a clearing and stopped dead in my tracks. I felt something falling inside myself, a brilliant, catastrophic toppling like the collapse of a star. Twenty yards from where I stood there was a fire burning. My father crouched beside it, chewing nonchalantly on a sandwich. Lost in the bush, I realized, I had walked in a perfect circle.

"I was starting to wonder about you," my father said. "Did you find any wood for the fire?"

It was hopeless. I walked toward him, empty-handed, convinced there was no way to fight destiny, that I would never be free of my father's luck.

The following summer my mother slipped into the same posture of defeat. She abandoned her attempts to force us into the shape she thought a happy family should take, began complaining of headaches, bowing out of regular excursions and events to stay at home alone. Her absence had been so habitual and familiar to my father for so many years that he barely registered this retreat. He took my sister and I to the movie matinees without her, bought us popcorn or candies, joking with my sister as if nothing had changed. I sat sullenly through war movies and westerns starring "The Durango Kid," or a white-hatted hero played by Rocky Lane. Even during bar room brawls that hat never left his head, as if it grew from his scalp like hair. Someone in the audience inevitably shouted, "Knock his hat off!" and everyone cheered. It was enough that he always came out on top. The hat was simply flaunting it.

When we arrived home I brought my mother tea or juice where she lay in the dusk of the heavy curtains in her bedroom, her hair splayed against the pillow like meadow grass cut and drying in a field. The air in the room was thick with the smell of cloistered bodies. "You're a prince," she murmured, distracted, as if I had woken her from a dream. It was all I could do to keep from crying. Winter was coming. The stars were aligned against me.

Fate is simply chance in a joker's hat.

The Black Rock ore deposits were discovered when the stones around a prospector's cooking fire began flaring, the seams of ore in the slag bursting into flame and melting. A snow storm threw my parents together for four days and they married. My father happened on his best friend by accident. In retrospect, it can all seem inevitable, unavoidable. I think about that now, how I might have gone on hating my father forever if not for the intervention of serendipity.

Two weeks before Christmas, the Company held its annual party for employees' children at the Star Hall. My mother stayed at home, complaining of a headache. I dressed, reluctantly, while my father and sister stood in the porch, sweating under coats and scarves, shouting at me to hurry. I lagged behind them on the street, scuffing snow with the toe of my boot. My sister was in my father's arms, and they were laughing. Other families on their way to the hall congregated around them. I walked more slowly, watching as the dark cluster of people and conversation moved farther and farther ahead of me, like a train leaving a town behind. Finally I stopped altogether, angry and curiously satisfied that they hadn't noticed I was no longer beside them. I could just hear their voices at the bottom of the street and then they turned the corner.

Back at the house I pulled off my boots in the porch, feeling vaguely triumphant. My mother and I could spend the evening playing Crazy Eights, drinking tea. I knocked my boots together to clear the bottoms of snow, then set them neatly by the wall. Beside Mr. Neary's boots. I walked into the kitchen in my stocking feet. Only the light over the stove was on, there was no sound. I was about to call when I heard my mother's voice from upstairs. "Who's there?" she shouted.

"It's me," I said.

"Where's your father?" Her voice was hard, but fragile, as if the hardness in it might suddenly shatter into fragments.

"Is Mr. Neary here?" I asked uncertainly.

"Russell, you go straight to the Star Hall. Right this minute. You hear me?"

I didn't know what to say. It was like walking into a house you think is your own, taking off your shoes and jacket, sitting at the kitchen table, and suddenly realizing you're in the middle of something completely unfamiliar and unexpected, something foreign. "I forgot my scarf," I lied.

Halfway to the Star Hall I met my father, on his way back to look for me. "Well," he said. "You're all right then."

I looked at his face, at the complete innocence of it. The wind had brought tears to his eyes and he was grinning his lop-sided grin at me. He had no idea. My mother and my father's best friend. For the first time in my life I felt sorry for him.

"I forgot my scarf," I lied again.

He turned toward the Hall and we walked together in the darkness. "If the wind dies down there'll be a decent frost tonight," my father said. "Tomorrow should be a good day to check the slips."

"I'd like that," I said. I reached out and held his arm through the bulk of his winter jacket. "I'd like that a lot."

1998

George Elliott
1923–1996

Elliott published his short-story collection The Kissing Man *in 1962 to a thundering silence. Clearly, though, this collection marked a change in the form of the short story in Canada, and it has always been appreciated by other writers. At the time, the prevailing fashion in short stories was for the Modernist story, traditionally structured, character-based, and realist. Elliott's stories were lyrical, elliptical, even mystical. It was an unexpected way to write about small-town Ontario, around the London area where Elliott grew up.*

*The first sentences of this story, from that collection, are highly poetic. Recurring and shifting sounds build on one another. Magical things, which are not explained, happen in this piece. They simply **are**. It is a story of character, but people are presented suggestively rather than explicitly or descriptively.*

Perhaps discouraged by the response to his first publication, but still seeing himself as a writer, Elliott went to work for an advertising firm in Toronto, where he moved from copy writer to top management.

Elliott's second collection, The Bittersweet Man *(1994), is more urban, more ironic, set in Montreal or Ottawa, where he moved to work as a high-level civil servant in the Prime Minister's office. With bittersweet tones in his own voice, Elliott described his first collection as "a young man's book." It is not really clear what he*

*meant about this work which is now highly regarded. Perhaps he
was referring to an almost romantic nostalgia that hovers over the
stories. They are set in a world close to nature, where a young mis-
fit could find someone who understood him, who mentored from a
distance, who showed him alternatives in a world harsh to someone
who did not like school.*

A Leaf for Everything Good

In those days there was a deep pond where the bowling greens
are now. It was formed by an earth dam that had been built to
make the fall for the water-power mill. The big willow, there,
put its branches out over the pond and dropped its leaves into the
water every autumn.

Men in work boots, young men in copper-toed boots, bare-
footed boys and girls and, later on, bicycles, firmed the earth down
around the edge of the pond and made a cool walk that began at the
mill and went upstream to the foot-bridge, then downstream to the
shadows under the willow tree.

The mill pond was a place to go, because there came the water
from springs far up country, water that flowed in long curves
through the low meadow-land and into the town where it was used
by the mill before it turned west for the lake. If a man's troubles
were not taken away downstream with the water that had to go that
way, they were at least cooled by September breezes as he sat on the
earth dam or as he dangled his feet in the water at the overflow gate.

The old man got the shape of the town clear in his heart by coming to the pond every Sunday and by walking once or maybe twice
around the path, then resting under the willow. When he got too
old to work, he took to spending all his afternoons on the banks of
the pond, in the sun on cool days, in the shade when it was warm.

The continuation school in those days was just beyond the pond.
Kids who lived in this end of the town naturally walked across the
earth dam going to and coming home from school.

The first-form kids were nervous about him. He sat with his back
against the willow, watching. The first-form kids whispered to each
other after they had passed safely over the earth dam and by the old

man. The ones who knew everything (there were always some in each new year) told the others it was only the old man who sat under the willow tree by the mill pond. He had always been there. He was too old to work. That's how the old man knew whose children were at school.

Finn was the only boy who stopped to talk to the old man.

"You'll be late for school, boy. She's rung the first bell."

"You be here after school?"

"Aren't I always? I'll be here."

That afternoon, Finn sat down on the grass, facing the old man.

"What did you learn today, son?"

"I didn't learn nothing. Don't you know who I am? I'm Finn, the dumbest first-former she ever had."

"I know who you are, all right. What's the matter? Don't you like school? Your maw certainly did."

"I got other things on my mind. Did you know my mother?"

"I knew her. I'll tell you about her. What have you got on your mind?"

"Oh, things. I don't know. I don't put my mind to algebra or anything like that."

The days went by, the way they do for a boy in school. Finn stopped nearly every day for a visit with the old man. On the days when he stopped to count milk bottles rattling into the steam cabinet at the dairy, he remembered to tell the old man, on the way by, that he would stop for a while after school, if she didn't keep him in.

One day the old man said to him, "You don't hang much with the other kids. What's the matter? You too quiet for them?"

"No, they laugh at me for being dumb in school. I don't mind. I make out all right."

"How'd you like to learn something they'll never know?"

"What about?"

"You see me sitting here every morning when you go to school, don't you? And you see me still here when school's out. I guess I should know something about this pond by now, eh?"

"I guess so."

"Take this willow tree. It was here before the town was. Look at those branches reaching up there. Think of what you could see if you could sit on the highest one. Under us, the roots go down and spread out all over, under the pond, under the school-yard. This willow is busy taking from the air, taking from the earth, taking what it needs, taking all the things we don't know but that travel in the earth and in the air. The love that's in an up-country man that can't be expressed. It's got to go somewhere. Maybe it goes in the air and is taken by this willow. The tears of a lonely girl who wants a friend. She might come and sit under this tree and cry her tears into the roots.

"What about the regrets of a father who never got to love a son who went away to die in a war? He'd come here to be alone. These leaves hold that. The remorse of a boy alone here in the dark with his girl. The compassion of an old man who knows he is going to outlive his wife."

"But the leaves fall into the water in October," Finn whispered.

"Yes. A leaf of love, a leaf of loneliness, a leaf of regret, a leaf of remorse, a leaf of compassion, a leaf for everything good and forgotten, for everything bad and always here. They fall into the pond and the trout eat them."

"The trout?"

"Sure. There are trout in the pond, son. Everybody in town thinks the trout have gone, but the big ones are still here in the pond. You've got to be patient to see them. That's all."

"I thought the pond was fished out long ago."

"This pond is never fished out. Look at it. A widening. Holding the water that comes down the creek, holding it back for a few minutes, then letting it through the mill-wheel and down the race and going on. That's what's important. Going on because it must. But here in the widening the pond catches all that falls from the willow and the trout eat it. The fish are there now, taking from what's upstream, staying here at the widening, taking from the tree, avoiding the lures, living, living."

"Do you believe that?" Finn got up to go.

"Believe? I know." It was a week before Finn spoke to the old man again.

Finn made himself go back and talk to the old man again because he saw that he was the only one who would. Besides the old man did not always talk as strangely as he did the last time. He was a friend, kind of, except for that.

He wondered what the old man was driving at. He worried a little, because he had said he knew Finn's mother. Maybe he was an old family friend of some kind. Maybe he was in cahoots with the teacher, the way the young doctor at the hospital was. He'd have to be careful. But there were the trout. He ought to know. Trout in the pond.

He slid down the dry clay by the iron bridge and over to the earth dam. He looked across and saw the old man was there. From that distance, the old man looked more shapeless than usual, huddled up and still.

"Hello there, son. Haven't seen you for a few days."

"Oh, I was going to school by the post office and the foot-bridge the past while."

"Kind of a change, eh?"

Finn noticed then the old man had a loosely woven robe wrapped around his shoulders under the faded blue smock coat.

"Say, have you been sick?"

The old man squirmed a little to shift the robe off his neck. "No, not exactly sick. Just getting on I guess."

"Maybe you shouldn't be sitting down here. The air is still kind of swampy."

The old man was impatient with Finn's concern. "You doing any better at school?"

"Same as usual, I guess. I don't expect I'll pass. Paw'll probably put me to work in the axe-handle factory this July if I fail."

"Your mother wouldn't have liked that."

"How come you knew my mother?"

"I happened to make a point of getting to know her when she got married, but nothing came of it. Your dad is a pretty sullen man, take him any way you care to."

In a way Finn wanted the old man to go on talking about his mother, but he was afraid if he did he'd not get to talking some more about the trout, so Finn interrupted.

"Uh, these trout. You think they'd be good eating?"

"Best eating in the world. That's if you could catch one."

The boy turned directly towards the old man. "Do you think I could?"

"Knowing your mother, I'd say yes. Knowing your father, I'm not so sure."

The boy couldn't figure out how his mother and father could have anything to do with catching trout. "What do you mean?"

"I mean the trout are for special people. They are not ordinary trout, you know. I explained that."

"Wouldn't they rise to a coachman?"

"I doubt it."

"A worm?"

"Not a chance."

"What, then?"

"Patience, maybe. And a kind of strength you're too young to understand yet."

"Maybe I understand more than you think I do."

"What do you understand?"

"You are an old friend of my mother's and you know that I don't get along so good in school and this whole trout business is a way you've got of telling me if I don't work better at school and if I don't make friends with the kids, you won't tell me how to catch the trout. If there are any."

"Is that all?"

Finn was excited and disappointed. He was afraid it was true and he was ashamed of the good times he had talking to the old man. He turned his head away and looked at the pond.

"I don't know."

"Well, maybe you better go away and try and figure out what I'm all about. Try and remember if you ever saw me talking to any of the other ones. Think about them for a while. Come and talk to me about it whenever you feel like it."

So Finn got up and went back up to the main street and along the store fronts and past the rink until he came to the blacksmith's shop. He stood in the doorway and watched for a few minutes but it didn't seem to matter, so he went home and lay on his bed and cried.

He avoided the pond and the willow tree again until the thought came to him that the old man was maybe not interested in his school work, but wondered what Finn was to do when he got out of school. What he had said that day he talked about the trout hadn't much to do with a boy, more for grown-ups. Maybe that was it.

He ran across the school-yard and down to the willow tree.

"Tell me again. Tell me about the tree and what it does and the river and a man's troubles. Tell me again so I can understand."

He called it as he came near the willow tree and the trunk of it was a pure cold grey and the leaves were a shivering green and the pond was a soft shiny black. The shade seemed a little damp. The old man was not there.

He ran up to the road, across the iron bridge and on to the main street. At Geddes's corner, where there were men sitting under the awning, he called out.

"Where is he? The old man who sits under the willow tree. Where is he?" And they looked down at him and said nothing and Finn wondered what there was about them to make them feel so proud of themselves. "Where is he?" he asked finally. They looked at each other and smiled a little.

Finn ran on. He ran across the street and down to the Queen's Hotel. There were men standing beside the hitching-post. "Where is he? Where does the old man live who sits under the willow tree?"

One of the men swept Finn up by the elbows and held him in the air, close to his red face.

"He lives in a cave and he'll eat you if you go near him."

The others laughed and Finn squirmed away from the red-faced one and ran catty-corner across to the bank. There was no one to ask. Maybe he was sick. He ran down the tunnel of oaks towards the hospital. His legs felt light and strong and he thought he would keep running until he found the old man, but he slowed down to a walk on the cinder path into the hospital.

The young doctor told him the old man was dead.

"But he promised to tell me something."

"Was he a relation of yours, sonny?"

"Are you sure he's dead?"

"I'm sorry. He's dead."

There was no feeling at the old man's funeral. It was one of those days when the sun was so clear it took the colour out of the leaves of the trees that shaded the street and left the church warm and dark and unfriendly. No branch moved and there was no sound, not even the bell. The sky was high and blue and the town lay dwarfed under it and they were going to bury the old man who didn't get a chance to speak to Finn again.

At the funeral, Finn said to himself it would have been all right to have gone to school by the dam those days he was avoiding the old man. He couldn't have said anything to hurt him. It was just that the old man knew. Finn wanted to know and the old man hinted and Finn was ashamed the hint wasn't enough. He watched the democrat with its grey canopy and velvet rope go down the street on the Fair Grounds road, down to where the cemetery was.

He came back this way towards home. He met his father at the corner and they walked together. Finn noticed the varnish stains were like ugly freckles on his father's hairy hands.

"You in school today?"

"I went to the old man's funeral. They buried the old man today."

"You skipped school for that?"

"They let me go. It doesn't matter."

"I thought you didn't like funerals."

"This was different. He knew maw, he said. Got to know her when you and she were married."

"Crazy. Crazy in the head."

"He was all right. We talked quite a bit together. He liked to talk to me."

"High time he died. Been sitting down in that swamp for as long as anybody can remember. Crazy in the head."

"He made sense. At least he'd've made sense to older people. Sometimes I didn't understand what he was driving at."

"Like you don't understand what that school is driving at, I suppose. You'd understand if you paid attention sometimes."

"I guess so. I guess that's right."

They were in the house then. It was dark, hot, and smelled of old cooked cabbage.

"And another thing mister, now that we're in the house, you'll ask me before you go to another funeral. I suppose you thought you'd sneak off to this one and me not know, eh?" The father hit Finn on the side of the head. Finn backed away.

"I didn't sneak anywhere. I told you where I was. I didn't try to hide anything."

"No back talk." He hit Finn again. "Get in the kitchen and get to work."

So Finn began to fish in the pond every morning before school. Naturally everybody laughed at him and asked him what he expected to catch.

Wouldn't you know? they asked. He's in a daze half the time at school. Never passes a term test. Can't answer a question. Stands around day-dreaming at the dairy or the blacksmith's shop. Wouldn't you know? With a father like that it's no wonder.

Others were kind and wished that someone would go gently to Finn and lead him away from the pond and explain to him that the fish had gone long ago. But there was no one gentle left in the town to do it. So the kind ones felt uncomfortable and hoped it wouldn't last for long.

He started off by using a cheap, store-bought royal coachman fly on a silk leader. In a few mornings he became expert at dropping the fly onto the surface of the water where he wanted it to go. Nothing happened, except that he became aware of the slight movement of the water in the direction of the earth dam. He never noticed that before.

When he changed from artificial flies to worms, he noticed that it was possible to see only part way into the water, that the worm dropped into it and soon disappeared. The odd leaf dropped from the willow tree and drifted along with the water to the dam, but he never got a bite.

Why does he stay at it so long? they asked. For goodness' sake, somebody tell him, they said. And the kind ones began to worry for Finn.

Once a third-form boy sneaked up behind him and pushed him towards the water. Finn's feet were soaked and he went to his knees in the clay mud. He had to go home and change.

Another time he was fishing from the overflow gate and lost track of the time. It was getting on for nine when the school kids tramped heavily across the gate, making it shiver. Finn held on to the top board with his fingers and held his fishing-rod between his knees until they had all passed. They stood on the other side of the pond and laughed at him.

All the excitement of getting the Fair Grounds ready for the Dominion Day[1] races didn't stop him. Neither did the final examinations at school. He was at the pond every morning at seven o'clock, trying every kind of bait. He never got a bite.

Examination results were to be pinned on the big bulletin board outside the principal's office on the last day of June. Finn knew what to expect there and knew what to expect when he took his report card home to his father. He kept on fishing.

That last school morning was a solemn one. The sun rose a glaring yellow through a dank, low mist back of the school. The little river mists spiralled up and disappeared. Finn was quiet, standing on the dam, his line making swishing noises through the air. The old willow drooped in the morning stillness and the picture of its roots the way the old man described them came to Finn. He could feel them under him and he could feel the process of taking from the earth. He saw a girl sitting under the willow, crying, and if he closed his eyes he could see her tears falling on the clay. He looked up and saw the top branches and it came back to him. He heard a noise behind him. He turned and saw the kids had started coming to school.

He reeled in his line, pressed the hook into the cork handle of the rod, tucked it under his arm and ran off to school.

There was an assembly of all the pupils in the school. The principal spoke and no one tittered or scuffled in their seats. Finn paid no attention. He wanted to get it over with. Everybody knew that one of the teachers was outside the room, pinning the results up. Everybody knew the classes would file out one at a time and go by the board and look for their names. Everybody knew what was to happen. Finn wanted to get it over with.

The principal's talk droned on. She couldn't speak very clearly and she had a lot to say. Finn supposed she would have something to say, not directly of course, about him. He didn't care.

The third-formers got up and lined up along the front, then shuffled out the door to go by the board. As the last of the third-formers went out, the second form got up. Finally the first-formers went out. Finn was last in line. His name wasn't on the list.

1. July 1, now called Canada Day.

He went into the classroom. The clock said five minutes to twelve. Finn gathered up his books without sitting down. The teacher asked what he thought he was doing.

"I expect I'm going home now," he said and went out the door. The others laughed uneasily.

He went by the bulletin board and looked again. His name was not there. He looked to make sure he was in front of the right list, then went out the door of the school, looked for a moment at the pond across the yard, then ran for the road as fast as he could go. He would beat his father home.

His father didn't come home for lunch that day. He probably stayed at the factory and ate a pick-up lunch from the café across the street.

Finn was disappointed that he couldn't get it all over with. He ate what there was at home, then picked up his fishing-rod and went to the pond. He sat quietly in the shade of the willow and cast the line into the pool regularly. When the whistle at the factory blew, Finn went home.

His father was there on the porch, waiting.

"Well?"

"I failed. My name wasn't on the list."

"I guess you know what that means."

"I guess you want me to start in at the factory."

"You're bloody right I do, you lazy little slut. I found out about you at noon today and you're to see Mister Penny at the horse barns tomorrow at one-thirty. And you'll be there, too."

"All right. I'll be there."

"And I'll be watching for you."

Dominion Day had a fair and promising morning that year. Nobody remembers it for that, though. Nobody except Finn. He was up as usual to get his father's breakfast. They didn't speak. His father went off to handle Mr. Penny's horse entered in the 2.28 at the track. As soon as he was around the corner, Finn set out for the pool. It was a good day.

Everybody was at the races, so no one saw or thought of Finn. About noon-time when things started to pick up at the Fair Grounds, Finn's father watched for him. He thought the boy would be around to see the horses warm up. There was no sign of him.

"Boy didn't show up, heh?" Mr. Penny said at a quarter to two.

After the races were all over and after the horses were in their vans on their way up county for the meet there next day, Finn's father came to the pool, looking for him. It was still light, but the shadows were long. He wondered if Finn might have fallen into the pond. He walked around the trampled path, went across the footbridge and down under the willow tree.

He found Finn's rod there and a grey old trout that measured nearly thirty-four inches long.

Later that night Emerson told him Finn got on the one-twenty flag-down.[2]

1962

Jacques Ferron
1921–1985

> *Ferron was a lively, somewhat controversial part of his beloved Quebec, a very public figure. He was born in Louiseville, Quebec, and educated at the conservative, elitist Jean de Brébeuf College. After graduating with a degree in medicine from Laval University, he worked as a doctor for many years in isolated areas of the Gaspé, where he came to appreciate the oral story-telling traditions of Quebec, including the contes, fables told to make a moral point or teach a lesson. He used that form in his own ways, creating modern fables to satirize attitudes he did not like.*
>
> *Irritated by the pomposity of political parties, Ferron created the Rhinoceros party as an alternative to mainstream politics. His sense of satire lifted off the page and into the culture he knew well, but it was mainly through his fiction and plays that Ferron spoke to Quebec and to the rest of Canada.*
>
> *As a doctor, Ferron became close to people in rural and working-class neighbourhoods. He saw how much they needed medical care and was especially irritated by his colleagues who offered glib solutions to people in real need. The medical fashion for psychological explanations, based loosely on Freudian theories, particularly an-*

---

2. The train stopped by a flagman at 1:20.

*noyed him. Explaining everything in terms of sex, in a society very
ambivalent about it, seemed irresponsible to Ferron.*

Many of Ferron's contes can be read in English in Tales *from
the Uncertain Country (1972), translated by Betty Bednarski. He
makes fun of Freudian language, pointedly, in a story like this one,
translated from* Contes anglais *(1964). Ferron uses the traditions
of the fable cleverly, twisting it to his own purposes. The usual animal imagery takes on Freudian, sexual connotations. Using whimsical humour and irony, the practical country doctor in Jacques
Ferron has a good laugh about human nature.*

Animal Husbandry

I went to a private school, at the end of the Fontarabie county[1]
road. The schoolmistress was a small, down-to-earth widow
with a bad reputation, nicknamed l'Allumette.[2] She told me
about the night life of Paris, and showed me the underside of life. I
came out of there quite depressed, followed by a pensive elephant
with a sad trunk. The people of Fontarabie, seeing me go by like
this, felt I was overdoing it. I couldn't help it and it was most embarrassing. But then, to make matters worse, the elephant got sick,
in the trunk, of course. I took him to Montreal to see a doctor. The
doctor said he was honoured, that it was a sickness one could be
proud of, and he cured me of it so quickly and completely that I
found myself, elephantless, riding a galloping unicorn back towards
the lovely county of Maskinongé. Three black dogs were with me,
their eyes red and their mouths on fire. It was more than I could
possibly have hoped for. So, when I got to Sainte Ursule, instead of
going on to Fontarabie, I spurred on towards the rectory. The dogs
were tumbling around in the flower beds. I went in alone with my
unicorn.

"A nice animal," said the priest.

"Sure, it's a nice animal, but it's leading me straight to hell."

And I showed him the wild black dogs sitting on their haunches
in the flower bed, their mouths on fire, like real hell-hounds.

1. A former county in Quebec. 2. The matchstick (French).

"You'd better get married," said the priest.

A week later it was done. My wife spoke as soft as a Charlesbourg mouse. She called me her big white rat. What could be more restful, especially after the elephant and the unicorn! I was happy and content. My wife could do anything she wanted with me. One fine morning she found a rat on the pillow, a big white rat. It was I. Now she was free as you please. At last she could open the closet in which, caught short by my proposal, she had locked up her lover a few days earlier. Out came the lover and my wife dusted him off. They were happy to see each other again. Meanwhile, I was running around the pillow.

"What's that?" asked the lover.

"It's a big white rat," replied my wife.

"A big white rat? Okay. But couldn't he run around somewhere else?"

"No," said my wife.

The lover was amazed.

"It's my husband," she added.

He wasn't surprised any more, but I kept on bothering him just the same; whenever he forgot about me, I would nibble his ears. A week later nothing was left of the love between them. He was always keeping an eye on me, and that had changed his looks. Why was he watching me like that? Innocently, I moved closer. With all his claws out he pounced! But I was expecting it, and immediately I barked. That took him completely by surprise. He couldn't get over it. It was a cat who ran away, not a lover. I chased him lazily, for fun, to stretch my limbs a bit, and then I returned and lay my muzzle on the knees of my unfaithful wife.

"Silly fool," she said, "why don't you grow up and be a man?"

That was all I was hoping for. And so it came to pass that, after various transformations, I became a good husband.

1964

Timothy Findley
1930–2002

> Born in Toronto, Findley has done for Toronto what James Joyce
> did for Dublin, writing its various districts into fiction. He began
> his career expecting to be an actor, until a kind colleague suggested
> that he might like to try writing. He became a towering figure in
> the Canadian and international literary scenes, an Officer of the
> Order of Canada.
>
> Findley published plays, short stories, essays, and prize-winning
> novels, including The Last of the Crazy People (1967), The Wars
> (1977), Not Wanted on the Voyage (1984), and Headhunter
> (1993). Stones (1988), from which this story comes, is one of his
> best-known short story collections. His newspaper columns, charm-
> ing, unpretentious reflections on his life in a rural area north of
> Toronto, were written with his partner, Bill Whitehead, and are
> gathered into From Stone Orchard (1998). Findley was a gracious,
> sophisticated man. He uses intricate fictional strategies which go al-
> most unnoticed, seamlessly worked into his stories.
>
> This story is Postmodern, set in the Toronto of upper-class urban
> professionals. Several parallel stories wind through it, exploring
> dreams and dream-like states, as well as the inadequacies and the
> power of psychiatry.
>
> Postmodern writers have resisted the idea of explanations for
> everything, especially scientific explanations. Modernist writers in
> the early part of the twentieth century were fascinated by psychiatry,
> by a whole new language of interpretation. Findley rejects the idea
> of the psychiatrist as ultimate authority. He does not expect the
> reader to act as psychiatrist, sorting out characters' conflicts. In the
> end, this story insists that some things cannot be accounted for,
> that we must learn to live with uncertainty, enigma, the not-yet-
> understood.

Dreams

Doctor Menlo was having a problem: he could not sleep and his wife—the other Doctor Menlo—was secretly staying awake in order to keep an eye on him. The trouble was that, in spite of her concern and in spite of all her efforts, Doctor Menlo—whose name was Mimi—was always nodding off because of her exhaustion.

She had tried drinking coffee, but this had no effect. She detested coffee and her system had a built-in rejection mechanism. She also prescribed herself a week's worth of Dexedrine to see if that would do the trick. *Five mg at bedtime*—all to no avail. And even though she put the plastic bottle of small orange hearts beneath her pillow and kept augmenting her intake, she would wake half an hour later with a dreadful start to discover the night was moving on to morning.

Everett Menlo had not yet declared the source of his problem. His restless condition had begun about ten days ago and had barely raised her interest. Soon, however, the time spent lying awake had increased from one to several hours and then, on Monday last, to all-night sessions. Now he lay in a state of rigid apprehension—eyes wide open, arms above his head, his hands in fists—like a man in pain unable to shut it out. His neck, his back and his shoulders constantly harried him with cramps and spasms. Everett Menlo had become a full-blown insomniac.

Clearly, Mimi Menlo concluded, her husband was refusing to sleep because he believed something dreadful was going to happen the moment he closed his eyes. She had encountered this sort of fear in one or two of her patients. Everett, on the other hand, would not discuss the subject. If the problem had been hers, he would have said *such things cannot occur if you have gained control of yourself.*

Mimi began to watch for the dawn. She would calculate its approach by listening for the increase of traffic down below the bedroom window. The Menlos' home was across the road from The Manulife Centre—corner of Bloor and Bay streets.[1] Mimi's first

---

1. Prominent business streets in Toronto.

sight of daylight always revealed the high, white shape of its terraced storeys. Their own apartment building was of a modest height and colour—twenty floors of smoky glass and polished brick. The shadow of the Manulife would crawl across the bedroom floor and climb the wall behind her, grey with fatigue and cold.

The Menlo beds were an arm's length apart, and lying like a rug between them was the shape of a large, black dog of unknown breed. All night long, in the dark of his well, the dog would dream and he would tell the content of his dreams the way that victims in a trance will tell of being pursued by posses of their nameless fears. He whimpered, he cried and sometimes he howled. His legs and his paws would jerk and flail and his claws would scrabble desperately against the parquet floor. Mimi—who loved this dog—would lay her hand against his side and let her fingers dabble in his coat in vain attempts to soothe him. Sometimes, she had to call his name in order to rouse him from his dreams because his heart would be racing. Other times, she smiled and thought: *at least there's one of us getting some sleep.* The dog's name was Thurber and he dreamed in beige and white.

Everett and Mimi Menlo were both psychiatrists. His field was schizophrenia; hers was autistic children. Mimi's venue was the Parkin Institute at the University of Toronto; Everett's was the Queen Street Mental Health Centre. Early in their marriage they had decided never to work as a team and not—unless it was a matter of financial life and death—to accept employment in the same institution. Both had always worked with the kind of physical intensity that kills, and yet they gave the impression this was the only tolerable way in which to function. It meant there was always a sense of peril in what they did, but the peril—according to Everett—made their lives worth living. This, at least, had been his theory twenty years ago when they were young.

Now, for whatever unnamed reason, peril had become his enemy and Everett Menlo had begun to look and behave and lose his sleep like a haunted man. But he refused to comment when Mimi asked him what was wrong. Instead, he gave the worst of all possible answers a psychiatrist can hear who seeks an explanation of a patient's silence: he said there was *absolutely nothing wrong.*

"You're sure you're not coming down with something?"

"Yes."

"And you wouldn't like a massage?"

"I've already told you: no."

"Can I get you anything?"

"No."

"And you don't want to talk?"

"That's right."

"Okay, Everett . . ."

"Okay, what?"

"Okay, nothing. I only hope you get some sleep tonight."

Everett stood up. "Have you been spying on me, Mimi?"

"What do you mean by *spying*?"

"Watching me all night long."

"Well, Everett, I don't see how I can fail to be aware you aren't asleep when we share this bedroom. I mean—I can hear you grinding your teeth. I can see you lying there wide awake."

"When?"

"All the time. You're staring at the ceiling."

"I've never stared at the ceiling in my whole life. I sleep on my stomach."

"You sleep on your stomach *if* you sleep. But you have not been sleeping. Period. No argument."

Everett Menlo went to his dresser and got out a pair of clean pyjamas. Turning his back on Mimi, he put them on.

Somewhat amused at the coyness of this gesture, Mimi asked what he was hiding.

"Nothing!" he shouted at her.

Mimi's mouth fell open. Everett never yelled. His anger wasn't like that; it manifested itself in other ways, in silence and withdrawal, never shouts.

Everett was staring at her defiantly. He had slammed the bottom drawer of his dresser. Now he was fumbling with the wrapper of a pack of cigarettes.

Mimi's stomach tied a knot.

Everett hadn't touched a cigarette for weeks.

"Please don't smoke those," she said. "You'll only be sorry if you do."

104 ✳ TIMOTHY FINDLEY

"And you," he said, "will be sorry if I don't."

"But, dear . . ." said Mimi.

"Leave me for Christ's sake alone!" Everett yelled.

Mimi gave up and sighed and then she said: "all right. Thurber and I will go and sleep in the living-room. Good-night."

Everett sat on the edge of his bed. His hands were shaking.

"Please," he said—apparently addressing the floor. "Don't leave me here alone. I couldn't bear that."

This was perhaps the most chilling thing he could have said to her. Mimi was alarmed; her husband was genuinely terrified of something and he would not say what it was. If she had not been who she was—if she had not known what she knew—if her years of training had not prepared her to watch for signs like this, she might have been better off. As it was, she had to face the possibility the strongest, most sensible man on earth was having a nervous breakdown of major proportions. Lots of people have breakdowns, of course; but not, she had thought, the gods of reason.

"All right," she said—her voice maintaining the kind of calm she knew a child afraid of the dark would appreciate. "In a minute I'll get us something to drink. But first, I'll go and change. . . ."

Mimi went into the sanctum of the bathroom, where her night-gown waited for her—a portable hiding-place hanging on the back of the door. "You stay there," she said to Thurber, who had padded after her. "Mama will be out in just a moment."

Even in the dark, she could gauge Everett's tension. His shadow—all she could see of him—twitched from time to time and the twitching took on a kind of lurching rhythm, something like the broken clock in their living-room.

Mimi lay on her side and tried to close her eyes. But her eyes were tied to a will of their own and would not obey her. Now she, too, was caught in the same irreversible tide of sleeplessness that bore her husband backward through the night. Four or five times she watched him lighting cigarettes—blowing out the matches, courting disaster in the bedclothes—conjuring the worst of deaths for the three of them: a flaming pyre on the twentieth floor.

All this behaviour was utterly unlike him; foreign to his code of disciplines and ethics; alien to everything he said and believed.

Openness, directness, sharing of ideas, encouraging imaginative response to every problem. Never hide troubles. Never allow despair . . . These were his directives in everything he did. Now, he had thrown them over.

One thing was certain. She was not the cause of his sleeplessness. She didn't have affairs and neither did he. He might be ill—but whenever he'd been ill before, there had been no trauma; never a trauma like this one, at any rate. Perhaps it was something about a patient—one of his tougher cases; a wall in the patient's condition they could not break through; some circumstance of someone's lack of progress—a sudden veering towards a catatonic state, for instance—something that Everett had not foreseen that had stymied him and was slowly . . . what? Destroying his sense of professional control? His self-esteem? His scientific certainty? If only he would speak.

Mimi thought about her own worst case: a child whose obstinate refusal to communicate was currently breaking her heart and, thus, her ability to help. If ever she had needed Everett to talk to, it was now. All her fellow doctors were locked in a battle over this child; they wanted to take him away from her. Mimi refused to give him up; he might as well have been her own flesh and blood. Everything had been done—from gentle holding sessions to violent bouts of manufactured anger—in her attempt to make the child react. She was staying with him every day from the moment he was roused to the moment he was induced to sleep with drugs.

His name was Brian Bassett and he was eight years old. He sat on the floor in the furthest corner he could achieve in one of the observation-isolation rooms where all the autistic children were placed when nothing else in their treatment—nothing of love or expertise—had managed to break their silence. Mostly, this was a signal they were coming to the end of life.

There in his four-square, glass-box room, surrounded by all that can tempt a child if a child can be tempted—toys and food and story-book companions—Brian Bassett was in the process, now, of fading away. His eyes were never closed and his arms were restrained. He was attached to three machines that nurtured him with all that science can offer. But of course, the spirit and the will to live cannot be fed by force to those who do not want to feed.

Now, in the light of Brian's Bassett's utter lack of willing contact with the world around him—his utter refusal to communicate— Mimi watched her husband through the night. Everett stared at the ceiling, lit by the Manulife building's distant lamps, borne on his back further and further out to sea. She had lost him, she was certain.

When, at last, he saw that Mimi had drifted into her own and welcome sleep, Everett rose from his bed and went out into the hall, past the simulated jungle of the solarium, until he reached the dining-room. There, all the way till dawn, he amused himself with two decks of cards and endless games of Dead Man's Solitaire.

Thurber rose and shuffled after him. The dining-room was one of Thurber's favourite places in all his confined but privileged world, for it was here—as in the kitchen—that from time to time a hand descended filled with the miracle of food. But whatever it was that his master was doing up there above him on the table-top, it wasn't anything to do with feeding or with being fed. The playing cards had an old and dusty dryness to their scent and they held no appeal for the dog. So he once again lay down and he took up his dreams, which at least gave his paws some exercise. This way, he failed to hear the advent of a new dimension to his master's problem. This occurred precisely at 5:45 A.M. when the telephone rang and Everett Menlo, having rushed to answer it, waited breathless for a minute while he listened and then said: "yes" in a curious, strangulated fashion. Thurber—had he been awake—would have recognized in his master's voice the signal for disaster.

For weeks now, Everett had been working with a patient who was severely and uniquely schizophrenic. This patient's name was Kenneth Albright, and while he was deeply suspicious, he was also oddly caring. Kenneth Albright loved the detritus of life, such as bits of woolly dust and wads of discarded paper. He loved all driedup leaves that had drifted from their parent trees and he loved the dead bees that had curled up to die along the window-sills of his ward. He also loved the spiderwebs seen high up in the corners of the rooms where he sat on plastic chairs and ate with plastic spoons.

Kenneth Albright talked a lot about his dreams. But his dreams had become, of late, a major stumbling block in the process of his recovery. Back in the days when Kenneth had first become Doctor Menlo's patient, the dreams had been overburdened with detail: "over-cast," as he would say, "with characters" and over-produced, again in Kenneth's phrase, "as if I were dreaming the dreams of Cecil B. de Mille."

Then he had said: "but a person can't really dream someone else's dreams. Or can they, Doctor Menlo?"

"No" had been Everett's answer—definite and certain.

Everett Menlo had been delighted, at first, with Kenneth Albright's dreams. They had been immensely entertaining—complex and filled with intriguing detail. Kenneth himself was at a loss to explain the meaning of these dreams, but as Everett had said, it wasn't Kenneth's job to explain. That was Everett's job. His job and his pleasure. For quite a long while, during these early sessions, Everett had written out the dreams, taken them home and recounted them to Mimi.

Kenneth Albright was a paranoid schizophrenic. Four times now, he had attempted suicide. He was a fiercely angry man at times—and at other times as gentle and as pleasant as a docile child. He had suffered so greatly, in the very worst moments of his disease, that he could no longer work. His job—it was almost an incidental detail in his life and had no importance for him, so it seemed—was returning reference books, in the Metro Library, to their places in the stacks. Sometimes—mostly late of an afternoon—he might begin a psychotic episode of such profound dimensions that he would attempt his suicide right behind the counter and even once, in the full view of everyone, while riding in the glass-walled elevator. It was after this last occasion that he was brought, in restraints, to be a resident patient at the Queen Street Mental Health Centre. He had slashed his wrists with a razor—but not before he had also slashed and destroyed an antique copy of *Don Quixote*, the pages of which he pasted to the walls with blood.

For a week thereafter, Kenneth Albright—just like Brian Bassett—had refused to speak or to move. Everett had him kept in an isolation cell, force-fed and drugged. Slowly, by dint of patience, encouragement and caring even Kenneth could recognize as genuine, Everett Menlo had broken through the barrier. Kenneth was removed from isolation, pampered with food and cigarettes, and he began relating his dreams.

At first there seemed to be only the dreams and nothing else in Kenneth's memory. Broken pencils, discarded toys and the telephone directory all had roles to play in these dreams but there were never any people. All the weather was bleak and all the landscapes were empty. Houses, motor cars and office buildings never made an appearance. Sounds and smells had some importance; the wind would blow, the scent of unseen fires was often described. Stairwells were plentiful, leading nowhere, all of them rising from a subterranean world that Kenneth either did not dare to visit or would not describe.

The dreams had little variation, one from another. The themes had mostly to do with loss and with being lost. The broken pencils were all given names and the discarded toys were given to one another as companions. The telephone books were the sources of recitations—hours and hours of repeated names and numbers, some of which—Everett had noted with surprise—were absolutely accurate.

All of this held fast until an incident occurred one morning that changed the face of Kenneth Albright's schizophrenia forever; an incident that stemmed—so it seemed—from something he had dreamed the night before.

Bearing in mind his previous attempts at suicide, it will be obvious that Kenneth Albright was never far from sight at the Queen Street Mental Health Centre. He was, in fact, under constant observation; constant, that is, as human beings and modern technology can manage. In the ward to which he was ultimately consigned, for instance, the toilet cabinets had no doors and the shower-rooms had no locks. Therefore, a person could not ever be alone with water, glass or shaving utensils. (All the razors were cordless automatics.) Scissors and knives were banned, as were pieces of string and rubber bands. A person could not even kill his feet and hands by binding up his wrists or ankles. Nothing poisonous was anywhere available. All the windows were barred. All the double doors between this ward and the corridors beyond were doors with triple locks and a guard was always near at hand.

Still, if people want to die, they will find a way. Mimi Menlo would discover this to her everlasting sorrow with Brian Bassett.

Everett Menlo would discover this to his everlasting horror with Kenneth Albright.

On the morning of April 19th, a Tuesday, Everett Menlo, in the best of health, had welcomed a brand-new patient into his office. This was Anne Marie Wilson, a young and brilliant pianist whose promising career had been halted mid-flight by a schizophrenic incident involving her ambition. She was, it seemed, no longer able to play and all her dreams were shattered. The cause was simple, to all appearances: Anne Marie had a sense of how, precisely, the music should be and she had not been able to master it accordingly. "Everything I attempt is terrible," she had said—in spite of all her critical accolades and all her professional success. Other doctors had tried and failed to break the barriers in Anne Marie, whose hands had taken on a life of their own, refusing altogether to work for her. Now it was Menlo's turn and hope was high.

Everett had been looking forward to his session with this prodigy. He loved all music and had thought to find some means within its discipline to reach her. She seemed so fragile, sitting there in the sunlight, and he had just begun to take his first notes when the door flew open and Louise, his secretary, had said: "I'm sorry, Doctor Menlo. There's a problem. Can you come with me at once?"

Everett excused himself.

Anne Marie was left in the sunlight to bide her time. Her fingers were moving around in her lap and she put them in her mouth to make them quiet.

Even as he'd heard his secretary speak, Everett had known the problem would be Kenneth Albright. Something in Kenneth's eyes had warned him there was trouble on the way: a certain wariness that indicated all was not as placid as it should have been, given his regimen of drugs. He had stayed long hours in one position, moving his fingers over his thighs as if to dry them on his trousers; watching his fellow patients come and go with abnormal interest—never, however, rising from his chair. An incident was on the horizon and Everett had been waiting for it, hoping it would not come.

Louise had said that Doctor Menlo was to go at once to Kenneth Albright's ward. Everett had run the whole way. Only after the attendant had let him in past the double doors, did he slow his pace to a hurried walk and wipe his brow. He didn't want Kenneth to know how alarmed he had been.

Coming to the appointed place, he paused before he entered, closing his eyes, preparing himself for whatever he might have to see. *Other people have killed themselves: I've seen it often enough*, he was thinking. *I simply won't let it affect me.* Then he went in.

The room was small and white—a dining-room—and Kenneth was sitting down in a corner, his back pressed out against the walls on either side of him. His head was bowed and his legs drawn up and he was obviously trying to hide without much success. An intern was standing above him and a nurse was kneeling down beside him. Several pieces of bandaging with blood on them were scattered near Kenneth's feet and there was a white enamel basin filled with pinkish water on the floor beside the nurse.

"Morowetz," Everett said to the intern. "Tell me what has happened here." He said this just the way he posed such questions when he took the interns through the wards at examination time, quizzing them on symptoms and prognoses.

But Morowetz the intern had no answer. He was puzzled. What had happened had no sane explanation.

Everett turned to Charterhouse, the nurse.

"On the morning of April 19th, at roughly ten-fifteen, I found Kenneth Albright covered with blood," Ms Charterhouse was to write in her report. "His hands, his arms, his face and his neck were stained. I would say the blood was fresh and the patient's clothing—mostly his shirt—was wet with it. Some—a very small amount of it—had dried on his forehead. The rest was uniformly the kind of blood you expect to find free-flowing from a wound. I called for assistance and meanwhile attempted to ascertain where Mister Albright might have been injured. I performed this examination without success. I could find no source of bleeding anywhere on Mister Albright's body."

Morowetz concurred.

The blood was someone else's.

"Was there a weapon of any kind?" Doctor Menlo had wanted to know.

"No, sir. Nothing," said Charterhouse.

"And was he alone when you found him?"

"Yes, sir. Just like this in the corner."

"And the others?"

"All the patients in the ward were examined," Morowetz told him.

"And?"

"Not one of them was bleeding."

Everett said: "I see."

He looked down at Kenneth.

"This is Doctor Menlo, Kenneth. Have you anything to tell me?"

Kenneth did not reply.

Everett said: "When you've got him back in his room and tranquillized, will you call me, please?"

Morowetz nodded.

The call never came. Kenneth had fallen asleep. Either the drugs he was given had knocked him out cold, or he had opted for silence. Either way, he was incommunicado.

No one was discovered bleeding. Nothing was found to indicate an accident, a violent attack, an epileptic seizure. A weapon was not located. Kenneth Albright had not a single scratch on his flesh from stem, as Everett put it, to gudgeon. The blood, it seemed, had fallen like the rain from heaven: unexplained and inexplicable.

Later, as the day was ending, Everett Menlo left the Queen Street Mental Health Centre. He made his way home on the Queen streetcar and the Bay bus. When he reached the apartment, Thurber was waiting for him. Mimi was at a goddamned meeting.

That was the night Everett Menlo suffered the first of his failures to sleep. It was occasioned by the fact that, when he wakened sometime after three, he had just been dreaming. This, of course, was not unusual—but the dream itself was perturbing. There was someone lying there, in the bright white landscape of a hospital dining-room. Whether it was a man or a woman could not be told, it was just a human body, lying down in a pool of blood.

Kenneth Albright was kneeling beside this body, pulling it open the way a child will pull a Christmas present open—yanking at its strings and ribbons, wanting only to see the contents. Everett saw this scene from several angles, never speaking, never being spoken to. In all the time he watched—the usual dream eternity—the si-

lence was broken only by the sound of water dripping from an unseen tap. Then, Kenneth Albright rose and was covered with blood,
the way he had been that morning. He stared at Doctor Menlo,
looked right through him and departed. Nothing remained in the
dining-room but plastic tables and plastic chairs and the bright red
thing on the floor that once had been a person. Everett Menlo did
not know and could not guess who this person might have been. He
only knew that Kenneth Albright had left this person's body in
Everett Menlo's dream.

Three nights running, the corpse remained in its place and every
time that Everett entered the dining-room in the nightmare he was
certain he would find out who it was. On the fourth night, fully expecting to discover he himself was the victim, he beheld the face
and saw it was a stranger.

But there are no strangers in dreams; he knew that now after
twenty years of practice. *There are no strangers; there are only people
in disguise.*

Mimi made one final attempt in Brian Bassett's behalf to turn away
the fate to which his other doctors—both medical and psychi-
atric—had consigned him. Not that, as a group, they had failed to
expend the full weight of all they knew and all they could do to save
him. One of his medical doctors—a woman whose name was Juliet
Bateman—had moved a cot into his isolation room and stayed with
him twenty-four hours a day for over a week. But her health had
been undermined by this and when she succumbed to the Shanghai
flu she removed herself for fear of infecting Brian Bassett.

The parents had come and gone on a daily basis for months in a
killing routine of visits. But parents, their presence and their loving,
are not the answer when a child has fallen into an autistic state.
They might as well have been strangers. And so they had been advised to stay away.

Brian Bassett was eight years old—*unlucky eight*, as one of his
therapists had said—and in every other way, in terms of physical development and mental capability, he had always been a perfectly
normal child. Now, in the final moments of his life, he weighed a
scant thirty pounds, when he should have weighed twice that much.

Brian had not been heard to speak a single word in over a year of constant observation. Earlier—long ago as seven months—a few expressions would visit his face from time to time. Never a smile—but often a kind of sneer, a passing of judgment, terrifying in its intensity. Other times, a pinched expression would appear—a signal of the shyness peculiar to autistic children, who think of light as being unfriendly.

Mimi's militant efforts in behalf of Brian had been exemplary. Her fellow doctors thought of her as *Bassett's crazy guardian angel*. They begged her to remove herself in order to preserve her health. Being wise, being practical, they saw that all her efforts would not save him. But Mimi's version of being a guardian angel was more like being a surrogate warrior: a hired gun or a samurai. Her cool determination to thwart the enemies of silence, stillness and starvation gave her strengths that even she had been unaware were hers to command.

Brian Bassett, seated in his corner on the floor, maintained a solemn composure that lent his features a kind of unearthly beauty. His back was straight, his hands were poised, his hair was so fine he looked the very picture of a spirit waiting to enter a newborn creature. Sometimes Mimi wondered if this creature Brian Bassett waited to inhabit could be human. She thought of all the animals she had ever seen in all her travels and she fell upon the image of a newborn fawn as being the most tranquil and the most in need of stillness in order to survive. If only all the natural energy and curiosity of a newborn beast could have entered into Brian Bassett, surely, they would have transformed the boy in the corner into a vibrant, joyous human being. But it was not to be.

On the 29th of April—one week and three days after Everett had entered into his crisis of insomnia—Mimi sat on the floor in Brian Bassett's isolation room, gently massaging his arms and legs as she held him in her lap.

His weight, by now, was shocking—and his skin had become translucent. His eyes had not been closed for days—for weeks—and their expression might have been carved in stone.

"Speak to me. Speak," she whispered to him as she cradled his head beneath her chin. "Please at least speak before you die."

Nothing happened. Only silence.

Juliet Bateman—wrapped in a blanket—was watching through

the observation glass as Mimi lifted up Brian Bassett and placed him in his cot. The cot had metal sides—and the sides were raised. Juliet Bateman could see Brian Bassett's eyes and his hands as Mimi stepped away.

Mimi looked at Juliet and shook her head. Juliet closed her eyes and pulled her blanket tighter like a skin that might protect her from the next five minutes.

Mimi went around the cot to the other side and dragged the IV stand in closer to the head. She fumbled for a moment with the long plastic lifelines—anti-dehydrants, nutrients—and she adjusted the needles and brought them down inside the nest of the cot where Brian Bassett lay and she lifted up his arm in order to insert the tubes and bind them into place with tape.

This was when it happened—just as Mimi Menlo was preparing to insert the second tube.

Brian Bassett looked at her and spoke.

"No," he said. "Don't."

Don't meant death.

Mimi paused—considered—and set the tube aside. Then she withdrew the tube already in place and she hung them both on the IV stand.

All right, she said to Brian Bassett in her mind, *you win.*

She looked down then with her arm along the side of the cot— and one hand trailing down so Brian Bassett could touch it if he wanted to. She smiled at him and said to him: "not to worry. Not to worry. None of us is ever going to trouble you again." He watched her carefully. "Goodbye, Brian," she said. "I love you."

Juliet Bateman saw Mimi Menlo say all this and was fairly sure she had read the words on Mimi's lips just as they had been spoken.

Mimi started out of the room. She was determined now there was no turning back and that Brian Bassett was free to go his way. But just as she was turning the handle and pressing her weight against the door—she heard Brian Bassett speak again.

"Goodbye," he said.

And died.

Mimi went back and Juliet Bateman, too, and they stayed with him another hour before they turned out his lights. "Someone else can cover his face," said Mimi. "I'm not going to do it." Juliet

agreed and they came back out to tell the nurse on duty that their
ward had died and their work with him was over.

On the 30th of April—a Saturday—Mimi stayed home and made
her notes and she wondered if and when she would weep for Brian
Bassett. Her hand, as she wrote, was steady and her throat was
not constricted and her eyes had no sensation beyond the burning
itch of fatigue. She wondered what she looked like in the mirror,
but resisted that discovery. Some things could wait. Outside it
rained. Thurber dreamed in the corner. Bay Street rumbled in the
basement.

Everett, in the meantime, had reached his own crisis and because
of his desperate straits a part of Mimi Menlo's mind was on her husband. Now he had not slept for almost ten days. *We really ought to
consign ourselves to hospital beds*, she thought. Somehow, the idea
held no persuasion. It occurred to her that laughter might do a better job, if only they could find it. The brain, when over-extended,
gives us the most surprisingly simple propositions, she concluded.
Stop, it says to us. *Lie down and sleep.*

Five minutes later, Mimi found herself still sitting at the desk,
with her fountain pen capped and her fingers raised to her lips in an
attitude of gentle prayer. It required some effort to re-adjust her
gaze and re-establish her focus on the surface of the window glass
beyond which her mind had wandered. Sitting up, she had been
asleep.

Thurber muttered something and stretched his legs and yawned,
still asleep. Mimi glanced in his direction. *We've both been dreaming*,
she thought, *but his dream continues.*

Somewhere behind her, the broken clock was attempting to
strike the hour of three. Its voice was dull and rusty, needing oil.

Looking down, she saw the words *BRIAN BASSETT* written on
the page before her and it occurred to her that, without his person,
the words were nothing more than extrapolations from the alphabet—something fanciful we call a "name" in the hope that, one day,
it will take on meaning.

She thought of Brian Bassett with his building blocks—pushing
the letters around on the floor and coming up with more acceptable
arrangements: *TINA STERABBS . . . IAN BRETT BASS . . . BEST STAB*

the RAIN: a sentence. He had known all along, of course, that *BRIAN BASSETT* wasn't what he wanted because it wasn't what he was. He had come here against his will, was held here against his better judgment, fought against his captors and finally escaped.

But where was here to Ian Brett Bass? Where was here to Tina Sterabbs? Like Brian Bassett, they had all been here in someone else's dreams, and had to wait for someone else to wake before they could make their getaway.

Slowly, Mimi uncapped her fountain pen and drew a firm, black line through Brian Bassett's name. *We dreamed him,* she wrote, *that's all. And then we let him go.*

Seeing Everett standing in the doorway, knowing he had just returned from another Kenneth Albright crisis, she had no sense of apprehension. All this was only as it should be. Given the way that everything was going, it stood to reason Kenneth Albright's crisis had to come in this moment. If he managed, at last, to kill himself then at least her husband might begin to sleep again.

Far in the back of her mind a carping, critical voice remarked that any such thoughts were *deeply unfeeling and verging on the barbaric.* But Mimi dismissed this voice and another part of her brain stepped forward in her defence. *I will weep for Kenneth Albright,* she thought, *when I can weep for Brian Bassett. Now, all that matters is that Everett and I survive.*

Then she strode forward and put out her hand for Everett's briefcase, set the briefcase down and helped him out of his topcoat. She was playing wife. It seemed to be the thing to do.

For the next twenty minutes Everett had nothing to say, and after he had poured himself a drink and after Mimi had done the same, they sat in their chairs and waited for Everett to catch his breath.

The first thing he said when he finally spoke was: "finish your notes?"

"Just about," Mimi told him. "I've written everything I can for now." She did not elaborate. "You're home early," she said, hoping to goad him into saying something new about Kenneth Albright.

"Yes," he said. "I am." But that was all.

Then he stood up—threw back the last of his drink and poured another. He lighted a cigarette and Mimi didn't even wince. He had been smoking now three days. The atmosphere between them had been, since then, enlivened with a magnetic kind of tension. But it was a moribund tension, slowly beginning to dissipate.

Mimi watched her husband's silent torment now with a kind of clinical detachment. This was the result, she liked to tell herself, of her training and her discipline. The lover in her could regard Everett warmly and with concern, but the psychiatrist in her could also watch him as someone suffering a nervous breakdown, someone who could not be helped until the symptoms had multiplied and declared themselves more openly.

Everett went into the darkest corner of the room and sat down hard in one of Mimi's straight-backed chairs: the ones inherited from her mother. He sat, prim, like a patient in a doctor's office, totally unrelaxed and nervy; expressionless. Either he had come to receive a deadly diagnosis, or he would get a clean bill of health.

Mimi glided over to the sofa in the window, plush and red and deeply comfortable; a place to recuperate. The view—if she chose to turn only slightly sideways—was one of the gentle rain that was falling onto Bay Street. Sopping-wet pigeons huddled on the window-sill; people across the street in the Manulife building were turning on their lights.

A renegade robin, nesting in their eaves, began to sing.

Everett Menlo began to talk.

"Please don't interrupt," he said at first.

"You know I won't," said Mimi. It was a rule that neither one should interrupt the telling of a case until they had been invited to do so.

Mimi put her fingers into her glass so the ice-cubes wouldn't click. She waited.

Everett spoke—but he spoke as if in someone else's voice, perhaps the voice of Kenneth Albright. This was not entirely unusual. Often, both Mimi and Everett Menlo spoke in the voices of their patients. What was unusual, this time, was that, speaking in Kenneth's voice, Everett began to sweat profusely—so profusely that Mimi was able to watch his shirt front darkening with perspiration.

"As you know," he said, "I have not been sleeping."

This was the understatement of the year. Mimi was silent.

"I have not been sleeping because—to put it in a nut-shell—I have been afraid to dream."

Mimi was somewhat startled by this. Not by the fact that Everett was afraid to dream, but only because she had just been thinking of dreams herself.

"I have been afraid to dream, because in all my dreams there have been bodies. Corpses. Murder victims."

Mimi—not really listening—idly wondered if she had been one of them.

"In all my dreams, there have been corpses," Everett repeated. "But I am not the murderer. Kenneth Albright is the murderer, and, up to this moment, he has left behind him fifteen bodies: none of them people I recognize."

Mimi nodded. The ice-cubes in her drink were beginning to freeze her fingers. Any minute now, she prayed, they would surely melt.

"I gave up dreaming almost a week ago," said Everett, "thinking that if I did, the killing pattern might be altered; broken." Then he said tersely; "it was not. The killings have continued. . . ."

"How do you know the killings have continued, Everett, if you've given up your dreaming? Wouldn't this mean he had no place to hide the bodies?"

In spite of the fact she had disobeyed their rule about not speaking, Everett answered her.

"I know they are being continued because I have seen the blood."

"Ah, yes. I see."

"No, Mimi. No. You do not see. The blood is not a figment of my imagination. The blood, in fact, is the only thing not dreamed." He explained the stains on Kenneth Albright's hands and arms and clothes and he said: "It happens every day. We have searched his person for signs of cuts and gashes—even for internal and rectal bleeding. Nothing. We have searched his quarters and all the other quarters in his ward. His ward is locked. His ward is isolated in the extreme. None of his fellow patients was ever found bleeding— never had cause to bleed. There were no injuries—no self-inflicted wounds. We thought of animals. Perhaps a mouse—a rat. But nothing. Nothing. Nothing . . . We also went so far as to strip-search all the members of the staff who entered that ward and I, too, offered myself for this experiment. Still nothing. Nothing. No one had bled."

Everett was now beginning to perspire so heavily he removed his jacket and threw it on the floor. Thurber woke and stared at it, startled. At first, it appeared to be the beast that had just pursued him through the woods and down the road. But, then, it sighed and settled and was just a coat; a rumpled jacket lying down on the rug.

Everett said: "we had taken samples of the blood on the patient's hands—on Kenneth Albright's hands and on his clothing and we had these samples analysed. No. It was not his own blood. No, it was not the blood of an animal. No, it was not the blood of a fellow patient. No, it was not the blood of any members of the staff. . . ."

Everett's voice had risen.

"Whose blood was it?" he almost cried. "Whose the hell was it?"

Mimi waited.

Everett Menlo lighted another cigarette. He took a great gulp of his drink.

"Well . . ." He was calmer now; calmer of necessity. He had to marshall the evidence. He had to put it all in order—bring it into line with reason. "Did this mean that—somehow—the patient had managed to leave the premises—do some bloody deed and return without our knowledge of it? That is, after all, the only possible explanation. Isn't it?"

Mimi waited.

"Isn't it?" he repeated.

"Yes," she said. "It's the only possible explanation."

"Except there is no way out of that place. There is absolutely no way out."

Now, there was a pause.

"But one," he added—his voice, again, a whisper.

Mimi was silent. Fearful—watching his twisted face.

"Tell me," Everett Menlo said—the perfect innocent, almost the perfect child in quest of forbidden knowledge. "Answer me this—be honest: is there blood in dreams?"

Mimi could not respond. She felt herself go pale. Her husband—after all, the sanest man alive—had just suggested something so completely mad he might as well have handed over his reason in a paper bag and said to her, *burn this.*

"The only place that Kenneth Albright goes, I tell you, is into dreams," Everett said. "That is the only place beyond the ward into which the patient can or does escape."

Another—briefer—pause.

"It is real blood, Mimi. Real. And he gets it all from dreams. *My dreams.*"

They waited for this to settle.

Everett said: "I'm tired. I'm tired. I cannot bear this any more. I'm tired. . . ."

Mimi thought, *good. No matter what else happens, he will sleep tonight.*

He did. And so, at last, did she.

Mimi's dreams were rarely of the kind that engender fear. She dreamt more gentle scenes with open spaces that did not intimidate. She would dream quite often of water and of animals. Always, she was nothing more than an observer; roles were not assigned her; often, this was sad. Somehow, she seemed at times locked out, unable to participate. These were the dreams she endured when Brian Bassett died: field trips to see him in some desert setting; underwater excursions to watch him floating amongst the seaweed. He never spoke, and, indeed, he never appeared to be aware of her presence.

That night, when Everett fell into his bed exhausted and she did likewise, Mimi's dream of Brian Bassett was the last she would ever have of him and somehow, in the dream, she knew this. What she saw was what, in magical terms, would be called a disappearing act. Brian Bassett vanished. Gone.

Sometime after midnight on May Day morning, Mimi Menlo awoke from her dream of Brian to the sound of Thurber thumping the floor in a dream of his own.

Everett was not in his bed and Mimi cursed. She put on her wrapper and her slippers and went beyond the bedroom into the hall.

No lights were shining but the street lamps far below and the windows gave no sign of stars.

Mimi made her way past the jungle, searching for Everett in the living-room. He was not there. She would dream of this one day; it was a certainty.

"Everett?"

He did not reply.

Mimi turned and went back through the bedroom.

"Everett?"

She heard him. He was in the bathroom and she went in through the door.

"Oh," she said, when she saw him. "Oh, my God."

Everett Menlo was standing in the bathtub, removing his pyjamas. They were soaking wet, but not with perspiration. They were soaking wet with blood.

For a moment, holding his jacket, letting its arms hang down across his belly and his groin, Everett stared at Mimi, blank-eyed from his nightmare.

Mimi raised her hands to her mouth. She felt as one must feel, if helpless, watching someone burn alive.

Everett threw the jacket down and started to remove his trousers. His pyjamas, made of cotton, had been green. His eyes were blinded now with blood and his hands reached out to find the shower taps.

"Please don't look at me," he said. "I . . . Please go away."

Mimi said: "no." She sat on the toilet seat. "I'm waiting here," she told him, "until we both wake up."

1988

Northrop Frye
1912–1991

Born in Sherbrooke, Quebec, Frye was educated at Victoria College and Emmanuel College, University of Toronto, then at Oxford University. He is usually associated with Victoria College at the University of Toronto, where he began teaching in 1939. Frye delighted in the academic environment, and his contributions to literary scholarship are among the most significant of his generation. His literary criticism was read by the public as well as by academics. He chose to continue teaching in the undergraduate class-

rooms of the University of Toronto, because he said they were the "boiler room of a society." Frye tested all his most erudite ideas about literature in the classroom. If his students could not understand him, he reasoned, no one else would be able to either.

Fearful Symmetry (1947), Anatomy of Criticism (1957), The Great Code (1982), and Words with Power (1990): these titles shaped ideas about literature and culture for literary scholars around the world. Frye's work begins in the traditions of English literature, which he loved, but it quickly moves into its own creative space.

Frye had far-reaching interests and tolerances, but he was scathing about intellectual or artistic laziness. The difference between good and bad art, he said, is that good art requires the exercise of the imagination. It reaches beyond the immediately obvious, lifting a reader or viewer with it.

This essay, taken from The Bush Garden: Essays on the Canadian Imagination (1971), is typical of the way Frye's mind worked. He begins by considering the actual work of two Canadian painters. He moves on, though, into seeing that work as a metaphor for other issues. In the differences between the works of the two painters, Frye sees an illustration of different attitudes to art. One painter challenges himself and his viewers. The other just gives people what they want.

Canadian and Colonial Painting

The countries men live in feed their minds as much as their bodies: the bodily food they provide is absorbed in farms and cities: the mental, in religion and arts. In all communities this process of material and imaginative *digestion* goes on. Thus a large tract of vacant land may well affect the people living near it as too much cake does a small boy: an unknown but quite possibly horrible Something stares at them in the dark: hide under the bedclothes as long as they will, sooner or later they must stare back. Explorers, tormented by a sense of the unreality of the unseen, are first: pioneers and traders follow. But the land is still not imaginatively absorbed, and the incubus[1] moves on to haunt the artists. It is a very real incubus. It glares through the sirens, gorgons, centaurs, griffins, cyclops, pygmies and chimeras[2] of the poems which followed the Greek colonies: there the historical defeat which left a world of mystery outside the Greek clearing increased the imaginative triumph. In our own day the exploration and settlement has been far more thorough and the artistic achievement proportionately less: the latter is typified in the novels of Conrad,[3] which are so often concerned with finding a dreary commonplace at the centre of the unknown. All of which is an elaborate prologue to the fact that I propose to compare Tom Thomson with Horatio Walker, as suggested by a recent showing of them at the Art Gallery of Toronto; still, when in Canadian history the sphinx of the unknown land takes its riddle from Frazer and Mackenzie[4] to Tom Thomson, no one can say that there has been an anti-climax.

Griffins and gorgons have no place in Thomson certainly, but the incubus is there, in the twisted stumps and sprawling rocks, the strident colouring, the scarecrow evergreens. In several pictures one has the feeling of something not quite emerging which is all the more sinister for its concealment. The metamorphic stratum is too old: the mind cannot contemplate the azoic[5] without turning it into the monstrous. But that is of minor importance. What is essential in Thomson is the imaginative instability, the emotional unrest and dissatisfaction one feels about a country which has not been lived in: the tension between the mind and a surrounding not integrated with it. This is the key to both his colour and his design. His underlying "colour harmony" is not a concord but a minor ninth. Sumachs and red maples are conceived, quite correctly, as a *surcharge* of colour: flaming reds and yellows are squeezed straight out of the tube on to an already brilliant background: in softer light ambers and pinks and blue-greens carry on a subdued cats' chorus. This in itself is mere fidelity to the subject, but it is not all. Thomson has a marked preference for the transitional over the full season:

1. A spirit that causes nightmares.
2. Imaginary, grotesque monsters.
3. Joseph Conrad, British novelist (1857–1924).

4. Scots explorers and writers in North America: Simon Frazer (1776–1862) and Sir Alexander Mackenzie (1763–1820).
5. Time on earth before life appeared.

he likes the delicate pink and green tints on the birches in early spring and the irresolute sifting of the first snow through the spruces; and his autumnal studies are sometimes a Shelleyan hectic decay in high winds and spinning leaves, sometimes a Keatsian[6] opulence and glut. His sense of design, which, of course, is derived from the trail and the canoe, is the exact opposite of the academic "establishing of foreground." He is primarily a painter of linear distance. Snowed-over paths wind endlessly through trees, rivers reach nearly to the horizon before they bend and disappear, rocks sink inch by inch under water, and the longest stretch of mountains dips somewhere and reveals the sky beyond. What is furthest in distance is often nearest in intensity. Or else we peer through a curtain of trees to a pool and an opposite shore. Even when there is no vista a long tree-trunk will lean away from us and the whole picture will be shattered by a straining and pointing diagonal.

This focussing on the farthest distance makes the foreground, of course, a shadowy blur: a foreground tree—even the tree in "West Wind"—may be only a green blob to be looked past, not at. Foreground leaves and flowers, even when carefully painted, are usually thought of as obstructing the vision and the eye comes back to them with a start. Thomson looks on a flat area with a naive Rousseauish[7] stare (see the "decorative panels"). In fact, of all important Canadian painters, only David Milne seems to have a consistent foreground focus, and even he is fond of the obstructive blur.

When the Canadian sphinx brought her riddle of unvisualized land to Thomson it did not occur to him to hide under the bedclothes, though she did not promise him money, fame, happiness or even self-confidence, and when she was through with him she scattered his bones in the wilderness. Horatio Walker, one of those wise and prudent men from whom the greater knowledges are concealed, felt differently. It was safety and bedclothes for him. He looked round wildly for some spot in Canada that had been thoroughly lived in, that had no ugly riddles and plenty of picturesque clichés. He found it in the Ile d'Orléans. That was a Fortunate Isle with

6. Like the English Romantic poets: Percy Bysshe Shelley (1792–1822) and John Keats (1795–1821).

7. Like the French philosopher and writer Jean-Jacques Rousseau (1712–1778).

rainbows and full moons instead of stumps and rocks: it had been cosily inhabited for centuries, and suggested relaxed easy-going narratives rather than inhuman landscapes. Pictures here were readymade. There was Honest Toil with the plough and the quaint Patient Oxen; there were pastoral epigrams of sheep-shearing and farmers trying to gather in hay before the storm broke; there was the note of Tender Humour supplied by small pigs and heraldic turkeys; there was the Simple Piety which bowed in Childlike Reverence before a roadside *calvaire*.[8] Why, it was as good as Europe, and had novelty besides. And for all Canadians and Americans under the bedclothes who wanted, not new problems of form and outlines, but the predigested picturesque, who preferred dreamy association-responses to detached efforts of organized vision, and who found in a queasy and maudlin[9] nostalgia the deepest appeal of art, Horatio Walker was just the thing. He sold and sold and sold.

1940

Hugh Garner
1913–1979

When he was six, Garner moved from Yorkshire, England, with his family to an area of Toronto which became the title of his best-known novel, Cabbagetown *(1950, 1968), named for the smell of the staple food of its residents.*

Garner said that he became a writer because it was the career which interfered least with his drinking, as he led the rough-and-ready life described in his autobiography, One Damn Thing After Another *(1973). His collection of stories,* Hugh Garner's Best Short Stories, *won the Governor General's Award for fiction in 1963.*

As a young man, living an itinerant life working one low-paying job or another, on farms and in factories, Garner met people on the fringes who knew what it was to be poor in the midst of a generally affluent society. In his stories, he presents them with sympathetic in-

8. Shrine.   9. Excessively sentimental, "mushy."

sight and no judgment or commentary on their situations. He leaves it to the reader to decide if they are brave—or foolish—in the decisions they make. He was one of the first Canadian writers to live and write in this way. His fiction was often unpolished, and when a "literary person" once criticized him for his bad grammar, he informed her that "he was not writing a grammar book."

After service in the Spanish Civil War (1936–39) and in the Second World War (1939–45), Garner returned to Toronto. He always claimed that he wrote the following story in an evening because he needed money to pay the rent. He said he thought of his mother as he wrote Mrs. Taylor, imagining what she would pack to take with her on a train trip.

A Modernist story, like others Garner wrote through the 1940s and 1950s, this piece was included in A Yellow Sweater and Other Stories *(1952). Character and personality, as affected by social situation, are always central in a Garner story. This one merges a character sketch with "social protest," which never becomes explicit in the story, but obviously informs its attitudes.*

A Trip for Mrs. Taylor

Mrs. Taylor got out of bed at five o'clock that morning; an hour ahead of her usual time for getting up. She moved around her attic room with the stealth of a burglar, making herself her morning cup of tea on the hotplate, and dressing quietly so as not to disturb her landlady, Mrs. Connell, on the floor below.

She dressed her tiny self carefully, donning a clean white camisole and her black Sunday frock. After she had drunk her tea and eaten a slice of thinly-margarined toast she washed her cup and saucer in some water she had drawn from the bathroom the evening before, and put them away on her "kitchen" shelf in the clothes closet. Then she tiptoed down the steep stairs to the bathroom and washed her face and hands; "a lick and a spit" as she called it.

When she returned to her room her seventy-six-year-old face shone with wrinkled cleanliness and the excitement of the day. She combed her thinning grey hair and did it up with pins into an unsevere bun at the back of her head. Then, half-guiltily, she powdered her face and touched her cheeks with a rouge-tipped finger. Going over to her old trunk in the corner she extracted from its depths two pieces of jewelry wrapped in tissue paper. One of the pieces was a gold locket holding a faded photograph of her dead husband Bert, while the other was an old-fashioned gold chain bangle with a small lock shaped like a heart. She had lost the key to the bangle long ago, but it did not matter; her hands were now so thin that it slipped easily over her wrist.

When she had adjusted the jewelry she took her old black straw hat from its paper bag and put it on, primping a bit before the Woolworth mirror on the wall, smiling at herself and wishing that her false teeth were a little whiter.

All through her preparations she had been taking hurried glances at the alarm clock on the dresser, but now, when she was ready to go, she saw that she still had nearly two hours before train time. The train left at seven o'clock Standard Time, which was eight o'clock Daylight Saving, and here it was only a quarter to six. Still, it would take a half hour to get downtown to the station, and she couldn't afford to be late on this day of days.

She unclasped her small cardboard suitcase and carefully checked its contents once again. There was a clean change of underwear, a towel and soap, some handkerchiefs, two pairs of black lisle stockings, Bert's picture in its frame, and one of the two boys in uniform, her blouse and blue serge skirt, and the red velvet dress that Mrs. Eisen had given her the year before. The dress didn't fit her, but she liked its rich color and the feeling of opulence it gave, just to possess it.

Picking up her heavy Bible from the top of the dresser she said to herself, "I really should take it along, I guess. It'll weigh me down, but I couldn't go anywhere without it." Quickly making up her mind she placed the Bible in the suitcase and fastened the lid. Then she sat down on the edge of the bed and let the wonderful coming events of the day take over her thoughts.

The idea for the trip had come to her about a week before, on the day she had received her July old-age pension cheque. She had been down to the main post-office, mailing a set of hand-crocheted runners to her daughter-in-law Ruth in Montreal when the idea struck her. Seeing all the holiday crowds hurrying into the maw of the station had prompted her to go in and enquire about train times.

The hurry and excitement of the place had brought back the nostalgic memories of those happier times when she and Bert and young Johnnie—yes, and young Bert too, who was killed in Italy—had gone away sometimes in the summer. Their trips hadn't been long ones, and their destination was usually the home of her dead cousin Flora in Jamesville, but they had been filled with all the hustle and bustle of getting ready, packing salmon and peanut-butter sandwiches for their lunches, and making sure Bert had the tickets. There had been the warm picnicky feeling going to the station on the streetcar, trying to keep young Bert from kneeling on the seat and brushing his feet on the man beside him (she wiped away a vagrant tear at the memory) and the awareness that she *belonged* to the crowds around her.

That was the thing she had missed most during the past few years, the feeling of being one with those about her. The knowledge that she was old and ignored by younger people sometimes caused her to wish she were dead, but then appalled by the irreverence of such thoughts she would take refuge in her Bible, which was now her only solace.

Her loneliness and the striving to live on her old-age pension made mere existence a hardship. Mrs. Connell, her landlady, was a kindly soul, not much younger than herself, but she had no conception of what it was like to be cooped up month after month in a dreary little room, without even a radio to keep you company, without even a cat or a dog or a canary—nothing but the four walls, an electric plate, a bed and a dresser.

Of course, she told herself, she could have gone to live with Johnnie and Ruth in Montreal, but she'd seen too much of that sort of thing in the past. When Johnnie had married down there after the war she had felt a sinking in the stomach at the thought that he too was leaving her. "Come on down there with me, Ma," he had said, but she had sensed the reluctance behind his words. "I'm not going to be a built-in baby sitter for my grandchildren," she had answered, trying to cover her sense of loss and disappointment under her bantering words. She was independent, a woman who had run her own home for years, and brought up her two boys on the skimpy and unreliable wages of a laborer husband. But sometimes her independence melted under her silent tears, and she wished that once, just once, somebody would need her again.

But today was not the time for such gloomy thoughts. She glanced at the clock and saw that it was after seven. She stood up, straightened her hat once more, and picking up the heavy suitcase, made her way from the room, closing the door silently behind her. She had no wish to waken Mrs. Connell and have to answer the surprised questions of that lady; this trip was going to be a secret one, known only to herself.

She hurried down the street through the cloying warmth of the summer morning as fast as the heavy bag would allow her. When she reached the streetcar stop she put the suitcase down on the sidewalk and searched in her purse for a car ticket. There was very little money left from her pension cheque, but by doing without a few things to eat over the past week she had managed to save the expenses for the trip.

When the streetcar came along she climbed aboard and sat down near the front of the car. She was aware of the stares from the men and girls who were going to work, and she felt important for the first time in months. There was something friendly in the glances they gave her, and perhaps even a slight envy that she should be going away while they could only look forward to another stifling day in their offices and factories.

The downtown streets at this hour of the day were strange to her, but there was a tired camaraderie among the people getting on and off the car which brought back memories she had almost forgotten; once again she saw herself as a young woman going to work as they were, stepping down from the open-sided cars they had in those days, proud of her narrow waist and new high-buttoned boots. She felt almost young again and smiled apologetically as a thin girl in slacks nearly tripped over her suitcase.

As they neared the station several people carrying pieces of luggage boarded the car, and Mrs. Taylor smiled at them as if they were partners in a conspiracy. Most of them smiled back at her, and she felt that the anticipation and preparation for a journey was only exceeded by its actual beginning.

When she alighted from the streetcar a young man in army uniform took her suitcase from her, and holding her by the arm, led
her across the street.

"This is a heavy bag for you to be carrying," he said in a conversational tone.

"It is a little heavy," she answered, "but I haven't far to go."

"Everybody seems to be going away today," he said. "I guess I
won't get a seat on the northbound train."

"That's a shame," Mrs. Taylor answered, trying to keep up with
the soldier's long strides. "Are you on leave?"

"Sort of. I was down here on a forty-eight hour pass from camp.
I should have been back last night."

"I hope you don't get into trouble," she said. She felt suddenly
sorry for the young man—only a boy really. She wanted to tell him
that both her sons had been overseas during the war, and that young
Bert had been killed. But then she thought he might think she was
bragging, or trying to make him feel bad because he'd been too
young to go.

As they entered the cathedral-like station concourse she said to
the young soldier, "I can manage now, thank you," and he stopped
and placed the bag on the floor.

"If you're taking the northbound train I'll carry the suitcase to
the gates for you," he offered.

"No. No, thank you. I'm taking the Montreal train," she
answered.

"Well then, I'll have to leave you. Goodbye. Have a nice holiday," he said.

"Yes," she whispered, her voice cracking with emotion. As he
walked away she shouted after him, "Good-luck, son!" She watched
him disappear into the crowd and felt a nameless dread for what
might be before him. He was such a nice polite young boy, but what
was more he was the first person outside Mrs. Connell and the man
at the grocery store that she had spoken to all week.

The man at the ticket window seemed surprised as she bought her
ticket, but he stamped it on the back and handed it to her without a
word. When she asked him where to get the Montreal train he
pointed across the station to a queue of people lined up before a pair

of gates, and she picked up her suitcase and made her way towards it.

The crowd was a good-natured one, as she had known it would be, and she spent several minutes taking stock of the other travelers. It was unbelievable that so many people had woke up this morning as she had done, with the idea of catching the same train. All night as she had tossed and turned in anticipation of the morning these other people had probably been doing the same thing, unknown to her. The knowledge that they all shared the same sense of immediacy seemed to bring them closer together, and they were united in their impatience to be going.

But Mrs. Taylor was not impatient. She knew the value of time—she who had so little of it left—and this waiting with the others in the crowded station was as exciting to her as reaching the end of her trip—more so in fact.

She looked about her at the young people with their overnight bags and their tennis rackets; at the older men carrying haversacks and fishing rods, each looking a little sheepish like boys caught playing hookey; the three girls in the brand-new clothes whispering together ahead of her in the line; the young couple with the baby in the go-cart standing outside the queue, smiling at one another and talking together in French; the two priests in white panama hats who nodded solemnly and looked hot and cool at the same time in their black alpaca jackets.

This was what she had looked forward to all week! It was just as she had expected it to be, and she didn't care if the gates never opened; the best part of any journey was the waiting for the train.

There was the sound of a small scuffle behind her, and a young woman's tired voice said, "Garry, stop that right now!"

Mrs. Taylor turned and saw a slight dark girl wearing a shabby suit trying vainly to hold a young baby in her arms while she tugged at a little boy who was swinging on the end of a harness. The boy was trying desperately to break away.

"Here, young man, where do you think you're going!" Mrs. Taylor said sternly, bending down and catching him around the waist. The child stopped struggling and looked at her in surprise.

"He's been a little devil all morning," his mother said. "He knows I can't do much with him while I've got the baby in my arms."

"Now you just stand still!" Mrs. Taylor warned, letting him go and smiling at the young woman to show that she did not mean to override her authority.

"He'll stop for you," the girl said. "At home he'll do anything for his grandma, but when he knows I've got the baby to look after, he takes advantage of it."

Mrs. Taylor nodded. "I know; I had two boys myself," she said. "Is the baby a boy, too?"

"Yes. Four months."

Mrs. Taylor reached over and pulled the light blanket from the baby's face. "He's a big boy for four months, isn't he?" she asked.

She learned that the young woman's name was Rawlinson, and that she was on her way to New Brunswick to join her husband who was in the Air Force. The girl's mother had wanted to come down to the station with her, but her arthritis had kept her at home. She also learned that the baby's name was Ian, and that his mother was twenty-two years old.

She in turn told the girl that she had lived alone since her oldest boy's marriage, and that Johnnie now lived with his wife and a young daughter in Montreal. In answer to the other's questions she also told the young woman that her husband and youngest son were dead, that she received the old-age pension, and that it wasn't enough in these days of high prices.

Mrs. Rawlinson said that a friend of her mother's went to the same church as Mrs. Taylor. Mrs. Taylor didn't recognize the woman's name, although she thought she knew whom the girl meant: a stout woman with short-bobbed bluish hair who wore a Persian lamb coat in the winter.

She realized now that she had been starved for conversation, and she was so grateful for having met the young woman with the children.

"They should be opening the gates pretty soon," said the girl, look-ing at her wristwatch. "The train is due to leave in twenty minutes."

From the loudspeaker came the voice of the station-master an-nouncing that the northbound train was due to leave. Mrs. Taylor thought about the nice young soldier who had overstayed his pass.

The little boy, Garry, indicated that he wanted to go to the toilet.

"Wait till we get on the train, dear," his mother pleaded desperately.

Mrs. Taylor said eagerly, "I'll hold the baby while you take him, if you like."

"Will you! Gee, that's swell!" the young woman exclaimed. She handed the baby over, and Mrs. Taylor cradled him in her arm, while the young mother and the little boy hurried away.

She pulled back the blanket once again from the baby's face and saw that he was awake. She placed her finger on his chin and smiled at him, and he smiled back at her. The moment took her back more years than she cared to remember, back to a time when young Bert was the same age. She was filled with the remembered happiness of those days, and she thought, "I'd give up every minute more I have to live just to be young again and have my boys as babies for one more day." Then to hide the quick tears that were starting from her eyes she began talking to the baby in her arms, rocking back and forth on her heels in a gesture not practised for years.

When the woman and the little boy returned she gave up the baby reluctantly. She and the young woman stood talking together like old friends, or like a mother and daughter-in-law. They discussed teething troubles, the housing shortage, and how hard it was to raise a family these days. They were so engrossed in their new-found friendship that they failed to notice when the man opened the gates.

The crowd began pushing them from behind, and Mrs. Taylor picked up her suitcase in one hand and grasped Garry's harness with the other. Then, followed by Mrs. Rawlinson and the baby, they climbed the set of iron stairs to the platform.

Mrs. Taylor's feet were aching after the long wait at the gates, but her face shone with happiness as she steered the small boy alongside the train. The boy's mother drew up to her, and they walked together to the day-coach steps where a trainman waited to help them aboard.

"You've got your hands full there, Granny," he said, picking up the little boy and depositing him in the vestibule of the car.

She was pleased that he mistook her for the children's grandmother, and she beamed at him, not attempting to correct his mistake.

Inside the coach she led the way to a pair of seats that faced each other at the end of the car, and dropped into one with a tired sigh.

Then she held the baby while its mother took the harness off Garry and placed her small case and shopping bags on the luggage rack.

"Am I ever glad to get aboard!" Mrs. Rawlinson exclaimed. "I'd been dreading the wait at the station. Now I've only got to change trains in Montreal and I'll be all set."

"It's quite a job travelling with children," Mrs. Taylor sympathized. "Don't worry, I know. I've done enough of it in my day," she said with slight exaggeration.

Mrs. Rawlinson laid the baby on the seat beside her, before sitting back and relaxing against the cushions. The coach soon filled up, and several people eyed their double seat enviously. Mrs. Taylor was glad she had been able to get well up in the queue at the gates.

When the train started she moved over close to the window and pointed out to the little boy the buildings and streets they passed, and the tiny inconsequential people they were leaving behind them. Young Garry shouted excitedly, "Choo-choo!" at every engine they passed in the yards.

The city looked hot and uncomfortable in the morning sun, and Mrs. Taylor was surprised that all the little ant-like people didn't simply jump on a train and get away from it. It was remarkable that the ones she could see walking the streets were strangers to her now, as if there was no connection between them and the people on the train. They were a race apart; an earth-bound race separated from herself by movement and time, and the sense of adventure of her and her fellows.

She picked out landmarks as the train gathered speed; the streets she had lived on as a girl, now turned into industrial sites; the spinning mill where she had once worked; the soot-blackened park where she and Bert had walked so many years ago. . . .

"We won't be getting into Montreal until supper time," Mrs. Rawlinson said from the opposite seat, intruding upon her memories.

"No."

"I'll bet you'll be glad to get there and see your granddaughter?"

Mrs. Taylor shook her head. "I'm not going to Montreal today," she said sadly. "I can't afford to go that far."[1]

---

1. At the time when Mrs. Taylor took the train from Toronto to Montreal, the approximately 500 kilometer journey would have lasted approximately five hours.

"But—but couldn't your son send you the fare?" asked the girl.

She had to protect Johnnie, who wasn't really mean, just forgetful. "Oh, he could, but I've never really cared to go that far," she lied.

"Well—well, where are you going then?" the young woman asked, her curiosity getting the best of her.

"Not very far. Just up the line a piece," Mrs. Taylor answered, smiling. "It's just a short trip."

The train seemed to flow across the underpasses marking the streets. Soon the industrial areas were left behind, and they began rushing through the residential districts.

Mrs. Taylor was enthralled with the sight of the rows of houses as seen from the rear; yards waving with drying clothes, and every house having an individuality of its own. She only recognized some of the familiar streets after the train had passed them, they looked so different when seen from her hurtling point of vantage.

In a few minutes the train began to slow down for an outlying station, and the conductor came along the car collecting tickets. When Mrs. Taylor handed him her small bit of pasteboard, he asked, "Are you getting off here, Madam?"

"Yes, I am," Mrs. Taylor replied, coloring with embarrassment.

"Have you any luggage?"

She pointed to the suitcase at her feet, ashamed to face the stares of those who were watching her.

"Fine. I'll carry it off for you," the conductor said calmly, as if old ladies took ten-cent train rides every day of the week.

She stood up then and said goodbye to the little boy, letting her hand rest for a long minute on his tousled head. She warned him to be a good boy and do what his mother told him.

"You must think I'm crazy just coming this far," she said to Mrs. Rawlinson. "You see, I've wanted to take a trip for so long, and this was sort of—pretending."

The young woman shook the surprised look from her face. "No I don't, Mrs. Taylor," she said. "I wish you were coming all the way. I don't know what I'd have ever done without you to help me with Garry."

"It was nice being able to help. You'll never know how much I enjoyed it," Mrs. Taylor answered, her face breaking into a shy smile. "Goodbye, dear, and God bless you. Have a nice journey."

"Goodbye," the young woman said. "Thanks! Thanks a lot!"

Mrs. Taylor stood on the station platform and waved at the young woman and her son, who waved back at her as the train began to move again. Then she picked up her bag and walked along the platform to the street.

When she boarded a streetcar the motorman looked down at her and said, "You look happy; you must have had a swell vacation."

She smiled at him. "I had a wonderful trip," she answered.

And it *had* been wonderful! While all the others in the train would get bored and tired after a few hours of travel, she could go back to her room and lie down on the bed, remembering only the excitement and thrill of going away, and the new friends she had made. It was wonderful, just wonderful, she said to herself. Perhaps next month, if she could afford it, she would take a trip to the suburbs on the Winnipeg train!

1952

Thomas Haliburton
1796–1865

Born in Windsor, Nova Scotia, Haliburton was educated at Canada's oldest university, King's College in Halifax, and went on to a highly successful career as a lawyer and judge. He was appointed to the Supreme Court of Nova Scotia and, after retiring to England, became a Member of Parliament there.

Haliburton's early writings were historical, as he hoped to present Nova Scotia to the world. Writing history was too tame for him, though, because it offered no way to comment on the society around him. He began writing a series of brief columns for a newspaper, The Novascotian, *featuring Sam Slick, a Yankee trader. Satirical and outspoken, they were very popular. As a judge, Haliburton traveled widely, so a picaresque style suited him well: Sam Slick and a narrator, a country squire, wander the province, commenting on what they see. Haliburton thought he was writing these pieces to affect politics and social attitudes, but it is likely fair to say that people read them because they enjoyed the absurd situations and Sam Slick's colourful, brash way of talking.*

Encouraged by their success, Haliburton gathered them into The Clockmaker; or The Sayings and Doings of Sam Slick of Slickville *(1836). It was the first Canadian bestseller and also highly popular in England, where people were interested in the conflict between the conservative squire and American commercial know-how.*

Each piece in the collection is a witty, clever social commentary, presented under the guise of story. The first-person narrator, the squire, is almost invisible. In eighteenth-century style, he merely reports what he observes, in a kind of pseudo-documentary: I was there and I saw what happened.

The Clockmaker

I had heard of Yankee clock pedlars, tin pedlars, and bible pedlars, especially of him who sold Polyglot[1] Bibles (*all in English*) to the amount of sixteen thousand pounds. The house of every substantial farmer had three substantial ornaments, a wooden clock, a tin reflector, and a Polyglot Bible. How is it that an American can sell his wares, at whatever price he pleases, where a blue-nose[2] would fail to make a sale at all? I will inquire of the Clockmaker the secret of his success.

What a pity it is, Mr. *Slick* (for such was his name), what a pity it is, said I, that you, who are so successful in teaching these people the value of *clocks,* could not also teach them the value of *time.* I guess, said he, they have got that ring to grow on their horns yet, which every four year old has in our country. We reckon hours and minutes to be dollars and cents. They do nothin in these parts but eat, drink, smoke, sleep, ride about, lounge at taverns, make speeches at temperance meetings, and talk about "*House of Assembly.*"[3] If a man don't hoe his corn, and he don't get a crop, he says it is all owin to the Bank; and if he runs into debt, and is sued, why he says lawyers are a cuss[4] to the country. They are a most idle set of folks, I tell *you.*

---

1. Many languages.
2. Nova Scotian.
3. Seat of government.
4. Curse.

But how is it, said I, that you manage to sell such an immense number of clocks (which certainly cannot be called necessary articles) among a people with whom there seems to be so great a scarcity of money?

Mr. Slick paused, as if considering the propriety of answering the question, and looking me in the face, said in a confidential tone, Why, I don't care if I do tell you, for the market is glutted, and I shall quit this circuit. It is done by a knowledge of *soft sawder*[5] and *human natur.* But here is Deacon Flint's, said he, I have but one clock left, and I guess I will sell it to him.

At the gate of a most comfortable-looking farm-house stood Deacon Flint, a respectable old man, who had understood the value of time better than most of his neighbours, if one might judge from the appearance of every thing about him. After the usual salutation, an invitation to "alight" was accepted by Mr. Slick, who said, he wished to take leave of Mrs. Flint before he left Colchester.

We had hardly entered the house, before the Clockmaker pointed to the view from the window, and addressing himself to me, said, If I was to tell them in Connecticut, there was such a farm as this away down east here in Nova Scotia, they wouldn't believe me—why there aint such a location in all New England. The Deacon has a hundred acres of dyke.—Seventy, said the Deacon, only seventy. Well seventy; but then there is your fine deep bottom, why I could run a ramrod into it.—Interval,[6] we call it, said the Deacon, who, though evidently pleased at this eulogium,[7] seemed to wish the experiment of the ramrod to be tried in the right place.—Well, interval, if you please, (though Professor Eleazer Cumstick, in his work on Ohio, calls them bottoms,) is just as good as dyke. Then there is that water privilege, worth 3,000 or 4,000 dollars, twice as good as what Governor Cass paid 15,000 dollars for. I wonder, Deacon, you don't put up a carding machine on it: the same works would carry a turning lathe, a shingle machine, a circular saw, grind bark, and ———. Too old, said the Deacon, too old for all those speculations.—Old, repeated the Clockmaker, not you, why you are worth half a dozen of

5. Slang: soft sawder = soft soap = flattery.
6. Dyke, bottom, interval are all terms
for rich, deep-soiled farm land.
7. A speech of praise.

the young men we see, now a-days, you are young enough to have—here he said something in a lower tone of voice, which I did not distinctly hear; but whatever it was, the Deacon was pleased, he smiled, and said he did not think of such things now.

But your beasts, dear me, your beasts must be put in and have a feed; saying which, he went out to order them to be taken to the stable.

As the old gentleman closed the door after him, Mr. Slick drew near to me, and said in an under tone, Now that is what I call "*soft sawder.*" An Englishman would pass that man as a sheep passes a hog in a pastur, without looking at him; or, said he, looking rather archly, if he was mounted on a pretty smart horse, I guess he'd trot away, *if he could.* Now I find—Here his lecture on "*soft sawder*" was cut short by the entrance of Mrs. Flint. Jist come to say good bye, Mrs. Flint.—What, have you sold all your clocks?—Yes, and very low, too, for money is scarce, and I wished to close the concarn; no, I am wrong in saying all, for I have jist one left. Neighbour Steel's wife asked to have the refusal of it, but I guess I won't sell it; I had but two of them, this one and the feller of it that I sold Governor Lincoln. General Green, the Secretary of State for Maine, said he'd give me 50 dollars for this here one—it has composition wheels and patent axles, it is a beautiful article—a real first chop[8]—no mistake, genuine superfine, but I guess I'll take it back; and beside, Squire Hawk might think it kinder harder that I didn't give him the offer. Dear me, said Mrs. Flint, I should like to see it; where is it? It is in a chist of mine over the way, at Tom Tape's store. I guess he can ship it on to Eastport. That's a good man, said Mrs. Flint, jist let's look at it.

Mr. Slick, willing to oblige, yielded to these entreaties, and soon produced the clock—a gawdy, highly varnished, trumpery-looking affair. He placed it on the chimney-piece, where its beauties were pointed out and duly appreciated by Mrs. Flint, whose admiration was about ending in a proposal, when Mr. Flint returned from giving his directions about the care of the horses. The Deacon praised the clock, he too thought it a handsome one; but the Deacon was a

8. Slang: first class.

prudent man, he had a watch—he was sorry, but he had no occasion for a clock. I guess you're in the wrong furrow this time, Deacon, it an't for sale, said Mr. Slick; and if it was, I reckon neighbour
Steel's wife would have it, for she gives me no peace about it. Mrs.
Flint said, that Mr. Steel had enough to do, poor man, to pay his interest, without buying clocks for his wife. It's no consarn of mine,
said Mr. Slick, so long as he pays me what he has to do, but I guess
I don't want to sell it, and besides it comes too high; that clock can't
be made at Rhode Island under 40 dollars. Why it an't possible, said
the Clockmaker, in apparent surprise, looking at his watch, why as
I'm alive, it is 4 o'clock, and if I hav'nt been two blessed hours
here—how on airth shall I reach River Philip to-night? I'll tell you
what, Mrs. Flint, I'll leave the clock in your care till I return on my
way to the States—I'll set it a goin, and put it to the right time.

As soon as this operation was performed, he delivered the key to
the Deacon with a sort of serio-comic injunction to wind up the
clock every Saturday night, which Mrs. Flint said she would take
care should be done, and promised to remind her husband of it, in
case he should chance to forget it.

That, said the Clockmaker, as soon as we were mounted, that I
call "*human natur!*" Now that clock is sold for 40 dollars—it cost
me jist 6 dollars and 50 cents. Mrs. Flint will never let Mrs. Steel
have the refusal—nor will the Deacon larn, until I call for the clock,
that having once indulged in the use of a superfluity, how difficult it
is to give it up. We can do without any article of luxury we never
had, but when once obtained, it isn't in "*human natur*" to surrender
it voluntarily. Of fifteen thousand sold by myself and partners in
this Province, twelve thousand were left in this manner, and only
ten clocks were ever returned—when we called for them, they in-
variably bought them. We trust to "*soft sawder*" to get them into the
house, and to "*human natur*" that they never come out of it.

1836

Claire Harris
b. 1937

Having lived and studied in various parts of the world before immigrating to Canada in 1966, Harris brings to Canadian literature the rich dialect of her native Trinidad, blended with standard English, in several collections of poems. This Postmodernist piece comes from Drawing Down a Daughter *(1992), a collage of poems, stories, songs, and recipes.*

Harris is interested in meeting points between dialects, cultures, literary forms. Her stories often have elements of metafiction, musings about what constitutes story, about how a story might be told. Each piece can include poems, pauses to reflect on the process, newspaper clippings, conversations, as well as more usual bits of narrative, sometimes so short they seem more like anecdote than story. Each story becomes a collage, where seemingly unconnected fragments are linked by theme, voice, imagery. Each one stretches a reader's expectations.

Endlessly curious, Harris is also intrigued by boundaries between realism and the supernatural, between observation and superstition. How are we to know anything, she wonders, especially if we give up the old ways of knowing that are so important in traditional communities of Trinidad? She also values the ways of oral story-telling.

In this story the narrator puzzles about what she is writing. It might be autobiography, it might be fiction. The world, she suggests, thinks that those are different genres, that autobiography is non-fiction. Lines blur, though, as she tries to track down a story she remembers from childhood. The narrator is uneasily aware that what we call "facts" do not make a story.

A Matter of Fact

It is a matter of fact that the girl waits till the man from the capital begins to dress before she asks diffidently, "Where you leave your car?"

Burri buttons his shirt carefully before he replies, "It on the other side, near the big house. It park round the bend near the temple. Why you ask?"

"We could go for a drive."

"We could go for a drive!" He smiles. "Jocelyn, you ain't see how late it is? What your mother go say, girl?" His smile broadens, he strikes a pose and asks again, "You want she coming after me with a cutlass?"

"Well we have to talk."

"Eh, eh! I thought we was talking. What you have to say you can't say here?" He is laughing as he says this.

"It too late to stay here . . . I can't afford to catch cold!"

With a flourish, "Here, put on my jacket." Then seeing her seriousness, "You see how warm you get." His arm goes around her shoulders. He nibbles on her ear and chuckles.

"Look, I want to talk!"

"SO, talk!" He still nibbles, moving down the column of her neck, his fingers turn her face away from the river to face him.

"I ain't get my menses this month, again."

"What you saying . . ." he begins casually, then suddenly alert he sits up. "You ain't get . . . Look girl, what you trying on me?" His voice is rough. His movements abrupt.

"Nothing! Is true. I pregnant."

"Well, that's great! . . . So, you see a doctor? When?"

"I get the results Monday."

He stares at her, frowning.

"I want you to come and see my mother."

He has decided to be cool, "Me! What I want with your mother!" His eyes are wide. He is smiling. He puts his arm around her. "Is you I want." He pats her stomach. "I'll bet is a boy!"

"How we go marry if you ain't talk?"

"Marry!" He is amazed. "Look girl, I ask you to marry me? Is the man does ask!" He scowls, "I ain't ready to marry nobody."

"But ain't you say you love me? What you think my mother go say? Where I go go?"

He is contemptuous. "Is town you go to school? You never hear about tablet? If is mine, ask your grandmother to give you a tea to drink, because I ain't marrying nobody." He begins to gather his things together. He checks his car keys, his wallet. Draws his Seiko on over his wrist.

"But I can't . . . I ain't never . . . nobody . . ."

Now he is gentle again. He takes her hand and seems to think. "Girl, I sorry. Don't do anything yet. I go think of a way. Don't say nothing if you frighten."

"What you mean?"

"A way to fix everything. What? You think I just go leave you?" He smiles, bends to kiss her, straightens, looks around. "But look how late you keep me here! Is a good thing it have moon. How else to see to go through all that bush?"

"When you coming back?"

"Thursday."

The lie trips from his tongue as smooth as butter, and the girl hears it though she is desperate to believe. She stands on the ledge by the falls watching him bound down the hill towards the river. His jacket slung over one shoulder flaps in his lean surefooted grace. He does not look back until he comes to the clump of bamboo before the bend in the river and sets foot on the path. She knows he has turned, because she can see the trim white shirt tucked neatly back into his pants, and the gleaming silver buckle in his belt. He has come to her straight from his clean civil service job in the intimidating red pile of the Legislature. She does not return his wave. But waits to stop the tears that come of their own volition. When she is no longer shuddering, she wipes her face and begins to plan how to get to her room at the back of the house without coming face to face with her mother. Later she will claim a headache. This at least is true. She begins to climb up to the road to the village. Her fingers stray to the medallion dangling against her sore breasts.

Of all this: the river valley, the girl Jocelyn, the pregnancy, Burri as snake, the old storyteller will say nothing. She has no truck with this simple form, with its order and its inherent possibility of justice. Though she speaks the language, she knows the real world where men wander is full of unseen presences, of interruptions, of rupture. In such a world, men have only tricks and magic. When she makes her old voice growl, or rise and fall on the gutter and flare of candlelight, her tale is not only a small meeting: chance and the implacable at the crossroads, i.e. in the individual. Her tale is a celebration, and a binding of community. Her theme is survival in the current of riverlife. Her eyes scan the gathered children fiercely, "You can learn how to deal with life; you cannot avoid what nests in you." There is something of the ancestral, of Africa in this. The children hear. They are polite. They nod solemnly. But their eyes lust after the story.

She laughs in the disconcerting way of old women, lights the candles, orders the electric lights switched off. Now she is ready.

"*See-ah,*" she growls.

"*See-ah,*" the children growl back.

"*See-ah Burri See-ah.*"

"*See-ah Burri See-ah,*" the children sing hugging their knees and moving closer, almost huddling.

"*It have a man,* Burri, he go see he girl by the river and he stay too late. They must have had talk or something because usually he leave while it light because he know about forest, riverbank, and La Diablesse.[1] Well, this Burri, he hurry long through the tunnel form by the arching bamboo. All time he watching the forest, looking round and thing. He ain't really 'fraid, but he know in a few minutes darkness be King. Only moon for light. He ain't running, but he walking real fast. He feel he got to get to the car quick. It seem to him he walking and walking but he ain't getting nowhere. He think perhaps he miss the crossing stones. But he can't see how he do that because it ain't got no turn off. Well, this Burri, he decide to stop for a minute and light a cigarette. Well is who tell Burri do that?"

"*See-ah Burri See-ah*
See-ah Burri Mammy oh.
See-ah Burri Mammy oh," respond the children.

"Crick-crack," says a small boy who wants to get on with the story.

"First thing he know he can't find his lighter anywhere. He check breast pocket, breast pocket say, 'check shirt pocket.' He check shirt pocket, shirt pocket say, 'check pant pocket.' He check pant pocket, pant pocket say, 'check jacket pocket.' He check jacket pocket, and jacket pocket say, 'ain't my business if you drop it.'

Is now he in big trouble. Pitch black and no way to make a light.

---

1. A female demon; succubus (French).

He begin to really hurry, and see heself looking straight into old eye of mappipi zanana. Snake straight and flat on the branch. Now he really begin to run. He run like he mad. Like snake chasing him. Branch catch at him, grass like it want to hold him back. A bird fly straight up out of the ground in front of him flapping and screaming. He running so hard that Burri half-way cross the clearing before he realize it.

He slow heself down. He bend over holding his knee like Olympic runner. When he heart return to he chest, he look back to the mouth of the bamboo grove. He ain't see nothing. He walk on now. He thinking how big and bright the moon. And is so it hanging low over the river. Well, is finally he come to the steppin stones and them. The water low in the river and he ain't think it go be slippery. And he standing there, shivering a little, because like is something cold trying to bind him, when he see a flash of something white. Like it moving in the trees on the other side of the river. Even before she come out in the moonlight he know is a woman. Is so some of those men does be. Anyhow she standing in the open looking frighten, and he see one time she pretty for so. Real pretty-pretty. And she got that high-boned face and full lips like the girl he just leave. Not that he thinking about she. What he thinking is how the moonlight so bright-bright, and how he clothes so mess up with all that running and thing. Instant he begin to fix up he shirt, and he jacket, he even take he tie out he pocket and put it back on.

And all the time he whistling. Like somebody give he something, and he real, real please . . ."

"*See-ah Burri See-ah*
Burri cross de river oh
Burri itch he scratch-oh.
Burri itch he scratch-oh," sang the children happily.

"Crick-crack," says the small boy who knows his role.

The old woman turns to the small boy, "You is man, all you don't have no real sense. Is not only what you see that there." She pauses a moment, "And not all what smell sweet does taste sweet." Then she begins again.

"Well, now that he tidy, Burri feel that he is who he is. He walk to the stones and all the whole time he smiling at the girl. He measure the first jump and he start crossing, jumping from stone to

stone, and like he showing off a little for the girl. So he look up to
see how she taking it, and he see her eyes. They like a lasso. They
like a fishline, and Burri hook. He fall. He slip and he fall and feel
heself struggling, the water close over he head, he thrash out and
kick up, and he know the water ain't deep. But he head butt against
sand, he eye open to the green wall of a pool. Current catch him, he
toss like twig. His chest heavy and hurting, he see stars, and white
light exploding, and red. Sudden he is boy again. This girl, Anita,
skin like clay pot, that colour, her hair trailing in the water, her
breast buds glistening, she floating on the surface of the river. Fragile and open as if she alone, as if none of the rest of them there. He
swim over to her quiet, quiet, then he grab a bud in his mouth.
How after the shock she scream and scream, and she grab his head
and hold it down in the river bottom. How the thin wiry legs scis-
sor and ride him. How the blood roar in he ears, and the darkness
catch him. And then the weight lift and the light break through.
How he jump and jerk and fight the line, the hooked finger. And
how in the end he flop on the bank. How he lungs burn in the
moonlight and water pour from eyes, nose, mouth. Meanwhile the
woman just standing there under the cocoa. She ain't say nothing.
He land on the riverbank at she feet where the skirt circle her in a
frothing green frill.

Well, Burri fright leave as he see the woman kind of smiling, like
she just too polite to laugh out loud. So now he start to feel stupid
for so! But the girl bend down and give he a hand, and he stand up,
and she say real nice, "You ain't careful, you catch cold!"

He just nod he head. Burri no fool, he figure he go let she do the
talking and just nod and thing. He know if she start feeling sorry
for him, he set. And right away he want to know she real, real well.

"You have far to go?" she voice have this sweet lilt.

Burri say, "It quite town I have to go!" He shiver a little bit then
he say, "Is only my chest I 'fraid."

"You could come by me and dry out. Is only my grandmother
there." And she smiling real sweet, and her voice like she promising
something.

Burri ain't stop to ask heself how come a girl standing out there
in the moonlight by sheself. He ain't ask heself how come he feeling so happy all of a sudden. He feeling happy, he just feel happy.

And the woman herself, she just looking prettier and prettier. The woman self, she too happy because normally she does have to beg, but this one he just coming with her easy-easy."

"*See-ah Burri See-ah.*" The old woman is drumming on her knees.

"*See-ah Burri See-ah.*" The boy has got a bottle an' spoon.

"*See-ah Burri See-ah*
Burri lock in a box oh
What lock he in, can't open oh."

Knees bent, turning slightly sideways, the old lady does a calypso shuffle, "*What lock he in, can't open oh.*"

Arms waving, pelvis shifting, the children dance around the room.

"*What lock he in, can't open oh*
See-ah Burri See-ah."

The boy gets tired of the bottle an' spoon. He decides to assert control.

"Crick-crack," he says. And again, "Crick-crack!" The old lady sighs, sits. The children collapse at her feet. The old lady eyes the boy. "Your pee ain't froth, you can't be man," she says. The boy's eyes go round with surprise. The girls giggle. The old lady is talking rudeness! For a moment her voice crackles as she picks up the tale.

"Well now, Burri, he going up the hill with the lady. And he noticing how sweet she smelling, like is flowers. And how she turn she head, and walk a little sideways. He thinking how lucky he is. And how he never realize Lopinot have so many pretty girls. His head so full a plans for the girl, he never notice she limping until they get to the car. Is when playing real gentleman he open the car door for she that he see the funny foot. Still his mind ain't tell him nothing. Is so when you talking love you don't see what you don't want to see. Burri get in the car, take out he car keys, and say to the girl, real formal, "So where do you live Miss . . . ?" and he kind of pause like he waiting for she to give he a name, but she ain't say no name. She just give him directions for a road near the ravine. The ravine about a mile and a half up the road. Burri thinking is so she want to play it? If she ain't give me a name, I ain't giving she one neither. He look at she sitting there beside him, and he thinking how smooth she skin, and he wondering what she grandmother going to say, and he hoping she real old. Perhaps is thinking of old that make he think of death. Anyway it suddenly hit him what the scent in the car remind him of. Is how the house smell when they bring all the wreaths for his mother funeral. Burri really love he mother now she dead. Just thinking about her could bring tears to his eye. The girl ain't saying nothing. She just sitting there smiling to sheself private like. Burri car have signal in the engine. But he begin to do show-off drive. He open the car window and begin to make pretty-pretty signal with his whole arm. Then he reach for he cigarettes. As soon as she see the cigarette, she begin to frown. She say "That does make me sick, yes?"

Burri forget all about he wet clothes, which practically dry by now. He thinking this woman bold, yes! She ask me for a lift. Now she telling me I can't smoke in my own car! Is right now to see who is boss. He say, "The window open, you don't see?" But she smart too. Quick as crazy ants her hand move to the dashboard, and she grab the extra lighter he does keep there. All the time she laughing like is joke. Burri ain't think is joke, but he laugh like he think is joke.

He smiling and he smiling, but he mind working overtime. "God!" he say, "but you stubborn yes! And in my own car too?" Is because he was looking at her that he see she face slip a little when he say "God!" He think, 'I ketch! Now is Lawd help me!' And he see she face. He see it slip. And she put she hand up to hide it, and he grab the lighter from she. The whole car filling up with the scent of dead flowers. And he light the cigarette."

"Ah, Burri!" the children exclaim.

"So what you think happen next?" the old lady asks. She is relaxed, at ease.

"*You lucky, eh Burri, You lucky.*"

The children vie with each other in their banshee wailing,

"*I woulda break you neck fuh you*
de devil eat you, Burri."

They try to fill the room with wild laughter.

"Well, then she disappear," the old lady says, "*Is so Burri tell me and now I come here to tell you.*"

A small girl fingers her face. "Ah, Burri," she sighs, eyes busy with the horror of a face slipping. Is it possible to be a La Diablesse and not know it, she wonders, where would you go when they found you out?

"But how she sitting here in the dark like that?"
"Girl, turn on the electricity and throw some light on things."

I'll try. But this isn't easy. For one thing, I doubt the ability of any-one to relate a series of facts accurately. For another, I doubt that it is possible to consider any event a fact except in the simplest use of that word. Take, for instance, the laughable, the incontrovertible idea that I am writing this. True, these are my hands that strike the keys. But I have so little control over what is being written that I know the story is writing me. I have been brooding over these events since I rediscovered them in 1983. Once I was determined to write a straightforward narrative. A soupçon[2] of horror. A fiction. Yet this has become an autobiography. Of sorts. And this short paragraph a kick against that fate. For we do not know if any of this really happened. Yet I remember the story being told. I remember the old woman. And I am sure the story was told as I have written it because that is how the books say Afro-Caribbean tales are told. Your books, I mean. But this is not really about style. This is about plot. For, a few years later, seven years after the telling, to be precise, I met John Burian Armstrong.

He was dressed all in white except for a navy shirt. Close-cropped greying hair topped what I was later on to learn was called an ageless face. At the time I thought that in spite of the deep crevasses that ran down to the corner of his mouth, he was young. There I was curled up in my father's chair on the verandah, reading, I am sure, though I am not sure what I was reading. He stood there smiling at me, sucking at his lower lip as if I reminded him of food, and in spite of his cane, or perhaps because of it, managing to look Mr. Cool.

"You must be Mr. Williams' daughter!"

It crossed my mind suddenly to say coldly, "Not really, I'm a La Diablesse in waiting."

Well . . . Not really.

2. A taste (French).

I'm trying for fact. A little artistic license here, a little there, and the next thing you know I'm writing history.

A few minutes later I heard him say to my father, "I'm John Burian Armstrong. People around here say I should talk to you."

I was not very surprised by this opening. "Talking to my father" was something the villagers did regularly. He was the recipient of their dreams and their fears. As the only educated black man who came to the village regularly, he was frequently asked to help when anything 'official' or unusual came into their lives. Sometimes, perhaps often, the villagers simply needed someone to know what life, or 'they who does run everything' had done to them, again. So when Armstrong introduced himself, my father sat back in his dark mahogany easy chair with the cushioned slats and prepared to listen.

"Oh! So what is it you have to tell me, Mr. Armstrong?"

"Everyone calls me 'Burri'."

"Burri, then."

"Sir what I have to say is God's truth! People say I was drunk. But that time I didn't drink. A drink now and then, yes. But drink to get drunk, no! Not even till today."

It was the name, Burri, that did it. "*See-ah Burri See-ah.*" I moved a Morris chair as close to the windows looking on the verandah as possible. Very quietly indeed I prepared to eavesdrop.

"Let me start from the beginning. Is true I get a girl pregnant. Is true I had no mind for marriage. We argue a bit and it get late. I leave her there and I start to walk along the river to get to the path what you cut there from the pool. Nothing so strange happen until I reach the steppin stones. Just before I cross to come to this side I see a girl standing on the bank, she just standing there on this side near the big cocoa tree where the steps begin."

"What time would that have been?"

"About what o'clock? About seven for the latest. I kind of wave to her and I start crossing. Half way I slip on the stones, fall into the water, and the current sweep me in to the little cave it have under the bank near the bend. I really thought I was gone. Every which way I turn I coming up water. Anyway the girl bend over and give me a hand."

"Did you see her do that yourself?"

"Well, Mr. Williams, there wasn't anybody else there! I figure it have to be her."

"Reasonable. But it's always better if you tell me exactly what you know for a fact. Not what you think it must have been."

"Well, when I get back my strength, I start talking and she offer to take me home with her to dry off my clothes. She tell me her mother gone to visit her sister in San Fernando, but the rest of the family, home. I ask her her name and she tell me 'Mera,' is short for 'Ramera.' I tell my name, Burri. Is true I never hear that name before, but they have lots of 'pagnol[3] people living up here, so I ain't surprise."

"And she didn't look like anyone you know? Not even a little? You know how moonlight is tricky."

"To tell you the truth she look a lot like the girl I was seeing. I thought they might have been some relation. But she herself I never see before."

"Go on."

"We come to the top of the road, and as I crossing over to the car I see she limping. I figure is a stone or something and I walk over to the other side. I open the car door and I get in. She tell me where she live and I start driving. The car smelling musty so I roll down the car window. I don't want the girl thinking my car nasty. Mosquitos start coming in the car so I reach for a cigarette. She say smoke does bother her. I reach for my lighter and my hand touch the bible with the Christopher medal my mother put there when I first buy the car. As God is my witness, Mr. Williams, I light the cigarette. The next thing I know the car rushing into the bank and I can't do anything. Sametime I look over, put out my hand, and the woman ain't there. Before the car hit the bank I see the whole thing. The car door stay close but the woman gone!

"The car crumple like somebody fold it up. I wait there half an hour before anybody come. Then they couldn't get me out."

"You never saw her again?"

"I'll tell you. While I was waiting for the ambulance and the police, I tell the people there was a woman in the car. I describe her. They say perhaps she fall out. They look all night. Nobody see any-

---

3. Espagnol = Spanish (French).

thing. Two days later the police come, question me. They say no-body reported missing. Nobody dead."

"You sure you didn't lose consciousness? Sometimes it's hard to tell."

"Well, I'll admit. My doctor tell me so too. So I come up here and I question everybody. Nobody ever hear of the family. Is that what convince me."

"You know you ought to write that down. One hears of these things, but no one ever has first-hand experience."

"But if a thing like that could happen what kind of world is this?"

What kind of world indeed! For Mr. Armstrong claimed to have had his amazing experience three years earlier. Four years after the night we had danced wildly around the back verandah chanting:

"de devil eat you, Burri"

First you point out to your sceptical parents that you have never be-fore or since heard the name Burri. Have they? No they haven't. In-fected by Newton[4] and the church, they insist on coincidence. You are invited to clean up your imagination, to attend daily Mass. But something lovely has been given to you. A world in which each fact like the legs of runners photographed at slow speeds is an amalgam of variations of itself. Myriad versions of event reaching out of time, out of space, individual to each observer.

It is March, 1954. Though he has friends among the villagers, we never see Mr. Armstrong again. My father, however, has discovered that his cane is merely a matter of fashion. "Just practising," he says, looking at me quizzically, "just practising."

The fiction persists that autobiography is non-fiction. A matter of fact. The question, of course, is what is fact: what is reality. Though the myth of La Diablesse sticks to convention, the stories them-selves are specific to a particular event. Is it possible that that old lady bodying forth a world in that long ago August night gave it flesh?

---

4. Sir Isaac Newton (1642–1727), English physicist famous for the theory of gravity.

Or was it Burri himself? The power of his experience/delusion stretching both backwards and forwards into time.

Or did the face of reality slip?

Here are the notes I made over thirty years ago for the last half of the story.

(i)   In the darkness he slips and breaks his legs.
(ii) The villagers hear him calling in delirium but are convinced that a spirit calls them to doom.
(iii) He calls the girl by name: there is a dream sequence.
(iv) He is found four days later by a hunting pack. Barely alive.
(v)   His leg never mends properly. (Serve him right!)

Sequel

He changes. Nice girl meets him and falls in love. He refuses to marry her and blight her life because of his leg. Somebody dies and leaves him a million dollars (US). The girl, who is poor, agrees to marry him because her little sister has nearly died from polio. The money helps them to buy better doctors. End on a kiss.

I could have been a romance novelist.

These I know to be facts: the 'Burri' tale; John Burian Armstrong; the Lopinot river; Jocelyn. By stopping here, I am being a purist. It is possible that the writing of this, this telling, began in 1983, when, on one of my rare trips to the island, I set out to visit the old lady, the storyteller of my childhood. I would have gone to see her anyway, but I also wanted to know if there had been an accident; more than that, I wanted to know where her story had come from. She was then 103 years old, this Great Aunt of mine, and she had the telegrams to prove it.

She looked at me cynically and observed, "All you so, ain't know what true from what ain't true!"

"You know. You tell me."

"You don't tell thing so to strangers."

"Come on! I am not a stranger!"

"Overseas water you blood! Don't know if you going or coming! Youself!"

She wouldn't sell me a plot of land either. She owned thirty acres, "All you had and you throw it away!"

But there had really been an accident. That much I had got from her.

I discovered that a friend, Dr. Harry Wilson-Janes of UWI,[5] could get me into the *Guardian* morgue. I wanted to find out if Mr. Armstrong's accident had been reported. It had been. Strong black lines to give it prominence. But I found it only by the merest fluke and in a paper dated *five* years after Mr. Armstrong's visit to my father:

AROUCA—The police are interested in interviewing the woman who was riding with Mr. John B. Armstrong when his car crashed near the half mile post on the Lopinot Road at approximately 7:40 p.m. on Thursday, February 18, 1959. A witness saw a young woman get into the car about 7:36 p.m. You are asked to contact Inspector Jarvis at the Arouca police station. (J. Badsee)

After a few days of dithering, I called the Arouca police station. Inspector Jarvis had retired. But the desk sergeant cheerfully gave me his number at home. Because I didn't have the nerve to ask a retired Superintendent of Police whether he remembered a traffic accident which had taken place twenty-four years earlier, face to face, I decided to phone him. It took me several tries to contact him, but when I did, his voice was strong and clear.

Mine was hesitant. Did he remember the Armstrong accident? He did. He certainly did. Why was I asking? Armstrong had been a friend of mine . . . I had been away . . . some very funny stories going around. When had the accident taken place? February 1959. He was certain. Had there been another accident in 1954? 1955? No. He was sure of it. Armstrong had had only one accident. God knows he had made it his business to find out everything there was to know

5. University of the West Indies.

about that man. And he went to his funeral in 1980, yes, and made sure to check out the coffin. Did he ever find the woman? That was a funny, funny thing happened there. He remembered it still. Couldn't get it out of his head.

(Here he paused for several minutes to check out my genealogy: Which Williams? Oh, so soandso is your cousin! Which brother was grandfather? Oh, so you relate to soandso!

In some quarters it takes three generations to establish trust. Both sides of the family.)

His next question was direct and much to the point. Did I believe in the old-time things? Convince me. I don't know what I believe. Like everybody else. Silence. W . . . ell, it was a long story, he would cut it short for me. When they got to the crash, Armstrong was conscious. Trapped. His legs twisted up. But his mind was clear. He said he picked up this woman and was taking her home when the car crashed. Asked him where the woman was. Funny look come over his face. Said he didn't know. To tell the truth, Jarvis thought it was going to be one of those gruesome cases. He and Sergeant Dick organized village search parties. Lanterns. Torchlight. Flambeaux. Ten groups of three spread out. Nothing. No woman. Next day, dogs and the police teams. Nothing. House to house; signals to every police station in the island. Signals to Tobago, Grenada. Nothing. He and Dick by themselves talked to every woman in the place. All the little tracks and hillhouses. Nothing.

By then the whole place started to panic. Country people. Taxi-drivers refused to drive after dark. Buses breaking down in the garage, come five-thirty. Visiting nurses sicken-off. Pressure! Pressure! He went to see Armstrong in the hospital, and Armstrong told him a strange, strange story. Went back to the accident reports. First thing, no skid marks. Yet that car, folded up like an accordion. De Silva, what own the plantation, he had called the station. Went back to see him. He wasn't there, he talked to his wife. The lady, English. At that time she was only here eight months. The lady didn't know anything about Trinidad. She swear she was sitting on her verandah having a drink after dinner. She, De Silva, and his brother. The car was parked under the hill, round the bend, after that is straight road. They saw the man come out the trees on the river track. They was watching for him. She know the girl young because she very slim, and though she had a limp she walk real queenly. Also she had on a very long skirt with a frill, like she was going to a ball. She thought it was funny to see that in the country, coming out of the bush. You know how those colonist type does think! She said it was bright moonlight.

Then the husband come in. He had hear all the rumours and he was kind of looking at Jarvis funny. Stressing that his wife English. He said they watch the couple get in the car. He stressed how modern they looked together. His wife laughed and said, "Like an advertisement." But then they get serious, and he said they watch the car drive real slow and kind of erratic as if the driver had only one hand on the wheel. Then the car head for the bank. De Silva gave him a queer look and said (he remembers his exact words), "The car head for the bank like it was going home. Quiet and peaceful. It hardly make any noise. The horn blare once and shut off." They stand on the verandah arguing about going down. His brother didn't believe the car crashed. They sent one of their men down to check and he came running back up the hill, shout up is a bad crash. De Silva said he didn't know why he asked him, but he ask his foreman, "How many people in the car?" The man said, "One."

There was a long silence. After a while I said, "Thank you. It's hard to get the truth of such a thing. The facts, I mean." Superintendent Jarvis wished me well. Then he said, "Nobody knows exactly what happen there that night. But is the kind of thing you think is story . . . You have to think is story."

1988

Anne Hébert
1916–2000

> *Hébert wrote the following essay for a special collection by prominent Canadian writers,* Century 1867–1967, *created for Canada's centennial. It appeared as a booklet in many of the country's newspapers.*
>
> *This piece demonstrates Hébert's deep love for her native Quebec, where she was born into its oldest family. In 1608, Louis Hébert and his wife, Marie Rollet, were the first European settlers*

in what is now Quebec City. Anne Hébert, a preeminent poet and novelist, has reason to think of Quebec as the place where it all began. She celebrates her country-within-a-country in the language of a poet, surveying its history and the sweep of its geography. She links Quebec to her own family, to her own memories of childhood in a way that, almost without our noticing, this public essay becomes personal.

Hébert's love of language shows in the way she creates lists: of towns, street names, foods, trees, insects. She enjoys the sounds of the words. Indeed, this essay comes close to poem and is perhaps best appreciated when read aloud.

The dark undertones of Hébert's writing come through in phrases such as "the flesh of this still-bitter fruit called Canada." French Canadians find it difficult to be a minority culture in a sea of English-speakers. This essay, in English, is still filled with the lyrical sounds of the French language.

Hébert enriches her essay with references to other writings, other literature, beginning with a notation Jacques Cartier inscribed on a cross, which she calls "The vocation of writing begun in the wilderness wind." She is a proud descendant of that vocation, continued into the twenty-first century.

The novel Kamouraska *(1970) is Hébert's best-known work in English-speaking Canada. For* Children of the Black Sabbath *(1975), she won France's treasured Prix Femina.*

Québec: The Proud Province

This province is a country within a country. Québec the original heart. The hardest and deepest kernel. The core of first time. All around, nine other provinces form the flesh of this still-bitter fruit called Canada.

The creation of the world took place on the rock of Québec. Face to the river. Adam and Eve were Louis Hébert and Marie Rollet. The first dwelling. The first land tilled. The first sheaf of grain reaped. The first bit of bread. The first child brought into life. The first body laid in earth.

The first written word. It was in 1534: "In the name of God and of the King of France." A cross planted at Gaspé by Jacques Cartier. The vocation of writing begun in the wilderness wind.

And then we were surrendered to time. Time followed its course. By turns we were shaken or lulled by time. Like logs drifting down rivers, we slipped by. A defeat in the heart. A rosary between the fingers. Like the dead. Musing on the song of Lazarus.[1] But see the thought give way to the word. The word becomes flesh. To possess the world. To seize and name the earth. Four and a half centuries of roots. The tree, no longer subterranean, admittedly in the light. Erect. Confronting the world. The Tree of Knowledge.[2] Not in the center of the garden. Those soft prenatal limbs outside paradise, in the accursed open land. At the hour of birth, a gate opens upon the round and total world.

The right of the adult to be and to do. His man's heart to take and to speak. His man's work to build and to proclaim.

"In Québec nothing changes." Once this was truth. Immobile, peasant-like. Beneath the snow, or the summer sun. Yet no Sleeping Beauty can pass unchanged the test of slumber. Beneath so many dreams and sorrows a duty is discerned. Take up thy bed and walk. The heaped-up treasure-hoard cracks and splits. Reclaim the heritage from foreign imposts.[3]

The river is salt like the sea. Waves beat upon seaweed-laden shores. Here the wind blows free for ten leagues[4] around. The adventure is boundless. Who can merely tell of it? One must shout it, hands forming a loud-hailer. The two banks narrowing together are thickly black with trees. It is on no human scale. Here man may labor only. Whoever speaks will speak savagely. With a voice of earth and water mixed.

Helter skelter land of wood and sea. North bank. South bank. Kamouraska, Saint-Vallier, Cap à l'Aigle, Saint-Jean-Port-Joli, Ile aux Lievres, Rimouski, Father Point, Sainte-Luce, Anse Pleureuse, Coin du Banc, Pic de l'Aurore, Gros Morne, Cloridorme, Ile Bonaventure.[5]

1. A reference to a man Jesus raised from the dead (John 11:43–44).
2. In the Garden of Eden (Genesis 2:9).
3. Taxes, duties.
4. Thirty miles.
5. Places along the St. Lawrence River.

Sea birds by thousands encrust the rock. Lift. Wheel. Raucous cries on the smell of the sea. Gannets, grebes, cormorants, gulls. Beneath the wind the rock seems to shake itself, like a wild beast attacked by superbly fantastic swarms of bees. Above, the sky.

A hundred thousand lakes. Streams with the strength of a river. Forests entangled by dead-falls. An axe in the hand like a cane. The tracks are those of caribou. Mosquitoes smoke upon your body like your own breath.

Burnt-over land as far as the eye can see. New growth of birch on the green moss. Long tendrils of moss, drawn from the soil, like garlands with fine sandy roots. Gathering blueberries. The barrens laden with blue fruit. That silvery mist clouding the fresh berries. That was when I was a child. Now the reign of the birches is threatened. The face of Charlebois is pitted by dead birches. Sad little white bones against the green of the forest.

Calm lakes, like water in the hollow of a hand. Lake Edward. We children were forbidden to go near the water. "Your hair the color of the fallow deer, your body of peacocks"—hunters might fire in error. The midges, the blackflies ambushed us. Thousands of needles. Was that the sound of a moose? It crosses the lake, swimming. As if it ploughed a mirror. Deer! A deer in the hayfield! A prodigy of a leap! There it is, out of range. Sheltering in the black spruce.

Sainte-Catherine. Each summer's end a brown bear ventured from the forest. Prowled the edges of the fields. While the golden hay assumed the color of fresh-baked bread. Children saw enormous tracks in the sand of the little strawberry woods. Games were erased. Sand castles crushed. The children gravely enchanted. As if in the night an heraldic beast had come from the high plains of the Countess de Segur, née Rostopchine,[6] claiming her tribute in Canadian land.

Sainte-Foy. Named for a bitter victory. There where the city, the new university city, now expands. During my childhood it was a little wood. A whole summer of holidays. A brook. Green grass-snakes. Symphonies of tree-frogs. Strawberries bordering the fields.

---

6. Popular French writer of books for children, (1799–1874).

Orchards. Apples succeeding apples—the green, the white, the transparents, the Fameuses. Four houses thick-shelled with white brick. Each with its garden and its orchard. The road was called the Avenue of the Four Bourgeois. It was the country.

Québec. That city where my parents were born. Where my ancestors prospered and were undone. The city is lived in. Above. Below. The city is ours. We need only plainly speak its name, this city. City on a crag. City of the New World. Upper Town. Lower Town. The secret province. Homogeneous. Certain of its identity. Dreaming behind its jalousies.[7] Taking its time. Sauntering through the narrow streets. Through the summer evenings. Releasing in full bloom the beauty of its daughters.

The long length of Dufferin Terrace. Rue Saint-Louis, rue de la Fabrique, Esplanade, rue des Grissons, rue des Glaçis, ruelle du Trésor, côte à Coton, côte de la Negresse, Latin Quarter, rue Dauphine, Jardin du Fort, Jardin du Gouveneur, rue sous le Cap, Petit Champlain. Little by little the aristocratic quarters move from the old city. A whole floating population camps within the walls. The tall dwellings divide into rented pigeonholes. They sell souvenirs. The port overflows with shipping. Whirlpools of gulls. Vast gates of the water. The sea begins. Clerical bands and coifs. A city of terraces and convents.

Sugar and syrup from the Beauce. Honey from Saint-Pierre-les-Becquets. Mushrooms from Waterloo. Cider from Saint-Hilaire. Brome Lake duck. Valcartier turkey. Real geography is learned at the table, in the breaking of bread.

Boucherville, Varennes, Verchères, Contrecœur, Saint-Antoine-de-Tilly, Sorel, Saint-Jean-sur-Richelieu. Old villages of the French regime. Fine stone houses in the style of manors. Elms, of all trees the most civilized; maples; an amiable river. A domesticated landscape. Ripe and reassuring age.

Rapid, rugged ice hockey. The log drive, perilous leap without a net, on rivers in full flood. Twenty-five thousand white geese alight

7. Shutters.

on Cap Tourmente. Take to the sky. Perfect formations. Passing above Québec. Their faraway raucous yelping, solid, unhearing, almost unreal, dominating the whole autumnal night sky—if you have never heard it, you have never felt the strange sensation of physical envelopment in a dream, never escaped above the earth.

Once this city was called Hochelaga. François-Xavier Garneau[8] wrote of it, "a half-hundred wooden habitations, fifty paces long and twelve to fifteen wide. In each house, walls hung with skins skilfully sewn together, several rooms opened upon a square room containing the hearth. The settlement was surrounded by a triple palisade." This city was called Ville-Marie. There mass was celebrated by the light of fireflies. "Should every tree on Montreal Island become an Iroquois, it is my duty there to found a colony, and I will go." Thus spoke Maisonneuve. This city is called Montreal. More than two million inhabitants. A vigorous, enterprising life. Creates. Defies. Struggles, gains, loses, rejoices in its destiny. Multiplies. Becomes complex. Accepts or rejects. Melting pot. Cultural broth. Constructs. Demolishes. Reconstructs. A perpetual factory. A city which has no age. Which burns its past. Of which its present pride is its future. At the high heat of its energy. At the peak of its endeavours. Victorian Sherbrooke Street is earthbound. Vive Dorchester Boulevard and its proud, fine skyscrapers. The calm of Westmount's little streets: Mount Stephen, Oliver, Kensington. Men, ideas, politics, commerce; business, the arts and daily life assert themselves, confront each other. With the rhythm of neon. Flashing in the immense city. By day as by night.

Country of water. Of the tumultuous strength of water. Untamed water harnessed. Like a hot-blooded team. Proud water tamed and mastered. The powerhouse of La Gabelle. The Beauharnois dam. Manicouagan. The greatest workshop in the world. Man's all-powerful hand set over the energy of the water.

Asbestos. Noranda. Bourlamaque. Gagnon. Arvida. Matagami. The darkness of the earth is opened. The black heart of the earth delivers up its treasures. Asbestos, copper, gold, zinc, aluminum,

8. Quebec historian and poet (1809–1866), ancestor of Anne Hébert.

iron. The shadows are heavy. The miner's lamp scarcely lights the depths of the workings. The patient slow efforts of the young master of the premises. Claiming his entire share.

To seize this province in flagrante delicto,[9] in the very act of existence. To understand. To do it justice. To put it into words. The task of a poet. The honor of living.

1967

Harold Horwood
b. 1923

Horwood's family, in St. John's, Newfoundland, were seafarers and writers. Horwood is one of the few Canadian writers who makes a living from his essays, non-fiction books, short stories, and novels. A founding member of the Writers Union of Canada, Horwood has always been a strong supporter of other writers. He had a brief career as a politician in the provincial legislature of Newfoundland, and he is a member of the Order of Canada.

As his children grew up, the house in Newfoundland became crowded. "I waited for them to leave," he mutters, "and they never did. So I did." He moved to the Annapolis Valley, Nova Scotia, where he built his own house and grows much of the food he and his younger family eat. It is typical of Horwood that he delivered one of his children on a canoe trip. He has a quick, searching intelligence and assumes that he can learn anything—as, it seems, he can.

Through newspaper writing and his non-fiction books, Horwood became well respected in Newfoundland. Death on the Ice *(1974), a book about the seal hunt written with Cassie Brown, brought people in to St. John's from the outports, looking for copies.* The Foxes of Beachy Cove *(1967) is a quiet book of observation and meditation, which draws attention to the natural world.*

Horwood wrote a number of novels, but became uneasy with the idea of fiction. He came to see it as a kind of "tarting up" of ideas

9. In the very midst of things (Latin).

and observations which were better presented directly, in literary non-fiction. This piece, from Dancing on the Shore *(1987), exemplifies Horwood's love of the natural world and his concerns about it. He is often impatient with people who cannot—or will not—see the damage we cause.*

Of Frogs and Fairy Godmothers

When the warm breath of April moves across our ponds, the first frogs begin to stir, poking small snouts out of the mud, sleepily swimming to a bank, and lying there to soak up the sun, which will soon regenerate them, send their blood surging on its way, and inspire them to lift their voices in the songs that we hear on warm evenings: the long-drawn notes of the toads like the bowing of a cello, the bright chirping of spring peepers, the deep, resonant bass of green frogs, all the more marvellous because this is perhaps the most ancient music in the world, changed little if at all from the music of amphibians who were singing long before the first bird flew, or the first dinosaur went sniffing among the tree ferns in the age of reptiles.

We are lucky to have toads and frogs and newts and salamanders in our part of the world, our small sanctuary in Nova Scotia, on the shore of the Bay of Fundy. So far we have escaped the apocalypse that has overtaken the amphibians in so many places where they were once plentiful. Whatever it is that is killing off the world's frogs has not reached us yet, or anyway not at lethal levels.

Lambs Lake on South Mountain, where we sometimes swim in summer, has a population of bullfrogs as well as green frogs and leopard frogs. Sometimes you can see myriads of their great, fat tadpoles in rocky pools near the shore. My daughter Leah, watching their activity, thought she might transfer a few of them to our ponds, where they might grow and breed and add their voices to the frog chorus. We had done this earlier with the tiny tadpoles of the spring peepers. But after thinking it over, I suggested leaving them where they were. I doubt that bullfrogs would be content to stay in ponds as small as ours. Likely, on reaching maturity, they'd take off, searching for broader waters. Besides this, if they reached adulthood

in our ponds, they'd likely eat the smaller frogs, and newts, and perhaps some of the small snakes as well. I think something like this
happened when Leah brought home a semi-wild Muscovy drake
caught in a nearby tidal creek. After this voracious bird had spent a
few months in our largest pond, there wasn't a tadpole in sight, and
newts, too, seemed very scarce. Fortunately we had other ponds
where small amphibians could flourish undisturbed by ducks.

The emergence of the frogs, a cardinal event of spring, seems always to have fascinated people. In ancient times peasants saw them
rising from the mud of the river Nile, and supposed they were not
just waking from sleep, but being created anew, that the mud, in
fact, was giving birth to them—an idea that now strikes us as absurd. It is not a long time, however, since people believed that rotting meat could generate flies, that a rotting fish might turn into
maggots, or even that the carcass of a lion might produce a swarm
of honeybees. "Spontaneous generation" was accepted as a fact until
Louis Pasteur, in a long series of experiments, disproved it in the
1860s, some ten years after Wallace and Darwin had published their
theory of evolution.

Frogs belong to an ancient branch of the animal kingdom, direct
descendants of the fishes. Originally, amphibians had scales, but all
modern ones have lost their scales, just as elephants, whales, mana-
tees, and humans have lost their fur. They seem to be vulnerable little animals, soft-bodied, not very fast, eagerly gobbled up by snakes,
herons, and ducks, and even by some house cats. Being egg layers,
they can reproduce rapidly if nothing stops them, but that's just
where they are now most vulnerable. Their eggs can be destroyed by
polluted water, by acid rain, or by excessive doses of ultraviolet B
pouring down from a sky drastically altered by human insanity.

Frogs look rather humanlike. When they swim they seem to be
doing the breast stroke. They are rather neckless and broad-bodied,
but they have hips, knees, ankles, five toes on each foot, and legs as
graceful as any dancer's. It is remarkable how this body type has persisted, though frogs and humans are separated by some quarter of a
billion years of evolution. Insects, meanwhile, have adopted shapes
as fanciful as anything we might imagine on the planets of Alpha
Centauri, birds have turned themselves into flying flowers, and dol-
phins have become imitation fish. Humans and frogs look much the

way they did when they first began to climb and hop. Like us, frogs
have survived the great natural disasters that have visited the world
time and again in the past quarter of a billion years, disasters that
caused most earthly creatures to become extinct. Now, in the midst
of what may be another great extinction, they may be facing their
greatest crisis. But then, we may be, too.

Even in other parts of the Atlantic Provinces frogs seem to be in
great trouble. They all but disappeared from Newfoundland, for example, and none of the field biologists there seemed to have an
explanation. Their near extinction was not a "natural population
fluctuation" as some people at first suggested. The green frog used to
be a very common animal on the Avalon and Bonavista Peninsulas.
Then they were gone—not completely, but almost. The cause in
Newfoundland was not destruction of habitat, because there has
been little habitat destruction there in recent decades. Surface pollution had reduced populations in many places, and might have been a
factor in a few Newfoundland waterways, but certainly not in most,
and certainly not in Labrador, where frogs have also been dying out.

Acid rain? Diseases? Weakened immune systems? None of it
seemed to be a satisfactory explanation.

Ultraviolet radiation (especially ultraviolet B, the part of the spectrum most directly linked to skin cancer) kills the eggs of some
species of amphibians. The Arctic ozone hole is therefore suspected
of being the chief culprit in the disappearance of frogs from the
northernmost parts of their range. This is certainly the cause in high
mountain lakes near the Pacific coast, where pollution of air and water is not a problem, but where the ultraviolet level has always been
high, and is now critically high because of ozone depletion. Field biologists studying mountain frogs in the far west discovered that
species laying eggs in areas open to the sky were declining because
few of their eggs were hatching. Those laying eggs in the shade cast
by vegetation or overhanging banks were doing much better.

It is tempting to look for a single, simple cause of a universal
phenomenon like the die-off of the small amphibians, but often the
causes are multiple and complex, rather than single or simple. In
Nova Scotia we cannot blame the decline of the frogs solely on elevated levels of ultraviolet, because the decline is most apparent on
the eastern side of the province, the Atlantic slope, where ultraviolet

levels are no more elevated than in central and western regions. What else may be killing them off? We cannot be sure, but the most likely culprit is acid rain, which affects lakes and rivers draining into the Atlantic much more severely than those draining into the Bay of Fundy.

The nearly worldwide population crash of small amphibians may well be an indicator of what lies in store for bigger and hardier creatures such as ourselves if we continue throwing wastes and poisons into the air and water, for though not all the data are complete, we know that ozone depletion, putrefaction of lakes and rivers, acid rain, and sewage pollution are all symptoms of a single problem—massive destruction caused by human irresponsibility and corporate decisions that profits are more important than lives—whether we're talking about the lives of frogs, newts, salamanders, or people.

Here on the shore of Annapolis Basin the merchants of death have not yet triumphed. The chorus of spring peepers, the cello notes of the toads, the percussion of the green frogs, the *basso profundo*[1] of the bullfrogs combine to lift up our hearts, to give us hope and reassurance that life is still fighting the good fight, hope that in the end it might triumph over corporate greed and the global market.

Just as we do not believe, today, that frogs emerge from mud without having burrowed into it first, so we believe that no living thing is a creation of the non-living world. *Ex nihilo nihil fit,*[2] to quote an axiom ascribed to Lucretius.[3] Not only did we discard the idea that living things might emerge from non-living matter, but also the idea that the universe was created *ex nihilo,* out of nothing, as theologians had insisted.

But now cosmologists have revived the idea of such creation, with the added refinement that god is removed from the picture. The universe is said to have created itself *ex nihilo.* A "quantum fluctuation," we are told, might have inflated itself by means of a Lagrangian[4] mathematical formula until it became a hundred bil-

---

1. Deep bass voice (Latin).
2. Out of nothing comes nothing (Latin).
3. Roman poet (98?–55 B.C.E.), author of *The Nature of Things.*

4. Joseph-Louis Lagrange laid the mechanical basis for wave mechanics. His work made it possible to treat waves, or "fluctuations," as absolute abstractions that might exist even in a total vacuum. "Field" phenomena are all based on Lagrange's work [Horwood's note].

lion trillion stars. Where the Lagrangian formula came from is another question. And in any case, as Huck Finn said, anybody who could believe that would suck eggs. It is an explanation in exactly the same class as a fairy godmother waving her wand. Except, of course, that there's no fairy godmother. Just a self-created wand. Take your choice: god, magic, or a Lagrangian.

No one has asked the frogs' opinion, but if you pay attention to them, they have words of wisdom for you just the same. We on this planet are "all in the same boat" and not nearly so all-fired smart as we thought we were back in the cocky days of the 1950s, before the world had so obviously started to fall apart. As I've mentioned, some people suspect that we may be in the midst of another great extinction, like the one that killed off the dinosaurs, this time not caused by comet, meteorite, drifting continents, or massive volcanic eruptions, but by the arrival of an animal with too much technical cleverness and not nearly enough intelligence to go with it.

1996

Hudson's Bay Company Officials

The original of this hand-written letter, composed in 1688, is now in the Hudson's Bay Company Archives, Archives of Manitoba. It is in fragile condition and so only a microfilm version is available to researchers.

Neither the recipient nor the writers are remembered as important figures in history. These were just businessmen doing their job. The notes in the margins, which highlight the main topics of the letter, were likely added at a meeting of company officials.

The astonishing thing to a twenty-first-century consciousness is that these people simply assumed their right to be "Masters" of the part of the world which they had named Hudson's Bay, and of its surrounding area. The writers warn of the possible treachery of the French, who might also want the territory, but there is no thought that the native people living there might have any claim to the land or its resources.

Each signature is in slightly different handwriting, so each of eight men signed the letter. It seems unlikely that a business letter today would be closed with "Your Very Loving Friends."

This letter has a strong, collective voice. It is very direct, without flourishes or decorative language. In the actual script, though, the letter begins with an elaborately stroked "W." Some of the signatures are dramatized with several loops of the pen. So are the capitals which begin paragraphs, although they are more modest than the signatures or the first letter. There is a firm dash of the pen at the end of each line of text. There are very few commas.

The spelling is sometimes puzzling, with unexpected extra "ee's." The letter also contains abbreviations. People who communicated through hand-written letters developed abbreviated or quick ways to convey the words they used frequently—in much the same way that email writers do.

London First June 1688

Capt. Leonard Edgcombe
Wee haveing Laden on Board your Shipp *John &
Thomas* what Goods Provisions &c. Wee intend, this
Present Voyage for Hudsons Bay It is therefore our Desire &
Wee Doe hereby require you upon receipt of this our order
to Weigh your Anchor & hasten from Gravesend with all
expedition as winde & weather will pmitt., endeavouring to
make your First port Yorke Fort in Hayes River neare Port
Nelson where when it shall please God you arrive in Safety
you are to Deliver to Capt. George Geyer, or any other our
Governor & Councell then being our Packett of Letters with
all such Goods Provisions &c. Consigned to them, And
you are to use your uttmost endeavour to prevent and detect
all Private Trade, And if you find any Interlopeing vessells
whatsoever Tradeing or Sayleing within Hudson's Bay
Without the Lycence of the Company, Wee Doe by these
presents by vertue of the Power & authority Given us by the
Kings Maties. Letters patents of Incorporacion and in
Pursuence of the King's Royall Proclamation lately issued
require & authorize you to Seize them and all the Goods
Aboard them the One halfe for the use of his Matie. &
the other halfe for the use of the Governor & Compa. of
Adventurers of England Tradeing into Hudsons Bay, For
the Doeing whereof you shalbe Saved harmelesse &
indemynifyed by the said Compa. agt. all such persons
whatsoever That shall sue or ymplead you for the same.

Wee Enjoyne you to endeavour what possible you Can to
keepe Compa. with our Ship the *Dering* Capt. James Young
Comander whoe is bound for Churchill River, as farr as your
Course lyes, that you may bee aideing and assisting to each
other as Occation shall require.

Wee Caution you to prevent any Treachery or Surprize
from the French, and *if they have Surprized any of our men
Forts or ships Wee expect from your Courage & Conduct, your
uttmost endeavour to recover them and that you will Repossesse
us, and make us Masters againe of them before you leave*

*Sayleing orders
or Instructions for
Capta.
Edgcombe*

*To Sayle to
Port Nelson*

*deliver our
packt of Letters
and goods &c.*

*If he meete
with any
Interlopers
to Seize them*

*To keepe
Compa. with
the Dering*

*Caution of the
French
if they have
taken any of
our Forts
to retake them*

the place, And Bee assured Wee shall bountifully reward any meritorious Service you Shall Doe therein, And for your further proceeding you are to Observe the Orders & Direccions of our Governor & Councell there, whome Wee have enjoyned to Call you to their Assistance in all theire Consultations dureing the tyme of your Stay with them Beleiveing you will all Unanimously endeavour to act all things as shall be for the Honour of the Nation and the Good and Welfare of your Present employers Soe Commending you to the Proteccion of the Almighty & wishing you a hapy and

Exd.   prosperouse Voyage Wee remaine

Your Very Loveing Freinds
CHURCHILL Governor
E. DERING Dep. Governor
JOHN HUBAND
WILL. YONGE
STEPHEN PITTS
NICO. HAYWARD
JOHN LETTEN
SAMUELL CLARKE

1688

Isabel Huggan
b. 1943

> *Huggan was born in Kitchener, Ontario, and educated at the University of Western Ontario in London. She grew up in the small town of Elmira, north of Kitchener, which was the thinly disguised setting for her first book of linked stories,* The Elizabeth Stories *(1984). Elizabeth, its main character, puzzles about the town where she finds herself, learns about sex in a butcher shop after hours, and yearns to be adult until she discovers that is not as easy as it might look. Many people in the area, who thought they recognized characters in the stories, were outraged by the book. At least one woman—who knew the butchers—stormed into a local bookstore, demanding her money back.*
>
> *Huggan's next collection of stories,* You Never Know *(1993), is about adult women in various places of the world. All her characters struggle to understand how to live honorable lives, often in the face of glib social assumptions.*

Her third book, Belonging *(2003), explores many of these same ideas in literary non-fiction. Writing in the quiet poetic voice of her own experience and observation, Huggan takes the reader into the many corners of the world where she has lived. As she learns about each place, she also learns about herself. This book won the Governor General's Award for non-fiction.*

In this selection from Belonging, *set in the Cévennes region of France, Huggan recognizes how "Canadian" she is when she simply cannot understand how a courier service can be shut down by a snow fall—especially when she is anxiously awaiting mail from home. Beginning in the traditions of travel writing, what might have been a documentary piece becomes a personal essay, using poetic imagery and strategies of narrative, especially characterization.*

Snow

Yesterday we had a snowstorm that lasted from early morning right on through the night, and now the world is clothed in white. Snowfall this heavy is rare, here on the lower edge of the Cévennes,[1] where the foothills begin rolling up out of the vineyards. Farther north and into the mountains, there's always enough to ensure winter skiing but in Latourne,[2] if it comes at all, it's only a light teasing tickle, a mere frosting. Today's snow, however, is thick and deep and means to stay. *This* snow would do Ottawa proud.

Shortly before dawn this morning—the sky still dark—the telephone rings, and a gruff male voice informs me that he is the courier service and has a package to deliver, and where is my house. He is calling on his cellphone from the *mairie*[3] on the main road, and he needs directions. I explain—I've memorized this patter in French—and when I get to the bit about his turning the corner around the monastery and continuing over the small bridge, he stops me.

He says he will not be able to come to my house, for not only are

---

1. Mountains in south-central France.
2. Village in the Cévennes region of France.

3. Town hall (French).

the narrow country roads leading to Mas Blanc[4] blocked with snow, but he will not attempt to cross the bridge. He understands now where I am located, and he knows that little bridge: it has no railing. Under the snow, the roads are sheer ice, he says, he could slide off. He will not do it. Don't I know that overnight everything has been freezing? It's too dangerous, *madame,* he says.

My stars, I say to myself, what a wimpy courier. But I do know that he has reason to be fearful, as I was out in the blizzard yesterday and saw for myself that cars were slipping and sliding out of control, several in accidents and even more headfirst in ditches along the highway. Of course, given the unlikelihood of this kind of weather, no one has snow tires, and there are no plows or machines to scatter sand and salt: one simply manages as best one can and waits for the snow to melt and disappear, which, ordinarily, it will do within hours.

Thus I am understanding and polite, and when he asks if I will come over to meet him, if he drives as far as the old church of St-Baudile across the way, I agree. It never occurs to me, I realize later, that I might ask *him* to walk to my house. No, and he wouldn't have done it, either.

I throw on clothes over my flannel pyjamas and pull on a pair of old winter boots I smartly brought back last summer from the attic where they'd been stored in Ottawa since I left in 1987. As soon as I step out the door and smell the silvery fragrance of new snow, I realize that this call has been a gift from the gods, for without it I would never have ventured out so early and would have missed this odd sensation of being enveloped in pastel light, as if I am dancing through a dream sequence in an old Hollywood musical. The rising sun, filtered through pearly clouds and reflected by the snow, shines everywhere. The eastern sky is rose grey streaked with lemony gold, and the vineyards are glowing blue and apricot. The world has turned, overnight, into an opal.

The birds are already at their feeder under the *micocoulier* tree, making busy little "*dix-huit, dix-huit*"[5] noises, but as I walk farther

---

4. White farm house (French) where the author lives.

5. Eighteen (French). Pronounced "deez wheet." *Micocoulier* tree: a Mediterranean nettletree, also known as hackberry.

down the lane I hear nothing and am struck by the solemn and ponderous nature of snow itself, the grave way it stifles sound. The silence feels like a secret I cannot tell.

As I walk across the narrow bridge and around the monastery, I see that the courier has been right, for the road is really quite icy under the snow, and he would easily have gone off into the stream that still runs merrily, not yet frozen over. I make my way through the vineyard instead of the road to reach the church, where I can see there's a small blue van parked and waiting. Inside sits the courier, a red-faced man about my age, who has been watching me scuff through the snow. I am wearing my old rabbit-fur hat held on by a plaid scarf, and he probably finds me pretty funny, for I see that he is laughing.

He gets out to give me the package—I have to sign for it—and we exchange a few pleasantries about the weather. I tell him I am Canadian and this is nothing, *monsieur,* really nothing, compared with what one encounters in Ottawa. If one has the correct tires, one can drive in snow like this with no problem, I say, but of course here. . . . I shrug meaningfully and let the sentence dangle, sharp criticism of France—and all things French—implied.

He laughs again and drives off, and I walk home with the sun, now fully up from behind the clouds, making everything ahead of me glitter and gleam. I feel a great ball of joy welling up in my throat, a balloon of laughter ready to float out into the bright air. White snow lies luminous everywhere and the package in my hands, I can see from the address, is from a Canadian publisher. Too curious to wait, I stop and tear open the end of the padded envelope and pull out a letter telling me that, at the author's request, I have been sent these galleys of her new novel, *A Student of Weather.*[6] Might I consider providing a comment and if so, could I. . . .

I spin around twice, kicking up snow and laughing out loud, and run then through the drifts onto the road, heading home happy but more than just happy, amazed—and as thrilled as a gambler by patterns of chance and probability. What else in the world but *this* book, so propitiously titled, might have called me out early to walk

6. Elizabeth Hay is the author of *A Student of Weather*. She is also the author of *Crossing the Snowlines* and *The Only Snow in Havana* [Huggan's note].

in the fresh snow? Am I not, this winter's morning, a true student of weather? Nevertheless, far stronger than the book's coincidental pull, is a new friendship that seems, suddenly, enormously powerful.

On the lane to the house, I stop for breath at the olive grove and think how strange the green oval leaves appear, so thickly covered with snow. I pull a branch toward me and stick out my tongue, licking the lovely stuff off in one sweeping mouthful. The instant prickle of melting snow explodes in my mouth—flakes disintegrate like stars—as it transforms itself to a swallow of water. A sweet, chalky taste, and then gone in a gulp. Another mouthful and another, and I stand there for a long time, thinking of you and eating snow . . . far away in another country but, in my heart, home.

2003

Linda Hutcheon
b. 1947

Hutcheon is an influential literary critic who was educated at the University of Toronto and Cornell University. She returned to the University of Toronto where she is a professor of English and Comparative literature. Hutcheon has published several books, including Narcissistic Narratives *(1980),* A Poetics of Postmodernism *(1988), and* Irony's Edge *(1995), which explore contemporary literature, with a special interest in unorthodox forms of writing that parody literature and social convention. The impact of her work rivals Northrop Frye's. Hutcheon has a strong suspicion that literary criticism serves social interests. As we approve of some writers and disapprove of others, she might say, we create the culture of a society. But who holds the power to decide what is good or acceptable and what is not?*

Hutcheon's writing describes and defines the Postmodernist movement in Canadian literature and beyond, which Hutcheon describes as caring about gender, genre, and race. Literary canons, she says, cannot be seen as value-free. She has worked to bring writing "from the margins" into public and critical attention, editing collections of fiction and interviews. She objects to critical attitudes that make forms like journals or letters less important than novels or the epic poem.

This essay was written for Language in Her Eye *(1990). The editors of that anthology invited several women to consider what the feminist movement has meant to them as writers. Hutcheon demonstrates that she has appreciated the freedom to write without having to leave her own experience aside. She can discuss herself as a reader and how that identity affects what she reads, as well as how she responds to it. By tracing her very personal experience, Hutcheon suggests, she can see far-ranging trends in literary criticism. She is glad to see them changing.*

Hutcheon's essay shows one of the directions an apparently personal essay can take—into considerations of much wider issues, which nevertheless must be grounded in the actual, in lived experience.

The Particular Meets the Universal

I sometimes wonder if I am the odd woman out. Or are there others out there who also went through their school years not really noticing that their teachers were, for the most part, men—especially at the more advanced levels? Not that this stopped me from thinking I, too, could join their ranks: I just proceeded, blithely unself-conscious about the relation between gender and knowledge, power and authority that played itself out daily before my eyes. It was during graduate school and especially when I first began teaching in the university that I realized I was somehow out of place. In a predominantly male, WASP,[1] middle-class academy, was there room for a female who also happened to be of working-class, Italian origins?

Since I am still teaching today, clearly there was and is room, but an important question still remains: why should gender, class or ethnicity even be issues in teaching and writing about "Literature?" Was I not taught throughout my liberal humanist education that

---

1. White Anglo-Saxon Protestant.

'Literature' and its values were eternal and universal? Where, then, would things like gender even be relevant?

The background to this particular humanist teaching is particularly interesting in the Canadian educational system as I experienced it. In my undergraduate years in the late nineteen-sixties, my professors at university were almost all male and they were rarely, if ever, Canadian: they were British or American. The Americans (who had often moved to Canada for political reasons) had been trained to be what were called "New Critics" and they therefore taught me how to read *texts*—not for the author's intent or the historical context, but for the text's own paradoxes, ironies and tensions which I—as a successful literature student—would learn to unify and reconcile. I didn't see the assumption underlying this at the time: that there was a single, true meaning that lay *within* the text itself, and therefore I missed the obvious logical fallacy: if so, then why did so many different interpretations about each text exist? The library was clearly full of them.

My other professors were British, which at that time usually meant that they came out of the F. R. Leavis—I. A. Richards—T. S. Eliot[2] tradition of author-oriented reading and general cultural conservatism. From them I learned that culture was the domain of universal values which are inherently civilized and civilizing *and* which will be passed on (and preserved by) an elite of sensitive intellectuals—to which I might perhaps aspire, or so I unthinkingly assumed. As you can tell, I cannot even articulate this today without some irony because I see in it my own lack of awareness at this time of issues like class, gender and race that have been argued today to underpin that particular definition of "universal," "human" values.

Thanks to this typically Canadian education—a historically apt mixture of the American and the British—I graduated with a B.A. and with the idea that the teacher/critic's task was to explicate texts (with a New Critical aim to unify textual oppositions) and also to evaluate them. Since, in our classes, we had only studied "great" works of art whose values were eternal and universal, that was clearly what was to be explicated and evaluated. I never had any

---

2. Mid-to-late twentieth century literary and linguistic theorists and writers. This piece mentions many such scholars throughout.

sense that what we today call the "canon" of accepted, institutional-
ized works was a construction of any kind. I never thought about
who defined what counts as "Literature." All this seemed self-
evident, given, natural. I never questioned that Leavis's notion of
"felt life"—the characteristic of the art of the "great tradition" he
outlined—would be discernible by me too, at least if I went on to
graduate school.

So, on I went. But this is where the story takes a sharp turn, for I
studied in both the United States and Italy in the heady days of the
first bloom of structuralism, semiotics and Russian formalism. The
appeal of an orderly and systematic way to analyze texts *as texts* soon
replaced Leavis's increasingly vague (at least, to me) concept of
"felt life." I had begun to wonder if maybe Canadians—or women—
weren't eligible for that "sensitive" elite that could gain access to it.
Here, timing is everything. These were the years when Althusser,
Derrida, Foucault, Lacan, Kristeva, and all those other structuralist,
feminist and poststructuralist theorists were just hitting their stride.
From them I learned much about the relation of what I had been
taught to see as humanist universals to something called "ideology,"
to what we tend to take for granted as natural and given, but which
really serves other purposes (such as, obviously, preventing the possibility of change by asserting eternal, universal value).

Shortly after this, I began to teach. I discovered that I could only
do so in a very self-conscious way, trying to make my theoretical assumptions and my critical preconceptions overt. I tried to "situate"
myself for my students, as Foucault and later Edward Said and
Catherine Belsey urged. This was especially necessary because I
taught (among other things) Canadian literature, which at that time
was not in the least canonical or even secure as part of the curricu-
lum of many Canadian universities. And what I specifically taught
was the literature written by women—not only out of feminist
principle, but because Canadian literature has been very much
dominated by its women writers in the last twenty years, and
even before. Their texts, combined with the rapid rise of feminist
critical practice, made me very aware that I had to learn to understand (and teach) cultural practices in general—not only literature—in the context of gender (that is, power) relations: how they
are constructed, then reproduced, and then, with any luck at all,

challenged. I learned to think about how gender is less biological than socially produced and—happily—therefore open to historical change.

My research and teaching in what has come to be called "critical theory" provided both a vocabulary and an intellectual and historical context in which to work. Foucault, Derrida, Lacan, Althusser, Irigaray, Kristeva—all conspired to combat any lingering traces of notions of certainty or stability of single meaning or of Truth—largely by pointing out their rhetorical strategies of exclusion. Pierce and Eco taught me that meaning was a matter of "unlimited semiosis"; Derrida, that meaning was constantly deferred. They all taught me that, as a teacher and a critic, my task was not to reconstitute something missing (but somehow present) in the text which was the "true" content of the work of art. Lacan further upset any illusions I might have been retaining about the role of language in the construction of the self and of the relation of language to ideology. So—as Freud had suggested too—the self was not perhaps the coherent, stable, autonomous, free agent that liberal humanism had taught me to assume?

In the classroom, the effect of this almost Copernican certainty-stealing for me was an overt questioning of the entire notion of authority. I didn't want to fall into the "bad faith" of claiming not to be an authority, while accepting a salary for it: I knew that I was institutionally bound to "pass on" something called my "knowledge" to students and also to "pass" on *their* knowledge. But instead of education being somehow a transmission of my knowledge directly to them, I now saw that my aim had to be more heuristic:[3] I could give them a wide range of literary "facts" and multiple critical tools—with their theoretical assumptions made explicit—and encourage them to develop an "informed capacity for independent thinking." This last phrase is a common one in educational circles, almost a trite truism of liberal humanism. But I think it has new meaning today: this will be independent thinking because it cannot help but be. Students—like their teachers—are particular, not general, in terms of race, gender, class, sexual orientation, ethnicity, and of their experience of both literature the world.

3. Aiding in the discovery of knowledge.

This waking up to the reality of the classroom experience (for both the instructor and the student) coincided with my interest in what our culture seems determined to call "postmodernism." Without engaging in the debate about the definition or evaluation of this phenomenon, let me just say that most commentators agree that the postmodern has meant, among many other things, a reconsideration of cultural positions of centrality in favour of the margins, the ex-centric;[4] it has also meant a valuing of the different over the same. Therefore, in the critical climate outlined above and with these postmodern values nudging me in the background, it became vital for me to define the position from which I read—and wrote and taught. How I performed each of these acts, I now saw, had everything to do with the fact that I was now a forty-three-year-old woman whose consciousness had been raised by feminist thought; that I was of working-class, Italian immigrant roots, though now camouflaged by middle-class academia and marital crypto-ethnicity[5] (the Hutcheon masking a Bortolotti); that I had been "formed" politically by the experience of the sixties and had been radicalized professionally by the experience of being a marginalized "gypsy scholar" on sessional appointments for six years before getting a "real" appointment.

This is the position from which I write and teach today. It will change; it must. But the particular critical perspective that has brought me to acknowledge this position (what has been labelled as "feminist poststructuralism") is happily one that will always force me to consider the relations between power, authority and knowledge, and these are not unimportant issues within the writing and university communities, perhaps especially in an age that might need to think a little more about the *responsibilities* that accompany the *rights* we have been so eager to assert.

1990

4. Outside the center (Latin), a pun on eccentric.

5. Apparent change of ethnicity through marriage, as for the author (Bartolotti is her maiden name).

J. B. Joe
b. 1948

> Born in Victoria, British Columbia, Joe grew up in the village of
> Wyah, which no longer exists. The West Coast Trail runs through
> where it used to be. Now living in Ladysmith, British Columbia,
> Joe is a Nootka writer and a member of the Penelakut Band. She
> has a Master of Fine Arts degree from the University of British Co-
> lumbia, with a focus on drama. In 1996, her full-length drama,
> Raven, was presented in Toronto.
>
> The following story appeared in Thomas King's All My Rela-
> tions (1990) and has since been included in other anthologies. It
> shifts the ground under the feet of a reader expecting the usual cul-
> tural traditions of western literature. This story supposes a universe
> with a Creatrix, a female creator and the Mother of All Things,
> who also becomes Spider Woman, and even a small spider spinning
> a web in the corner of a room. At the centre of all creativity, she
> communicates without words. She is the source of wisdom and con-
> solation for a young woman who has suffered in the "cement world"
> of cities and bars.
>
> The story's atmosphere might be described as dreamlike. It may
> be the world of meditation, of a dream quest, seeking answers be-
> yond what we think of as "reality." It is a disciplined and deliberate
> search, not careless or an accident, taking the narrator into odd
> places, showing her strength she did not know she had.
>
> Joe's interest in drama shows through in this story. It has strong
> performative elements, as well as links to the rhythms of oral story-
> telling.

Cement Woman

I'm going to dress all in greys today. Grey socks under grey
boots, grey pantyhose under my grey panties, grey bra under
grey slip, grey sweater over a long, grey skirt . . . grey blouse.
This is my grey day.

There's just a sliver of purple light squeezing through a critch in
my purple blinds. The dawn has arrived. I lie on my narrow cot,
holding the edge of my quilt just under my chin. My body is per-

fectly straight, my toes aligned. I can feel my body settle into nothingness. In the far corner of the room a spider is preparing a web. She's a big, black spider, with red-gold tinges underneath her belly. Could be she's pregnant. I narrow my eyelids to slits, my pupils get large and the web becomes blue and dust flies from it as she works. There are sparks flying every which way, slowly becoming more and more blue until the room is filled with blue dust. Blue sparks from a pregnant spider. Outside giant ravens clink-clink together as they swoop over the river. I blink and the room returns to its normal hue. My body is in stillness underneath the quilt. I hear the stream running quickly and rippling along the jagged edges of yellow grasses clinging to the shore. A raven lets out a long screech.

There is always time to fling away the everyday.

I would hold the ashtray just under Wustenaxsun's chin. He would tell me to fling away the everyday. He was too weak to hold up his head, and sometimes to blink. He would lay there on his deathbed, telling me over and over again. There is always time to fling away the everyday. Always time. Always. I would flick the ashes from his cigarette with a long-handled paintbrush (number seven) as he sighed into his sleep. He wouldn't take long drags, just little intakes of breath to smell the smoke. He lay on his bed for four weeks like that. People came, but only to the doorway. He would not allow anyone else in the room.

The spider continues to work slowly and precisely. I get up from the cot and pick up my drum. The drum holds a new song for today and I beat it slowly, slowly, taking turns about the room. The light from the blinds follows as I beat the drum. I beat faster. I place my knees wide apart and spread my legs. I can feel pulls from deep in my stomach. I take small steps, increasing the speed of the drumming. The song is about a woman who learns all the ways of the hunt. She studies stories about Raven and his trickster ways to hunt. She studies how the air changes when a big animal enters her territory. She studies how her own body slips into the very breezes until she smells like her prey. Pieces of flesh line her bag. Flesh of the deer, the bear, the bait. She kills and recovers life for the old and for the children. The veins in my arms stick out like blue ribbons on the back of a garter snake. I can feel the pull in my stomach becoming almost unbearable. I continue to drum and to move about the room, with the new knowledge that the pain I feel is a signal. I feel myself falling forward and I stumble, but do not miss a beat. I feel the importance building and building. The song turns to high notes that last and last, my head tilts further and further back, and I can feel my hair brushing the small of my back. The song tells of the woman hunter entering the body of the deer. She feels his fear; she feels her blood rushing from one end of her body to the other in flashes of hot, lightning-like rushes. I kneel further back until the back of my head touches the floor and my pelvis is arched upward. I stay that way, letting the drum fall.

The song is ended and I get up slowly and I see that I have left blood on the floor. I go over to my dresser and open the top drawer. Inside is my jar of *tumulth*.[1] I spread the red cream on my face until I see only my brown eyes. I go to my full-length mirror and proceed to spread *tumulth* all over myself. There is a soft coolness all over my body as the cream mixes with my sweat.

I walk like that, through my kitchen and then through my small living room and out the door. Outside it is cool and the sun is shedding its first light. The light hits the tips of the trees and casts long, thin lines of white dust-lines between the trees and among the branches of cedar. I place my feet into the stream. The yellow grasses tickle my feet. I enter slowly and walk to the middle of the stream until I am submerged. I close my eyes and I can feel my pupils filling everything.

I open my eyes and I am in a cave filled with the old ones and a golden light surrounds them. They have red bodies and all are naked. Their hair flies about their faces in a beautiful slow motion as they dance around a fire. I can feel Wustenaxsun. He is near. Oh, dear, dear Wustenaxsun. My husband. I see him. He is coming to me. I know that smile. I enter his eyes and we laugh together. He is restored to youth and he is strong again.

The flames from the fire light the cave until it is as bright as daylight, only, with a golden glow. The old ones come to Wustenaxsun and me and they kiss the tips of our fingers. They float away and continue dancing. They begin to chant, "The Mother of All Things waits," over and over again. There is a new knowledge for me. The

---

1. A cream made from red clay taken from sacred caves.

Mother is waiting for me. I feel that knowledge very strongly. It tells me that if I turn to the entrance of the cave, she will be there. I am filled with the desire to see her and I turn. She is not there. I turn back to the fire and I find myself walking into the flames. Wustenaxsun lets me go and I can see him walking away as the flames wrap themselves around me. The *tumulth* crumbles from my body. I hear the chanting become faster and then all I hear is the whu-whu-whu over and over again. The flames unwrap themselves and I step out of the fire.

From deep inside of me I feel steel glowing red-hot and hardening all in the same instant. There is a movement of time that hits me. It feels like slow motion and divides itself into FLASHES OF FRACTIONS OF SECONDS! I scream. My pupils grow inside my eyes, filling everything. The steel becomes hard and cold. I align my toes and make my body still. The steel helps me. I close my eyes.

When I open them, I am in a shopping mall. There are people hurrying by me and they are grim-faced. Some of them pull angry babies. I look down and I am pulling my own angry baby. I have all grey clothes on and I turn to a man with powerfully built arms and legs. I smile at him. He wears soft, rich woollen clothes and he picks me up by the waist. The child falls on his face and screams. I scream. Blood falls from my eyes and I push the man away. He disappears and I close my eyes.

I open them and I am on a large, white ship and I am ordering *Oncorhynchus kisutch* from a waiter. I use only my eyes to place the order. He scampers away yelling, "The lady wants coho!" I wear a gold dress. The dress has no top and my breasts rest on top of the table. There are eyes sitting on the edges of the table and I glare back at them. Blood begins to fall from their sockets and I drink it from cups placed at exactly measured intervals around the table, which turns from square, to oblong, to round as I pick up each cup. I find an eyeball in the cup, too late. It slips down my throat. I yell, "Take a number!" and it pops back out. I pick up a fork and poke at it. It winks at me and wobbles away. I reach down to pick it up and the gold from my dress falls from my body like dust and scatters underneath the table and then it changes into the entrails of a deer. I put my face into the entrails and enter a room of spinning lights.

I fly and weave in and out of shadows. There are pinpricks of lights in my eye and they annoy me. I look down and I see that I have wings. They flutter only at the tips. They carry me about not by my power, not my power. It is the power of this room. Tears drop from my eyes and my pupils grow into everything. The dancing lights fade and everything is white and then darker shapes form themselves. The shapes are the people in the cave and they have stopped their blood. Time does not move. The shadows are still against the white walls. I breathe and my breath comes out in streams of pink and blue and orange and turquoise and purple and red and green and yellow.

I know she is here. I feel her blinking at me. The blinks are slow and steady, like a heartbeat. I turn away from the shadows and see an entrance. I hear the whu-whu-whu and it becomes more and more insistent, yet not louder. She stands there. She is blinking slowly, slowly. Blue air surrounds her. She sighs and her breath, too, is pink and blue and orange and turquoise and purple and red and green and yellow. I see my colours blending with her breath. She sits down, cross-legged.

I fly over and land just to her right. She turns to me and I enter her eyes. "I am the Mother of All Things," she says with her blink. Lights from our breath dance around our bodies and twinkle in the pupils of her eyes.

I tremble and she blinks that we, she and I are mothers. We are mothers of gods. Indeed, she says, you are the mother of Wustenaxsun, who is himself a god. She said she was the fire and the water and the coloured air. She saw me before I was born. She told me I existed in the fire and the water and the air. I told her I was lonely all my life. I told her Wustenaxsun came and made me a whole new life. She said yes, he did that. She blinked that I, too, made my new life. She told me my new life was my own wish. It was the wish to become who I am. It was the wish of the cave-dancers. It was the wish of the Mother of All Things. It was my own wish. We are one. We are one with our wishes. She blinked these words at me and I sighed into her breath.

I blinked that I lived with the cement people. They wished me to be one of them and I lived as one of them. I lived a life in the cold streets. I performed before them, dancing in the dimness of a beaten-down old beer hall. I made them put dollars into my clothing. I closed my eyes. She said you do not live among the cement people, now. I opened my eyes and she blinked my life. She blinked that I live in the mountains. I live in the forest. I live in the house beside the stream. I live with the ravens. The steel bends inside and I am sad. She emits a long stream and her breath captures my breath. She closes her eyes and fades away. The coloured streams turn back to white.

I close my eyes, feeling the tears dropping onto my breasts. I open them and I am back in the cave. The fire is no longer burning and I see Wustenaxsun's image on the cave wall. I see images of the old ones on the cave wall, their hair flying in graceful folds in the hard rock of the cave. I fly back to the shopping mall, through the hurrying crowd of grim-faced people and back to the white ship and back to the stream. I walk out of the stream and go back into my house.

There is always time to fling away the everyday.

Wustenaxsun would sit in the chair and tell me over and over that our life together would not be ordinary. He told me he would see that I would not miss the cement people. I would assure him that I did not miss anything of the town, the long roads, the noise of the traffic. We would go to the stream and bathe while he sang the songs. He would sing and the ravens would clink-clink in the trees. He made our song about our meeting. It told of a dying man who wished to have a wife. It told of a young woman living in the land of cement. She was dancing for money in a run-down beer hall and he sang how he, Wustenaxsun, travelled into the land of cement and found her. The song told about how she struggled with her past life after she moved into his house. Wustenaxsun sang about how her past belonged with the crumbled rocks at the bottom of the ocean.

I go and take my grey clothes from my closet. They fit me perfectly and I pick up my rattle and, suddenly, I hear the Mother of All Things. She tells me to put aside fear. She tells me the steel remains and keeps me strong in the face of real substances. The substances that make up the cement, the fire and the water and the coloured air, are also the substances that make up my own self, the same substances that make up the Mother of All Things. She is in the cement. She is all. She is one. We are one.

I shake the rattle and I see my future. It contains my children. Their faces are smiling and round, their heads shining from their bathwater. They run and hide among the trees and count petals that fall from their fingertips. My children. I am a mother. I am a child.

I put away the rattle and the steel inside remains stronger than ever. I will go and find my future. I will go and find my husband who waits in the land of the cement people. Wustenaxsun found me. I will find my husband. I already picture him in my mind. He has brown hair and brown skin, golden from the sun, and his eyes have pupils that never narrow down. Who knows but the wind and the rain that the man is not blond? I am at the centre of the universe. I place the rattle in a soft cloth bag.

1990

Linda Kenyon
b. 1957

Kenyon used to write and publish stories of "normal" length. "But they started getting shorter," she says. "And shorter. I wondered for a while if they would disappear altogether."

This kind of story has been given several names: postcard fiction, postscript fiction, sudden fiction, short short story. It might be written onto postcards and mailed, so that lots of people get a chance to read it. It might be left on a subway seat, or in a bus station. Kenyon describes a short short story as being like a drift of melody on the wind, heard in passing. That experience is different from listening to a longer, fuller piece of music. The fragment caught on the wind lingers, makes us wonder what the rest might be. What came before—or after? As we ponder those questions, we move in closer, participate, become a part of the story. And, sometimes, we do not need to know the rest; what is on the page is enough.

Short short stories may look casual, but they are carefully formed. They usually depend heavily on one or two elements of fiction: on voice, imagery, character, atmosphere, or plot. Often, they have a turn at the end, into some unexpected place.

Although Kenyon was born in Collingwood, Ontario, she has lived much of her adult life, as writer and editor, near Kitchener, Ontario, which is the setting for the cycle of stories, You Are Here *(1995). Its pieces are linked by the tones of the narrator's voice and by recurring images of food, birds, plants, loss. In this one, voice becomes another theme, as questions arise about what is voiced, to whom, and what is kept silent. It also raises lingering questions about what matters between a man and a woman; how is one to know what the other is thinking?*

Say For Me That I'm All Right

I f you see him say hello.

Tell him I saw a heron in the park the other morning, on the bank of the creek, beside the culvert that runs under the railway tracks. I was so close I could see the scraggy blue feathers on its throat, and one yellow eye.

Tell him I made basil lasagna the other night, and now there's a pan of cold lasagna in my fridge, and a bowl of the olives he likes.

Tell him I found a black plastic spider ring in the park the other day. It's really quite convincing. And the deadly nightshade along the railway track is a tangle of purple flowers and red and green berries right now. Really, he should see it.

Don't tell him I was sitting by myself on the end of the culvert, drinking coffee from a paper cup, when I found the spider ring.

Tell him I'm reading an article about people who bore holes in their heads to allow their consciousness to expand, to free their imaginations from the constraints of adulthood. What I want to know is do they ever get tired of it, do they ever wish that, just for a few minutes, they could go back to the way they were before?

Tell him yesterday I watched two swallows chasing each other, skimming the surface of the creek sometimes, but never falling in.

Don't tell him that sometimes I wake up in the middle of the night, I don't know why, and I lie in bed and look at the pattern the headlights make on the wall and listen to the cars go by. The street-sweepers come out around four-thirty, then the garbage trucks.

Tell him not to worry, I don't even own a drill.

Tell him there's a silly gondola in the park now. When the weather's fine, a young man in tight black pants poles couples around the muddy pond. Who would want to do that. Tell him there's always a silver vase with a single red rose in it balanced on the bow of the boat, and the back of the passengers' seat is shaped like a big heart.

Don't tell him I bought a new dress, ivory silk with a dropped waist, and matching silk shoes. He'd laugh about the shoes, but don't tell him. And don't tell him I bought a new slip, and gold-coloured eye pencil, and when I put it all on, I look so beautiful his heart would stand still if he saw me.

No, if you see him, don't tell him anything at all. Just say hello.

1996

Thomas King
b. 1943

Of Cherokee and Greek descent, King grew up in California. He teaches at the University of Guelph, in Ontario. King is a popular—and effective—speaker. He supports other writers, especially native writers, editing An Anthology of Short Fiction by Native Writers in Canada *(1988) and* All My Relations: An Anthology of Contemporary Canadian Native Writing *(1990).*

King's novels, Medicine River *(1990) and* Green Grass, Running Water *(1993) are lively in form as well as content. They fuse oral and written traditions, creating new fictional structures. Char-*

acters are developed through their voices, in dialogue with one another. Their exchanges are short and often pointed, often very funny in their understatement. Underneath the humour are respectful explorations of old myths and parodies of current values.

King especially likes the Trickster, the mythic hero who is a creator figure, an artist, who makes new things happen, but almost always with some element of self-interest.

This story from One Good Story, That One (1993) demonstrates King's skills as a fiction writer. Joe and Red are vividly boorish, living their lives by stereotypes. It is tempting to speculate about what kind of beer they drink. The older native men are ordinary people who just want to drink their lemon water and enjoy one another's company. The fun comes in through the trickster impulse to manipulate those stereotypes to make something good—and more than a little self-interested—happen. This satiric social comment has high performance value. The setting is a simple one, a vegetable garden. The conversation is fast-paced, dramatic, especially funny when read aloud, a parody of films-about-Indians made in the 1950s.

King delivered the 2003 Massey lectures on CBC radio. Those presentations demonstrate how important stories are, how we must be careful about which ones we tell. They are gathered as The Truth About Stories (2003).

A Seat in the Garden

Joe Hovaugh settled into the garden on his knees and began pulling at the wet, slippery weeds that had sprung up between the neat rows of beets. He trowelled his way around the zucchini and up and down the lines of carrots, and he did not notice the big Indian at all until he stopped at the tomatoes, sat back, and tried to remember where he had set the ball of twine and the wooden stakes.

The big Indian was naked to the waist. His hair was braided and wrapped with white ermine and strips of red cloth. He wore a single feather held in place by a leather band stretched around his head, and, even though his arms were folded tightly across his chest, Joe could see the glitter and flash of silver and turquoise on each finger.

"If you build it, they will come," said the big Indian.

Joe rolled forward and shielded his eyes from the morning sun.

"If you build it, they will come," said the big Indian again.

"Christ sakes," Joe shouted. "Get the hell out of the corn, will ya!"

"If you build it . . ."

"Yeah, yeah. Hey! This is private property. You people ever hear of private property?"

". . . they will come."

Joe struggled to his feet and got his shovel from the shed. But when he got back to the garden, the big Indian was gone.

"Alright!" Joe shouted and drove the nose of the shovel into the ground. "Come out of that corn!"

The corn stalks were only about a foot tall. Nevertheless, Joe walked each row, the shovel held at the ready just in case the big Indian tried to take him by surprise.

When Red Mathews came by in the afternoon, Joe poured him a cup of coffee and told him about the big Indian and what he had said, and Red told Joe that he had seen the movie.[1]

"Wasn't a movie, Red, damn it. It was a real Indian. He was just standing there in the corn."

"You probably scared him away."

"You can't let them go standing in your garden whenever they feel like it."

"That's the truth."

The next day, when Joe came out to the garden to finish staking the tomatoes, the big Indian was waiting for him. The man looked as though he was asleep, but, as soon as he saw Joe, he straightened up and crossed his arms on his chest.

"You again!"

"If you build it . . ."

"I'm going to call the police. You hear me. The police are going to come and haul you away."

---

1. *Field of Dreams.* "If you build it, they will come" is a refrain from the film, which was based on the novel *Shoeless Joe* by the Canadian author W. P. Kinsella.

". . . they will come."

Joe turned around and marched back into the house and phoned the RCMP,[2] who said they would send someone over that very afternoon.

"Afternoon? What am I supposed to do with him until then. Feed him lunch?"

The RCMP officer told Joe that it might be best if he stayed in his house. There was the chance, the officer said, that the big Indian might be drunk or on drugs and, if that were the case, it was better if Joe didn't antagonize him.

"He's walking on my corn. Does that mean anything to you?"

The RCMP officer assured Joe that it meant a great deal to him, that his wife was a gardener, and he knew how she would feel if someone walked on her corn.

"Still," said the officer, "it's best if you don't do anything."

What Joe did do was to call Red, and, when Red arrived, the big Indian was still in the garden waiting.

"Wow, he's a big sucker, alright," said Red. "You know, he looks a little like Jeff Chandler."[3]

"I called the police, and they said not to antagonize him."

"Hey, there are two of us, right?"

"That's right," said Joe.

"You bet it's right."

Joe got the shovel and a hoe from the shed, and he and Red wandered out into the garden as if nothing was wrong.

"He's watching us," said Red.

"Don't step on the tomatoes," said Joe.

Joe walked around the zucchini, casually dragging the shovel behind him. Red ambled through the beets, the hoe slung over his shoulder.

"If you build it, they will come."

"Get him!" shouted Joe. And before Red could do anything, Joe was charging through the carrots, the shovel held out in front like a lance.

"Wait a minute, Joe," yelled Red, the hoe still on his shoulder.

2. Royal Canadian Mounted Police.

3. Actor (1918–1961) who played the Apache Chief Cochise in several films.

But Joe was already into the tomatoes. He was closing on the big Indian, who hadn't moved, when he stepped on the bundle of wooden stakes and went down in a heap.

"Hey," said Red. "You okay?"

Red helped Joe to his feet, and, when the two men looked around, the big Indian was gone.

"Where'd he go?" said Joe.

"Beats me," said Red. "What'd you do to get him so angry?"

Red helped Joe to the house, wrapped an ice pack on his ankle, and told him to put his leg on the chair.

"I saw a movie a couple of years back about a housing development that was built on top of an ancient Indian burial mound."

"I would have got him, if I hadn't tripped."

"They finally had to get an authentic medicine man to come in and appease the spirits."

"Did you see the look on his face when he saw me coming?"

"And you should have seen some of those spirits."

When the RCMP arrived, Joe showed the officer where the Indian had stood, how he had run at him with the shovel, and how he had stumbled over the bundle of stakes.

After Joe got up and brushed himself off, the RCMP officer asked him if he recognized the big Indian.

"Not likely," said Joe. "There aren't any Indians around here."

"Yes, there are," said Red. "Remember those three guys who come around on weekends every so often."

"The old winos?" said Joe.

"They have that grocery cart, and they pick up cans."

"They don't count."

"They sit down there by the hydrangea and crush the cans and eat their lunch. Sometimes they get to singing."

"You mean drink their lunch."

"Well, they could have anything in that bottle."

"Most likely Lysol."

The RCMP officer walked through the garden with Joe and Red and made a great many notes. He shook hands with both men and told Joe to call him if there was any more trouble.

"Did you ever wonder," said Red, after the officer left, "just what he wants you to build or who 'they' are?"

"I suppose you saw a movie."

"Maybe we should ask the Indians."

"The drunks?"

"Maybe they could translate for us."

"The guy speaks English."

"That's right, Joe. God, this gets stranger all the time. Ed Ames,[4] that's who he reminds me of."

On Saturday morning, when Joe and Red walked out on the porch, the big Indian was waiting patiently for them in the corn. They were too far away to hear him, but they could see his mouth moving.

"Okay," said Red. "All we got to do is wait for the Indians to show up."

The Indians showed up around noon. One man had a green knapsack. The other two pushed a grocery cart in front of them. It was full of cans and bottles. They were old, Joe noticed, and even from the porch, he imagined he could smell them. They walked to a corner of the garden behind the hydrangea where the sprinklers didn't reach. It was a dry, scraggly wedge that Joe had never bothered to cultivate. As soon as the men stopped the cart and sat down on the ground, Red got to his feet and stretched.

"Come on. Can't hurt to talk with them. Grab a couple of beers, so they know we're friendly."

"A good whack with the shovel would be easier."

"Hey, this is kind of exciting. Don't you think this is kind of exciting?"

"I wouldn't trip this time."

When Joe and Red got to the corner, the three men were busy crushing the cans. One man would put a can on a flat stone and the second man would step on it. The third man picked up the crushed can and put it in a brown grocery bag. They were older than Joe had thought, and they didn't smell as bad as he had expected.

---

4. Singer and actor (b. 1927), part of "The Ames Brothers" singing group. He played the Indian sidekick Mingo in the 1960's TV series *Daniel Boone*.

"Hi," said Red. "That's a nice collection of cans."

"Good morning," said the first Indian.

"Getting pretty hot," said the second Indian.

"You fellows like a drink?" said the third Indian, and he took a large glass bottle out of the knapsack.

"No thanks," said Red. "You fellows like a beer?"

"Lemon water," said the third Indian. "My wife makes it without any sugar so it's not as sweet as most people like."

"How can you guys drink that stuff?" said Joe.

"You get used to it," said the second Indian. "And it's better for you than pop."

As the first Indian twisted the lid off the bottle and took a long drink, Joe looked around to make sure none of his neighbors were watching him.

"I'll bet you guys know just about everything there is to know about Indians," said Red.

"Well," said the first Indian, "Jimmy and Frank are Nootka and I'm Cree. You guys reporters or something?"

"Reporters? No."

"You never know," said the second Indian. "Last month, a couple of reporters did a story on us. Took pictures and everything."

"It's good that these kinds of problems are brought to the public's attention," said Red.

"You bet," said the third Indian. "Everyone's got to help. Otherwise there's going to be more garbage than people."

Joe was already bored with the conversation. He looked back to see if the big Indian was still there.

"This is all nice and friendly," said Joe. "But we've got a problem that we were hoping you might be able to help us with."

"Sure," said the first Indian. "What's the problem?"

Joe snapped the tab on one of the beers, took a long swig, and jerked his thumb in the direction of the garden. "I've got this big Indian who likes to stand in my garden."

"Where?" asked the second Indian.

"Right there," said Joe.

"Right where?" asked the third Indian.

"If you build it, they will come," shouted the big Indian.

"There, there," said Joe. "Did you hear that?"

"Hear what?" said the first Indian.

"They're embarrassed," said Red under his breath. "Let me handle this."

"This is beginning to piss me off," said Joe, and he took another pull on the beer.

"We were just wondering," Red began. "If you woke up one day and found a big Indian standing in your cornfield and all he would say was, 'If you build it, they will come,' what would you do?"

"I'd stop drinking," said the second Indian, and the other two Indians covered their faces with their hands.

"No, no," said Red. "That's not what I mean. Well . . . you see that big Indian over there in the cornfield, don't you?"

The Indians looked at each other, and then they looked at Joe and Red.

"Okay," said the first Indian. "Sure, I see him."

"Oh, yeah," said the second Indian. "He's right there, all right. In the . . . beets?"

"Corn," said Joe.

"Right," said the third Indian. "In the corn. I can see him, too. Clear as day."

"That's our problem," said Red. "We think maybe he's a spirit or something."

"No, we don't," said Joe.

"Yes, we do," said Red, who was just getting going. "We figure he wants us to build something to appease him so he'll go away."

"Sort of like . . . a spirit?" said the first Indian.

"Hey," said the second Indian, "remember that movie we saw about that community that was built . . ."

"That's the one," said Red. "What we have to figure out is what he wants us to build. You guys got any ideas?"

The three Indians looked at each other. The first Indian looked at the cornfield. Then he looked at Joe and Red.

"Tell you what," he said. "We'll go over there and talk to him and see what he wants. He looks . . . Cree. You guys stay here, okay."

Joe and Red watched as the three Indians walked into the garden. They stood together facing the beets.

"Hey," shouted Joe. "You guys blind? He's behind you."

The first Indian waved his hand and smiled, and the three men turned around. Red could see them talking, and he tried to watch their lips, but he couldn't figure out what they were saying. After a while, the Indians waved at the rows of carrots and came back over to where Joe and Red were waiting.

"Well," said Red. "Did you talk to him?"

"Yes," said the first Indian. "You were right. He is a spirit."

"I knew it!" shouted Red. "What does he want?"

The first Indian looked back to the cornfield. "He's tired of standing, he says. He wants a place to sit down. But he doesn't want to mess up the garden. He says he would like it if you would build him a . . . a . . . bench right about . . . here."

"A bench?" said Joe.

"That's what he said."

"So he can sit down?"

"He gets tired standing."

"The hell you say."

"Do you still see him?" asked the second Indian.

"You blind? Of course I still see him."

"Then I'd get started on the bench right away," said the third Indian.

"Come on, Red," said Joe, and he threw the empty beer can into the hydrangea and opened the other one. "We got to talk."

Joe put the pad of paper on the kitchen table and drew a square. "This is the garden," he said. "These are the carrots. These are the beets. These are the beans. And this is the corn. The big Indian is right about here."

"That's right," said Red. "But what does it mean?"

"Here's where those winos crush their cans and drink their Lysol," Joe continued, marking a spot on the pad and drawing a line to it.

"Lemon water."

"You listening?"

"Sure."

"If you draw lines from the house to where the big Indian stands and from there to where the winos crush their cans and back to the house . . . Now do you see it?"

"Hey, that's pretty good, Joe."

"What does it remind you of?"

"A bench?"

"No," said Joe. "A triangle."

"Okay, I can see that."

"And if you look at it like this, you can see clearly that the winos and the big Indian are there, and the house where you and I are is here."

"What if you looked at it this way, Joe," said Red and he turned the paper a half turn to the right. "Now the house is there and the old guys and the big Indian are here."

"That's not the way you look at it. That's not the way it works."

"Does that mean we're not going to build the bench?"

"It's our battle plan."

"A bench might be simpler," said Red.

"I'll attack him from the house along this line. You take him from the street along that line. We'll catch him between us."

"I don't know that this is going to work."

"Just don't step on the tomatoes."

The next morning, Red waited behind the hydrangea. He was carrying the hoe and a camera. Joe crouched by the corner of the house with the shovel.

"Charge!" yelled Joe, and he broke from his hiding place and lumbered across the yard and into the garden. Red leaped through the hydrangea and struggled up the slight incline to the cornfield.

"If you build it, they will come," shouted the Indian.

"Build it yourself," shouted Joe, and he swung the shovel at the big Indian's legs. Red, who was slower, stopped at the edge of the cornfield to watch Joe whack the Indian with his shovel and to take a picture, so he saw Joe and his shovel run right through the Indian and crash into the compost mound.

"Joe, Joe . . . you alright? God, you should have seen it. You ran right through that guy. Just like he wasn't there. I got a great picture. Wait till you see the picture. Just around the eyes, he looks a little like Sal Mineo."[5]

Red helped Joe back to the house and cleaned the cuts on Joe's

5. Actor (1939–1976) known for his role as James Dean's outcast friend in *Rebel Without a Cause* (1955). He also played a Sioux brave in *Tonka* (1958).

face. He wrapped another ice pack on Joe's ankle and then drove down to the one-hour photo store and turned the film in. By the time he got back to the house, Joe was standing on the porch, leaning on the railing.

"You won't believe it, Joe," said Red. "Look at this."

Red fished a photograph out of the pack. It showed Joe and the shovel in mid-swing, plunging through the corn. The colors were brilliant.

Joe looked at the photograph for a minute and then he looked at the cornfield. "Where's the big Indian?"

"That's just it. He's not there."

"Christ!"

"Does that mean we're going to build the bench?"

The bench was a handsome affair with a concrete base and a wooden seat. The Indians came by the very next Saturday with their knapsack and grocery cart, and Red could tell that they were impressed.

"Boy," said the first Indian, "that's a good-looking bench."

"You think this will take care of the problem?" asked Red.

"That Indian still in the cornfield?" said the second Indian.

"Of course he's still there," said Joe. "Can't you hear him?"

"I don't know," said the third Indian, and he twisted the lid off the bottle and took a drink. "I don't think he's one of ours."

"What should we do?"

"Don't throw your cans in the hydrangea," said the first Indian. "It's hard to get them out. We're not as young as we used to be."

Joe and Red spent the rest of the day sitting on the porch, drinking beer, and watching the big Indian in the garden. He looked a little like Victor Mature, Red thought, now that he had time to think about it, or maybe Anthony Quinn,[6] only he was taller. And there was an air about the man that made Red believe—believe with all his heart—that he had met this Indian before.

1990

6. Actor Anthony Quinn (1915–2001) played the chief of the Seminole tribe in *Seminole* (1953). Actor Victor Mature (1915–1999) played the title role in *Chief Crazy Horse* (1955).

Stephen Leacock
1869–1944

Canada's best-known humorous writer, Leacock was born in Swanmore, England. His father took his family to South Africa and Kansas, then to the centre of Ontario, near Lake Simcoe, where he continued his habit of failing at farming. He deserted his wife and their eleven children. Leacock managed to educate himself, and he was for many years the chair of the Department of Economics and Political Science at McGill University, Montreal. Arts students there now gather in the Leacock Building.

Leacock's summer home near Orillia, Ontario, was the setting for the gently satirical Sunshine Sketches of a Little Town *(1912). Many residents of Orillia were outraged by Leacock's book. He was making fun of them—and he was an outsider. Those sketches do poke fun at the citizens of Orillia, but Leacock was motivated by a deep concern for small towns as the economy shifted steadily to large urban centres. He was recording a passing way of life, where human nature was writ large. He worried that people and their humanity would be lost in the anonymity of big cities.*

Opinion varies about whether or not Leacock's works like this one should be considered "fiction." He himself called them sketches, avoiding the issue. He obviously saw them as close to essays, although he uses strategies of character development, conversation and setting to develop the humour. The unobtrusive speaker in most of these pieces seems like a closely observing narrator, but in the following piece, he becomes the central character.

When Leacock wrote this piece, from Literary Lapses *(1910), he was a respected academic in the area of economics and economic institutions. He was supposed to understand such institutions, and above all, he was supposed to know how to function in them. So while this piece made fun of the pompous bank, its author/narrator was also laughing at himself.*

My Financial Career

When I go into a bank I get rattled. The clerks rattle me; the wickets rattle me; the sight of the money rattles me; everything rattles me.

The moment I cross the threshold of a bank and attempt to transact business there, I become an irresponsible idiot.

I knew this beforehand, but my salary had been raised to fifty dollars a month and I felt that the bank was the only place for it.

So I shambled in and looked timidly round at the clerks. I had an idea that a person about to open an account must needs consult the manager.

I went up to a wicket marked "Accountant." The accountant was a tall, cool devil. The very sight of him rattled me. My voice was sepulchral.

"Can I see the manager?" I said, and added solemnly, "alone." I don't know why I said "alone."

"Certainly," said the accountant, and fetched him.

The manager was a grave, calm man. I held my fifty-six dollars clutched in a crumpled ball in my pocket.

"Are you the manager?" I said. God knows I didn't doubt it.

"Yes," he said.

"Can I see you," I asked, "alone?" I didn't want to say "alone" again, but without it the thing seemed self-evident.

The manager looked at me in some alarm. He felt that I had an awful secret to reveal.

"Come in here," he said, and led the way to a private room. He turned the key in the lock.

"We are safe from interruption here," he said. "Sit down."

We both sat down and looked at each other. I found no voice to speak.

"You are one of Pinkerton's men, I presume," he said.

He had gathered from my mysterious manner that I was a detective. I knew what he was thinking, and it made me worse.

"No, not from Pinkerton's," I said, seeming to imply that I came from a rival agency.

"To tell the truth," I went on, as if I had been prompted to lie about it, "I am not a detective at all. I have come to open an account. I intend to keep all my money in this bank."

The manager looked relieved but still serious; he concluded now that I was a son of Baron Rothschild or a young Gould.

"A large account, I suppose," he said.

"Fairly large," I whispered. "I propose to deposit fifty-six dollars now and fifty dollars a month regularly."

The manager got up and opened the door. He called to the accountant.

"Mr. Montgomery," he said unkindly loud, "this gentleman is opening an account, he will deposit fifty-six dollars. Good morning."

I rose.

A big iron door stood open at the side of the room.

"Good morning," I said, and stepped into the safe.

"Come out," said the manager coldly, and showed me the other way.

I went up to the accountant's wicket and poked the ball of money at him with a quick convulsive movement as if I were doing a conjuring trick.

My face was ghastly pale.

"Here," I said, "deposit it." The tone of the words seemed to mean, "Let us do this painful thing while the fit is on us."

He took the money and gave it to another clerk.

He made me write the sum on a slip and sign my name in a book. I no longer knew what I was doing. The bank swam before my eyes.

"Is it deposited?" I asked in a hollow, vibrating voice.

"It is," said the accountant.

"Then I want to draw a cheque."

My idea was to draw out six dollars of it for present use. Someone gave me a cheque-book through a wicket and someone else began telling me how to write it out. The people in the bank had the impression that I was an invalid millionaire. I wrote something on the cheque and thrust it in at the clerk. He looked at it.

"What! are you drawing it all out again?" he asked in surprise. Then I realised that I had written fifty-six instead of six. I was too far gone to reason now. I had a feeling that it was impossible to explain the thing. All the clerks had stopped writing to look at me.

Reckless with misery, I made a plunge.

"Yes, the whole thing."

"You withdraw your money from the bank?"

"Every cent of it."

"Are you not going to deposit any more?" said the clerk, astonished.

"Never."

An idiot hope struck me that they might think something had insulted me while I was writing the cheque and that I had changed my mind. I made a wretched attempt to look like a man with a fearfully quick temper.

The clerk prepared to pay the money.

"How will you have it?" he said.

"What?"

"How will you have it?"

"Oh"—I caught his meaning and answered without even trying to think—"in fifties."

He gave me a fifty-dollar bill.

"And the six?" he asked dryly.

"In sixes," I said.

He gave it me and I rushed out.

As the big door swung behind me I caught the echo of a roar of laughter that went up to the ceiling of the bank. Since then I bank no more. I keep my money in cash in my trousers pocket and my savings in silver dollars in a sock.

1910

Annabel Lyon
b. 1971

One of Canada's emerging writers, Lyon took the literary world by storm with the publication of Oxygen *(2000), a collection of short fiction. Her second book is* The Best Thing For You; Three Novellas *(2004). Reviewers use words like "savvy, subversive, succinct," to describe her writing.*

Lyon graduated from the Master's program in creative writing at the University of British Columbia, Vancouver, where she now lives. She is outspoken about people who say that writing cannot be taught, believing that a writer always benefits from feedback and criticism. Certainly, it seems that she has. She earns her living as a freelance journalist, writing reviews and articles for newspapers and magazines.

In an article in Geist magazine, Lyon considered theorists discussing the question of ethics in works of literature. It is an old habit, she says, to read literature looking for ethical guidance. This is no longer the usual way of approaching literature, but ethics do come up in a consideration of this story from Oxygen.

These characters are utterly amoral, responding only to situations directly in front of them, motivated by self-interest and greed. They do not seem to consider any possible consequences of their acts. They live in an urban world, with little human connection to anyone outside their peer group.

Lyon makes no judgment on these characters. She presents them in a spare, clear style devoid of sentimentality. At the end of the Geist article, Lyon writes, "We take a risk when we close our eyes to the 'lessons' of great literature. We risk, at our peril, forgetting what tragedy is." It is a statement which resonates eerily with this story.

Song

Two boys went into a house. A girl waited in the car.

It happened like this. The boys went into the house while the girl waited in the car. When they came out the girl drove them away. For some time it wasn't clear to her what had happened.

Shit, whispered the one. Shit, shit. He was the younger one, with straw hair and an intemperate personality. He sat next to her in the front.

She herself was sweet on the older one, who sat on the back seat. He kept his hands in front of his face and appeared to be praying or thinking hard.

Did you get? she asked. But the boys wouldn't talk to her. They weren't talking at that point.

Names—Craig, Marco, and Sherry.

Sherry was sixteen then, Craig fifteen. Marco was eighteen. These were facts. At trial, no one disputed that Sherry stayed in the car.

I got some on my pants, Craig said as she drove. Hey, man. Will you look at this.

Marco leaned forward to look over the bench seat.

It happened like this. Sherry imagined an old woman who lived alone. She would be frightened and give them her money.

It happened like this. Marco knew of a widow, the mother of a man who had once ripped off his father. The man had shaken a fist in his father's face. He had ripped up an invoice and laughed. His father wouldn't care about this old woman or what his son might do to this old woman. She would be sleeping, and wake to find vengeance had been and gone and robbed her blind while she had been sleeping.

Craig didn't give a fuck.

Two boys went into a house. The girl waited in the car. She felt sick. She tried to remember why money had seemed like such a good idea, what she wanted it for. CDs? Lipsticks? I don't want any more lipsticks, she thought. She sat in the car with the engine running, the exhaust going up like a white signal, thumbtacking them to the map of the cold curved street.

They walked out slowly. Marco closed the front door behind him and gave it a little tug to make sure it was locked. Neither of them was carrying anything.

It was Craig's idea, the electrician's tape.

It was Marco's idea, the electrician's tape. Sit still, he told the old woman. She was crying. He hated to touch her skin. He wound the tape around her wrists, behind her back, round and round, binding rather than taping, freeing the tape from the roll in snatches. Craig had gone down the hall to the left while Marco did this thing. This was fast. This was happening fast.

No hurry now, she remembered at trial. Craig or Marco had said it. One or the other.

No hurry now.

What happened? she asked. She was driving. They were a ways away and she wanted to know. How much did—?

Sherry, said Marco.

There was a smell. She caught it then.

Oh, she said. You.

She stopped the car. Craig fell out his door and threw up onto the ground.

It was him, Marco said. It wasn't me.

Craig went down the hall to the left while Marco tied her up in the kitchen.

The curtains were drawn in all the rooms. The beds were made. It was like underwater. He didn't want to go in the rooms, didn't want to take anything any more. He wanted to go through the motions so as not to anger the older boy, and then he wanted to leave. He felt nervous and guilty. He knew what he was doing was wrong. Yes, he was afraid of violence, he was afraid. Yes, he was afraid.

Marco went up the stairs to the right while Craig watched the old woman in the kitchen. He was looking white so Marco didn't try to get him to do anything. When Marco went upstairs Craig was just standing there looking white. Marco had given the old woman a cuff to keep her quiet and told Craig just to stand there and not do anything. The cuff was nothing, like you would deal a puppy.

Upstairs the carpet was thick and pale and took the imprint of his steps like stains. He had to drag his feet to smudge them out. There was a bedroom with a cheap computer and a small bathroom with a sloped ceiling. He wasn't taking much in. He heard a sound like a puppy and headed back down the stairs to get the younger boy out of there. It had been a lot for one day.

———

She waited in the car.

They had been to the beach at White Rock, the three of them. This was the day before. Sitting on a picnic table overlooking the wide sands they had teased her, calling her a Surrey girl, which meant slut. It had been nice sitting there in the open with the ocean and birds in the air and a boy she liked and the three of them laughing. They didn't know each other very well, except that none of them felt like going to school that day or the next.

It happened like this. The boys were shouting at each other while she drove. She couldn't understand it. Finally Marco said, Stop the car.

He got out and slammed the door hard. He started to walk, he started to run toward the intersection. He ran against the electric hand telling him not to cross and they saw him slam his palm down on the hood of a car which had had to brake hard for him, almost at his hip. He ran out of their sight.

He hit her hard, Craig said when Sherry looked at him.

When she looked back at the street she saw the vanilla man come on for the walkers as though to say, That's right.

It was him, Craig said. It wasn't me.

Before they went into the house they had each kissed her for luck. They must have talked about it beforehand because she was not expecting it and afterwards they were both smiling and would not look at her or each other. The blond boy had done it first, shyly on the cheek, and then the dark boy. He had leaned over the back seat and touched her ear and when she turned to him he smiled and touched her hair and kissed her mouth. Then they got out of the car and proceeded up the front path to the house, smiling at nothing at all.

Craig was abused.

Marco was abused.

Sherry was abused.

———

Two boys went into a house. There were knives in the sink, knives
in a block, knives in drawers. The hands of the clock were a knife
and fork. There were knives in the bathroom, knives in the bedroom, knives in the carpet and knives hanging from the ceiling.

Forensic reports revealed a single weak blow to the head and seventeen stab wounds to the back, neck, and head. The knife was a
poor choice, blunt and serrated, probably a steak knife.

Marco tried to think what would anger him least. Good boy, he
said. He was sure that was what he had said, watching the blade in
the other boy's fist. You did what you had to do.

Craig tried to think what would anger him least. Shit, he said.
But he couldn't speak after that. The older boy had put the knife
down and grabbed him to stop him falling. That was how the blood
came to be on his clothes.

They washed at the sink like brothers, or unlike brothers.

When Craig got his knees back under him they got out of that
house. It had all been pretty quiet but Marco locked the door behind them anyway, just to slow whoever came next.

Before they went into the house they had each kissed her for luck.
They must have talked about it beforehand because she was not expecting it and afterwards they were both smiling. The older boy put
his face to her ear and bit her while the younger one leaned forward
to kiss her on the mouth. She felt tongue, teeth. They were both at
her at once and then they were gone, out of the car and proceeding
up the front path to the house, walking straight and tall with their
animal heads like something horrible out of Egypt.

The sun had slipped from its place in the sky. This was the day before. Sherry was getting cold. They sat on a picnic table at White
Rock with their collars up against the cold, smoking and talking
quietly as the last daylight pooled in the ocean. Her hands were
white and cold. Christmas was coming.

The idea had been with them all that day and they had enjoyed
talking about it, planning it and taking themselves seriously. They
each wanted a little bit of money, that was all, for little things they
each wanted.

———

It happened like this. As Marco came down the stairs he saw Craig standing behind the woman tied to the chair. Both had their backs to him. Craig was leaning forward and then Marco saw him unsheath the knife from her body. That would have been the last time, number seventeen. He had had to stab between the railings of the chair. Her clothes were black with it.

It happened like this. When Craig came back from the bedrooms to the kitchen he saw what at first seemed to be a badly applied coat of red lipstick on the woman's mouth. She was still tied to the chair. The older boy was behind her, leaning forward as though to whisper in her ear. Then she started to drool and it was red.

Later at the sink when he saw the older boy wash blood and particles from the knife he started to cry.

Two boys went into a house. At trial she would be asked whether one or both of them had acted strangely that day or before. Meaning: which one and why?

The younger boy had tender shadows under his eyes and a childish temper, subject to bizarre triggers—seagulls, hunger, kissing. He had flown into a rage when he caught Marco laughing with Sherry behind the White Rock 7-Eleven, his little face all twisted, almost crying. He had gone in to buy liquorice while they waited outside but when he came out he couldn't see them right away and thought they had taken off.

Marco had carved obscenities into the picnic table with a Scout knife while Craig and Sherry ate the liquorice. Then he tried to sink the knife to its hilt in the wood of the table. He and Craig took turns gripping and wiggling it, trying to work it in deeper while Sherry ate the liquorice. It was somewhat stupid behaviour, she thought, but it did not detract from the sweet thing she had for Marco or the general good feeling of the day.

Two boys went into a house. Marco knocked on the door while Craig looked over his shoulder.

Don't, Marco said.

The door opened. Yes, the woman said.

Marco leaned down and hugged her. He picked her up off the

ground in a hug and carried her into the house. Craig followed, pulling the door closed behind him. Anyone watching would have seen a young man giving an old woman a nice big hug.

Don't you hurt me, she said. I've seen your faces.

Two boys went into a house.

Don't you hurt me, she said. I'm not afraid of you.

As he came towards her she cried out but he walked past, behind her back, like he was going upstairs.

It happened like this. Sherry was alone in the car.

She was driving down Hastings Street in the blue hour when tail-lights are rubies and people are feeling good. She had felt good herself yesterday at this time at White Rock when they saw the streetlights come on like someone switching on the night. That was a hundred years ago. Now this thing was in between. She realized her life would be divided now into before and after.

Two boys went into a house. What happened? She tried to imagine. It happened like this. Two boys went into a house. She looked down at the passenger seat of the stolen Jetta and saw long stains. Carefully she signalled and crossed into the slower lane. She signalled again and parallel parked and pushed the gearshift into Park and ratcheted up the handbrake. She turned around to look at the back seat and it was there too. It was then she saw the electrician's tape snatched from the roll, the aquarium light of the bedrooms, the footprints in the carpet, the hands of the cutlery clock, the black clothes and new lipstick, and the boys leaning down each in turn as though to kiss or whisper in her ear.

But I was in the car, she thought. I was in the car. I was in the car. I was in the car.

Across the street glowed a payphone with a white light both harsh and soft. She went to it. Soon she could hear the long rising praise of sirens. Much later, after the prescribed period of tales and contradictions, her companions were duly convicted, the younger one as a child, the elder as an adult, and they were sent to different places. Two boys went into a house—yes they did.

At trial, she wondered if he still liked her.

2000

Alistair MacLeod

b. 1936

> *MacLeod has become the voice of the quiet Scots men of Cape Breton, Nova Scotia. Just because a man isn't saying anything doesn't mean he isn't thinking anything, MacLeod says. These men, descendants of people deported from Scotland during the Highland clearances, are facing the end of their way of life in the mines, in the woods, and on the fishing boats. The narrator's voice in MacLeod's stories becomes bardic, the voice of a poet telling the stories of his people.*
>
> *Each word in a MacLeod story is deliberately placed. Drawing heavily on oral traditions, the language comes alive when read aloud. MacLeod says it takes him longer to write a sentence than it takes him to write a novel. Several of his stories have been translated into Scots Gaelic, as well as other languages. Often, their imagery is recurring, braided, in the way of Celtic knotwork.*
>
> *MacLeod was born in North Battleford, Saskatchewan, half a continent away from Cape Breton, but he grew up among the people he writes about. He has published only two collections of short stories:* The Lost Salt Gift of Blood *(1976) and* As Birds Bring Forth the Sun *(1986), collected into* Island *(2000), and one novel,* No Great Mischief *(1999), which won the largest literary prize of the English-speaking world: the IMPAC Dublin Literary Award. This story comes from his second collection, and also has been published as a book with the subtitle: "A Cape Breton Christmas Story," with illustrations by Peter Rankin (2004).*
>
> *The young people of Cape Breton have been moving away, making lives for themselves in the cities of the interior, but like MacLeod himself, a professor of English and creative writing at Ontario's University of Windsor, they are drawn back to their families, often traveling great distances on dangerous roads to be with them. In this story a small brother is learning their codes, finding his place among them, coming of age.*

To Every Thing There Is a Season

I am speaking here of a time when I was eleven and lived with my family on our small farm on the west coast of Cape Breton. My family had been there for a long, long time and so it seemed had I. And much of that time seems like the proverbial yesterday. Yet when I speak on this Christmas 1977, I am not sure how much I speak with the voice of that time or how much in the voice of what I have since become. And I am not sure how many liberties I may be taking with the boy I think I was. For Christmas is a time of both past and present and often the two are imperfectly blended. As we step into its nowness we often look behind.

We have been waiting now, it seems, forever. Actually, it has been most intense since Halloween when the first snow fell upon us as we moved like muffled mummers upon darkened country roads. The large flakes were soft and new then and almost generous and the earth to which they fell was still warm and as yet unfrozen. They fell in silence into the puddles and into the sea where they disappeared at the moment of contact. They disappeared, too, upon touching the heated redness of our necks and hands or the faces of those who did not wear masks. We carried our pillowcases from house to house, knocking on doors to become silhouettes in the light thrown out from kitchens (white pillowcases held out by whitened forms). The snow fell between us and the doors and was transformed in shimmering golden beams. When we turned to leave, it fell upon our footprints and as the night wore on obliterated them and all the records of our movements. In the morning everything was soft and still and November had come upon us.

My brother Kenneth, who is two and a half, is unsure of his last Christmas. It is Halloween that looms largest in his memory as an exceptional time of being up late in magic darkness and falling snow. "Who are you going to dress up as at Christmas?" he asks. "I think I'll be a snowman." All of us laugh at that and tell him Santa Claus will find him if he is good and that he need not dress up at all. We go about our appointed tasks waiting for it to happen.

I am troubled myself about the nature of Santa Claus and I am trying to hang on to him in any way that I can. It is true that at my age I no longer *really* believe in him yet I have hoped in all his possibilities as fiercely as I can; much in the same way, I think, that the drowning man waves desperately to the lights of the passing ship on the high sea's darkness. For without him, as without the man's ship, it seems our fragile lives would be so much more desperate.

My mother has been fairly tolerant of my attempted perpetuation. Perhaps because she has encountered it before. Once I overheard her speaking about my sister Anne to one of her neighbours. "I thought Anne would *believe* forever," she said. "I practically had to tell her." I have somehow always wished I had not heard her say that as I seek sanctuary and reinforcement even in an ignorance I know I dare not trust.

Kenneth, however, believes with an unadulterated fervour, and so do Bruce and Barry who are six-year-old twins. Beyond me there is Anne who is thirteen and Mary who is fifteen, both of whom seem to be leaving childhood at an alarming rate. My mother has told us that she was already married when she was seventeen, which is only two years older than Mary is now. That too seems strange to contemplate and perhaps childhood is shorter for some than it is for others. I think of this sometimes in the evenings when we have finished our chores and the supper dishes have been cleared away and we are supposed to be doing our homework. I glance sideways at my mother, who is always knitting or mending, and at my father, who mostly sits by the stove coughing quietly with his handkerchief at his mouth. He has "not been well" for over two years and has difficulty breathing whenever he moves at more than the slowest pace. He is most sympathetic of all concerning my extended hopes and says we should hang on to the good things in our lives as long as we are able. As I look at him out of the corner of my eye, it does not seem that he has many of them left. He is old, we think, at forty-two.

Yet Christmas, in spite of all the doubts of our different ages, is a fine and splendid time, and now as we pass the midpoint of December our expectations are heightened by the increasing coldness that has settled down upon us. The ocean is flat and calm and along the coast, in the scooped-out coves, has turned to an icy slush. The brook that flows past our house is almost totally frozen and there is only a small channel of rushing water that flows openly at its very centre. When we let the cattle out to drink, we chop holes with the axe at the brook's edge so that they can drink without venturing onto the ice.

The sheep move in and out of their lean-to shelter restlessly stamping their feet or huddling together in tightly packed groups. A conspiracy of wool against the cold. The hens perch high on their roosts with their feathers fluffed out about them, hardly feeling it worthwhile to descend to the floor for their few scant kernels of grain. The pig, who has little time before his butchering, squeals his displeasure to the cold and with his snout tosses his wooden trough high in the icy air. The splendid young horse paws the planking of his stall and gnaws the wooden cribwork of his manger.

We have put a protective barricade of spruce boughs about our kitchen door and banked our house with additional boughs and billows of eel grass. Still, the pail of water we leave standing in the porch is solid in the morning and has to be broken with the hammer. The clothes my mother hangs on the line are frozen almost instantly and sway and creak from their suspending clothespins like sections of dismantled robots: the stiff-legged rasping trousers and the shirts and sweaters with unyielding arms outstretched. In the morning we race from our frigid upstairs bedrooms to finish dressing around the kitchen stove.

We would extend our coldness half a continent away to the Great Lakes of Ontario so that it might hasten the Christmas coming of my oldest brother, Neil. He is nineteen and employed on the "lake boats," the long flat carriers of grain and iron ore whose season ends any day after December 10, depending on the ice conditions. We wish it to be cold, cold on the Great Lakes of Ontario, so that he may come home to us as soon as possible. Already his cartons have arrived. They come from different places: Cobourg, Toronto, St. Catharines, Welland, Windsor, Sarnia, Sault Ste. Marie. Places that we, with the exception of my father, have never been. We locate them excitedly on the map, tracing their outlines with eager fingers. The cartons bear the lettering of Canada Steamship Lines, and are bound with rope knotted intricately in the fashion of sailors. My mother says they contain his "clothes" and we are not allowed to open them.

For us it is impossible to know the time or manner of his coming. If the lakes freeze early, he may come by train because it is cheaper. If the lakes stay open until December 20, he will have to fly because his time will be more precious than his money. He will hitchhike the last sixty or hundred miles from either station or airport. On our part, we can do nothing but listen with straining ears to radio reports of distant ice formations. His coming seems to depend on so many factors which are out there far beyond us and over which we lack control.

The days go by in fevered slowness until finally on the morning of December 23 the strange car rolls into our yard. My mother touches her hand to her lips and whispers "Thank God." My father gets up unsteadily from his chair to look through the window. Their longed-for son and our golden older brother is here at last. He is here with his reddish hair and beard and we can hear his hearty laugh. He will be happy and strong and confident for us all.

There are three other young men with him who look much the same as he. They too are from the boats and are trying to get home to Newfoundland. They must still drive a hundred miles to reach the ferry at North Sydney. The car seems very old. They purchased it in Thorold for two hundred dollars because they were too late to make any reservations, and they have driven steadily since they began. In northern New Brunswick their windshield wipers failed but instead of stopping they tied lengths of cord to the wipers' arms and passed them through the front window vents. Since that time, in whatever precipitation, one of them has pulled the cords back and forth to make the wipers function. This information falls tiredly but excitedly from their lips and we greedily gather it in. My father pours them drinks of rum and my mother takes out her mincemeat and the fruitcakes she has been carefully hoarding. We lean on the furniture or look from the safety of sheltered doorways. We would like to hug our brother but are too shy with strangers present. In the kitchen's warmth, the young men begin to nod and doze, their heads dropping suddenly to their chests. They nudge each other with their feet in an attempt to keep awake. They will not stay and rest because they have come so far and tomorrow is Christmas Eve and stretches of mountains and water still lie between them and those they love.

After they leave we pounce upon our brother physically and verbally. He laughs and shouts and lifts us over his head and swings us in his muscular arms. Yet in spite of his happiness he seems surprised at the appearance of his father whom he has not seen since March. My father merely smiles at him while my mother bites her lip.

Now that he is here there is a great flurry of activity. We have left everything we could until the time he might be with us. Eagerly I show him the fir tree on the hill which I have been watching for months and marvel at how easily he fells it and carries it down the hill. We fall over one another in the excitement of decoration.

He promises that on Christmas Eve he will take us to church in the sleigh behind the splendid horse that until his coming we are all afraid to handle. And on the afternoon of Christmas Eve he shoes the horse, lifting each hoof and rasping it fine and hammering the cherry-red horseshoes into shape upon the anvil. Later he drops them hissingly into the steaming tub of water. My father sits beside him on an overturned pail and tells him what to do. Sometimes we argue with our father, but our brother does everything he says.

That night, bundled in hay and voluminous coats, and with heated stones at our feet, we start upon our journey. Our parents and Kenneth remain at home but all the rest of us go. Before we leave we feed the cattle and sheep and even the pig all that they can possibly eat so that they will be contented on Christmas Eve. Our parents wave to us from the doorway. We go four miles across the mountain road. It is a primitive logging trail and there will be no cars or other vehicles upon it. At first the horse is wild with excitement and lack of exercise and my brother has to stand at the front of the sleigh and lean backwards on the reins. Later he settles down to a trot and still later to a walk as the mountain rises before him. We sing all the Christmas songs we know and watch for the rabbits and foxes scudding across the open patches of snow and listen to the drumming of partridge wings. We are never cold.

When we descend to the country church we tie the horse in a grove of trees where he will be sheltered and not frightened by the many cars. We put a blanket over him and give him oats. At the church door the neighbours shake hands with my brother. "Hello, Neil," they say. "How is your father?"

"Oh," he says, just "Oh."

The church is very beautiful at night with its festooned branches and glowing candles and the booming, joyous sounds that come from the choir loft. We go through the service as if we are mesmerized.

On the way home, although the stones have cooled, we remain happy and warm. We listen to the creak of the leather harness and the hiss of runners on the snow and begin to think of the potentiality of presents. When we are about a mile from home the horse senses his destination and breaks into a trot and then into a confident lope. My brother lets him go and we move across the winter landscape like figures freed from a Christmas card. The snow from the horse's hooves falls about our heads like the whiteness of the stars.

After we have stabled the horse we talk with our parents and eat the meal our mother has prepared. And then I am sleepy and it is time for the younger children to be in bed. But tonight my father says to me, "We would like you to stay up with us a while," and so I stay quietly with the older members of my family.

When all is silent upstairs Neil brings in the cartons that contain his "clothes" and begins to open them. He unties the intricate knots quickly, their whorls falling away before his agile fingers. The boxes are filled with gifts neatly wrapped and bearing tags. The ones for my younger brothers say "from Santa Claus" but mine are not among them anymore, as I know with certainty they will never be again. Yet I am not so much surprised as touched by a pang of loss at being here on the adult side of the world. It is as if I have suddenly moved into another room and heard a door click lastingly behind me. I am jabbed by my own small wound.

But then I look at those before me. I look at my parents drawn together before the Christmas tree. My mother has her hand upon my father's shoulder and he is holding his ever-present handkerchief. I look at my sisters who have crossed this threshold ahead of me and now each day journey farther from the lives they knew as girls. I look at my magic older brother who has come to us this Christmas from half a continent away, bringing everything he has and is. All of them are captured in the tableau of their care.

"Every man moves on," says my father quietly, and I think he speaks of Santa Claus, "but there is no need to grieve. He leaves good things behind."

1977

Eric McCormack
b. 1938

McCormack has a wickedly Scots sense of humour. He delights in telling interviewers different versions of his life story, testing to see how outrageous he can make the accounts, how much he can get away with. He seems to have settled on this one included as the Introduction to Inspecting the Vaults *(1987).*

What is likely true is that he was born in Scotland and grew up in working-class Glasgow, coming to Canada as an adult. He says that his favourite book is Robert Louis Stevenson's Treasure Island. *He also appreciates the fictional strategies of the Argentinian writer Jorge Luis Borges, especially in a short-fiction collection like* Ficciones. *Certainly, McCormack's own writing shows an interest in exotic places and strange characters as well as inventive fictional structures. Above all, McCormack loves language, often creating lists of words for the sheer pleasure of using them. His widely appreciated novels include* Paradise Motel *(1989),* The Mysterium *(1992),* First Blast of the Trumpet Against the Monstrous Regiment of Women *(1997), and* The Dutch Wife *(2002).*

Underneath the playfulness of style in McCormack's fiction lurk serious issues. He satirizes social attitudes, the church, education, the medical profession. It is easy to miss those under the surface extravagance which some readers consider Gothic and even bizarre.

In this story, McCormack shows how language can break down into the almost incomprehensible. Perhaps less obvious is an exploration of the father-son relationship usually presented more directly. Suggestions about the difficulties of the writer/artist also hover around this story. The twins are a way of understanding what happens when a person has to speak with two voices, one socially acceptable and the other perhaps less so. McCormack does tell us that he grew up in a world hostile to writers and reading.

Introduction to *Inspecting the Vaults*

I heard recently about an elderly man in some gulag. He had endured solitary confinement for many years, for a forgotten political crime. The only light that ever brightened his cold cell would occur briefly at midnight every night. The guard on duty would pull a switch to turn on the recessed ceiling bulbs in all of the cells, then he would stroll along the stone corridor to check the prisoners. The elderly man was always ready. As soon as the light came on, even though the glare stung his eyes, he would force them to focus on the page of a book he was holding, and try to read a sentence or two. The guard would peer in through the grill, slide it back shut, and move on to the next cell. The entire process would take about two minutes. Then darkness again for another twenty-four hours.

For those who enjoy reading, the idea is nightmarish. To be deprived in this way of one of the major pleasures in life seems an unendurable torment. The elderly man is a heroic lover of books, his fate pathetic. What book, we wonder, is he reading? How many years will it take him to get through, say, *Crime and Punishment*[1] (that's the one I think he has), or *Being and Nothingness*[2] (God forbid) at such a rate?

The story of the prisoner in the gulag is testimony to the power of the written word. In the Scottish village where I was born, I had my first experience of that same power. The people were workers without much education (a neighbour asked my mother what "definitely" meant, in a War Office telegram that said her husband was "definitely missing in action"), and they admired the ability to use words well. When I was about five or six, a letter arrived for my father from an uncle in London. After our family had read it over a hundred times—learnt it by heart almost—I got hold of it, fairly tattered by this time, and kept it with me for weeks, reading choice parts to anyone who'd listen. When that thrill wore off, I traded the letter to Phil Duffy, a schoolmate, for something I had never owned—a penknife (it had a fine bone handle, but the blades were broken). It was a fair exchange. No one in his family had ever received a private letter, and they were grateful for even a vicarious one at last.

That was my first literary transaction, a fairly mercenary one.

1. (1866) a long Russian novel by Fyodor Dostoevsky.

2. (1943) a long philosophical treatise on existentialism by the French philosopher and novelist Jean-Paul Sartre.

Till I was twenty-six, Canada was a fantasy known to me only through films, TV and books. When I arrived here, I could hardly believe the beauty of the place. Were these real trees, squirrels, cars, buses, houses? Were these people real? I couldn't keep my eyes off them, the way they moved, smiled. The men were manly, the women absurdly beautiful. Their voices were soothing to the soul and the ear of a man who'd spent a lifetime amidst the chain-saw burr and the violent glottal stops of Scottish speech. And the size of the place: on the train west from Montreal, I was convinced that one lake after another must be Lake Superior, they seemed so huge after the "great lakes" of Scotland—Loch Lomond and Loch Ness.

Eventually, in the Winnipeg winter of 1966, less pleasant realities struck. For the first time, my bare eyeballs felt the pain caused by freezing cold air. The hairs in my nose turned into wire. And that winter, my good Scottish overcoat, with its foam rubber lining, actually split in halves, right down the join at the back, when I took it off. It lay there on the floor like the broken shell of a dead sea-creature. I think now I was shedding more than just a Scottish coat that day.

I've lived and worked in Canada for more than twenty years now. I'm taken by surprise when someone comments on my accent. I can't hear it any more. But perhaps my writing still has it. Many of my stories, I think, dabble in the marginal, slightly alien areas of everyday experience—such as that of the elderly man in the gulag. The need to write about them is probably like the need to drink whisky, or to take drugs, or to do all three at the same time. And the reasons for the need are as complex. The writer may be in love, or in love with words. He may be in despair at the state of the world, or at his own state. Or he may be, in a roundabout way, just celebrating, having a great time. Perhaps it's his way of shouting his hurrahs for being, at last, by the purest of luck, in a good place. For many of us who are travellers, in mind or in body, that's what Canada is—one of the last of the good places.

1978

Twins

People swarm from north and south, abandon the rituals of Saturday afternoon shopping expeditions and ball-game attendances, in favour of him. One thing: no children. He demands no admission fee, so he is entitled to say "No children." ("Say" won't do. Even that woman, his mother, the crutch on which he has limped his eighteen years, can never be sure of what he "says." He, therefore, writes. And has written, with his right hand, and with his left hand, "NO CHILDREN.") For children are always the enemy: they suspect something, frown at him, tire of his performances, spoil everything. (As for dogs, they are wary too when they see him out walking. They sheath their tails. They slink growling to the opposite side of the road.) But, ah! The adults! The benches of the old church hall sag under the weight of their veneration. His devotees. How they admire him, how they nod their approval of his enigmatic sermons. He bestows upon them tears perhaps of gratitude, howls perhaps of execration. Either way, his votaries (the tall man with the blue eyes sits among them) are content.

The name of the one they come to hear? Malachi. That, at least, is sure. He has a sickness (is there a name for it?). His sickness attracts them. He is the one who speaks with two voices, two different voices, at the same time. One of the voices trolls smoothly from the right side of his mouth. The other crackles from the left corner. How memorable, how remarkable, the sound of those two voices emanating from that one flexible mouth.

Is his affliction, then, a miracle? No matter, it certainly complicates his life. It might be easier to bear if the two voices would speak in turns. But whenever he wants to say something, both voices chime in, overlap, each using an exactly equal number of syllables. Without euphony. There is discord in the sounds, there is dissent in the things said. What allures is the eeriness of it. The right-side voice thanks the tall man with the blue eyes for a gift he has brought:

"Thanks a lot."

But the left-side voice remarks simultaneously:

"You're a fool."

(Or is it vice-versa? Often it is hard to tell.) The hearing is a difficult experience. Words sometimes twine together, like this—

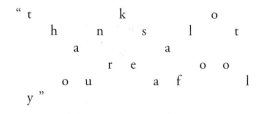

—braided like two snakes. Or a discrepancy in timing produces a long, alien word: "*thyaounksreaalfoolot.*" Or exact synchronization causes a triple grunt: "*thyaounksre aalfootol.*" Leaving the hearer to rummage among fragments of words, palimpsests of phrases. Did he hear, "you're a lot," "thanks a fool," "yanks a lol," "thou're a foot?"

A disease of words. When Malachi was a child, nobody was willing to diagnose his problem. No father to turn to. His mother never revealed who fathered him in the bed of her clapboard house, imitation brick, a mile north of town. Malachi squirmed out of the womb, purple. Let loose his inhuman shrieks. It was presumed his brain was not right.

See him at the age of ten. A boy unable to cope with anything scholastic. No one understands his noises, the drooling, the maddening grunts. Then, lying on the floor on a Sunday morning in June, in his mother's presence, tiger stripes of sun through the shutters on his prone body, he who has never written a word, picks up two pencils, one in each hand, and writes two messages simultaneously on a sheet of paper. With his right hand, a neat firm line:

"Help me, Mother."

With his left hand a scrawl:

"Leave me alone."

She stares at the paper, squints at his mouth, understands at last.

The why of it? How can such a thing have happened to her son? She expounds her theory to the tall man. (He has blue eyes, fine lines web the corners.) Malachi, she says, is meant to be twins, but somehow the division has not occurred, and he has been born, two people condemned to one body. Reverse Siamese twins. When she speaks of her theory in Malachi's presence, his face seems to confirm it. The right side blooms smooth, an innocent boy's. The left side shimmers with defiance. His head becomes unsteady, wobbles like an erratic planet with orbiting satellite eyes.

The German pastor is the force behind the audiences. He has spoken at some length to the tall man with the unflinching blue eyes. The pastor suggests to the mother that it will be good for the boy's confidence to exhibit himself. Is the pastor concerned about therapy or theology? Is he convinced that ultimately one voice or the other will prevail in open combat? Is he enthusiastic because he himself marvels at the sight? (Understands something?) He never misses an audience, sits rapt, engrossed in the turmoil in the face, the voice, of Malachi.

A sudden change. In the middle of the eighteenth year, tranquility. The harsh voice silent, the soft voice alone emerges from the twisted mouth, unencumbered. The left side of the mouth still curls, the left cheek still twitches, the left eye still glares. People still cringe ready for the snarl. But they wait in vain. And Malachi appears one morning wearing a black cloth patch over the left side of his face. A black triangle.

They ask him, "What has happened to your other voice?"

He seems surprised at the question, as though unaware of the years of struggle. Soon, no one asks him any more, everyone becomes used to his masked face. They admire it, a portentous half moon. Malachi is a kind-hearted boy. His long illness is forgotten.

Three years later, he dies. At the age of twenty-one, he is sucked into the spirals of the river on a dark night. The verdict at the inquest: death by accident. The pathologist does not fail to take note of Malachi's remarkable tongue, wide as two normal tongues, linked by a membrane of skin. It must have made breathing difficult in those final moments. Malachi's mother attends the inquest, too distraught to be called as a witness. Afterwards, in the car park, the tall man catches up to her. He is about her age. (He has blue eyes. Fine lines web the corners.) He is silent. The sun beats down, mid-July, a day that ridicules mourning. She is still a woman of some beauty.

"It would have happened long ago," she says, "but for a pact. Three years ago I made them agree to it. One voice was to be in command all day, then after dark the other would take over. They just shifted the patch. But the girl drove them against each other again. They were jealous over her. They couldn't share her any longer. They needed to fight it out. But there was only the one body to hurt."

She can no longer control herself. She sobs, and begs the man to leave her alone. A neighbour takes her by the arm to a waiting car. The man with blue eyes watches her go. He knows what must be done.

He drives to where the girl lives, a country motel, a run-down place, peeling green paint. She greets him solemnly, invites him up to her room. A lank-haired girl, not beautiful. He savours her quiet voice.

"He was a good friend to me," telling of Malachi. "I could trust him. On sunny days, we just sat by the river and talked. He said everything was under control. I was not to worry about his moods at night. I told him I liked him just as much at night when he switched the patch and changed his voice. At night, he would drink and drink, and make love. I told him how much I loved the feel of his tongue on my body. I suppose he didn't believe me."

She asks the man with the blue eyes to wait with her for a while. He stays, consoles her. It is dark when he leaves.

Ten years have passed. I am on an assignment to this country town. It is a pleasant summer's morning with, strangely, an arc of moon still visible in the bright sky like a single heelprint on glare ice. I am here to observe two children. They are twins, I am told. I am a little afraid of what I may find. I have a fear of children.

They don't look especially alike. One is fair, composed, the other dark and fidgety. They are ten years old. They speak in a babble no one has been able to understand. Aside from themselves, that is, for they seem to understand each other.

I am here with the other observers because of a curious development. The twins have discovered how to communicate with the world. When they wish to be understood by others, we are told, they join hands and speak in unison. The sounds blend together and produce words that are intelligible.

The twins do not seem happy to meet our group of linguists, philologists, semanticists, etymologists, cynics, believers. Amongst us, the tall man with blue eyes. Fine lines web the corners. He seems anxious.

At length the boys' mother, who has not changed much over the years, asks them to speak to us. They hesitate, resolve to please her. They join hands. The two solo voices that, separately, are incomprehensible to the audience, blend together in a curious duet:

"Please help us, Father," they cry.

This evokes great delight on the part of the other observers. They demand more. But the two little boys stand firm, hand-in-hand. They look directly at me. They repeat, for me, their shy, angry chant:

"Please help us, Father," they plead.

They are staring directly at the man with blue eyes. He glances around fearfully, understands that the boys are making their appeal only to him. He looks at me in desperation. He can no longer refuse to acknowledge me. I, for my part, am ready to acknowledge him. I try to control my terror. I extend my hand to him. I find I am alone. Alone, for the first time, with my children.

1978

Rohinton Mistry
b. 1952

> Born in Bombay, India, Mistry immigrated to Canada in 1975. He earned a B.A. from the University of Toronto and lives near Toronto, a full-time writer of best-selling, prize-winning novels: Such a Long Journey *(1991),* A Fine Balance *(1995), and* Family Matters *(2002). Mistry's short stories are collected in* Tales from Firoszha Baag *(1987). His is one of the multicultural voices which have enriched Canadian writing over the last decades, making it part of the international postcolonial writing scene.*
>
> Most of Mistry's fiction takes place in India, blending its words into English so that they are clear in context. The linked short pieces in his collection follow an imaginative young boy as he grows up, learning about people in his apartment block and about story-telling. This piece is the last story in the collection, when the boy has become a young man. It is set in a Toronto apartment building,

where people are surprisingly like the ones in India—with some key differences. To the young man's amazement, they are inclined to walk around in scanty clothing.

There are parallel stories here. As this narrator discovers Toronto and delights in its swimming pools, his mother and father are reading his letters at home in India. Full of reports on the weather, the standard Canadian topic of polite conversation, these letters annoy his father who complains that he could read about weather in newspapers. He has no way of knowing that the reports mean his son is gradually fitting into Canadian society.

The story becomes metafiction, as the mother and father comment on their son's writing style and on his book, which he finally sends them. His father has theories about it. His mother is impatient with theory.

Swimming Lessons

The old man's wheelchair is audible today as he creaks by in the hallway: on some days it's just a smooth whirr. Maybe the way he slumps in it, or the way his weight rests has something to do with it. Down to the lobby he goes, and sits there most of the time, talking to people on their way out or in. That's where he first spoke to me a few days ago. I was waiting for the elevator, back from Eaton's[1] with my new pair of swimming-trunks.

"Hullo," he said. I nodded, smiled.

"Beautiful summer day we've got."

"Yes," I said, "it's lovely outside."

He shifted the wheelchair to face me squarely. "How old do you think I am?"

I looked at him blankly, and he said, "Go on, take a guess."

I understood the game; he seemed about seventy-five although the hair was still black, so I said, "Sixty-five?" He made a sound between a chuckle and a wheeze: "I'll be seventy-seven next month." Close enough.

I've heard him ask that question several times since, and everyone

---

1. A Canadian department store.

plays by the rules. Their faked guesses range from sixty to seventy. They pick a lower number when he's more depressed than usual. He reminds me of Grandpa as he sits on the sofa in the lobby, staring out vacantly at the parking lot. Only difference is, he sits with the stillness of stroke victims, while Grandpa's Parkinson's disease would bounce his thighs and legs and arms all over the place. When he could no longer hold the *Bombay Samachar* steady enough to read, Grandpa took to sitting on the veranda and staring emptily at the traffic passing outside Firozsha Baag. Or waving to anyone who went by in the compound: Rustomji, Nariman Hansotia in his 1932 Mercedes-Benz, the fat ayah Jaakaylee with her shopping-bag, the *kuchrawalli* with her basket and long bamboo broom.

The Portuguese woman across the hall has told me a little about the old man. She is the communicator for the apartment building. To gather and disseminate information, she takes the liberty of un-abashedly throwing open her door when newsworthy events tran-spire. Not for Portuguese Woman the furtive peerings from thin cracks or spyholes. She reminds me of a character in a movie, *Bare-foot In The Park* I think it was, who left empty beer cans by the landing for anyone passing to stumble and give her the signal. But PW does not need beer cans. The gutang-khutang of the elevator opening and closing is enough.

The old man's daughter looks after him. He was living alone till his stroke, which coincided with his youngest daughter's divorce in Vancouver. She returned to him and they moved into this low-rise in Don Mills. PW says the daughter talks to no one in the building but takes good care of her father.

Mummy used to take good care of Grandpa, too, till things be-came complicated and he was moved to the Parsi General Hospital. Parkinsonism and osteoporosis laid him low. The doctor explained that Grandpa's hip did not break because he fell, but he fell because the hip, gradually growing brittle, snapped on that fatal day. That's what osteoporosis does, hollows out the bones and turns effect into cause. It has an unusually high incidence in the Parsi community,[2] he said, but did not say why. Just one of those mysterious things.

---

2. Descendants of Persians who fled to India in the seventh and eighth centuries to escape religious prosecution.

We are the chosen people where osteoporosis is concerned. And divorce. The Parsi community has the highest divorce rate in India. It also claims to be the most westernized community in India. Which is the result of the other? Confusion again, of cause and effect.

The hip was put in traction. Single-handed, Mummy struggled valiantly with bedpans and dressings for bedsores which soon appeared like grim spectres on his back. *Mamaiji*, bent double with her weak back, could give no assistance. My help would be enlisted to roll him over on his side while Mummy changed the dressing. But after three months, the doctor pronounced a patch upon Grandpa's lungs, and the male ward of Parsi General swallowed him up. There was no money for a private nursing home. I went to see him once, at Mummy's insistence. She used to say that the blessings of an old person were the most valuable and potent of all, they would last my whole life long. The ward had rows and rows of beds; the din was enormous, the smells nauseating, and it was just as well that Grandpa passed most of his time in a less than conscious state.

But I should have gone to see him more often. Whenever Grandpa went out, while he still could in the days before parkinsonism, he would bring back pink and white sugar-coated almonds for Percy and me. Every time I remember Grandpa, I remember that; and then I think: I should have gone to see him more often. That's what I also thought when our telephone-owning neighbour, esteemed by all for that reason, sent his son to tell us the hospital had phoned that Grandpa died an hour ago.

The postman rang the doorbell the way he always did, long and continuous; Mother went to open it, wanting to give him a piece of her mind but thought better of it, she did not want to risk the vengeance of postmen, it was so easy for them to destroy letters; workers nowadays thought no end of themselves, strutting around like peacocks, ever since all this Shiv Sena agitation about Maharashtra for Maharashtrians, threatening strikes and Bombay bundh all the time, with no respect for the public; bus drivers and conductors were the worst, behaving as if they owned the buses and were doing favours to commuters, pulling the bell before you were in the bus, the driver purposely braking and moving with big jerks to make the standees lose their balance, the conductor so rude if you did not have the right change.

But when she saw the airmail envelope with a Canadian stamp her face lit up, she said wait to the postman, and went in for a fifty paisa piece, a little baksheesh *for you, she told him, then shut the door and kissed the envelope, went in running, saying my son has written, my son has sent a letter, and Father looked up from the newspaper and said, don't get too excited, first read it, you know what kind of letters he writes, a few lines of empty words, I'm fine, hope you are all right, your loving son—that kind of writing I don't call letter-writing.*

Then Mother opened the envelope and took out one small page and began to read silently, and the joy brought to her face by the letter's arrival began to ebb; Father saw it happening and knew he was right, he said read aloud, let me also hear what our son is writing this time, so Mother read: My dear Mummy and Daddy, Last winter was terrible, we had record-breaking low temperatures all through February and March, and the first official day of spring was colder than the first official day of winter had been, but it's getting warmer now. Looks like it will be a nice warm summer. You asked about my new apartment. It's small, but not bad at all. This is just a quick note to let you know I'm fine, so you won't worry about me. Hope everything is okay at home.

After Mother put it back in the envelope, Father said everything about his life is locked in silence and secrecy, I still don't understand why he bothered to visit us last year if he had nothing to say; every letter of his has been a quick note so we won't worry—what does he think we worry about, his health, in that country everyone eats well whether they work or not, he should be worrying about us with all the black market and rationing, has he forgotten already how he used to go to the ration-shop and wait in line every week; and what kind of apartment description is that, not bad at all; and if it is a Canadian weather report I need from him, I can go with Nariman Hansotia from A Block to the Cawasji Framji Memorial Library and read all about it, there they get newspapers from all over the world.

The sun is hot today. Two women are sunbathing on the stretch of patchy lawn at the periphery of the parking lot. I can see them clearly from my kitchen. They're wearing bikinis and I'd love to take a closer look. But I have no binoculars. Nor do I have a car to saunter out to and pretend to look under the hood. They're both luscious and gleaming. From time to time they smear lotion over their skin, on the bellies, on the inside of the thighs, on the shoulders. Then one of them gets the other to undo the string of her top and spread some there. She lies on her stomach with the straps undone. I wait. I pray that the heat and haze make her forget, when it's time to turn over, that the straps are undone.

But the sun is not hot enough to work this magic for me. When it's time to come in, she flips over, deftly holding up the cups, and reties the top. They arise, pick up towels, lotions and magazines, and return to the building.

This is my chance to see them closer. I race down the stairs to the lobby. The old man says hullo. "Down again?"

"My mailbox," I mumble.

"It's Saturday," he chortles. For some reason he finds it extremely funny. My eye is on the door leading in from the parking lot.

Through the glass panel I see them approaching. I hurry to the elevator and wait. In the dimly lit lobby I can see their eyes are having trouble adjusting after the bright sun. They don't seem as attractive as they did from the kitchen window. The elevator arrives and I hold it open, inviting them in with what I think is a gallant flourish. Under the fluorescent glare in the elevator I see their wrinkled skin, aging hands, sagging bottoms, varicose veins. The lustrous trick of sun and lotion and distance has ended.

I step out and they continue to the third floor. I have Monday night to look forward to, my first swimming lesson. The high school behind the apartment building is offering, among its usual assortment of macramé and ceramics and pottery classes, a class for non-swimming adults.

The woman at the registration desk is quite friendly. She even gives me the opening to satisfy the compulsion I have about explaining my non-swimming status.

"Are you from India?" she asks. I nod. "I hope you don't mind my asking, but I was curious because an Indian couple, husband and wife, also registered a few minutes ago. Is swimming not encouraged in India?"

"On the contrary," I say. "Most Indians swim like fish. I'm an exception to the rule. My house was five minutes walking distance from Chaupatty beach in Bombay. It's one of the most beautiful beaches in Bombay, or was, before the filth took over. Anyway, even though we lived so close to it, I never learned to swim. It's just one of those things."

"Well," says the woman, "that happens sometimes. Take me, for instance. I never learned to ride a bicycle. It was the mounting that used to scare me, I was afraid of falling." People have lined up behind me. "It's been very nice talking to you," she says, "hope you enjoy the course."

The art of swimming had been trapped between the devil and the deep blue sea. The devil was money, always scarce, and kept the private swimming clubs out of reach; the deep blue sea of Chaupatty beach was grey and murky with garbage, too filthy to swim in. Every so often we would muster our courage and Mummy would take me there to try and teach me. But a few minutes of paddling was all we could endure. Sooner or later something would float up against our legs or thighs or waists, depending on how deep we'd gone in, and we'd be revulsed and stride out to the sand.

Water imagery in my life is recurring. Chaupatty beach, now the high-school swimming pool. The universal symbol of life and re-generation did nothing but frustrate me. Perhaps the swimming pool will overturn that failure.

When images and symbols abound in this manner, sprawling or rolling across the page without guile or artifice, one is prone to say, how obvious, how skilless; symbols, after all, should be still and gentle as dewdrops, tiny, yet shining with a world of meaning. But what happens when, on the page of life itself, one encounters the ever-moving, all-engirdling sprawl of the filthy sea? Dewdrops and oceans both have their rightful places; Nariman Hansotia certainly knew that when he told his stories to the boys of Firozsha Baag.

The sea of Chaupatty was fated to endure the finales of life's everyday functions. It seemed that the dirtier it became, the more crowds it attracted: street urchins and beggars and beachcombers, looking through the junk that washed up. (Or was it the crowds that made it dirtier?—another instance of cause and effect blurring and evading identification.)

Too many religious festivals also used the sea as repository for their finales. Its use should have been rationed, like rice and kerosene. On Ganesh Chaturthi, clay idols of the god Ganesh, adorned with garlands and all manner of finery, were carried in processions to the accompaniment of drums and a variety of wind instruments. The music got more frenzied the closer the procession got to Chaupatty and to the moment of immersion.

Then there was Coconut Day, which was never as popular as Ganesh Chaturthi. From a bystander's viewpoint, coconuts chucked into the sea do not provide as much of a spectacle. We used the sea, too, to deposit the leftovers from Parsi religious ceremonies, things such as flowers, or the ashes of the sacred sandalwood fire, which just could not be dumped with the regular garbage but had to be entrusted to the care of Avan Yazad, the guardian of the sea. And things which were of no use but which no one had the heart to destroy were also given to Avan Yazad. Such as old photographs.

After Grandpa died, some of his things were flung out to sea. It was high tide; we always checked the newspaper when going to perform these disposals; an ebb would mean a long walk in squelchy sand before finding water. Most of the things were probably washed up on shore. But we tried to throw them as far out as possible, then waited a few minutes; if they did not float back right away we would pretend they were in the permanent safekeeping of Avan Yazad, which was a comforting thought. I can't remember everything we sent out to sea, but his brush and comb were in the parcel, his *kusti*, and some Kemadrin pills, which he used to take to keep the parkinsonism under control.

Our paddling sessions stopped for lack of enthusiasm on my part. Mummy wasn't too keen either, because of the filth. But my main concern was the little guttersnipes, like naked fish with little buoyant penises, taunting me with their skills, swimming underwater and emerging unexpectedly all around me, or pretending to masturbate—I think they were too young to achieve ejaculation. It was embarrassing. When I look back, I'm surprised that Mummy and I kept going as long as we did.

I examine the swimming-trunks I bought last week. Surf King, says the label, Made in Canada-Fabriqué Au Canada. I've been learning bits and pieces of French from bilingual labels at the supermarket too. These trunks are extremely sleek and streamlined hipsters, the distance from waistband to pouch tip the barest minimum. I wonder how everything will stay in place, not that I'm boastful about my endowments. I try them on, and feel that the tip of my member lingers perilously close to the exit. Too close, in fact, to conceal the exigencies of my swimming lesson fantasy: a gorgeous woman in the class for non-swimmers, at whose sight I will be instantly aroused, and she, spying the shape of my desire, will look me straight in the eye with her intentions; she will come home with me, to taste the pleasures of my delectable Asian brown body whose strangeness has intrigued her and unleashed uncontrollable surges of passion inside her throughout the duration of the swimming lesson.

I drop the Eaton's bag and wrapper in the garbage can. The swimming-trunks cost fifteen dollars, same as the fee for the ten weekly lessons. The garbage bag is almost full. I tie it up and take it outside. There is a medicinal smell in the hallway; the old man must have just returned to his apartment.

PW opens her door and says, "Two ladies from the third floor were lying in the sun this morning. In bikinis."

"That's nice," I say, and walk to the incinerator chute. She reminds me of Najamai in Firozsha Baag, except that Najamai employed a bit more subtlety while going about her life's chosen work.

PW withdraws and shuts her door.

Mother had to reply because Father said he did not want to write to his son till his son had something sensible to write to him, his questions had been ignored long enough, and if he wanted to keep his life a secret, fine, he would get no letters from his father.

But after Mother started the letter he went and looked over her shoulder, telling her what to ask him, because if they kept on writing the same questions, maybe he would understand how interested they were in knowing about things over there; Father said go on, ask him what his work is at the insurance company, tell him to take some courses at night school, that's how everyone moves ahead over there, tell him not to be discouraged if his job is just clerical right now, hard work will get him ahead, remind him he is a Zoroastrian:[3] manashni, gavashni, kunashni, better write the translation also: good thoughts, good words, good deeds—he must have forgotten what it means, and tell him to say prayers and do kusti *at least twice a day.*

---

3. Member of the religion founded by Zoroaster in Iran in the seventh century.

Writing it all down sadly, Mother did not believe he wore his sudra *and* kusti *anymore, she would be very surprised if he remembered any of the prayers; when she had asked him if he needed new* sudras *he said not to take any trouble because the Zoroastrian Society of Ontario imported them from Bombay for their members, and this sounded like a story he was making up, but she was leaving it in the hands of God, ten thousand miles away there was nothing she could do but write a letter and hope for the best.*

Then she sealed it, and Father wrote the address on it as usual because his writing was much neater than hers, handwriting was important in the address and she did not want the postman in Canada to make any mistake; she took it to the post office herself, it was impossible to trust anyone to mail it ever since the postage rates went up because people just tore off the stamps for their own use and threw away the letter, the only safe way was to hand it over the counter and make the clerk cancel the stamps before your own eyes.

Berthe, the building superintendent, is yelling at her son in the parking lot. He tinkers away with his van. This happens every fine-weathered Sunday. It must be the van that Berthe dislikes because I've seen mother and son together in other quite amicable situations.

Berthe is a big Yugoslavian with high cheekbones. Her nationality was disclosed to me by PW. Berthe speaks a very rough-hewn English, I've overheard her in the lobby scolding tenants for late rents and leaving dirty lint screens in the dryers. It's exciting to listen to her, her words fall like rocks and boulders, and one can never tell where or how the next few will drop. But her Slavic yells at her son are a different matter, the words fly swift and true, well-aimed missiles that never miss. Finally, the son slams down the hood in disgust, wipes his hands on a rag, accompanies mother Berthe inside.

Berthe's husband has a job in a factory. But he loses several days of work every month when he succumbs to the booze, a word Berthe uses often in her Slavic tirades on those days, the only one I can understand, as it clunks down heavily out of the tight-flying formation of Yugoslavian sentences. He lolls around in the lobby, submitting passively to his wife's tongue-lashings. The bags under his bloodshot eyes, his stringy moustache, stubbled chin, dirty hair are so vulnerable to the poison-laden barbs (poison works the same way in any language) emanating from deep within the powerful watermelon bosom. No one's presence can embarrass or dignify her into silence.

No one except the old man who arrives now. "Good morning," he says, and Berthe turns, stops yelling, and smiles. Her husband rises, positions the wheelchair at the favourite angle. The lobby will be peaceful as long as the old man is there.

It was hopeless. My first swimming lesson. The water terrified me. When did that happen, I wonder, I used to love splashing at Chaupatty, carried about by the waves. And this was only a swimming pool. Where did all that terror come from? I'm trying to remember.

Armed with my Surf King I enter the high school and go to the pool area. A sheet with instructions for the new class is pinned to the bulletin board. All students must shower and then assemble at eight by the shallow end. As I enter the showers three young boys, probably from a previous class, emerge. One of them holds his nose. The second begins to hum, under his breath: Paki Paki, smell like curry. The third says to the first two: pretty soon all the water's going to taste of curry. They leave.

It's a mixed class, but the gorgeous woman of my fantasy is missing. I have to settle for another, in a pink one-piece suit, with brown hair and a bit of a stomach. She must be about thirty-five. Plain-looking.

The instructor is called Ron. He gives us a pep talk, sensing some nervousness in the group. We're finally all in the water, in the shallow end. He demonstrates floating on the back, then asks for a volunteer. The pink one-piece suit wades forward. He supports her, tells her to lean back and let her head drop in the water.

She does very well. And as we all regard her floating body, I see what was not visible outside the pool: her bush, curly bits of it, straying out at the pink Spandex V. Tongues of water lapping against her delta, as if caressing it teasingly, make the brown hair come alive in a most tantalizing manner. The crests and troughs of little waves, set off by the movement of our bodies in a circle around her, dutifully irrigate her; the curls alternately wave free inside the crest, then adhere to her wet thighs, beached by the inevitable trough. I could watch this forever, and I wish the floating demonstration would never end.

Next we are shown how to grasp the rail and paddle, face down in the water. Between practising floating and paddling, the hour is almost gone. I have been trying to observe the pink one-piece suit, getting glimpses of her straying pubic hair from various angles. Finally, Ron wants a volunteer for the last demonstration, and I go forward. To my horror he leads the class to the deep end. Fifteen feet of water. It is so blue, and I can see the bottom. He picks up a metal hoop attached to a long wooden stick. He wants me to grasp the hoop, jump in the water, and paddle, while he guides me by the stick. Perfectly safe, he tells me. A demonstration of how paddling propels the body.

It's too late to back out; besides, I'm so terrified I couldn't find the words to do so even if I wanted to. Everything he says I do as if in a trance. I don't remember the moment of jumping. The next thing I know is, I'm swallowing water and floundering, hanging on to the hoop for dear life. Ron draws me to the rails and helps me out. The class applauds.

We disperse and one thought is on my mind: what if I'd lost my grip? Fifteen feet of water under me. I shudder and take deep breaths. This is it. I'm not coming next week. This instructor is an irresponsible person. Or he does not value the lives of non-white immigrants. I remember the three teenagers. Maybe the swimming pool is the hangout of some racist group, bent on eliminating all non-white swimmers, to keep their waters pure and their white sisters unogled.

The elevator takes me upstairs. Then gutang-khutang. PW opens her door as I turn the corridor of medicinal smells. "Berthe was screaming loudly at her husband tonight," she tells me.

"Good for her," I say, and she frowns indignantly at me.

The old man is in the lobby. He's wearing thick wool gloves. He wants to know how the swimming was, must have seen me leaving with my towel yesterday. Not bad, I say.

"I used to swim a lot. Very good for the circulation." He wheezes. "My feet are cold all the time. Cold as ice. Hands too."

Summer is winding down, so I say stupidly, "Yes, it's not so warm any more."

The thought of the next swimming lesson sickens me. But as I comb through the memories of that terrifying Monday, I come upon the straying curls of brown pubic hair. Inexorably drawn by them, I decide to go.

It's a mistake, of course. This time I'm scared even to venture in the shallow end. When everyone has entered the water and I'm the only one outside, I feel a little foolish and slide in.

Instructor Ron says we should start by reviewing the floating technique. I'm in no hurry. I watch the pink one-piece pull the swim-suit down around her cheeks and flip back to achieve perfect flotation. And then reap disappointment. The pink Spandex triangle is perfectly streamlined today, nothing strays, not a trace of fuzz, not one filament, not even a sign of post-depilation irritation. Like the airbrushed parts of glamour magazine models. The barrenness of her impeccably packaged apex is a betrayal. Now she is shorn like the other women in the class. Why did she have to do it?

The weight of this disappointment makes the water less manageable, more lung-penetrating. With trepidation, I float and paddle my way through the remainder of the hour, jerking my head out every two seconds and breathing deeply, to continually shore up a supply of precious, precious air without, at the same time, seeming too anxious and losing my dignity.

I don't attend the remaining classes. After I've missed three, Ron the instructor telephones. I tell him I've had the flu and am still feeling poorly, but I'll try to be there the following week.

He does not call again. My Surf King is relegated to an unused drawer. Total losses: one fantasy plus thirty dollars. And no watery rebirth. The swimming pool, like Chaupatty beach, has produced a stillbirth. But there is a difference. Water means regeneration only if it is pure and cleansing. Chaupatty was filthy, the pool was not. Failure to swim through filth must mean something other than failure of rebirth—failure of symbolic death? Does that equal success of symbolic life? death of a symbolic failure? death of a symbol? What is the equation?

The postman did not bring a letter but a parcel, he was smiling because he knew that every time something came from Canada his baksheesh was guaranteed, and this time because it was a parcel Mother gave him a whole rupee, she was quite excited, there were so many stickers on it besides the stamps, one for Small Parcel, another Printed Papers, a red sticker saying Insured; she showed it to Father, and opened it, then put both hands on her cheeks, not able to speak because the surprise and happiness was so great, tears came to her eyes and she could not stop smiling, till Father became impatient to know and finally got up and came to the table.

When he saw it he was surprised and happy too, he began to grin, then hugged Mother saying our son is a writer, and we didn't even know it, he never told us a thing, here we are thinking he is still clerking away at the insurance company, and he has written a book of stories, all these years in school and college he kept his talent hidden, making us think he was just like one of the boys in the Baag, shouting and playing the fool in the compound, and now what a surprise; then Father opened the book and began reading it, heading back to the easy chair, and Mother so excited, still holding his arm, walked with him, saying it was not fair him reading it first, she wanted to read it too, and they agreed that he would read the first story, then give it to her so she could also read it, and they would take turns in that manner.

Mother removed the staples from the padded envelope in which he had mailed the book, and threw them away, then straightened the folded edges of the envelope and put it away safely with the other envelopes and letters she had collected since he left.

The leaves are beginning to fall. The only ones I can identify are maple. The days are dwindling like the leaves. I've started a habit of taking long walks every evening. The old man is in the lobby when I leave, he waves as I go by. By the time I'm back, the lobby is usually empty.

Today I was woken up by a grating sound outside that made my flesh crawl. I went to the window and saw Berthe raking the leaves in the parking lot. Not in the expanse of patchy lawn on the periphery, but in the parking lot proper. She was raking the black tarred surface. I went back to bed and dragged a pillow over my head, not releasing it till noon.

When I return from my walk in the evening, PW, summoned by

the elevator's gutang-khutang, says, "Berthe filled six big black garbage bags with leaves today."

"Six bags!" I say. "Wow!"

Since the weather turned cold, Berthe's son does not tinker with his van on Sundays under my window. I'm able to sleep late.

Around eleven, there's a commotion outside. I reach out and switch on the clock radio. It's a sunny day, the window curtains are bright. I get up, curious, and see a black Olds Ninety-Eight in the parking lot, by the entrance to the building. The old man is in his wheelchair, bundled up, with a scarf wound several times round his neck as though to immobilize it, like a surgical collar. His daughter and another man, the car-owner, are helping him from the wheelchair into the front seat, encouraging him with words like: that's it, easy does it, attaboy. From the open door of the lobby, Berthe is shouting encouragement too, but hers is confined to one word: yah, repeated at different levels of pitch and volume, with variations on vowel-length. The stranger could be the old man's son, he has the same jet black hair and piercing eyes.

Maybe the old man is not well, it's an emergency. But I quickly scrap that thought—this isn't Bombay, an ambulance would have arrived. They're probably taking him out for a ride. If he is his son, where has he been all this time, I wonder.

The old man finally settles in the front seat, the wheelchair goes in the trunk, and they're off. The one I think is the son looks up and catches me at the window before I can move away, so I wave, and he waves back.

In the afternoon I take down a load of clothes to the laundry room. Both machines have completed their cycles, the clothes inside are waiting to be transferred to dryers. Should I remove them and place them on top of a dryer, or wait? I decide to wait. After a few minutes, two women arrive, they are in bathrobes, and smoking. It takes me a while to realize that these are the two disappointments who were sunbathing in bikinis last summer.

"You didn't have to wait, you could have removed the clothes and carried on, dear," says one. She has a Scottish accent. It's one of the few I've learned to identify. Like maple leaves.

"Well," I say, "some people might not like strangers touching their clothes."

"You're not a stranger, dear," she says, "you live in this building, we've seen you before."

"Besides, your hands are clean," the other one pipes in. "You can touch my things any time you like."

Horny old cow. I wonder what they've got on under their bathrobes. Not much, I find, as they bend over to place their clothes in the dryers.

"See you soon," they say, and exit, leaving me behind in an erotic wake of smoke and perfume and deep images of cleavages. I start the washers and depart, and when I come back later, the dryers are empty.

PW tells me, "The old man's son took him out for a drive today. He has a big beautiful black car."

I see my chance, and shoot back: "Olds Ninety-Eight."

"What?"

"The car," I explain, "it's an Oldsmobile Ninety-Eight."

She does not like this at all, my giving her information. She is visibly nettled, and retreats with a sour face.

Mother and Father read the first five stories, and she was very sad after reading some of them, she said he must be so unhappy there, all his stories are about Bombay, he remembers every little thing about his childhood, he is thinking about it all the time even though he is ten thousand miles away, my poor son, I think he misses his home and us and everything he left behind, because if he likes it over there why would he not write stories about that, there must be so many new ideas that his new life could give him.

But Father did not agree with this, he said it did not mean that he was unhappy, all writers worked in the same way, they used their memories and experiences and made stories out of them, changing some things, adding some, imagining some, all writers were very good at remembering details of their lives.

Mother said, how can you be sure that he is remembering because he is a writer, or whether he started to write because he is unhappy and thinks of his past, and wants to save it all by making stories of it; and

Father said that is not a sensible question, anyway, it is now my turn to read the next story.

The first snow has fallen, and the air is crisp. It's not very deep, about two inches, just right to go for a walk in. I've been told that immigrants from hot countries always enjoy the snow the first year, maybe for a couple of years more, then inevitably the dread sets in, and the approach of winter gets them fretting and moping. On the other hand, if it hadn't been for my conversation with the woman at the swimming registration desk, they might now be saying that India is a nation of non-swimmers.

Berthe is outside, shovelling the snow off the walkway in the parking lot. She has a heavy, wide pusher which she wields expertly.

The old radiators in the apartment alarm me incessantly. They continue to broadcast a series of variations on death throes, and go from hot to cold and cold to hot at will, there's no controlling their temperature. I speak to Berthe about it in the lobby. The old man is there too, his chin seems to have sunk deeper into his chest, and his face is a yellowish grey.

"Nothing, not to worry about anything," says Berthe, dropping rough-hewn chunks of language around me. "Radiator no work, you tell me. You feel cold, you come to me, I keep you warm," and she opens her arms wide, laughing. I step back, and she advances, her breasts preceding her like the gallant prows of two ice-breakers. She looks at the old man to see if he is appreciating the act: "You no feel scared, I keep you safe and warm."

But the old man is staring outside, at the flakes of falling snow. What thoughts is he thinking as he watches them? Of childhood days, perhaps, and snowmen with hats and pipes, and snowball fights, and white Christmases, and Christmas trees? What will I think of, old in this country, when I sit and watch the snow come down? For me, it is already too late for snowmen and snowball fights, and all I will have is thoughts about childhood thoughts and dreams, built around snowscapes and winter-wonderlands on the Christmas cards so popular in Bombay; my snowmen and snowball fights and Christmas trees are in the pages of Enid Blyton's[4] books,

4. Widely read English writer (1897–1968) of children's books.

dispersed amidst the adventures of the Famous Five, and the Five Find-Outers, and the Secret Seven. My snowflakes are even less forgettable than the old man's, for they never melt.

It finally happened. The heat went. Not the usual intermittent coming and going, but out completely. Stone cold. The radiators are like ice. And so is everything else. There's no hot water. Naturally. It's the hot water that goes through the rads and heats them. Or is it the other way around? Is there no hot water because the rads have stopped circulating it? I don't care, I'm too cold to sort out the cause and effect relationship. Maybe there is no connection at all.

I dress quickly, put on my winter jacket, and go down to the lobby. The elevator is not working because the power is out, so I take the stairs. Several people are gathered, and Berthe has announced that she has telephoned the office, they are sending a man. I go back up the stairs. It's only one floor, the elevator is just a bad habit. Back in Firozsha Baag they were broken most of the time. The stairway enters the corridor outside the old man's apartment, and I think of his cold feet and hands. Poor man, it must be horrible for him without heat.

As I walk down the long hallway, I feel there's something different but can't pin it down. I look at the carpet, the ceiling, the wallpaper: it all seems the same. Maybe it's the freezing cold that imparts a feeling of difference.

PW opens her door: "The old man had another stroke yesterday. They took him to the hospital."

The medicinal smell. That's it. It's not in the hallway any more.

In the stories that he'd read so far Father said that all the Parsi families were poor or middle-class, but that was okay; nor did he mind that the seeds for the stories were picked from the sufferings of their own lives; but there should also have been something positive about Parsis, there was so much to be proud of: the great Tatas and their contribution to the steel industry, or Sir Dinshaw Petit in the textile industry who made Bombay the Manchester of the East, or Dadabhai Naoroji in the freedom movement, where he was the first to use the word swaraj, *and the first to be elected to the British Parliament where he carried on his campaign; he should have found some way to bring some of these wonderful* facts into his stories, what would people reading these stories think, those who did not know about Parsis—that the whole community was full of cranky, bigoted people; and in reality it was the richest, most advanced and philanthropic community in India, and he did not need to tell his own son that Parsis had a reputation for being generous and family-oriented. And he could have written something also about the historic background, how Parsis came to India from Persia because of Islamic persecution in the seventh century, and were the descendants of Cyrus the Great and the magnificent Persian Empire. He could have made a story of all this, couldn't he?

Mother said what she liked best was his remembering everything so well, how beautifully he wrote about it all, even the sad things, and though he changed some of it, and used his imagination, there was truth in it.

My hope is, Father said, that there will be some story based on his Canadian experience, that way we will know something about our son's life there, if not through his letters then in his stories; so far they are all about Parsis and Bombay, and the one with a little bit about Toronto, where a man perches on top of the toilet, is shameful and disgusting, although it is funny at times and did make me laugh, I have to admit, but where does he get such an imagination from, what is the point of such a fantasy; and Mother said that she would also enjoy some stories about Toronto and the people there; it puzzles me, she said, why he writes nothing about it, especially since you say that writers use their own experience to make stories out of.

Then Father said this is true, but he is probably not using his Toronto experience because it is too early; what do you mean, too early; asked Mother and Father explained it takes a writer about ten years time after an experience before he is able to use it in his writing, it takes that long to be absorbed internally and understood, thought out and thought about, over and over again, he haunts it and it haunts him if it is valuable enough, till the writer is comfortable with it to be able to use it as he wants; but this is only one theory I read somewhere, it may or may not be true.

That means, said Mother, that his childhood in Bombay and our home here is the most valuable thing in his life just now, because he is able to remember it all to write about it, and you were so bitterly saying he is forgetting where he came from; and that may be true, said Father, *but that is not what the theory means, according to the theory he is writing of these things because they are far enough in the past for him to deal with objectively, he is able to achieve what critics call artistic distance, without emotions interfering; and what do you mean emotions, said Mother, you are saying he does not feel anything for his characters, how can he write so beautifully about so many sad things without any feelings in his heart?*

But before Father could explain more, about beauty and emotion and inspiration and imagination, Mother took the book and said it was her turn now and too much theory she did not want to listen to, it was confusing and did not make as much sense as reading the stories, she would read them her way and Father could read them his.

My books on the windowsill have been damaged. Ice has been forming on the inside ledge, which I did not notice, and melting when the sun shines in. I spread them in a corner of the living-room to dry out.

The winter drags on. Berthe wields her snow pusher as expertly as ever, but there are signs of weariness in her performance. Neither husband nor son is ever seen outside with a shovel. Or anywhere else, for that matter. It occurs to me that the son's van is missing, too.

The medicinal smell is in the hall again, I sniff happily and look forward to seeing the old man in the lobby. I go downstairs and peer into the mailbox, see the blue and magenta of an Indian aerogramme with Don Mills, Ontario, Canada in Father's flawless hand through the slot.

I pocket the letter and enter the main lobby. The old man is there, but not in his usual place. He is not looking out through the glass door. His wheelchair is facing a bare wall where the wallpaper is torn in places. As though he is not interested in the outside world any more, having finished with all that, and now it's time to see inside. What does he see inside, I wonder? I go up to him and say hullo. He says hullo without raising his sunken chin. After a few seconds his grey countenance faces me. "How old do you think I am?" His eyes are dull and glazed; he is looking even further inside than I first presumed.

"Well, let's see, you're probably close to sixty-four."

"I'll be seventy-eight next August." But he does not chuckle or wheeze. Instead, he continues softly, "I wish my feet did not feel so cold all the time. And my hands." He lets his chin fall again.

In the elevator I start opening the aerogramme, a tricky business because a crooked tear means lost words. Absorbed in this while emerging, I don't notice PW occupying the centre of the hallway, arms folded across her chest: "They had a big fight. Both of them have left."

I don't immediately understand her agitation. "What . . . who?"

"Berthe. Husband and son both left her. Now she is all alone."

Her tone and stance suggest that we should not be standing here talking but do something to bring Berthe's family back. "That's very sad," I say, and go in. I picture father and son in the van, driving away, driving across the snow-covered country, in the dead of winter, away from wife and mother; away to where? how far will they go? Not son's van nor father's booze can take them far enough. And the further they go, the more they'll remember, they can take it from me.

All the stories were read by Father and Mother, and they were sorry when the book was finished, they felt they had come to know their son better now, yet there was much more to know, they wished there were many more stories; and this is what they mean, said Father, when they say that the whole story can never be told, the whole truth can never be known; what do you mean, they say, asked Mother, who they, and Father said writers, poets, philosophers. I don't care what they say, said Mother, my son will write as much or as little as he wants to, and if I can read it I will be happy.

The last story they liked the best of all because it had the most in it about Canada, and now they felt they knew at least a little bit, even if it was a very little bit, about his day-to-day life in his apartment; and Father said if he continues to write about such things he will become popular because I am sure they are interested there in reading about life through the eyes of an immigrant, it provides a different viewpoint; the only danger is if he changes and becomes so much like them that he will write like one of them and lose the important difference.

The bathroom needs cleaning. I open a new can of Ajax and scour the tub. Sloshing with mug from bucket was standard bathing procedure in the bathrooms of Firozsha Baag, so my preference now is always for a shower. I've never used the tub as yet; besides, it would be too much like Chaupatty or the swimming pool, wallowing in my own dirt. Still, it must be cleaned.

When I've finished, I prepare for a shower. But the clean gleaming tub and the nearness of the vernal equinox give me the urge to do something different today. I find the drain plug in the bathroom cabinet, and run the bath.

I've spoken so often to the old man, but I don't know his name. I should have asked him the last time I saw him, when his wheelchair was facing the bare wall because he had seen all there was to see outside and it was time to see what was inside. Well, tomorrow. Or better yet, I can look it up in the directory in the lobby. Why didn't I think of that before? It will only have an initial and a last name, but then I can surprise him with: hullo Mr Wilson, or whatever it is.

The bath is full. Water imagery is recurring in my life: Chaupatty beach, swimming pool, bathtub. I step in and immerse myself up to the neck. It feels good. The hot water loses its opacity when the chlorine, or whatever it is, has cleared. My hair is still dry. I close my eyes, hold my breath, and dunk my head. Fighting the panic, I stay under and count to thirty. I come out, clear my lungs and breathe deeply.

I do it again. This time I open my eyes under water, and stare blindly without seeing, it takes all my will to keep the lids from closing. Then I am slowly able to discern the underwater objects. The drain plug looks different, slightly distorted; there is a hair trapped between the hole and the plug, it waves and dances with the movement of the water. I come up, refresh my lungs, examine quickly the overwater world of the washroom, and go in again. I do it several times, over and over. The world outside the water I have seen a lot of, it is now time to see what is inside.

The spring session for adult non-swimmers will begin in a few days at the high school. I must not forget the registration date.

The dwindled days of winter are now all but forgotten; they have grown and attained a respectable span. I resume my evening walks, it's spring, and a vigorous thaw is on. The snowbanks are melting, the sound of water on its gushing, gurgling journey to the drains is beautiful. I plan to buy a book of trees, so I can identify more than the maple as they begin to bloom.

When I return to the building, I wipe my feet energetically on the mat because some people are entering behind me, and I want to set a good example. Then I go to the board with its little plastic letters and numbers. The old man's apartment is the one on the corner by the stairway, that makes it number 201. I run down the list, come to 201, but there are no little white plastic letters beside it. Just the empty black rectangle with holes where the letters would be squeezed in. That's strange. Well, I can introduce myself to him, then ask his name.

However, the lobby is empty. I take the elevator, exit at the second floor, wait for the gutang-khutang. It does not come: the door closes noiselessly, smoothly. Berthe has been at work, or has made sure someone else has. PW's cue has been lubricated out of existence.

But she must have the ears of a cockroach. She is waiting for me. I whistle my way down the corridor. She fixes me with an accusing look. She waits till I stop whistling, then says: "You know the old man died last night."

I cease groping for my key. She turns to go and I take a step towards her, my hand still in my trouser pocket. "Did you know his name?" I ask, but she leaves without answering.

Then Mother said, the part I like best in the last story is about Grandpa, where he wonders if Grandpa's spirit is really watching him and blessing him, because you know I really told him that, I told him helping an old suffering person who is near death is the most blessed thing to do, because that person will ever after watch over you from heaven, I told him this when he was disgusted with Grandpa's urine-bottle and would not touch it, would not hand it to him even when I was not at home.

Are you sure, said Father, that you really told him this, or you believe you told him because you like the sound of it, you said yourself the other day that he changes and adds and alters things in the stories but he writes it all so beautifully that it seems true, so how can you be sure; this sounds like another theory, said Mother, but I don't care, he says I told him and I believe now I told him, so even if I did not tell him then it does not matter now.

Don't you see, said Father, that you are confusing fiction with facts, fiction does not create facts, fiction can come from facts, it can grow out of facts by compounding, transposing, augmenting, diminishing, or altering them in any way; but you must not confuse cause and effect, you must not confuse what really happened with what the story says happened, you must not loose your grasp on reality, that way madness lies.

Then Mother stopped listening because, as she told Father so often, she was not very fond of theories, and she took out her writing pad and started a letter to her son; Father looked over her shoulder, telling her to say how proud they were of him and were waiting for his next book, he also said, leave a little space for me at the end, I want to write a few lines when I put the address on the envelope.

1992

Susanna Moodie
1803–1885

Moodie is a successor to people like David Thompson, explorers who mapped the interior of North America. Born in Suffolk, England, she was part of the literary Strickland family, and through all her troubles in the early settlements of what is now eastern Ontario, Moodie was determined to be a writer. She has been a figurehead, if not a model, for other women writing in Canada.

Moodie's Roughing it in the Bush *(1852) is now a Canadian classic, but it was written for people like herself in England to discourage them from emigrating to a difficult life in the wilderness. Unlike the early explorers who were passing through and recording what they saw, Moodie tells stories about trying to make a home in this strange—to her—place.*

Writing in the early nineteenth century, Susanna Moodie was heavily influenced by its style, which valued emotional reaction to anything observed or experienced. She records her feelings about the grandeur of nature, the ignorance of people she meets, her difficulties in unfamiliar situations, and her nostalgia for home, represented by things like fine china.

This piece is taken from Roughing it in the Bush, *which was supposedly a diary of Moodie's life in the woods. Although it is non-fiction and heavily documentary, it was obviously written for publication and uses conversation, character development, and even loosely constructed plot. Moodie's writing often blurs the line between fact and fiction, but is always presented through her own sensibility, in the fashion of her time.*

Sisters in the Wilderness *(1999) by Charlotte Gray is a highly readable biography of Susanna Moodie and her sister Catherine Parr Traill, who also wrote about early British settlement in Canada.*

A Journey to the Woods

'Tis well for us poor denizens of earth
That God conceals the future from our gaze;
Or Hope, the blessed watcher on Life's tower,
Would fold her wings, and on the dreary waste
Close the bright eye that through the murky clouds
Of blank Despair still sees the glorious sun.

It was a bright, frosty morning when I bade adieu to the farm, the birthplace of my little Agnes, who, nestled beneath my cloak, was sweetly sleeping on my knee, unconscious of the long journey before us into the wilderness. The sun had not as yet risen. Anxious to get to our place of destination before dark, we started as early as we could. Our own fine team had been sold the day before for forty pounds; and one of our neighbours, a Mr. D——,[1] was to convey us and our household goods to Douro[2] for the sum of twenty dollars. During the week he had made several journeys, with furniture and stores; and all that now remained was to be conveyed to the woods in two large lumber-sleighs, one driven by himself, the other by a younger brother.

---

1. Early nineteenth-century convention of not using proper names in print, a mark of respect.

2. Settlement in eastern Ontario.

It was not without regret that I left Melsetter, for so my husband had called the place, after his father's estate in Orkney. It was a beautiful, picturesque spot; and, in spite of the evil neighbourhood, I had learned to love it; indeed, it was much against my wish that it was sold. I had a great dislike to removing, which involves a necessary loss, and is apt to give to the emigrant roving and unsettled habits. But all regrets were now useless; and happily unconscious of the life of toil and anxiety that awaited us in those dreadful woods, I tried my best to be cheerful, and to regard the future with a hopeful eye.

Our driver was a shrewd, clever man, for his opportunities. He took charge of the living cargo, which consisted of my husband, our maid-servant, the two little children, and myself—besides a large hamper, full of poultry—a dog, and a cat. The lordly sultan of the imprisoned seraglio thought fit to conduct himself in a very eccentric manner, for at every barnyard we happened to pass, he clapped his wings, and crowed so long and loud that it afforded great amusement to the whole party, and doubtless was very edifying to the poor hens, who lay huddled together as mute as mice.

"That 'ere rooster thinks he's on the top of the heap," said our driver, laughing. "I guess he's not used to travelling in a close conveyance. Listen! How all the crowers in the neighbourhood give him back a note of defiance! But he knows that he's safe enough at the bottom of the basket."

The day was so bright for the time of year (the first week in February), that we suffered no inconvenience from the cold. Little Katie was enchanted with the jingling of the sleigh-bells, and, nestled among the packages, kept singing or talking to the horses in her baby lingo. Trifling as these little incidents were, before we had proceeded ten miles on our long journey, they revived my drooping spirits, and I began to feel a lively interest in the scenes through which we were passing.

The first twenty miles of the way was over a hilly and well-cleared country; and as in winter the deep snow fills up the inequalities, and makes all roads alike, we glided as swiftly and steadily along as if they had been the best highways in the world. Anon, the clearings began to diminish, and tall woods arose on either side of the path; their solemn aspect, and the deep silence that brooded over their vast solitudes, inspiring the mind with a strange awe. Not a breath of wind stirred the leafless branches, whose huge shadows, reflected upon the dazzling white covering of snow, lay so perfectly still, that it seemed as if Nature had suspended her operations, that life and motion had ceased, and that she was sleeping in her winding-sheet, upon the bier of death.

"I guess you will find the woods pretty lonesome," said our driver, whose thoughts had been evidently employed on the same subject as our own. "We were once in the woods, but emigration has stepped ahead of us, and made our'n a cleared part of the country. When I was a boy, all this country, for thirty miles on every side of us, was bush land. As to Peterborough, the place was unknown; not a settler had ever passed through the great swamp, and some of them believed that it was the end of the world."

"What swamp is that?" asked I.

"Oh, the great Cavan swamp. We are just two miles from it; and I tell you the horses will need a good rest, and ourselves a good dinner, by the time we are through it. Ah! Mrs. Moodie, if ever you travel that way in summer, you will know something about corduroy roads. I was 'most jolted to death last fall; I thought it would have been no bad notion to have insured my teeth before I left C——. I really expected that they would have been shook out of my head before we had done manœuvering over the big logs."

"How will my crockery stand it in the next sleigh?" quoth I. "If the road is such as you describe, I am afraid that I shall not bring a whole plate to Douro."

"Oh! the snow is a great leveller—it makes all rough places smooth. But with regard to this swamp, I have something to tell you. About ten years ago, no one had ever seen the other side of it; and if pigs or cattle strayed away into it, they fell a prey to the wolves and bears, and were seldom recovered.

"An old Scotch emigrant, who had located himself on this side of it, so often lost his beasts that he determined during the summer season to try and explore the place, and see if there were any end to it. So he takes an axe on his shoulder, and a bag of provisions for the week, not forgetting a flask of whiskey, and off he starts all alone, and tells his wife that if he never returned, she and little Jock must try and carry on the farm without him; but he was determined to

see the end of the swamp, even if it led to the other world. He fell
upon a fresh cattle-track, which he followed all that day; and towards night he found himself in the heart of a tangled wilderness of
bushes, and himself half eaten up with mosquitoes and black-flies.
He was more than tempted to give in, and return home by the first
glimpse of light.

"The Scotch are a tough people; they are not easily daunted—a
few difficulties only seem to make them more eager to get on; and
he felt ashamed the next moment, as he told me, of giving up. So he
finds out a large, thick cedar-tree for his bed, climbs up, and coiling
himself among the branches like a bear, he was soon fast asleep.

"The next morning, by daylight, he continued his journey, not
forgetting to blaze with his axe the trees to the right and left as he
went along. The ground was so spongy and wet that at every step he
plunged up to his knees in water, but he seemed no nearer the end
of the swamp than he had been the day before. He saw several deer,
a raccoon, and a groundhog, during his walk, but was unmolested
by bears or wolves. Having passed through several creeks, and killed
a great many snakes, he felt so weary towards the second day that he
determined to go home the next morning. But just as he began to
think his search was fruitless, he observed that the cedars and tama-
racks which had obstructed his path became less numerous, and
were succeeded by bass and soft maple. The ground, also, became
less moist, and he was soon ascending a rising slope, covered with
oak and beech, which shaded land of the very best quality. The old
man was now fully convinced that he had cleared the great swamp;
and that, instead of leading to the other world, it had conducted
him to a country that would yield the very best returns for cultiva-
tion. His favourable report led to the formation of the road that we
are about to cross, and to the settlement of Peterborough, which is
one of the most promising new settlements in this district, and is
surrounded by a splendid back country."

We were descending a very steep hill, and encountered an ox-
sleigh, which was crawling slowly up it in a contrary direction.
Three people were seated at the bottom of the vehicle upon straw,
which made a cheap substitute for buffalo robes. Perched, as we
were, upon the crown of the height, we looked completely down
into the sleigh, and during the whole course of my life I never saw

three uglier mortals collected into such a narrow space. The man was blear-eyed, with a hare-lip, through which protruded two dreadful yellow teeth which resembled the tusks of a boar. The woman was long-faced, high cheek-boned, red-haired, and freckled all over like a toad. The boy resembled his hideous mother, but with the addition of a villainous obliquity of vision which rendered him the most disgusting object in this singular trio.

As we passed them, our driver gave a knowing nod to my husband, directing, at the same time, the most quizzical glance towards the strangers, as he exclaimed, "We are in luck, sir! I think that 'ere sleigh may be called Beauty's egg-basket!"

We made ourselves very merry at the poor people's expense, and Mr. D——, with his odd stories and Yankeefied expressions, amused the tedium of our progress through the great swamp, which in summer presents for several miles one uniform bridge of rough and unequal logs, all laid loosely across huge sleepers, so that they jumped up and down, when pressed by the wheels, like the keys of a piano. The rough motion and jolting occasioned by this collision is so distressing that it never fails to entail upon the traveller sore bones and an aching head for the rest of the day. The path is so narrow over these logs that two wagons cannot pass without great difficulty, which is rendered more dangerous by the deep natural ditches on either side of the bridge, formed by broad creeks that flow out of the swamp, and often terminate in mud-holes of very ominous dimensions. The snow, however, hid from us all the ugly features of the road, and Mr. D—— steered us through it in perfect safety, and landed us at the door of a little log house which crowned the steep hill on the other side of the swamp, and which he dignified with the name of a tavern.

It was now two o'clock. We had been on the road since seven; and men, women, and children were all ready for the good dinner that Mr. D—— had promised us at this splendid house of entertainment, where we were destined to stay for two hours, to refresh ourselves and rest the horses.

"Well, Mrs. J——, what have you got for our dinner?" said the driver, after he had seen to the accommodation of his teams.

"Pritters and pork, sir. Nothing else to be had in the woods. Thank God, we have enough of that!"

D—— shrugged up his shoulders, and looked at us.

"We've plenty of that same at home. But hunger's good sauce. Come, be spry, widow, and see about it, for I am very hungry."

I inquired for a private room for myself and the children, but there were no private rooms in the house. The apartment we occupied was like the cobbler's stall in the old song, and I was obliged to attend upon them in public.

"You have much to learn, ma'am, if you are going to the woods," said Mrs. J——.

"To unlearn, you mean," said Mr. D——. "To tell you the truth, Mrs. Moodie, ladies and gentlemen have no business in the woods. Eddication spoils man or woman for that location. So, widow (turning to our hostess), you are not tired of living alone yet?"

"No, sir; I have no wish for a second husband. I had enough of the first. I like to have my own way—to lie down mistress, and get up master."

"You don't like to be put out of your *old* way," returned he, with a mischievous glance.

She coloured very red; but it might be the heat of the fire over which she was frying the pork for our dinner.

I was very hungry, but I felt no appetite for the dish she was preparing for us. It proved salt, hard, and unsavoury.

D—— pronounced it very bad, and the whiskey still worse, with which he washed it down.

I asked for a cup of tea and a slice of bread. But they were out of tea, and the hop-rising had failed, and there was no bread in the house. For this disgusting meal we paid at the rate of a quarter of a dollar a-head.

I was glad when, the horses being again put to, we escaped from the rank odour of the fried pork, and were once more in the fresh air.

"Well, mister; did not you grudge your money for that bad meat?" said D——, when we were once more seated in the sleigh. "But in these parts, the worse the fare the higher the charge."

"I would not have cared," said I, "if I could have got a cup of tea."

"Tea! it's poor trash. I never could drink tea in my life. But I like coffee, when 'tis boiled till it's quite black. But coffee is not good without plenty of trimmings."

"What do you mean by trimmings?"

He laughed. "Good sugar, and sweet cream. Coffee is not worth drinking without trimmings."

Often in after years have I recalled the coffee trimmings, when endeavouring to drink the vile stuff which goes by the name of coffee in the houses of entertainment in the country.

We had now passed through the narrow strip of clearing which surrounded the tavern, and again entered upon the woods. It was near sunset, and we were rapidly descending a steep hill, when one of the traces that held our sleigh suddenly broke. D—— pulled up in order to repair the damage. His brother's team was close behind, and our unexpected stand-still brought the horses upon us before J. D—— could stop them. I received so violent a blow from the head of one of them, just in the back of the neck, that for a few minutes I was stunned and insensible. When I recovered, I was supported in the arms of my husband, over whose knees I was leaning, and D—— was rubbing my hands and temples with snow.

"There, Mr. Moodie, she's coming to. I thought she was killed. I have seen a man before now killed by a blow from a horse's head in the like manner." As soon as we could, we resumed our places in the sleigh; but all enjoyment of our journey, had it been otherwise possible, was gone.

When we reached Peterborough, Moodie wished us to remain at the inn all night, as we had still eleven miles of our journey to perform, and that through a blazed forest-road, little travelled, and very much impeded by fallen trees and other obstacles; but D—— was anxious to get back as soon as possible to his own home, and he urged us very pathetically to proceed.

The moon arose during our stay at the inn, and gleamed upon the straggling frame houses which then formed the now populous and thriving town of Peterborough. We crossed the wild, rushing, beautiful Otonabee river by a rude bridge, and soon found ourselves journeying over the plains or level heights beyond the village, which were thinly wooded with picturesque groups of oak and pine, and very much resembled a gentleman's park at home. Far below, to our right (for we were upon the Smith-town side) we heard the rushing of the river, whose rapid waters never receive curb from the iron chain of winter. Even while the rocky banks are coated with ice, and the frost-king suspends from every twig and branch the most beautiful and fantastic crystals, the black waters rush foaming along, a thick steam rising constantly above the rapids, as from a boiling pot. The shores vibrate and tremble beneath the force of the impetuous flood, as it whirls round cedar-crowned islands and opposing rocks, and hurries on to pour its tribute into the Rice Lake, to swell the calm, majestic grandeur of the Trent, till its waters are lost in the beautiful bay of Quinté, and finally merged in the blue ocean of Ontario.[3]

The most renowned of our English rivers dwindle into little muddy rills when compared with the sublimity of the Canadian waters. No language can adequately express the solemn grandeur of her lake and river scenery; the glorious islands that float, like visions from fairy land, upon the bosom of these azure mirrors of her cloudless skies. No dreary breadth of marshes, covered with flags,[4] hide from our gaze the expanse of heaven-tinted waters; no foul mud-banks spread their unwholesome exhalations around. The rocky shores are crowned with the cedar, the birch, the alder, and soft maple, that dip their long tresses in the pure stream; from every crevice in the limestone the harebell and Canadian rose wave their graceful blossoms.

The fiercest droughts of summer may diminish the volume and power of these romantic streams, but it never leaves their rocky channels bare, nor checks the mournful music of their dancing waves. Through the openings in the forest, we now and then caught the silver gleam of the river tumbling on in moonlight splendour, while the hoarse chiding of the wind in the lofty pines above us gave a fitting response to the melancholy cadence of the waters.

The children had fallen asleep. A deep silence pervaded the party. Night was above us with her mysterious stars. The ancient forest stretched around us on every side, and a foreboding sadness sunk upon my heart. Memory was busy with the events of many years. I retraced step by step the pilgrimage of my past life, until arriving at that passage in its sombre history, I gazed through tears upon the singularly savage scene around me, and secretly marvelled, "What brought me here?"

3. Lake Ontario.   4. Flowers: irises.

"Providence,"[5] was the answer which the soul gave. "Not for your own welfare, perhaps, but for the welfare of your children, the unerring hand of the great Father has led you here. You form a connecting link in the destinies of many. It is impossible for any human creature to live for himself alone. It may be your lot to suffer, but others will reap a benefit from your trials. Look up with confidence to Heaven, and the sun of hope will yet shed a cheering beam through the forbidden depths of this tangled wilderness."

The road became so bad that Mr. D—— was obliged to dismount, and lead his horses through the more intricate passages. The animals themselves, weary with their long journey and heavy load, proceeded at foot-fall. The moon, too, had deserted us, and the only light we had to guide us through the dim arches of the forest was from the snow and the stars, which now peered down upon us through the leafless branches of the trees, with uncommon brilliancy.

"It will be past midnight before we reach your brother's clearing," (where we expected to spend the night,) said D——. "I wish, Mr. Moodie, we had followed your advice, and staid at Peterborough. How fares it with you, Mrs. Moodie, and the young ones? It is growing very cold."

We were now in the heart of a dark cedar swamp, and my mind was haunted with visions of wolves and bears; but beyond the long, wild howl of a solitary wolf, no other sound awoke the sepulchral silence of that dismal-looking wood.

"What a gloomy spot," said I to my husband. "In the old country, superstition would people it with ghosts."

"Ghosts! There are no ghosts in Canada!" said Mr. D——. "The country is too new for ghosts. No Canadian is afeard of ghosts. It is only in old countries, like your'n, that are full of sin and wickedness, that people believe in such nonsense. No human habitation has ever been erected in this wood through which you are passing. Until a very few years ago, few white persons had ever passed through it; and the Red Man would not pitch his tent in such a place as this. Now, ghosts, as I understand the word, are the spirits of bad men, that are not allowed by Providence to rest in their

5. God.

graves, but, for a punishment, are made to haunt the spots where their worst deeds were committed. I don't believe in all this; but, supposing it to be true, bad men must have died here before their spirits could haunt the place. Now, it is more than probable that no person ever ended his days in this forest, so that it would be folly to think of seeing his ghost."

This theory of Mr. D——'s had the merit of originality, and it is not improbable that the utter disbelief in supernatural appearances, which is common to most native-born Canadians, is the result of the same very reasonable mode of arguing. The unpeopled wastes of Canada must present the same aspect to the new settler that the world did to our first parents after their expulsion from the garden of Eden; all the sin which could defile the spot, or haunt it with the association of departed evil, is concentrated in their own persons. Bad spirits cannot be supposed to linger near a place where crime has never been committed. The belief in ghosts, so prevalent in old countries, must first have had its foundation in the consciousness of guilt.

After clearing this low, swampy portion of the wood, with much difficulty, and the frequent application of the axe, to cut away the fallen timber that impeded our progress, our ears were assailed by a low, roaring, rushing sound, as of the falling of waters.

"That is Herriot's Falls," said our guide. "We are within two miles of our destination."

Oh, welcome sound! But those two miles appeared more lengthy than the whole journey. Thick clouds, that threatened a snow-storm, had blotted out the stars, and we continued to grope our way through a narrow, rocky path, upon the edge of the river, in almost total darkness. I now felt the chillness of the midnight hour, and the fatigue of the long journey, with double force, and envied the servant and children, who had been sleeping ever since we left Peter-borough. We now descended the steep bank, and prepared to cross the rapids.

Dark as it was, I looked with a feeling of dread upon the foaming waters as they tumbled over their bed of rocks, their white crests flashing, life-like, amid the darkness of the night.

"This is an ugly bridge over such a dangerous place," said D——, as he stood up in the sleigh and urged his tired team across the miserable, insecure log-bridge, where darkness and death raged below, and one false step of his jaded horses would have plunged us into both. I must confess I drew a freer breath when the bridge was crossed, and D—— congratulated us on our safe arrival in Douro.

We now continued our journey along the left bank of the river, but when in sight of Mr. S——'s clearing, a large pine-tree, which had newly fallen across the narrow path, brought the teams to a stand-still. The mighty trunk which had lately formed one of the stately pillars in the sylvan temple of Nature, was of too large dimensions to chop in two with axes; and after half-an-hour's labour, which to me, poor, cold, weary wight![6] seemed an age, the males of the party abandoned the task in despair. To go round it was impossible; its roots were concealed in an impenetrable wall of cedar-jungle on the right-hand side of the road, and its huge branches hung over the precipitous bank of the river.

"We must try and make the horses jump over it," said D——. "We may get an upset, but there is no help for it; we must either make the experiment, or stay here all night, and I am too cold and hungry for that—so here goes." He urged his horses to leap the log; restraining their ardour for a moment as the sleigh rested on the top of the formidable barrier, but so nicely balanced, that the difference of a straw would almost have overturned the heavily laden vehicle and its helpless inmates. We, however, cleared it in safety. He now stopped, and gave directions to his brother to follow the same plan that he had adopted; but whether the young man had less coolness, or the horses in his team were more difficult to manage, I cannot tell: the sleigh, as it hung poised upon the top of the log, was overturned with a loud crash, and all my household goods and chattels were scattered over the road. Alas, for my crockery and stone china! scarcely one article remained unbroken.

"Never fret about the china," said Moodie; "thank God, the man and the horses are uninjured."

I should have felt more thankful had the crocks been spared too; for, like most of my sex, I had a tender regard for china, and I knew that no fresh supply could be obtained in this part of the world. Leaving his brother to collect the scattered fragments, D—— proceeded

6. Person.

on his journey. We left the road, and were winding our way over a steep hill, covered with heaps of brush and fallen timber, and as we reached the top, a light gleamed cheerily from the windows of a log house, and the next moment we were at my brother's door.

I thought my journey was at an end; but here I was doomed to fresh disappointment. His wife was absent on a visit to her friends, and it had been arranged that we were to to stay with my sister, Mrs. T——, and her husband. With all this I was unacquainted; and I was about to quit the sleigh and seek the warmth of the fire when I was told that I had yet further to go. Its cheerful glow was to shed no warmth on me, and, tired as I was, I actually buried my face and wept upon the neck of a hound which Moodie had given to Mr. S——, and which sprang up upon the sleigh to lick my face and hands. This was my first halt in that weary wilderness, where I endured so many bitter years of toil and sorrow. My brother-in-law and his family had retired to rest, but they instantly rose to receive the way-worn travellers; and I never enjoyed more heartily a warm welcome after a long day of intense fatigue, than I did that night of my first sojourn in the backwoods.

1852

Alice Munro
b. 1931

> Munro was born and grew up in Wingham, in southwestern Ontario, near Lake Huron. She lived for about twenty years in British Columbia, but then returned to Clinton, Ontario, to the area central to her work. Munro is Canada's celebrated and best-known writer of short fiction. She has published some ten volumes of stories, most of them prize winning. Each volume is as accomplished as the last, beginning with Dance of the Happy Shades (1968), which won the Governor General's Award. Munro's fiction often appears in The New Yorker and has been translated into many languages. Runaway (2004) is Munro's second book of short stories to win the Giller Prize, and she has been awarded the Governor General's Award for Fiction three times.

Munro says that she does not read a story only to find out what happens. The experience is, she suggests, more like entering a house and moving from room to room, investigating what is there, looking out through the windows to see how the world looks from in there.

Munro leaves a great deal unsaid in her stories, as do the people she writes about. But much happens in these silences. They can be ignored, bridged, filled in from events in the story itself, or added to from the reader's own life and imagining. These open spaces often make reading a Munro story seem like reading a novel.

The epilogue is a frequent Munro strategy to bring unexpected turns to a seemingly straightforward story. This piece from Friend of My Youth *(1990), like many of Munro's stories, includes several styles: poem, gossip, documentary, wishful thinking, newspaper report, obituary, tombstone inscription, and metafiction—fiction about fiction.*

Meneseteung

I

Columbine, bloodroot,
And wild bergamot,
Gathering armfuls,
Giddily we go.

*O*fferings the book is called. Gold lettering on a dull-blue cover. The author's full name underneath: Almeda Joynt Roth. The local paper, the *Vidette*, referred to her as "our poetess." There seems to be a mixture of respect and contempt, both for her calling and for her sex—or for their predictable conjuncture. In the front of the book is a photograph, with the photographer's name in one corner, and the date: 1865. The book was published later, in 1873.

The poetess has a long face; a rather long nose; full, sombre dark eyes, which seem ready to roll down her cheeks like giant tears; a lot of dark hair gathered around her face in droopy rolls and curtains. A streak of gray hair plain to see, although she is, in this picture, only twenty-five. Not a pretty girl but the sort of woman who may age well, who probably won't get fat. She wears a tucked and braid-trimmed dark dress or jacket, with a lacy, floppy arrangement of white material—frills or a bow—filling the deep V at the neck. She also wears a hat, which might be made of velvet, in a dark color to match the dress. It's the untrimmed, shapeless hat, something like a soft beret, that makes me see artistic intentions, or at least a shy and stubborn eccentricity, in this young woman, whose long neck and forward-inclining head indicate as well that she is tall and slender and somewhat awkward. From the waist up, she looks like a young nobleman of another century. But perhaps it was the fashion.

"In 1854," she writes in the preface to her book, "my father brought us—my mother, my sister Catherine, my brother William, and me—to the wilds of Canada West (as it then was). My father was a harness-maker by trade, but a cultivated man who could quote by heart from the Bible, Shakespeare, and the writings of Edmund Burke. He prospered in this newly opened land and was able to set up a harness and leather-goods store, and after a year to build the comfortable house in which I live (alone) today. I was fourteen years old, the eldest of the children, when we came into this country from Kingston, a town whose handsome streets I have not seen again but often remember. My sister was eleven and my brother nine. The third summer that we lived here, my brother and sister were taken ill of a prevalent fever and died within a few days of each other. My dear mother did not regain her spirits after this blow to our family. Her health declined, and after another three years she died. I then became housekeeper to my father and was happy to make his home for twelve years, until he died suddenly one morning at his shop.

"From my earliest years I have delighted in verse and I have occupied myself—and sometimes allayed my griefs, which have been no more, I know, than any sojourner on earth must encounter—with many floundering efforts at its composition. My fingers, indeed, were always too clumsy for crochetwork, and those dazzling productions of embroidery which one sees often today—the overflowing fruit and flower baskets, the little Dutch boys, the bonneted maidens with their watering cans—have likewise proved to be beyond my skill. So I offer instead, as the product of my leisure hours, these rude posies, these ballads, couplets, reflections."

Titles of some of the poems: "Children at Their Games," "The Gypsy Fair," "A Visit to My Family," "Angels in the Snow," "Champlain at the Mouth of the Meneseteung," "The Passing of the Old Forest," and "A Garden Medley." There are other, shorter poems, about birds and wildflowers and snowstorms. There is some comically intentioned doggerel about what people are thinking about as they listen to the sermon in church.

"Children at Their Games": The writer, a child, is playing with her brother and sister—one of those games in which children on different sides try to entice and catch each other. She plays on in the deepening twilight, until she realizes that she is alone, and much older. Still she hears the (ghostly) voices of her brother and sister calling. *Come over, come over, let Meda come over.* (Perhaps Almeda was called Meda in the family, or perhaps she shortened her name to fit the poem.)

"The Gypsy Fair": The Gypsies have an encampment near the town, a "fair," where they sell cloth and trinkets, and the writer as a child is afraid that she may be stolen by them, taken away from her family. Instead, her family has been taken away from her, stolen by Gypsies she can't locate or bargain with.

"A Visit to My Family": A visit to the cemetery, a one-sided conversation.

"Angels in the Snow": The writer once taught her brother and sister to make "angels" by lying down in the snow and moving their arms to create wing shapes. Her brother always jumped up carelessly, leaving an angel with a crippled wing. Will this be made perfect in Heaven, or will he be flying with his own makeshift, in circles?

"Champlain at the Mouth of the Meneseteung": This poem celebrates the popular, untrue belief that the explorer sailed down the eastern shore of Lake Huron and landed at the mouth of the major river.

"The Passing of the Old Forest": A list of all the trees—their names, appearance, and uses—that were cut down in the original forest, with a general description of the bears, wolves, eagles, deer, waterfowl.

"A Garden Medley": Perhaps planned as a companion to the forest poem. Catalogue of plants brought from European countries, with bits of history and legend attached, and final Canadianness resulting from this mixture.

The poems are written in quatrains or couplets. There are a couple of attempts at sonnets, but mostly the rhyme scheme is simple—*a b a b* or *a b c b*. The rhyme used is what was once called "masculine" ("shore"/"before"), though once in a while it is "feminine" ("quiver"/"river"). Are those terms familiar anymore? No poem is unrhymed.

II

White roses cold as snow
Bloom where those "angels" lie.
Do they but rest below
Or, in God's wonder, fly?

In 1879, Almeda Roth was still living in the house at the corner of Pearl and Dufferin streets, the house her father had built for his family. The house is there today; the manager of the liquor store lives in it. It's covered with aluminum siding; a closed-in porch has replaced the veranda. The woodshed, the fence, the gates, the privy, the barn—all these are gone. A photograph taken in the eighteen-eighties shows them all in place. The house and fence look a little shabby, in need of paint, but perhaps that is just because of the bleached-out look of the brownish photograph. The lace-curtained windows look like white eyes. No big shade tree is in sight, and, in fact, the tall elms that overshadowed the town until the nineteen-fifties, as well as the maples that shade it now, are skinny young trees with rough fences around them to protect them from the cows. Without the shelter of those trees, there is a great exposure—back yards, clotheslines, woodpiles, patchy sheds and barns and privies—all bare, exposed, provisional-looking. Few houses would have anything like a lawn, just a patch of plantains and anthills and raked dirt. Perhaps petunias growing on top of a stump, in a round box. Only the main street is gravelled; the other streets are dirt roads, muddy or dusty according to season. Yards must be fenced to keep animals out. Cows are tethered in vacant lots or pastured in back yards, but sometimes they get loose. Pigs get loose, too, and dogs roam free or nap in a lordly way on the boardwalks. The town has taken root, it's not going to vanish, yet it still has some of the look of an encampment. And, like an encampment, it's busy all the time—full of people, who, within the town, usually walk wherever they're going; full of animals, which leave horse buns, cow pats, dog turds that ladies have to hitch up their skirts for; full of the noise of building and of drivers shouting at their horses and of the trains that come in several times a day.

I read about that life in the *Vidette*.

The population is younger than it is now, than it will ever be again. People past fifty usually don't come to a raw, new place. There are quite a few people in the cemetery already, but most of them died young, in accidents or childbirth or epidemics. It's youth that's in evidence in town. Children—boys—rove through the streets in gangs. School is compulsory for only four months a year, and there are lots of occasional jobs that even a child of eight or nine can do—pulling flax, holding horses, delivering groceries, sweeping the boardwalk in front of stores. A good deal of time they spend looking for adventures. One day they follow an old woman, a drunk nicknamed Queen Aggie. They get her into a wheelbarrow and trundle her all over town, then dump her into a ditch to sober her up. They also spend a lot of time around the railway station. They jump on shunting cars and dart between them and dare each other to take chances, which once in a while result in their getting maimed or killed. And they keep an eye out for any strangers coming into town. They follow them, offer to carry their bags, and direct them (for a five-cent piece) to a hotel. Strangers who don't look so prosperous are taunted and tormented. Speculation surrounds all of them—it's like a cloud of flies. Are they coming to town to start up a new business, to persuade people to invest in some scheme, to sell cures or gimmicks, to preach on the street corners? All these things are possible any day of the week. Be on your guard, the *Vidette* tells people. These are times of opportunity and danger. Tramps, confidence men, hucksters, shysters, plain thieves are travelling the roads, and particularly the railroads. Thefts are announced: money invested and never seen again, a pair of trousers taken from the clothesline, wood from the woodpile, eggs from the henhouse. Such incidents increase in the hot weather.

Hot weather brings accidents, too. More horses run wild then, upsetting buggies. Hands caught in the wringer while doing the washing, a man lopped in two at the sawmill, a leaping boy killed in a fall of lumber at the lumberyard. Nobody sleeps well. Babies wither with summer complaint, and fat people can't catch their breath. Bodies must be buried in a hurry. One day a man goes through the streets ringing a cowbell and calling, "Repent! Repent!" It's not a stranger this time, it's a young man who works at the butcher shop. Take him home, wrap him in cold wet cloths, give him some nerve medicine, keep him in bed, pray for his wits. If he doesn't recover, he must go to the asylum.

Almeda Roth's house faces on Dufferin Street, which is a street of considerable respectability. On this street, merchants, a mill owner, an operator of salt wells have their houses. But Pearl Street, which her back windows overlook and her back gate opens onto, is another story. Workmen's houses are adjacent to hers. Small but decent row houses—that is all right. Things deteriorate toward the end of the block, and the next, last one becomes dismal. Nobody but the poorest people, the unrespectable and undeserving poor, would live there at the edge of a boghole (drained since then), called the Pearl Street Swamp. Bushy and luxuriant weeds grow there, makeshift shacks have been put up, there are piles of refuse and debris and crowds of runty children, slops are flung from doorways. The town tries to compel these people to build privies, but they would just as soon go in the bushes. If a gang of boys goes down there in search of adventure, it's likely they'll get more than they bargained for. It is said that even the town constable won't go down Pearl Street on a Saturday night. Almeda Roth has never walked past the row housing. In one of those houses lives the young girl Annie, who helps her with her housecleaning. That young girl herself, being a decent girl, has never walked down to the last block or the swamp. No decent woman ever would.

But that same swamp, lying to the east of Almeda Roth's house, presents a fine sight at dawn. Almeda sleeps at the back of the house. She keeps to the same bedroom she once shared with her sister Catherine—she would not think of moving to the large front bedroom, where her mother used to lie in bed all day, and which was later the solitary domain of her father. From her window she can see the sun rising, the swamp mist filling with light, the bulky, nearest trees floating against that mist and the trees behind turning transparent. Swamp oaks, soft maples, tamarack, bitternut.

III

Here where the river meets the inland sea,
Spreading her blue skirts from the solemn wood,
I think of birds and beasts and vanished men,
Whose pointed dwellings on these pale sands stood.

One of the strangers who arrived at the railway station a few years ago was Jarvis Poulter, who now occupies the next house to Almeda Roth's—separated from hers by a vacant lot, which he has bought, on Dufferin Street. The house is plainer than the Roth house and has no fruit trees or flowers planted around it. It is understood that this is a natural result of Jarvis Poulter's being a widower and living alone. A man may keep his house decent, but he will never—if he is a proper man—do much to decorate it. Marriage forces him to live with more ornament as well as sentiment, and it protects him, also, from the extremities of his own nature—from a frigid parsimony or a luxuriant sloth, from squalor, and from excessive sleeping or reading, drinking, smoking, or freethinking.

In the interests of economy, it is believed, a certain estimable gentleman of our town persists in fetching water form the public tap and supplementing his fuel supply by picking up the loose coal along the railway track. Does he think to repay the town or the railway company with a supply of free salt?

This is the *Vidette*, full of shy jokes, innuendo, plain accusation that no newspaper would get away with today. It's Jarvis Poulter they're talking about—though in other passages he is spoken of with great respect, as a civil magistrate, an employer, a churchman. He is close, that's all. An eccentric, to a degree. All of which may be a result of his single condition, his widower's life. Even carrying his water from the town tap and filling his coal pail along the railway track. This is a decent citizen, prosperous: a tall—slightly paunchy?—man in a dark suit with polished boots. A beard? Black hair streaked with gray. A severe and self-possessed air, and a large pale wart among the bushy hairs of one eyebrow? People talk about a young, pretty, beloved wife, dead in childbirth or some horrible accident, like a house fire or a railway disaster. There is no ground for this, but it adds interest. All he has told them is that his wife is dead.

He came to this part of the country looking for oil. The first oil well in the world was sunk in Lambton County, south of here, in the eighteen-fifties. Drilling for oil, Jarvis Poulter discovered salt. He set to work to make the most of that. When he walks home from church with Almeda Roth, he tells her about his salt wells. They are twelve hundred feet deep. Heated water is pumped down into them, and that dissolves the salt. Then the brine is pumped to the surface. It is poured into great evaporator pans over slow, steady fires, so that the water is steamed off and the pure, excellent salt remains. A commodity for which the demand will never fail.

"The salt of the earth," Almeda says.

"Yes," he says, frowning. He may think this disrespectful. She did not intend it so. He speaks of competitors in other towns who are following his lead and trying to hog the market. Fortunately, their wells are not drilled so deep, or their evaporating is not done so efficiently. There is salt everywhere under this land, but it is not so easy to come by as some people think.

Does this not mean, Almeda says, that there was once a great sea?

Very likely, Jarvis Poulter says. Very likely. He goes on to tell her about other enterprises of his—a brickyard, a limekiln. And he explains to her how this operates, and where the good clay is found. He also owns two farms, whose woodlots supply the fuel for his operations.

Among the couples strolling home from church on a recent, sunny Sabbath morning we noted a certain salty gentleman and literary lady, not perhaps in their first youth but by no means blighted by the frosts of age. May we surmise?

This kind of thing pops up in the *Vidette* all the time.

May they surmise, and is this courting? Almeda Roth has a bit of

money, which her father left her, and she has her house. She is not
too old to have a couple of children. She is a good enough housekeeper, with the tendency toward fancy iced cakes and decorated
tarts that is seen fairly often in old maids. (Honorable mention at
the Fall Fair.) There is nothing wrong with her looks, and naturally
she is in better shape than most married women of her age, not having been loaded down with work and children. But why was she
passed over in her earlier, more marriageable years, in a place that
needs women to be partnered and fruitful? She was a rather gloomy
girl—that may have been the trouble. The deaths of her brother and
sister, and then of her mother, who lost her reason, in fact, a year
before she died, and lay in her bed talking nonsense—those
weighed on her, so she was not lively company. And all that reading
and poetry—it seemed more of a drawback, a barrier, an obsession,
in the young girl than in the middle-aged woman, who needed
something, after all, to fill her time. Anyway, it's five years since her
book was published, so perhaps she has got over that. Perhaps it was
the proud, bookish father encouraging her?

Everyone takes it for granted that Almeda Roth is thinking of
Jarvis Poulter as a husband and would say yes if he asked her. And
she is thinking of him. She doesn't want to get her hopes up too
much, she doesn't want to make a fool of herself. She would like a
signal. If he attended church on Sunday evenings, there would be a
chance, during some months of the year, to walk home after dark.
He would carry a lantern. (There is as yet no street lighting in
town.) He would swing the lantern to light the way in front of the
lady's feet and observe their narrow and delicate shape. He might
catch her arm as they step off the boardwalk. But he does not go to
church at night.

Nor does he call for her, and walk with her *to* church on Sunday
mornings. That would be a declaration. He walks her home, past
his gate as far as hers; he lifts his hat then and leaves her. She does
not invite him to come in—a woman living alone could never do
such a thing. As soon as a man and woman of almost any age are
alone together within four walls, it is assumed that anything may
happen. Spontaneous combustion, instant fornication, an attack of
passion. Brute instinct, triumph of the senses. What possibilities
men and women must see in each other to infer such dangers. Or,

believing in the dangers, how often they must think about the possibilities.

When they walk side by side, she can smell his shaving soap, the barber's oil, his pipe tobacco, the wool and linen and leather smell of his manly clothes. The correct, orderly, heavy clothes are like those she used to brush and starch and iron for her father. She misses that job—her father's appreciation, his dark, kind authority. Jarvis Poulter's garments, his smell, his movements all cause the skin on the side of her body next to him to tingle hopefully, and a meek shiver raises the hairs on her arms. Is this to be taken as a sign of love? She thinks of him coming into her—*their*—bedroom in his long underwear and his hat. She knows this outfit is ridiculous, but in her mind he does not look so; he has the solemn effrontery of a figure in a dream. He comes into the room and lies down on the bed beside her, preparing to take her in his arms. Surely he removes his hat? She doesn't know, for at this point a fit of welcome and submission overtakes her, a buried gasp. He would be her husband.

One thing she has noticed about married women, and that is how many of them have to go about creating their husbands. They have to start ascribing preferences, opinions, dictatorial ways. Oh, yes, they say, my husband is very particular. He won't touch turnips. He won't eat fried meat. (Or he will only eat fried meat.) He likes me to wear blue (brown) all the time. He can't stand organ music. He hates to see a woman go out bareheaded. He would kill me if I took one puff of tobacco. This way, bewildered, sidelong-looking men are made over, made into husbands, heads of households. Almeda Roth cannot imagine herself doing that. She wants a man who doesn't have to be made, who is firm already and determined and mysterious to her. She does not look for companionship. Men—except for her father—seem to her deprived in some way, incurious. No doubt that is necessary, so that they will do what they have to do. Would she herself, knowing that there was salt in the earth, discover how to get it out and sell it? Not likely. She would be thinking about the ancient sea. That kind of speculation is what Jarvis Poulter has, quite properly, no time for.

Instead of calling for her and walking her to church, Jarvis Poulter might make another, more venturesome declaration. He could hire a horse and take her for a drive out to the country. If he did this, she would be both glad and sorry. Glad to be beside him, driven by him, receiving this attention from him in front of the world. And sorry to have the countryside removed for her—filmed over, in a way, by his talk and preoccupations. The countryside that she has written about in her poems actually takes diligence and determination to see. Some things must be disregarded. Manure piles, of course, and boggy fields full of high, charred stumps, and great heaps of brush waiting for a good day for burning. The meandering creeks have been straightened, turned into ditches with high, muddy banks. Some of the crop fields and pasture fields are fenced with big, clumsy uprooted stumps; others are held in a crude stitchery of rail fences. The trees have all been cleared back to the woodlots. And the woodlots are all second growth. No trees along the roads or lanes or around the farmhouses, except a few that are newly planted, young and weedy-looking. Clusters of log barns—the grand barns that are to dominate the countryside for the next hundred years are just beginning to be built—and mean-looking log houses, and every four or five miles a ragged little settlement with a church and school and store and a blacksmith shop. A raw countryside just wrenched from the forest, but swarming with people. Every hundred acres is a farm, every farm has a family, most families have ten or twelve children. (This is the country that will send out wave after wave of settlers—it's already starting to send them—to northern Ontario and the West.) It's true that you can gather wildflowers in spring in the woodlots, but you'd have to walk through herds of horned cows to get to them.

IV

The Gypsies have departed.
Their camping-ground is bare.
Oh, boldly would I bargain now
At the Gypsy Fair.

Almeda suffers a good deal from sleeplessness, and the doctor has given her bromides and nerve medicine. She takes the bromides, but the drops gave her dreams that were too vivid and disturbing, so she has put the bottle by for an emergency. She told the doctor her eyeballs felt dry, like hot glass, and her joints ached. Don't read so much, he said, don't study; get yourself good and tired out with housework, take exercise. He believes that her troubles would clear up if she got married. He believes this in spite of the fact that most of his nerve medicine is prescribed for married women.

So Almeda cleans house and helps clean the church, she lends a hand to friends who are wallpapering or getting ready for a wedding, she bakes one of her famous cakes for the Sunday-school picnic. On a hot Saturday in August, she decides to make some grape jelly. Little jars of grape jelly will make fine Christmas presents, or offerings to the sick. But she started late in the day and the jelly is not made by nightfall. In fact, the hot pulp has just been dumped into the cheesecloth bag to strain out the juice. Almeda drinks some tea and eats a slice of cake with butter (a childish indulgence of hers), and that's all she wants for supper. She washes her hair at the sink and sponges off her body to be clean for Sunday. She doesn't light a lamp. She lies down on the bed with the window wide open and a sheet just up to her waist, and she does feel wonderfully tired. She can even feel a little breeze.

When she wakes up, the night seems fiery hot and full of threats. She lies sweating on her bed, and she has the impression that the noises she hears are knives and saws and axes—all angry implements chopping and jabbing and boring within her head. But it isn't true. As she comes further awake, she recognizes the sounds that she has heard sometimes before—the fracas of a summer Saturday night on Pearl Street. Usually the noise centers on a fight. People are drunk, there is a lot of protest and encouragement concerning the fight, somebody will scream, "Murder!" Once, there was a murder. But it didn't happen in a fight. An old man was stabbed to death in his shack, perhaps for a few dollars he kept in the mattress.

She gets out of bed and goes to the window. The night sky is clear, with no moon and with bright stars. Pegasus hangs straight ahead, over the swamp. Her father taught her that constellation— automatically, she counts its stars. Now she can make out distinct voices, individual contributions to the row. Some people, like herself, have evidently been wakened from sleep. "Shut up!" they are yelling. "Shut up that caterwauling or I'm going to come down and tan the arse off yez!"

But nobody shuts up. It's as if there were a ball of fire rolling up Pearl Street, shooting off sparks—only the fire is noise; it's yells and laughter and shrieks and curses, and the sparks are voices that shoot off alone. Two voices gradually distinguish themselves—a rising and falling howling cry and a steady throbbing, low-pitched stream of abuse that contains all those words which Almeda associates with danger and depravity and foul smells and disgusting sights. Some-one—the person crying out, "Kill me! Kill me now!"—is being beaten. A woman is being beaten. She keeps crying, "Kill me! Kill me!" and sometimes her mouth seems choked with blood. Yet there is something taunting and triumphant about her cry. There is some-thing theatrical about it. And the people around are calling out, "Stop it! Stop that!" or "Kill her! Kill her!" in a frenzy, as if at the theatre or a sporting match or a prizefight. Yes, thinks Almeda, she has noticed that before—it is always partly a charade with these people; there is a clumsy sort of parody, an exaggeration, a missed connection. As if anything they did—even a murder—might be something they didn't quite believe but were powerless to stop.

Now there is the sound of something thrown—a chair, a plank?—and of a woodpile or part of a fence giving way. A lot of newly surprised cries, the sound of running, people getting out of the way, and the commotion has come much closer. Almeda can see a figure in a light dress, bent over and running. That will be the woman. She has got hold of something like a stick of wood or a shingle, and she turns and flings it at the darker figure running after her.

"Ah, go get her!" the voices cry. "Go baste her one!"

Many fall back now; just the two figures come on and grapple, and break loose again, and finally fall down against Almeda's fence. The sound they make becomes very confused—gagging, vomiting, grunting, pounding. Then a long, vibrating, choking sound of pain and self-abasement, self-abandonment, which could come from ei-ther or both of them.

Almeda has backed away from the window and sat down on the bed. Is that the sound of murder she has heard? What is to be done, what is she to do? She must light a lantern, she must go downstairs and light a lantern—she must go out into the yard, she must go downstairs. Into the yard. The lantern. She falls over on her bed and pulls the pillow to her face. In a minute. The stairs, the lantern. She sees herself already down there, in the back hall, drawing the bolt of the back door. She falls asleep.

She wakes, startled, in the early light. She thinks there is a big crow sitting on her windowsill, talking in a disapproving but unsurprised way about the events of the night before. "Wake up and move the wheelbarrow!" it says to her, scolding, and she understands that it means something else by "wheelbarrow"—something foul and sorrowful. Then she is awake and sees that there is no such bird. She gets up at once and looks out the window.

Down against her fence there is a pale lump pressed—a body. *Wheelbarrow.*

She puts a wrapper over her nightdress and goes downstairs. The front rooms are still shadowy, the blinds down in the kitchen. Something goes *plop, plup,* in a leisurely, censorious way, reminding her of the conversation of the crow. It's just the grape juice, straining overnight. She pulls the bolt and goes out the back door. Spiders have draped their webs over the doorway in the night, and the hollyhocks are drooping, heavy with dew. By the fence, she parts the sticky hollyhocks and looks down and she can see.

A woman's body heaped up there, turned on her side with her face squashed down into the earth. Almeda can't see her face. But there is a bare breast let loose, brown nipple pulled long like a cow's teat, and a bare haunch and leg, the haunch showing a bruise as big as a sunflower. The unbruised skin is grayish, like a plucked, raw drumstick. Some kind of nightgown or all-purpose dress she has on. Smelling of vomit. Urine, drink, vomit.

Barefoot, in her nightgown and flimsy wrapper, Almeda runs away. She runs around the side of her house between the apple trees and the veranda; she opens the front gate and flees down Dufferin Street to Jarvis Poulter's house, which is the nearest to hers. She slaps the flat of her hand many times against the door.

"There is the body of a woman," she says when Jarvis Poulter appears at last. He is in his dark trousers, held up with braces, and his shirt is half unbuttoned, his face unshaven, his hair standing up on his head. "Mr. Poulter, excuse me. A body of a woman. At my back gate."

He looks at her fiercely. "Is she dead?"

His breath is dank, his face creased, his eyes bloodshot.

"Yes. I think murdered," says Almeda. She can see a little of his cheerless front hall. His hat on a chair. "In the night I woke up. I heard a racket down on Pearl Street," she says, struggling to keep her voice low and sensible. "I could hear this—pair. I could hear a man and a woman fighting."

He picks up his hat and puts it on his head. He closes and locks the front door, and puts the key in his pocket. They walk along the boardwalk and she sees that she is in her bare feet. She holds back what she feels a need to say next—that she is responsible, she could have run out with a lantern, she could have screamed (but who needed more screams?), she could have beat the man off. She could have run for help then, not now.

They turn down Pearl Street, instead of entering the Roth yard. Of course the body is still there. Hunched up, half bare, the same as before.

Jarvis Poulter doesn't hurry or halt. He walks straight over to the body and looks down at it, nudges the leg with the toe of his boot, just as you'd nudge a dog or a sow.

"You," he says, not too loudly but firmly, and nudges again.

Almeda tastes bile at the back of her throat.

"Alive," says Jarvis Poulter, and the woman confirms this. She stirs, she grunts weakly.

Almeda says, "I will get the doctor." If she had touched the woman, if she had forced herself to touch her, she would not have made such a mistake.

"Wait," says Jarvis Poulter. "Wait. Let's see if she can get up."

"Get up, now," he says to the woman. "Come on. Up, now. Up."

Now a startling thing happens. The body heaves itself onto all fours, the head is lifted—the hair all matted with blood and vomit—and the woman begins to bang this head, hard and rhythmically, against Almeda Roth's picket fence. As she bangs her head, she finds her voice and lets out an openmouthed yowl, full of strength and what sounds like an anguished pleasure.

"Far from dead," says Jarvis Poulter. "And I wouldn't bother the doctor."

"There's blood," says Almeda as the woman turns her smeared face.

"From her nose," he says. "Not fresh." He bends down and catches the horrid hair close to the scalp to stop the head-banging.

"You stop that, now," he says. "Stop it. Gwan home, now. Gwan home, where you belong." The sound coming out of the woman's mouth has stopped. He shakes her head slightly, warning her, before he lets go of her hair. "Gwan home!"

Released, the woman lunges forward, pulls herself to her feet. She can walk. She weaves and stumbles down the street, making intermittent, cautious noises of protest. Jarvis Poulter watches her for a moment to make sure that she's on her way. Then he finds a large burdock leaf, on which he wipes his hand. He says, "There goes your dead body!"

The back gate being locked, they walk around to the front. The front gate stands open. Almeda still feels sick. Her abdomen is bloated; she is hot and dizzy.

"The front door is locked," she says faintly. "I came out by the kitchen." If only he would leave her, she could go straight to the privy. But he follows. He follows her as far as the back door and into the back hall. He speaks to her in a tone of harsh joviality that she has never before heard from him. "No need for alarm," he says. "It's only the consequences of drink. A lady oughtn't to be living alone so close to a bad neighborhood." He takes hold of her arm just above the elbow. She can't open her mouth to speak to him, to say thank you. If she opened her mouth, she would retch.

What Jarvis Poulter feels for Almeda Roth at this moment is just what he has not felt during all those circumspect walks and all his own solitary calculations of her probable worth, undoubted respectability, adequate comeliness. He has not been able to imagine her as a wife. Now that is possible. He is sufficiently stirred by her loosened hair—prematurely gray but thick and soft—her flushed face, her light clothing, which nobody but a husband should see. And by her indiscretion, her agitation, her foolishness, her need?

"I will call on you later," he says to her. "I will walk with you to church."

At the corner of Pearl and Dufferin streets last Sunday morning there was discovered, by a lady resident there, the body of a certain woman of Pearl Street, thought to be dead but only, as it turned out, dead drunk.

She was roused from her heavenly—or otherwise—stupor by the firm
persuasion of Mr. Poulter, a neighbour and a Civil Magistrate, who
had been summoned by the lady resident. Incidents of this sort, un-
seemly, troublesome, and disgraceful to our town, have of late become all
too common.

V

I sit at the bottom of sleep,
As on the floor of the sea.
And fanciful Citizens of the Deep
Are graciously greeting me.

As soon as Jarvis Poulter has gone and she has heard her front gate
close, Almeda rushes to the privy. Her relief is not complete, however, and she realizes that the pain and fullness in her lower body
come from an accumulation of menstrual blood that has not yet
started to flow. She closes and locks the back door. Then, remembering Jarvis Poulter's words about church, she writes on a piece of
paper, "I am not well, and wish to rest today." She sticks this firmly
into the outside frame of the little window in the front door. She
locks that door, too. She is trembling, as if from a great shock or
danger. But she builds a fire, so that she can make tea. She boils water, measures the tea leaves, makes a large pot of tea, whose steam
and smell sicken her further. She pours out a cup while the tea is
still quite weak and adds to it several dark drops of nerve medicine.
She sits to drink it without raising the kitchen blind. There, in the
middle of the floor, is the cheesecloth bag hanging on its broom
handle between the two chairbacks. The grape pulp and juice has
stained the swollen cloth a dark purple. *Plop, plup*, into the basin
beneath. She can't sit and look at such a thing. She takes her cup,
the teapot, and the bottle of medicine into the dining room.

She is still sitting there when the horses start to go by on the way
to church, stirring up clouds of dust. The roads will be getting hot
as ashes. She is there when the gate is opened and a man's confident
steps sound on her veranda. Her hearing is so sharp she seems to
hear the paper taken out of the frame and unfolded—she can almost hear him reading it, hear the words in his mind. Then the

footsteps go the other way, down the steps. The gate closes. An image comes to her of tombstones—it makes her laugh. Tombstones are marching down the street on their little booted feet, their long bodies inclined forward, their expressions preoccupied and severe. The church bells are ringing.

Then the clock in the hall strikes twelve and an hour has passed.

The house is getting hot. She drinks more tea and adds more medicine. She knows that the medicine is affecting her. It is responsible for her extraordinary languor, her perfect immobility, her unresisting surrender to her surroundings. That is all right. It seems necessary.

Her surroundings—some of her surroundings—in the dining room are these: walls covered with dark-green garlanded wallpaper, lace curtains and mulberry velvet curtains on the windows, a table with a crocheted cloth and a bowl of wax fruit, a pinkish-gray carpet with nosegays of blue and pink roses, a sideboard spread with embroidered runners and holding various patterned plates and jugs and the silver tea things. A lot of things to watch. For every one of these patterns, decorations seems charged with life, ready to move and flow and alter. Or possibly to explode. Almeda Roth's occupation throughout the day is to keep an eye on them. Not to prevent their alteration so much as to catch them at it—to understand it, to be a part of it. So much is going on in this room that there is no need to leave it. There is not even the thought of leaving it.

Of course, Almeda in her observations cannot escape words. She may think she can, but she can't. Soon this glowing and swelling begins to suggest words—not specific words but a flow of words somewhere, just about ready to make themselves known to her. Poems, even. Yes, again, poems. Or one poem. Isn't that the idea—one very great poem that will contain everything and, oh, that will make all the other poems, the poems she has written, inconsequential, mere trial and error, mere rags? Stars and flowers and birds and trees and angels in the snow and dead children at twilight—that is not the half of it. You have to get in the obscene racket on Pearl Street and the polished toe of Jarvis Poulter's boot and the plucked-chicken haunch with its blue-black flower. Almeda is a long way now from human sympathies or fears or cozy household considerations. She doesn't think about what could be done for that woman or about keeping Jarvis Poulter's dinner warm and hanging his long underwear on the line. The basin of grape juice has overflowed and is running over her kitchen floor, staining the boards of the floor, and the stain will never come out.

She has to think of so many things at once—Champlain and the naked Indians and the salt deep in the earth, but as well as the salt the money, the money-making intent brewing forever in heads like Jarvis Poulter's. Also the brutal storms of winter and the clumsy and benighted deeds on Pearl Street. The changes of climate are often violent, and if you think about it there is no peace even in the stars. All this can be borne only if it is channelled into a poem, and the word "channelled" is appropriate, because the name of the poem will be—it *is*—"The Meneseteung." The name of the poem is the name of the river. No, in fact it is the river, the Meneseteung, that is the poem—with its deep holes and rapids and blissful pools under the summer trees and its grinding blocks of ice thrown up at the end of winter and its desolating spring floods. Almeda looks deep, deep into the river of her mind and into the tablecloth, and she sees the crocheted roses floating. They look bunchy and foolish, her mother's crocheted roses—they don't look much like real flowers. But their effort, their floating independence, their pleasure in their silly selves do seem to her so admirable. A hopeful sign. *Meneseteung.*

She doesn't leave the room until dusk, when she goes out to the privy again and discovers that she is bleeding, her flow has started. She will have to get a towel, strap it on, bandage herself up. Never before, in health, has she passed a whole day in her nightdress. She doesn't feel any particular anxiety about this. On her way through the kitchen, she walks through the pool of grape juice. She knows that she will have to mop it up, but not yet, and she walks upstairs leaving purple footprints and smelling her escaping blood and the sweat of her body that has sat all day in the closed hot room.

No need for alarm.

For she hasn't thought that crocheted roses could float away or that tombstones could hurry down the street. She doesn't mistake that for reality, and neither does she mistake anything else for reality, and that is how she knows that she is sane.

VI

I dream of you by night,
I visit you by day.
Father, Mother,
Sister, Brother,
Have you no word to say?

April 22, 1903. At her residence, on Tuesday last, between three and four o'clock in the afternoon, there passed away a lady of talent and refinement whose pen, in days gone by, enriched our local literature with a volume of sensitive, eloquent verse. It is a sad misfortune that in later years the mind of this fine person had become somewhat clouded and her behaviour, in consequence, somewhat rash and unusual. Her attention to decorum and to the care and adornment of her person had suffered, to the degree that she had become, in the eyes of those unmindful of her former pride and daintiness, a familiar eccentric, or even, sadly, a figure of fun. But now all such lapses pass from memory and what is recalled is her excellent published verse, her labours in former days in the Sunday school, her dutiful care of her parents, her noble womanly nature, charitable concerns, and unfailing religious faith. Her last illness was of mercifully short duration. She caught cold, after having become thoroughly wet from a ramble in the Pearl Street bog. (It has been said that some urchins chased her into the water, and such is the boldness and cruelty of some of our youth, and their observed persecution of this lady, that the tale cannot be entirely discounted.) The cold developed into pneumonia, and she died, attended at the last by a former neighbour, Mrs. Bert (Annie) Friels, who witnessed her calm and faithful end.

January, 1904. One of the founders of our community, an early maker and shaker of this town, was abruptly removed from our midst on Monday morning last, whilst attending to his correspondence in the office of his company. Mr. Jarvis Poulter possessed a keen and lively commercial spirit, which was instrumental in the creation of not one but several local enterprises, bringing the benefits of industry, productivity, and employment to our town.

So the *Vidette* runs on, copious and assured. Hardly a death goes undescribed, or a life unevaluated.

I looked for Almeda Roth in the graveyard. I found the family stone. There was just one name on it—Roth. Then I noticed two flat stones in the ground, a distance of a few feet—six feet?—from the upright stone. One of these said "Papa," the other "Mama." Farther out from these I found two other flat stones, with the names William and Catherine on them. I had to clear away some overgrowing grass and dirt to see the full name of Catherine. No birth or death dates for anybody, nothing about being dearly beloved. It was a private sort of memorializing, not for the world. There were no roses, either—no sign of a rose-bush. But perhaps it was taken out. The grounds keeper doesn't like such things; they are a nuisance to the lawnmower, and if there is nobody left to object he will pull them out.

I thought that Almeda must have been buried somewhere else. When this plot was bought—at the time of the two children's deaths—she would still have been expected to marry, and to lie finally beside her husband. They might not have left room for her here. Then I saw that the stones in the ground fanned out from the upright stone. First the two for the parents, then the two for the children, but these were placed in such a way that there was room for a third, to complete the fan. I paced out from "Catherine" the same number of steps that it took to get from "Catherine" to "William," and at this spot I began pulling grass and scrabbling in the dirt with my bare hands. Soon I felt the stone and knew that I was right. I worked away and got the whole stone clear and I read the name "Meda." There it was with the others, staring at the sky.

I made sure I had got to the edge of the stone. That was all the name there was—Meda. So it was true that she was called by that name in the family. Not just in the poem. Or perhaps she chose her name from the poem, to be written on her stone.

I thought that there wasn't anybody alive in the world but me who would know this, who would make the connection. And I would be the last person to do so. But perhaps this isn't so. People are curious. A few people are. They will be driven to find things out, even trivial things. They will put things together. You see them going around with notebooks, scraping the dirt off gravestones, reading microfilm, just in the hope of seeing this trickle in time, making a connection, rescuing one thing from the rubbish.

And they may get it wrong, after all. I may have got it wrong. I don't know if she ever took laudanum. Many ladies did. I don't know if she ever made grape jelly.

1990

P. K. Page
b. 1916

One of Canada's most acclaimed poets, Page was born in Swanage, England. When she was three, her family came to Canada, so she grew up in Alberta. She has, though, spent a life moving around the world, first to study art in Brazil and in New York City, then working in New Brunswick and in Montreal. After she married a diplomat, she moved with him—to Australia, Brazil and Mexico. As P. K. Irwin, she has been a widely appreciated painter. She eventually returned to Victoria, British Columbia.

Page's poems have always had clear natural imagery, but they often move into an other-worldly vision. She has always been interested in the metaphysical, the visionary, and she acknowledges the influence of Sufi poetry. Her stories have been scattered, published as part of her collections of poetry, or in literary journals, but A Kind of Fiction *(2001) draws them together. They have many of her poems' qualities.*

This piece has the control of form identified with Page. Presented in a documentary style, it quickly becomes pseudo-documentary, trying to be a journal, recording what is observed, as it happens. But the timeline breaks down, impossible to keep track of in the face of astonishing events. The documentary proves inadequate.

This could be seen as a science fiction story about the end of the world. It also lends itself to metaphorical reading, opening into several different themes or ideas. The narrator has a special kind of insight, shared with only a few people—artists? mystics? the insane?

People who have it recognize one another but rarely speak of it to others. This insight is a gift which makes everything else bearable. Tough and delicate, Page's writing lingers in the imagination.

Unless the Eye Catch Fire

Unless the eye catch fire
The God will not be seen . . .
Where the Wasteland Ends, *Theodore Rosak*

Wednesday, **September 17.** The day began normally enough. The quail cockaded as antique foot soldiers, arrived while I was having my breakfast. The males blackfaced, white-necklaced, cinnamon-crowned, with short, sharp, dark plumes. Square bibs, Payne's grey; belly and sides with a pattern of small stitches. Reassuring, the flock of them. They tell me the macadamization[1] of the world is not complete.

A sudden alarm, and as if they had one brain among them, they were gone in a rush—a sideways ascending Niagara—shutting out the light, obscuring the sky and exposing a rectangle of lawn, unexpectedly emerald. How bright the berries on the cotoneaster. Random leaves on the cherry twirled like gold spinners. The garden was high-keyed, vivid, locked in aspic.

Without warning, and as if I were looking down the tube of a kaleidoscope, the merest shake occurred—moiréed[2] the garden—rectified itself. Or, more precisely, as if a range-finder through which I had been sighting found of itself a more accurate focus. Sharpened, in fact, to an excoriating exactness.

And then the colours changed. Shifted to a higher octave—a *bright spectrum.* Each colour with its own *light,* its own *shape.* The leaves of the trees, the berries, the grasses—as if shedding successive films—disclosed layer after layer of hidden perfections. And upon these rapidly changing surfaces the "range-finder"—to really play hob with metaphor!—sharpened its small invisible blades.

I don't know how to describe the intensity and speed of focus of this gratuitous zoom lens through which I stared, or the swift and

---

1. Asphalt surfacing.   2. With a wavy pattern, like watered silk.

dizzying adjustments within me. I became a "sleeping top," perfectly centred, perfectly sighted. The colours vibrated beyond the visible range of the spectrum. Yet I saw them. With some matching eye. Whole galaxies of them, blazing and glowing, flowing in rivulets, gushing in fountains—volatile, mercurial, and making lacklustre and off-key the colours of the rainbow.

I had no time or inclination to wonder, intellectualize. My mind seemed astonishingly clear and quite still. Like a crystal. A burning glass.

And then the range-finder sharpened once again. To alter space.

The lawn, the bushes, the trees—still super-brilliant—were no longer *there*. *There*, in fact, had ceased to exist. They were now, of all places in the world, *here*. Right in the centre of my being. Occupying an immense inner space. Part of me. Mine. Except the whole idea of ownership was beside the point. As true to say I was theirs as they mine. I and they were here; they and I, there. (*There, here . . .* odd . . . but for an irrelevant, inconsequential "t" which comes and goes, the words are the same.)

As suddenly as the world had altered, it returned to normal. I looked at my watch. A ridiculous mechanical habit. As I had no idea when the experience began it was impossible to know how long it had lasted. What had seemed eternity couldn't have been more than a minute or so. My coffee was still steaming in its mug.

The garden, through the window, was as it had always been. Yet not as it had always been. Less. Like listening to mono after hearing stereo. But with a far greater loss of dimension. A grievous loss.

I rubbed my eyes. Wondered, not without alarm, if this was the onset of some disease of the retina—glaucoma or some cellular change in the eye itself—superlatively packaged, fatally sweet as the marzipan cherry I ate as a child and *knew* was poison.

If it *is* a disease, the symptoms will recur. It will happen again.

Tuesday, September 23. It *has* happened again.

Tonight, taking Dexter for his late walk, I looked up at the crocheted tangle of boughs against the sky. Dark silhouettes against the lesser dark, but beating now with an extraordinary black brilliance. The golden glints in obsidian or the lurking embers in black opals are the nearest I can come to describing them. But it's a false description, emphasizing as it does the wrong end of the scale. This was a *dark spectrum*. As if the starry heavens were translated into densities of black—black Mars, black Saturn, black Jupiter; or a master jeweller had crossed his jewels with jet and set them to burn and wink in the branches and twigs of oaks whose leaves shone luminous—a leafy Milky Way—fired by black chlorophyll.

Dexter stopped as dead as I. Transfixed. His thick honey-coloured coat and amber eyes, glowing with their own intense brightness, suggested yet another spectrum. A *spectrum of light*. He was a constellated dog, shining, supra-real, against the foothills and mountain ranges of midnight.

I am reminded now, as I write, of a collection of lepidoptera in Brazil—one entire wall covered with butterflies, creatures of daylight—enormous or tiny—blue, orange, black. Strong-coloured. And on the opposite wall their antiselves—pale night flyers spanning such a range of silver and white and lightest snuff-colour that once one entered their spectral scale there was no end to the subtleties and delicate nuances. But I didn't think like this then. All thought, all comparisons were prevented by the startling infinities of darkness and light.

Then, as before, the additional shake occurred and the two spectrums moved swiftly from without to within. As if two equal and complementary circles centred inside me—or I in them. How explain that I not only *saw* but actually *was* the two spectrums? (I underline a simple, but in this case exactly appropriate, anagram.)[3]

Then the range-finder lost its focus and the world, once again, was back to normal. Dexter, a pale, blurred blob, bounded about within the field of my peripheral vision, going on with his doggy interests just as if a moment before he had not been frozen in his tracks, a dog entranced.

I am no longer concerned about my eyesight. Wonder only if we are both mad, Dexter and I? Angelically mad, sharing hallucinations of epiphany. *Folie à deux?*[4]

Friday, October 3. It's hard to account for my secrecy, for I *have* been secretive. As if the cat had my tongue. It's not that I don't long

---

3. A word made from shifting the letters of another: *saw* and *was*.

4. A delusion shared with someone loved (French).

to talk about the colours but I can't risk the wrong response—(as Gaby once said of a companion after a faultless performance of *Giselle:* "If she had criticized the least detail of it, I'd have hit her!").

Once or twice I've gone so far as to say, "I had the most extraordinary experience the other day . . ." hoping to find some look or phrase, some answering, "So did I." None has been forthcoming.

I can't forget the beauty. Can't get it out of my head. Startling, unearthly, indescribable. Infuriatingly indescribable. A glimpse of— somewhere else. Somewhere alive, miraculous, newly made yet timeless. And more important still—significant, luminous, with a meaning of which I was part. Except that I—the I who is writing this—did not exist: was flooded out, dissolved in that immensity where subject and object are one.

I have to make a deliberate effort now not to live my life in terms of it; not to sit, immobilized, awaiting the shake that heralds a new world. Awaiting the transfiguration.

Luckily the necessities of life keep me busy. But upstream of my actions, behind a kind of plate glass, some part of me waits, listens, maintains a total attention.

Tuesday, October 7. Things are moving very fast.

Some nights ago my eye was caught by a news item. "Trucker Blames Colours," went the headline. Reading on: "R. T. Ballantyne, driver for Island Trucks, failed to stop on a red light at the intersection of Fernhill and Spender. Questioned by traffic police, Ballantyne replied: 'I didn't see it, that's all. There was this shake, then all these colours suddenly in the trees. Real bright ones I'd never seen before. I guess they must have blinded me.' A breathalyzer test proved negative." Full stop.

I had an overpowering desire to talk to R. T. Ballantyne. Even looked him up in the telephone book. Not listed. I debated reaching him through Island Trucks in the morning.

Hoping for some mention of the story, I switched on the local radio station, caught the announcer mid-sentence:

". . . to come to the studio and talk to us. So far no one has been able to describe just what the 'new' colours are, but perhaps Ruby Howard can. Ruby, you say you actually *saw* 'new' colours?"

What might have been a flat, rather ordinary female voice was sharpened by wonder. "I was out in the garden, putting it to bed, you might say, getting it ready for winter. The hydrangeas are dried out—you know the way they go. Soft beiges and greys. And I was thinking maybe I should cut them back, when there was this— shake, like—and there they were shining. Pink. And blue. But not like they are in life. Different. Brighter. With little lights, like . . ."

The announcer's voice cut in, "You say 'not like they are in life.' D'you think this wasn't life? I mean, do you think maybe you were dreaming?"

"Oh, no," answered my good Mrs Howard, positive, clear, totally unrattled. "Oh, no, I wasn't *dreaming*. Not *dreaming*—. . . Why— *this* is more like dreaming. "She was quiet a moment and then, in a matter-of-fact voice, "I can't expect you to believe it," she said. "Why should you? I wouldn't believe it myself if I hadn't seen it." Her voice expressed a kind of compassion as if she was really sorry for the announcer.

I picked up the telephone book for the second time, looked up the number of the station. I had decided to tell Mrs Howard what I had seen. I dialled, got a busy signal, depressed the bar and waited, cradle in hand. I dialled again. And again.

Later. J. just phoned. Curious how she and I play the same game over and over.

J: Were you watching Channel 8?
ME: No, I . . .
J: An interview. With a lunatic. One who sees colours and flashing lights.
ME: Tell me about it.
J: He was a logger—a high-rigger—not that that has anything to do with it. He's retired now and lives in an apartment and has a window-box with geraniums. This morning the flowers were like neon, he said, flashing and shining . . . *Honestly!*
ME: Perhaps he saw something you can't . . .
J: (*Amused*) I might have known you'd take his side. Seriously, what *could* he have seen?
ME: Flashing and shining—as he said.
J: But they couldn't. Not geraniums. And you know it as well as I

do. *Honestly*, Babe . . . (She is the only person left who calls me the name my mother called me.) Why are you always so perverse?

I felt faithless. I put down the receiver, as if I had not borne witness to my God.

October 22. Floods of letters to the papers. Endless interviews on radio and TV. Pros, cons, inevitable spoofs.

One develops an eye for authenticity. It's as easy to spot as sunlight. However they may vary in detail, true accounts of the colours have an unmistakable common factor—a common factor as difficult to convey as sweetness to those who know only salt. True accounts are inarticulate, diffuse, unlikely—impossible.

It's recently crossed my mind that there may be some relationship between having seen the colours and their actual manifestation— something as improbable as *the more one sees them the more they are able to be seen*. Perhaps they are always there in some normally invisible part of the electro-magnetic spectrum and only become visible to certain people at certain times. A combination of circumstances or some subtle refinement in the organ of sight. And then—from quantity to quality perhaps, like water to ice—a whole community changes, is able to see, catches fire.

For example, it was seven days between the first time I saw the colours and the second. During that time there were no reports to the media. But once the reports began, the time between lessened appreciably *for me*. Not proof, of course, but worth noting. And I can't help wondering why some people see the colours and others don't. Do some of us have extra vision? Are some so conditioned that they're virtually blind to what's there before their very noses? Is it a question of more, or less?

Reports come in from farther and farther afield; from all walks of life. I think now there is no portion of the inhabited globe without "shake freaks" and no acceptable reason for the sightings. Often, only one member of a family will testify to the heightened vision. In my own small circle, I am the only witness—or so I think. I feel curiously hypocritical as I listen to my friends denouncing the "shakers." Drugs, they say. Irrational—possibly dangerous. Although no sinister incidents have occurred yet—just some mild shake-baiting here and there—one is uneasily reminded of Salem.[5]

Scientists pronounce us hallucinated or mistaken, pointing out that so far there is no hard evidence, no objective proof. That means, I suppose, no photographs, no spectroscopic measurement—if such is possible. Interestingly, seismographs show very minor earthquake tremors—showers of them, like shooting stars in August. Pundits claim 'shake fever'—as it has come to be called—is a variant on flying saucer fever and that it will subside in its own time. Beneficent physiologists suggest we are suffering (why is it *always* suffering, never enjoying?) a distorted form of *ocular spectrum* or after-image. (An after-image of what?) Psychologists disagree among themselves. All in all, it is not surprising that some of us prefer to keep our experiences to ourselves.

January 9. Something new has occurred. Something impossible. Disturbing. So disturbing, in fact, that according to rumour it is already being taken with the utmost seriousness at the highest levels. TV, press and radio—with good reason—talk of little else.

What seemingly began as a mild winter has assumed sinister overtones. Farmers in southern Alberta are claiming the earth is unnaturally hot to the touch. Golfers at Harrison complain that the soles of their feet burn. Here on the coast, we notice it less. Benign winters are our specialty.

Already we don't lack for explanations as to why the earth could not be hotter than usual, nor why it is naturally "un-naturally" hot. Vague notes of reassurance creep into the speeches of public men. They may be unable to explain the issue, but they can no longer ignore it.

To confuse matters further, reports on temperatures seem curiously inconsistent. What information we get comes mainly from self-appointed "earth touchers." And now that the least thing can fire an argument, their conflicting readings lead often enough to inflammatory debate.

For myself, I can detect no change at all in my own garden.

5. The Massachusetts town where witch hunts occurred (1692).

Thursday . . . ? There is no longer any doubt. The temperature of the earth's surface *is* increasing.

It is unnerving, horrible, to go out and feel the ground like some great beast, warm, beneath one's feet. As if another presence—vast, invisible—attends one. Dexter, too, is perplexed. He barks at the earth with the same indignation and, I suppose, fear, with which he barks at the first rumblings of earthquake.

Air temperatures, curiously, don't increase proportionately—or so we're told. It doesn't make sense, but at the moment nothing makes sense. Countless explanations have been offered. Elaborate explanations. None adequate. The fact that the air temperature remains temperate despite the higher ground heat must, I think, be helping to keep panic down. Even so, these are times of great tension.

Hard to understand these two unexplained—unrelated?—phenomena: the first capable of dividing families; the second menacing us all. We are like animals trapped in a burning building.

Later. J. just phoned. Terrified. Why don't I move in with her, she urges. After all she has the space and we have known each other forty years. (Hard to believe when I don't feel even forty!) She can't bear it—the loneliness.

Poor J. Always so protected, insulated by her money. And her charm. What one didn't provide, the other did . . . diversions, services, attention.

What do I think is responsible for the heat, she asks. But it turns out she means who. Her personal theory is that the "shake-freaks" are causing it—involuntarily, perhaps, but the two are surely linked.

"How could they possibly cause it?" I enquire. "By what reach of the imagination . . . ?"

"Search *me!*" she protests. "How on earth should *I* know?" And the sound of the dated slang makes me really laugh.

But suddenly she is close to tears. "How can you *laugh?*" she calls. "This is nightmare. Nightmare!"

Dear J. I wish I could help but the only comfort I could offer would terrify her still more.

September. Summer calmed us down. If the earth was hot, well, summers *are* hot. And we were simply having an abnormally hot one.

Now that it is fall—the season of cool nights, light frosts—and the earth like a feverish child remains worryingly hot, won't cool down, apprehension mounts.

At last we are given official readings. For months the authorities have assured us with irrefutable logic that the temperature of the earth could not be increasing. Now, without any apparent period of indecision or confusion, they are warning us with equal conviction and accurate statistical documentation that it has, in fact, increased. Something anyone with a pocket-handkerchief of lawn has known for some time.

Weather stations, science faculties, astronomical observatories all over the world are measuring and reporting. Intricate computerized tables are quoted. Special departments of Government have been set up. We speak now of a new Triassic Age[6]—the Neo-Triassic—and of the accelerated melting of the ice caps. But we are elaborately assured that this could not, repeat not, occur in our lifetime.

Interpreters and analysts flourish. The media are filled with theories and explanations. The increased temperature has been attributed to impersonal agencies such as bacteria from outer space; a thinning of the earth's atmosphere; a build-up of carbon-dioxide in the air; some axial irregularity;[7] a change in the earth's core (geologists are reported to have begun test borings). No theory is too far-fetched to have its supporters. And because man likes a scapegoat, blame has been laid upon NASA, atomic physicists, politicians, the occupants of flying saucers and finally upon mankind at large—improvident, greedy mankind—whose polluted, strike-ridden world is endangered now by the fabled flames of hell.

Yet, astonishingly, life goes on. The Pollack baby was born last week. I received the news as if it were a death. Nothing has brought the irony of our situation home to me so poignantly. And when I saw the perfect little creature in its mother's arms, the look of adoration on her face, I found myself saying the things one always says to a new mother—exactly as if the world had not changed. Exactly as if our radio was not informing us that Nostradamus, the Bible, and Jeane Dixon[8] have all foreseen our plight. A new paperback, *Let*

6. The geologic periods which saw the rise of dinosaurs.

7. Change in the tilt of the earth in relation to the sun.

8. American syndicated astrologer and psychic (1918–1997).

Edgar Cayce Tell You Why sold out in a matter of days. Attendance at churches has doubled. Cults proliferate. Yet even in this atmosphere, we, the "shake freaks," are considered lunatic fringe. Odd men out. In certain quarters I believe we are seriously held responsible for the escalating heat, so J. is not alone. There have now been one or two nasty incidents. It is not surprising that even the most vocal among us have grown less willing to talk. I am glad to have kept silent. As a woman living alone, the less I draw attention to myself the better.

But, at the same time, we have suddenly all become neighbours. Total strangers greet each other on the street. And the almost invisible couple behind the high hedge appears every time I pass with Dexter—wanting to talk. Desperately wanting to talk.

For our lives are greatly altered by this overhanging sense of doom. It is already hard to buy certain commodities. Dairy products are in very short supply. On the other hand, the market is flooded with citrus fruits. We are threatened with severe shortages for the future. The authorities are resisting rationing but it will have to come, if only to prevent artificial shortages resulting from hoarding.

Luckily the colours are an almost daily event. I see them now, as it were, with my entire being. It is as if all my cells respond to their brilliance and become light too. At such times I feel I might shine in the dark.

No idea of the date. It is evening and I am tired but I am so far behind in my notes I want to get something down. Events have moved too fast for me.

Gardens, parks—every tillable inch of soil—have been appropriated for food crops. As an able, if aging body, with an acre of land and some knowledge of gardening, I have been made responsible for soybeans—small trifoliate plants rich with the promise of protein. Neat rows of them cover what were once my vegetable garden, flower beds, lawn.

Young men from the Department of Agriculture came last month, bulldozed, cultivated, planted. Efficient, noisy desecrators of my twenty years of landscaping. Dexter barked at them from the moment they appeared and I admit I would have shared his indignation had the water shortage not already created its own desolation.

As a Government gardener I'm a member of a new privileged

class. I have watering and driving permits and coupons for gasoline and boots—an indication of what is to come. So far there has been no clothes rationing.

Daily instructions—when to water and how much, details of mulching, spraying—reach me from the Government radio station to which I tune first thing in the morning. It also provides temperature readings, weather forecasts and the latest news releases on emergency measures, curfews, rationing, insulation. From the way things are going I think it will soon be our only station. I doubt that newspapers will be able to print much longer. In any event, I have already given them up. At first it was interesting to see how quickly drugs, pollution, education, women's lib., all became bygone issues; and, initially, I was fascinated to see how we rationalized. Then I became bored. Then disheartened. Now I am too busy.

Evening. A call came from J. Will I come for Christmas?

Christmas! Extraordinary thought. Like a word from another language learned in my youth, now forgotten.

"I've still got some Heidsieck.[9] We can get tight."

The word takes me back to my teens. "Like old times . . ."

"Yes." She is eager. I hate to let her down. "J., I can't. How could I get to you?"

"In your *car*, silly. *You* still have gas. You're the only one of us who has." Do I detect a slight hint of accusation, as if I had acquired it illegally?

"But J., it's only for emergencies."

"My God, Babe, d'you think *this* isn't an emergency?"

"J., dear . . ."

"*Please*, Babe," she pleads. "I'm so afraid. Of the looters. The eeriness. You must be afraid too. *Please!*"

I should have said, yes, that of course I was afraid. It's only natural to be afraid. Or, unable to say that, I should have made the soothing noises a mother makes to her child. Instead, "There's no reason to be afraid, J.," I said. It must have sounded insufferably pompous.

"No reason!" She was exasperated with me. "I'd have thought there was every reason."

---

9. Champagne.

She will phone again. In the night perhaps when she can't sleep. Poor J. She feels so alone. She *is* so alone. And so idle. I don't suppose it's occurred to her yet that telephones will soon go. That a whole way of life is vanishing completely.

It's different for me. I have the soybeans which keep me busy all the daylight hours. And Dexter. And above all I have the colours and with them the knowledge that there are others, other people, whose sensibilities I share. We are as invisibly, inviolably related to one another as the components of a molecule. I say "we." Perhaps I should speak only for myself, yet I feel as sure of these others as if they had spoken. Like the quail, we share one brain—no, I think it is one heart—between us. How do I know this? How *do* I know? I know by knowing. We are less alarmed by the increasing heat than those who have not seen the colours. I can't explain why. But seeing the colours seems to change one—just as certain diagnostic procedures cure the complaint they are attempting to diagnose.

In all honesty I admit to having had moments when this sense of community was not enough, when I have had a great longing for my own kind—for so have I come to think of these others—in the way one has a great longing for someone one loves. Their presence in the world is not enough. One must see them. Touch them. Speak with them.

But lately that longing has lessened. All longing, in fact. And fear. Even my once great dread that I might cease to see the colours has vanished. It is as if through seeing them I have learned to see them. Have learned to be ready to see—passive; not striving to see—active. It keeps me very wide awake. Transparent even. Still.

The colours come daily now. Dizzying. Transforming. Lifegiving. My sometimes back-breaking toil in the garden is lightened, made full of wonder, by the incredible colours shooting in the manner of children's sparklers from the plants themselves and from my own work-worn hands. I hadn't realized that I too am part of this vibrating luminescence.

Later. I have no idea how long it is since I abandoned these notes. Without seasons to measure its passing, without normal activities—preparations for festivals, occasional outings—time feels longer, shorter or—more curious still—simultaneous, undifferentiated. Future and past fused in the present. Linearity broken.

I had intended to write regularly, but the soybeans keep me busy pretty well all day and by evening I'm usually ready for bed. I'm sorry however to have missed recording the day-by-day changes. They were more or less minor at first. But once the heat began its deadly escalation, the world as we have known it—"our world"—had you been able to put it alongside "this world"—would have seemed almost entirely different.

No one, I think, could have foreseen the speed with which everything has broken down. For instance, the elaborate plans made to maintain transportation became useless in a matter of months. Private traffic was first curtailed, then forbidden. If a man from another planet had looked in on us, he would have been astonished to see us trapped who were apparently free.

The big changes only really began after the first panic evacuations from the cities. Insulated by concrete, sewer pipes and underground parkades, high density areas responded slowly to the increasing temperatures. But once the heat penetrated their insulations, Gehennas[1] were created overnight and whole populations fled in hysterical exodus, jamming highways in their futile attempts to escape.

Prior to this the Government had not publicly acknowledged a crisis situation. They had taken certain precautions, brought in temporary measures to ease shortages and dealt with new developments on an *ad hoc* basis. Endeavoured to play it cool. Or so it seemed. Now they levelled with us. It was obvious that they must have been planning for months, only awaiting the right psychological moment to take everything over. That moment had clearly come. What we had previously thought of as a free world ended. We could no longer eat, drink, move without permits or coupons. This was full-scale emergency.

Yet nothing proceeds logically. Plans are made only to be remade to accommodate new and totally unexpected developments. The heat, unpatterned as disseminated sclerosis, attacks first here, then there. Areas of high temperature suddenly and inexplicably cool off—or vice versa. Agronomists are doing everything possible to

---

1. The valley of slaughter in the Old Testament, where sacrifices were made to Baal and Moloch (Jeremiah 7:30–32).

keep crops coming—taking advantage of hot-house conditions to force two crops where one had grown before—frantically playing a kind of agricultural roulette, gambling on the length of time a specific region might continue to grow temperate-zone produce.

Mails have long since stopped. And newspapers. And telephones. As a member of a new privileged class, I have been equipped with a two-way radio and a permit to drive on Government business. Schools have of course closed. An attempt was made for a time to provide lessons over TV. Thankfully the looting and rioting seem over. Those desperate gangs of angry citizens who for some time made life additionally difficult, have now disappeared. We seem at last to understand that we are all in this together.

Life is very simple without electricity. I get up with the light and go to bed as darkness falls. My food supply is still substantial and because of the soybean crop I am all right for water. Dexter has adapted well to his new life. He is outdoors less than he used to be and has switched to a mainly vegetable diet without too much difficulty.

Evening. This morning a new order over the radio. All of us with special driving privileges were asked to report to our zone garage to have our tires treated with heat-resistant plastic.

I had not been into town for months. I felt rather as one does on returning home from hospital—that the world is unexpectedly large, with voluminous airy spaces. This was exaggerated perhaps by the fact that our whole zone had been given over to soybeans. Everywhere the same rows of green plants—small pods already formed—march across gardens and boulevards. I was glad to see the climate prove so favourable. But there was little else to make me rejoice as I drove through ominously deserted streets, paint blistering and peeling on fences and houses, while overhead a haze of dust, now always with us, created a green sun.

The prolonged heat has made bleak the little park opposite the garage. A rocky little park, once all mosses and rhododendrons, it is bare now, and brown. I was seeing the day as everyone saw it. Untransmuted.

As I stepped out of my car to speak to the attendant I cursed that I had not brought my insulators. The burning tarmac made me shift rapidly from foot to foot. Anyone from another planet would have wondered at this extraordinary quirk of earthlings. But my feet were forgotten as my eyes alighted a second time on the park across the way. I had never before seen so dazzling and variegated a display of colours. How could there be such prismed brilliance in the range of greys and browns? It was as if the perceiving organ—wherever it is—sensitized by earlier experience, was now correctly tuned for this further perception.

The process was as before: the merest shake and the whole park was "rainbow, rainbow, rainbow." A further shake brought the park from *there* to *here*. Interior. But this time the interior space had increased. Doubled. By a kind of instant knowledge that rid me of all doubt, I knew that the garage attendant was seeing it too. *We saw the colours.*

Then, with that slight shift of focus, as if a gelatinous film had moved briefly across my sight, everything slipped back.

I really looked at the attendant for the first time. He was a skinny young man standing up naked inside a pair of loose striped overalls cut off at the knee, *sidney* embroidered in red over his left breast pocket. He was blond, small-boned, with nothing about him to stick in the memory except his clear eyes which at that moment bore an expression of total comprehension.

"You . . ." we began together and laughed.

"Have you seen them before?" I asked. But it was rather as one would say "how do you do"—not so much a question as a salutation.

We looked at each other for a long time, as if committing each other to memory.

"Do you know anyone else?" I said.

"One or two. Three, actually. Do you?"

I shook my head. "You are the first. Is it . . . is it . . . always like that?"

"You mean . . . ?" he gestured towards his heart.

I nodded.

"Yes," he said. "Yes, it is."

There didn't seem anything more to talk about. Your right hand hasn't much to say to your left, or one eye to the other. There was comfort in the experience, if comfort is the word, which it isn't. More as if an old faculty had been extended. Or a new one activated.

Sidney put my car on the hoist and sprayed its tires.

Some time later. I have not seen Sidney again. Two weeks ago when I went back he was not there and as of yesterday, cars have become obsolete. Not that we will use that word publicly. The official word is *suspended.*

Strange to be idle after months of hard labour. A lull only before the boys from the Department of Agriculture come back to prepare the land again. I am pleased that the soybeans are harvested, that I was able to nurse them along to maturity despite the scorching sun, the intermittent plagues and the problems with water. Often the pressure was too low to turn the sprinklers and I would stand, hour after hour, hose in hand, trying to get the most use from the tiny trickle spilling from the nozzle.

Sometimes my heart turns over as I look through the kitchen window and see the plants shrivelled and grotesque, the baked earth scored by a web of fine cracks like the glaze on a plate subjected to too high an oven. Then it comes to me in a flash that of course, the beans are gone, the harvest is over.

The world is uncannily quiet. I don't think anyone had any idea of how much noise even distant traffic made until we were without it. It is rare indeed for vehicles other than Government mini-cars to be seen on the streets. And there are fewer and fewer pedestrians. Those who do venture out move on their thick insulators with the slow gait of rocking-horses. Surreal and alien, they heighten rather than lessen one's sense of isolation. For one *is* isolated. We have grown used to the sight of helicopters like large dragon-flies hovering overhead—addressing us through their P.A. systems, dropping supplies—welcome but impersonal.

Dexter is my only physical contact. He is delighted to have me inside again. The heat is too great for him in the garden and as, officially, he no longer exists, we only go out under cover of dark.

The order to destroy pets, when it came, indicated more clearly than anything that had gone before, that the Government had abandoned hope. In an animal-loving culture, only direct necessity could validate such an order. It fell upon us like a heavy pall.

When the Government truck stopped by for Dexter, I reported him dead. Now that the welfare of so many depends upon our co-operation with authority, law-breaking is a serious offence. But I am not uneasy about breaking this law. As long as he remains healthy and happy, Dexter and I will share our dwindling provisions.

No need to be an ecologist or dependent on non-existent media to know all life is dying and the very atmosphere of our planet is changing radically. Already no birds sing in the hideous hot dawns as the sun, rising through a haze of dust, sheds its curious bronze-green light on a brown world. The trees that once gave us shade stand leafless now in an infernal winter. Yet as if in the masts and riggings of ships, St. Elmo's fire[2] flickers and shines in their high branches, and bioplasmic pyrotechnics light the dying soybeans. I am reminded of how the ghostly form of a limb remains attached to the body from which it has been amputated. And I can't help thinking of all the people who don't see the colours, the practical earth-touchers with only their blunt senses to inform them. I wonder about J. and if, since we last talked, she has perhaps been able to see the colours too. But I think not. After so many years of friendship, surely I would be able to sense her, had she broken through.

Evening . . . ? The heat has increased greatly in the last few weeks—in a quantum leap. This has resulted immediately in two things: a steady rising of the sea level throughout the world—with panic re-actions and mild flooding in coastal areas; and, at last, a noticeably higher air temperature. It is causing great physical discomfort.

It was against this probability that the authorities provided us with insulator spray. Like giant cans of pressurized shaving cream. I have shut all rooms but the kitchen and by concentrating my insu-lating zeal on this one small area, we have managed to keep fairly cool. The word is relative, of course. The radio has stopped giving temperature readings and I have no thermometer. I have filled all cracks and crannies with the foaming plastic, even applied a layer to the exterior wall. There are no baths, of course, and no cold drinks. On the other hand I've abandoned clothes and given Dexter a shave and a haircut. Myself as well. We are a fine pair. Hairless and naked.

When the world state of emergency was declared we didn't need to be told that science had given up. The official line had been that the process would reverse itself as inexplicably as it had begun. The

---

2. Luminous electrical discharge sometimes seen in a ship's rigging during storms.

official policy—to hold out as long as possible. With this in mind, task forces worked day and night on survival strategy. On the municipal level, which is all I really knew about, everything that could be centralized was. Telephone exchanges, hydro plants, radio stations became centres around which vital activities took place. Research teams investigated the effects of heat on water mains, sewer pipes, electrical wiring; work crews were employed to prevent, protect or even destroy incipient causes of fire, flood and asphyxiation.

For some time now the city has been zoned. In each zone a large building has been selected, stocked with food, medical supplies and insulating materials. We have been provided with zone maps and an instruction sheet telling us to stay where we are until ordered to move to what is euphemistically called our "home." When ordered, we are to load our cars with whatever we still have of provisions and medicines and drive off *at once*. Helicopters have already dropped kits with enough gasoline for the trip and a small packet, somewhat surprisingly labelled "emergency rations" which contains one cyanide capsule—grim reminder that all may not go as the planners plan. We have been asked to mark our maps, in advance, with the shortest route from our house to our "home," so that in a crisis we will know what we are doing. These instructions are repeated *ad nauseam* over the radio, along with hearty assurances that everything is under control and that there is no cause for alarm. The Government station is now all that remains of our multimedia. When it is not broadcasting instructions, its mainly pre-recorded tapes sound inanely complacent and repetitive. Evacuation Day, as we have been told again and again, will be announced by whistle blast. Anyone who runs out of food before that or who is in need of medical aid is to use the special gas ration and go "home" at once.

As a long-time preserver of fruits and vegetables, I hope to hold out until E. Day. When that time comes it will be a sign that broadcasts are no longer possible, that contact can no longer be maintained between the various areas of the community, that the process will not reverse itself in time and that, in fact, our world is well on the way to becoming—oh, wonder of the modern kitchen—a self-cleaning oven.

Spring, Summer, Winter, Fall. What season is it after all? I sense the hours by some inner clock. I have applied so many layers of insulating spray that almost no heat comes through from outside. But we have to have air and the small window I have left exposed acts like a furnace. Yet through it I see the dazzling colours; sense my fellow-men.

Noon. The sun is hidden directly overhead. The world is topaz. I see it through the minute eye of my window. I, the perceiving organ that peers through the house's only aperture. We are one, the house and I—parts of some vibrating sensitive organism in which Dexter plays his differentiated but integral role. The light enters us, dissolves us. We are the golden motes in the jewel.

Midnight. The sun is directly below. Beneath the burning soles of my arching feet it shines, a globe on fire. Its rays penetrate the earth. Upward beaming, they support and sustain us. We are held aloft, a perfectly balanced ball in the jet of a golden fountain. Light, dancing, infinitely upheld.

Who knows how much later. I have just "buried" Dexter.

This morning I realized this hot little cell was no longer a possible place for a dog.

I had saved one can of dog food against this day. As I opened it Dexter's eyes swivelled in the direction of so unexpected and delicious a smell. He struggled to his feet, joyous, animated. The old Dexter. I was almost persuaded to delay, to wait and see if the heat subsided. What if tomorrow we awakened to rain? But something in me, stronger than this wavering self, carried on with its purpose.

He sat up, begging, expectant.

I slipped the meat out of the can.

"You're going to have a really good dinner," I said, but as my voice was unsteady, I stopped.

I scooped a generous portion of the meat into his dish and placed it on the floor. He was excited, and as always when excited about food, he was curiously ceremonial, unhurried—approaching his dish and backing away from it, only to approach it again at a slightly different angle. As if the exact position was of the greatest importance. It was one of his most amusing and endearing characteristics. I let him eat his meal in his own leisurely and appreciative manner and then, as I have done so many times before, I fed him his final *bonne bouche*[3] by hand. The cyanide pill, provided by a beneficent Government for me, went down in a gulp.

I hadn't expected it to be so sudden. Life and death so close. His small frame convulsed violently, then collapsed. Simultaneously, as if synchronized, the familiar "shake" occurred in my vision. Dexter glowed brightly, whitely, like phosphorus. In that dazzling, light-filled moment he was no longer a small dead dog lying there. I could have thought him a lion, my sense of scale had so altered. His beautiful body blinded me with its fires.

With the second "shake" his consciousness must have entered mine for I felt a surge in my heart as if his loyalty and love had flooded it. And like a kind of ground bass, I was aware of scents and sounds I had not known before. Then a great peace filled me—an immense space, light and sweet—and I realized that this was death. Dexter's death.

But how describe what is beyond description?

As the fires emanating from his slight frame died down, glowed weakly, residually, I put on my insulators and carried his body into the now fever-hot garden. I laid him on what had been at one time an azalea bed. I was unable to dig a grave in the baked earth or to cover him with leaves. But there are no predators now to pick the flesh from his bones. Only the heat which will, in time, desiccate it.

I returned to the house, opening the door as little as possible to prevent the barbs and briars of burning air from entering with me. I sealed the door from inside with foam sealer.

The smell of the canned dog food permeated the kitchen. It rang in my nostrils. Olfactory chimes, lingering, delicious. I was intensely aware of Dexter. Dexter immanent. I contained him as simply as a dish contains water. But the simile is not exact. For I missed his physical presence. One relies on the physical more than I had known. My hands sought palpable contact. The flesh forgets slowly.

Idly, abstractedly, I turned on the radio. I seldom do now as the batteries are low and they are my last. Also, there is little incentive. Broadcasts are intermittent and I've heard the old tapes over and over.

3. A treat, especially at the end of a meal (French).

But the Government station was on the air. I tuned with extreme care and placed my ear close to the speaker. A voice, faint, broken by static, sounded like that of the Prime Minister.

". . . all human beings can do, your Government has done for you." (Surely not a political speech *now?*) "But we have failed. Failed to hold back the heat. Failed to protect ourselves against it; to protect you against it. It is with profound grief that I send this farewell message to you all." I realized that this, too, had been pre-recorded, reserved for the final broadcast. "Even now, let us not give up hope . . ."

And then, blasting through the speech, monstrously loud in the stone-silent world, the screech of the whistle summoning us "home." I could no longer hear the P.M.'s words.

I began automatically, obediently, to collect my few remaining foodstuffs, reaching for a can of raspberries, the last of the crop to have grown in my garden when dawns were dewy and cool and noon sun fell upon us like golden pollen. My hand stopped in mid-air.

I would not go "home."

The whistle shrilled for a very long time. A curious great steam-driven cry—man's last. Weird that our final utterance should be this anguished inhuman wail.

The end. Now that it is virtually too late, I regret not having kept a daily record. Now that the part of me that writes has become nearly absorbed, I feel obliged to do the best I can.

I am down to the last of my food and water. Have lived on little for some days—weeks, perhaps. How can one measure passing time? Eternal time grows like a tree, its roots in my heart. If I lie on my back I see winds moving in its high branches and a chorus of birds is singing in its leaves. The song is sweeter than any music I have ever heard.

My kitchen is as strange as I am myself. Its walls bulge with many layers of spray. It is without geometry. Like the inside of an eccentric Styrofoam coconut. Yet, with some inner eye, I see its intricate mathematical structure. It is as ordered and no more random than an atom.

My face is unrecognizable in the mirror. Wisps of short damp hair. Enormous eyes. I swim in their irises. Could I drown in the pits of their pupils?

Through my tiny window when I raise the blind, a dead world shines. Sometimes dust storms fill the air with myriad particles burning bright and white as the lion body of Dexter. Sometimes great clouds swirl, like those from which saints receive revelations.

The colours are almost constant now. There are times when, light-headed, I dance a dizzying dance, feel part of that whirling incandescent matter—what I might once have called inorganic matter!

On still days the blameless air, bright as a glistening wing, hangs over us, hangs its extraordinary beneficence over us.

We are together now, united, indissoluble. Bonded.

Because there is no expectation, there is no frustration.

Because there is nothing we can have, there is nothing we can want.

We are hungry of course. Have cramps and weakness. But they are as if in *another body*. Our body is inviolate. Inviolable.

We share one heart.

We are one with the starry heavens and our bodies are stars.

Inner and outer are the same. A continuum. The water in the locks is level. We move to a higher water. A high sea.

A ship could pass through.

1979

Catherine Richards

A professor in the Department of Visual Arts at the University of Ottawa, Richards has worked extensively on the intersections between technology and art. As she points out in this essay, those are usually seen as opposed to one another, but she has used various computer and biological technologies to create her art. The title of one of her projects, Spectral Bodies, *shows Richards's concern about bringing the body into visual art through such techniques. She has written numerous articles about these strategies and possibilities.*

This essay is an example of what has come to be known as "hypertext," writing done for the computer. It is characterized by those highlighted words which a reader can click on to go somewhere else, usually to look for further explanations of a word or additional information.

This particular text takes that technique further. The medium could be said to be its message, because while Richards discusses the connections among nature, technology and art, she makes it possible to watch them, through words and moving images. When this piece is read at <www.innovation.ca>, these "hot links" invite a reader to leave this text behind and go into another place, such as a virtual art gallery, to see a work of art Richards made.

Richards's essay challenges our conception of the non-fiction essay, written to be read on the page. There are issues to be considered in such work. Is it a good idea to interrupt reading by accessing hot links? Will a reader ever come back? Does it matter? An important consideration is that such a piece should be able to stand alone, without the links into other places.

Excitable Tissues and Virtual Worlds: Art, Science and Technology

How is it that science and technology, often considered indifferent to art, can now be found deeply entwined in its domain?

Historically, in the west, the business of artificial worlds—of visualizing our relations, fears, desires, and how we understand ourselves to be—has been the almost exclusive domain of artists. But that has changed. Now, our new information technologies are deeply involved in the ways we re-imagine ourselves.

As humans become increasingly disconnected from nature and technologically linked to a virtual world, our multiple senses are increasingly mediated. Where do our psyche and physiology begin and end? What do we imagine ourselves to be? The answers lie in the new territory where the worlds of art, science, and technology converge.

Charged Hearts (1997)[1] occupies this new Territory. The piece shamelessly mixes the look of an early science lab with an early

---

1. Art work by Catherine Richards.

nineteenth-century art museum display of collectibles under glass. Upon entering, the first impression is visually alluring and seems familiar. The art-gallery experience appears to tell the visitor, "look, contemplate, but don't touch." Observe three simple brass cabinets. The two shorter ones are identical, each displaying a bell jar with a single, life-sized blown-glass heart. Inside each jar, an electrode emerges from a copper spool and descends into the main artery of the heart. Between these cabinets is a slightly taller one displaying a large, glass sphere with a small, dark sphere inside. Glass-blown onto two sides of the large sphere are electronic wires.

In the "don't touch" art-gallery experience, the boundaries between the visitor and the objects are well defined. It is understood where each begins and ends. But in *Charged Hearts*, the boundaries are blurred or non-existent. The point of this work begins when the visitor picks up the bell jar in the cabinet and turns the piece inside out. As the heart is grasped, it excites and begins to beat luminescently. Simultaneously the sphere, the terrella[2] excites, forming a luminescent plasma cloud of electromagnetic weather, a miniature version of the unimaginable wireless dynamo that surrounds the earth and hides in our household television sets. Holding hearts, plugging in, spectators are literally and figuratively part of the electromagnetic fields, a phenomenon they can barely see but can sense.

Plugging Ourselves into the Electronic World

Charged Hearts asks a question and responds aesthetically. What is it like for us—human, flesh, blood, driven by heartbeats of living electromagnetic charges—to plug into the electromagnetic world that surrounds us? Our new technological environment is electromagnetic. And so are we. Excitation is both the means and the end. Excite, say physicists observing electron energy. Excite, we say when our hearts are moved. Excite, say doctors watching heart tissue beat. We can change heartbeats by a warm embrace, a cold dream, a fearful image, or an electric charge. We are plugging one electromagnetic system into another: ourselves into the electronic world. We can change heartbeats and we can change minds.

2. A magnetized sphere.

This brings us to the brain. The heart is an excitable tissue. So too is the brain. The follow-up piece to *Charged Hearts* is called *I was scared to death / I could have died from joy* (2000). In the piece, two stainless "clean" tables stand in a large, dim room, one at either end. On each table is an oversized test tube containing a blown-glass half brain, life-sized, with spinal nerves. As the viewer approaches, the brain suddenly appears to pulsate as the tube glows with luminescent gas in vertebrae-like patterns. As the viewer touches the tube, an excited plasma follows the fingers.

These particular art works set out to aesthetically investigate the conditions of our culture's massive project: to engage our senses in artificial worlds that are technologically simulated and aim to surpass the natural world.

Virtual Reality as an Art Experience

Some events can be called "found art." Watching a human form tethered by wires, blinded by a helmet and computer images, gesturing with a gloved hand at the unseen, and followed by handlers, is one of these "events." A kind of found performance art. These were the images of the first virtual-reality system when it became a civilian event as NASA, the U.S. space agency, moved technology from weapons development to a virtual environment lab. Since the user literally wore the technology, it was an enticing snapshot of immersion in new media environments. The technology was all over the body, tracking, so close to the senses that it seemed to be dealing directly with our ability to create mental images, plugging us directly into a system.

As virtual reality has became more accessible, the popular understanding of it has grown more confused. Many claim it as an immersion in a realm of pure mind, seemingly abstract and bloodless, and at last leaving behind the troublesome flesh. This commonly held opinion appeared to reconstruct the mind/body split, which is puzzling since it was an outdated paradigm in science and unfashionable even in conventional medical circles.

In the late 1980s, the question of finding a way to investigate these issues was not easily answered. The Banff Center for the Arts in Banff, Alberta, was one of the few places in the world that could welcome a multidisciplinary residency in virtual reality, the body, and art practice. In 1991, this project became the BIOAPPARATUS residency that played its part in setting the stage for the convergence of these issues (at the same time, crucial support from the Canada Council for the Arts meant travelling to Edmonton to work in the first Canadian lab with immersive virtual-reality gear).

On the scientific research agenda was the question of simulating presence in virtual worlds. But if we were attempting to simulate presence in virtual bodies, we first had to ask a question: How did we know if we were present in our material bodies? This question led to scientific expertise in the sense of proprioception, that is, the sense of inhabiting our bodies (how we know we are). Remarkably, the research demonstrated that this habitation of our material bodies turns out to be quite unstable. Household technology used on a blindfolded subject could illicit illusions of displaced bodies: an arm can be felt to be somewhere other than where it is, even inside the body. Artists at Banff became the willing victims of my inquiry. Fundamentally, the question became this: What might happen if we displaced this bodily presence and found a way to map it into virtual bodies?

The art pieces I have attempted to bring to life here result from years of research and collaboration with scientists who were tuned to complementary intuitions: neuroscientists, perceptual psychologists, physicists, electrical engineers, medical researchers, computer scientists, and mathematicians. Since the technology is an integral part of each piece's intention, much of it is specifically developed including: programming, evacuating glass tubes and filling them with gases, and constructing high-voltage supplies (not to mention the installation of a prototype at 4 A.M. the day of the exhibition opening that is intended to run continuously for months of tactile accessibility to the public).

Simulating Our Senses through Technology

Canada has a history of artistic expression that perceives information technology as a cultural artefact and artist terrain. The 1960s and 1970s were an explosive period of art happenings, multimedia art events, performance art, video art, the first portopaks, satellite live art, art installations, and Telidon (the first consumer graphic work station and used by artists). Artists took Marshall McLuhan's lament perversely to heart. On one hand, McLuhan described media technologies as wreaking drastic shifts in society. On the other hand, he singled out the artist's role: "In the history of human culture there is no example of a conscious adjustment . . . to new extensions (technologies) except in the puny and peripheral efforts of artists."

McLuhan was preceded by such Canadian thinkers as Harold Innis and George Grant who were part of a general climate that included institutions like the National Research Council, the National Film Board, the Department of Communications, the Canada Council for the Arts; research labs like the Structured Sound Synthesis Project at the University of Toronto; and companies such as Alias Research and Softimage. It was a climate that recognized the convergence of media technologies, science, art, and culture. The artworks described here extend this historical thread of awareness. It is an awareness that understood that, by technically simulating our senses, we appropriate that power over our imaginations.

In contemporary terms, these early threads have spun further and further into the social matrix. New information technology has became more than computer image making, user interface developments, and displays. There are now new visualization methods such as evolutionary algorithms and visualization of complex data and data mining. The technology has deeply implicated the viewer by imaging the formerly inaccessible, such as the interior of the human body and its processes. It is also profoundly implicated in the myriad of surveillance and tracking techniques that can read minute physiological body changes, as well as feed into complex models of dynamic systems. And it is becoming deeply enmeshed in day-to-day life be it smart houses, smart agents, smart fabrics, or smart toys.

While creating *Charged Hearts* in 1995 and reflecting on the slippery language of physics and emotion, we were considering which areas would be the next subject for simulation and mediation. Consequently, our first project on emotion and intimacy was a Web site linked to the glass hearts in *Charged Hearts*. The Web site was an ironical look at an intimacy simulation: a real time, interactive, emergent game of hearts where one's heartbeat could become dangerously over excited, have a heart attack, or become comatose. Its life depended on the relationship with other users' hearts, which could be called in, dragging in their malcontent friends' heartbeats with them. With our slim resources, we cheerfully called it the slowest game. However, it anticipated a move in information technologies to model emotion, now among a trend of related ways to "make alive" new technological representations.

The moment when representations are "alive" may be seen in the well-known first cinematic public event, when the audience fled a film projection of an oncoming train. Looking back further to the mid-1700s, it was also revealed when French philosopher Denis Diderot recounted his experience of entering a painting and being flooded with "sensations délicieuses." Currently, the same kind of moment may be seen when virtual reality users declare they leave their bodies behind, or evolutionary algorithms are said to be alive and evolving.

By 2000, the project of emotions, intimate interactions, and mediation evolved into *Method and Apparatus for Finding Love*, a work of art that takes the form of a patent. The form was chosen as a way to implicate both the world of art and the world of invention in the construction of desire. As such, it critiques how technology is developed and rationalized in North American culture. The patent is a description of an art piece and a device: a wireless, embedded, handheld, information technology device that will simultaneously act as a new kind of person information technology, and an instrument that will collect data on its and the user's behaviour. In its first exhibition, a young woman sat at a desk placed next to a locked room. To enter the room, viewers were asked to sign a non-disclosure agreement promising not to reveal the contents of the artwork.

As the research progresses, it will present an opportunity to investigate a speculative issue on the relationship of humans and intelligent systems. There is continuing discussion that we are becoming "post human" and mixed with intelligent machines that take on human attributes. These works of art raise further questions. Is the initial pleasure, the enticement of the mind and senses in both art and media related to the obsession to "make alive" a world of representation? Is this an extension of aesthetics? If so, then the aesthetic project has been taken up by media and now information technologies. If this seems to be the case, then the aesthetic project appears to go to exceeding lengths to re-invent that moment of disbelief, with the consequences played out in the human landscape.

2002

Leon Rooke
b. 1934

Born in North Carolina, Rooke moved, to Victoria, British Columbia, and then to Erin Mills, Ontario. He now lives in Winnipeg and in Mexico. Beginning with Last One Home Sleeps in the Yellow Bed *(1977), he has published many volumes of short stories, among them* Who Do You Love? *(1992), which includes this story. He has also published six novels.*

Hard-working and productive, Rooke has perhaps not had the attention he deserves. In some ways, it is difficult to "place" him. He sets his stories in many locales, with many dialects, including Elizabethan English in Shakespeare's Dog *(1983), which won a Governor General's Award for Fiction.*

Rooke is a tolerant and generous supporter of other writers. He has said that we may never know the best ones. He created and chaired the popular, influential Eden Mills Writers' Festival, which has provided a reading platform for countless established and emerging writers. He has also been writer-in-residence at several Canadian universities.

Short fiction has more in common with poetry than with the novel, and this is especially true in Rooke's stories, which seem to be his favourite form. He has published some 300, and he likely has written several more collections-worth. They have the lyrical tone often associated with poetry, but they also share its compression, intensity, suggestiveness, and sheer delight in language.

In this story, Rooke explores the line between life and art. How do we know where one begins and the other ends? This story can seem slight, clever, amusing, delicate. But it carries significant questions—about the making of art and people's understanding or appreciation of it. It is very much story, though, and not essay.

Art

I told the woman I wanted that bunch down near the pine grove by the rippling stream.

Where the cow is? she asked.

I told her yep, that was the spot.

She said I'd have to wait until the milking was done.

The cow mooed a time or two as we waited. It was all very peaceful.

How much if you throw in the maiden? I asked.

Without the cow? she asked, or *with*?

Both would be nice, I said.

But it turned out a Not For Sale sign had already gone up on the girl. Too bad. It was sweet enough with her out of the picture, but not quite the same.

I took my cut bunch of flowers and plodded on behind the cow over to the next field. I wanted a horse too, if I could get one cheap.

Any horses? I asked.

Not today, they said.

Strawberries?

Not the season, I was told. At home, I threw out the old bunch and put the new crop in a vase by the picture window so the wife might marvel at them when she came in from her hard day's grind.

I staked the cow out front where the grass was still doing pretty well.

It was touch-and-go, whether we'd be able to do the milking ourselves. It would be rough without a shed or stall.

Oh, hand-painted! the wife said when she came in.

I propped her up in the easy chair and put up her feet. She looked a trifle wind-blown.

Hard day? I asked.

So-so, she said.

I mixed up a gin and tonic, nice as I knew how, and lugged that in.

A touch flat, she said, but the lemon wedge has a nice effect.

I pointed out the cow, which was tranquilly grazing.

Sweet, she said. Very sweet. What a lovely idea.

I put on the stereo for her.

That needle needs re-doing, she observed. The tip needs retouching, I mean.

It will have to wait until tomorrow, I told her.

She gave me a sorrowful look, though one without any dire reproach in it. She pecked me a benign one on the cheek. A little wet. I wiped it off before it could do any damage.

The flowers were a good thought, she said. I appreciate the flowers.

Well, you know how it is, I said. What I meant was that one did the best one could—though I didn't really have to tell her that. It was what she was always telling me.

She was snoozing away in the chair as I tiptoed off to bed. I was beginning to flake a little myself. Needed a good touch-up job from an expert.

We all do, I guess. The dampness, the mildew, the *rot*—it gets into the system somehow.

Not much to be done about it, however.

I thought about the cow. Wondered if I hadn't made a mistake on that. Without the maiden to milk her, there didn't seem to be much *point* in having a cow. Go back tomorrow, I thought. Offer a good price for the maiden, the stream, and the whole damned field.

Of course, I could go the other way: find a nice seascape somewhere. Hang that up.

Well, sleep on it, I thought.

The wife slipped into bed about two in the morning. That's approximate. The paint job on the hour hand wasn't holding up very well. The undercoating was beginning to show through on the entire clock face, and a big crack was developing down in the six o'clock area.

Shoddy goods, I thought. Shoddy artisanship.

Still, we'd been around a bit. Undated, unsigned, but somewhere in the nineteenth century was my guess. It was hard to remember. I just wished the painter had been more careful. I wished he'd given me more chest, and made the bed less rumpled.

Sorry, baby, she said. Sorry I waked you.

She whispered something else, which I couldn't hear, and settled down far away on her side of the bed. I waited for her to roll into me and embrace me. I waited for her warmth, but she remained where she was and I thought all this very strange.

What's wrong? I said.

She stayed very quiet and did not move. I could feel her holding herself in place, could hear her shallow, irregular breathing, and I caught the sweep of one arm as she brought it up to cover her face. She started shivering.

I am so sorry, she said. I am so sorry. She said that over and over.

Tell me what's wrong, I said.

No, she said, please don't touch me, please don't, please don't even think about touching me. She went on like this for some seconds, her voice rising, growing in alarm, and I thought to myself: Well, I have done something to upset her, I must have said or done something unforgivable, and I lay there with my eyes open wide, trying to think what it might be.

I am so sorry, she said. So very very sorry.

I reached for her hand, out of that hurting need we have for warmth and reassurance, and it was then that I found her hand had gone all wet and muddy and smeary.

Don't! she said, oh please don't, I don't want you to hurt yourself!

Her voice was wan and low and she had a catch in her voice and a note of forlorn panic. I lifted my hand away quickly from her wetness, though not quickly enough for I knew the damage already had been done. The tips of my fingers were moist and cold, and the pain, bad enough but not yet severe, was slowly seeping up my arm.

My drink spilled, she said. She snapped that out so I would know.

Christ, I thought. Oh Jesus Christ. God help us.

I shifted quickly away to the far side of the bed, my side, away from her, far as I could get, for I was frightened now and all I could think was that I must get away from her, I must not let her wetness touch me any more than it had.

Yes, she said shivering, do that, stay there, you must try and save yourself, oh darling I am so sorry.

We lay in the darkness, on our backs, separated by all that distance, yet I could still feel her warmth and her tremors and I knew there was nothing I could do to save her.

Her wonderful scent was already going and her weight on the bed was already decreasing.

I slithered up high on the sheets, keeping my body away from her, and ran my good hand through her hair and down around her warm neck and brought my face up against her.

I know it hurts, I said. You're being so brave.

Do you hurt much? she said. I am so terribly, terribly sorry. I was dozing in the chair and opened my eyes and saw the dark shape of the cow out on the lawn and for an instant I didn't know what it was and it scared me. I hope I haven't hurt you. I've always loved you and the life we had in here. My own wounds aren't so bad now. I don't feel much of anything anymore. I know the water has gone all through me and how frightful I must look to you. Oh please forgive me, it hurts and I'm afraid I can't think straight.

I couldn't look at her. I looked down at my own hand and saw that the stain had spread. It had spread up to my elbow and in a small puddle where my arm lay, but it seemed to have stopped there. I couldn't look at her. I knew her agony must be very great and I marveled a little that she was being so brave for I knew that in such circumstances I would be weak and angry and able to think only of myself.

Water damage, I thought, that's the hardest part to come to terms with. The fear that's over you like a curse. Every day you think you've reconciled yourself to it and come to terms with how susceptible you are, and unprotected you are, and then something else happens. But you never think you will do it to yourself.

Oil stands up best, I thought. Oh holy Christ why couldn't we have been done in oil.

You get confident, you get to thinking what a good life you have, so you go out and buy yourself flowers and a goddamn cow.

I wish I could kiss you, she moaned. I wish I could.

My good hand was already behind her neck and I wanted to bring my head down on her breasts and put my hand there too. I wanted to close my eyes and stroke her all over and lose myself in the last sweetness I'd ever know.

I will too, I thought. I'll do it.

Although I tried, I couldn't, not all over, so I stroked my hand through her hair and rolled my head over till my lips gently touched hers.

She sobbed and broke away.

It's too much, she said. I'm going to cry. I am, I know I am.

Don't, I said. Don't. If you do that will be the end of you.

The tears burst and I spun above her, wrenching inside, gripping the sheet and wiping it furiously about her eyes.

I can't stop it! she said. It's no use. It burns so much but I can't stop it, it's so sad but I've got to cry!

She kept on crying.

Soon there was just a smear of muddled color on the pillow where her face had been, and then the pillow was washing away.

The moisture spread, reaching out and touching me, filling the bed until at last it and I collapsed on the floor.

Yet the stain continued widening.

I had the curious feeling that people were already coming in, that someone already was disassembling our frame, pressing us flat, saying, Well here's one we can throw out. You can see how the house, the cow, etc., have all bled together. You can't recognize the woman anymore, or see that this once was a bed and . . . well it's all a big puddle except those flowers. Flowers are a dime a dozen but these are pretty good, we could snip out the flowers, I guess, give them their own small frame. Might fetch a dollar or two, what do you say?

1992

Sinclair Ross
1908–1996

Born on a homestead in Saskatchewan, near Prince Albert, Ross grew up on the prairie he writes about in his short stories and well-known novels, like As For Me and My House *(1941). He was a realist, describing the harsh life there as he and people around him experienced it. His work was highly influential for other writers, demonstrating that it was possible to write about your own place. "He showed me that fiction didn't have to be about lords and ladies in castles," Margaret Laurence said. Through the difficult time of the 1930s and 1940s, Ross's short stories were published in small magazines, especially* The Queen's Quarterly. *They were not published in a collection until 1968, as* The Lamp at Noon and Other Stories.

Snow storms, sand storms, and drought almost become characters in Ross's fiction. They have moods and voices, as well as destructive intentions. People struggle against them, against their awesome power. Dreams, especially the dreams of men, are consumed by the elements which wipe out crops and kill livestock. Women are forced into devastating isolation and loneliness.

In this harsh environment, people's lives become distorted and Ross's characters betray themselves and one another. The third-person narrators in Ross's fiction do not take sides, however. Often, gender expectations are puzzling. Men do not know how to be the men women want, while women feel neglected in the face of the love men have for the land or their animals. Anyone with artistic inclinations has a hard time, women yearn for the beautiful things in life while men work doggedly to survive, and emotional expression is a foolish luxury at best, a weakness at worst.

The Painted Door

Straight across the hills it was five miles from John's farm to his father's. But in winter, with the roads impassable, a team had to make a wide detour and skirt the hills, so that from five the distance was more than trebled to seventeen.

"I think I'll walk," John said at breakfast to his wife. "The drifts in the hills wouldn't hold a horse, but they'll carry me all right. If I leave early I can spend a few hours helping him with his chores, and still be back by suppertime."

She went to the window, and thawing a clear place in the frost with her breath, stood looking across the snowswept farmyard to the huddle of stables and sheds. "There was a double wheel around the moon last night," she countered presently. "You said yourself we could expect a storm. It isn't right to leave me here alone. Surely I'm as important as your father."

He glanced up uneasily, then drinking off his coffee tried to reassure her. "But there's nothing to be afraid of—even supposing it does start to storm. You won't need to go near the stable. Everything's fed and watered now to last till night. I'll be back at the latest by seven or eight."

She went on blowing against the frosted pane, carefully elongating the clear place until it was oval-shaped and symmetrical. He watched her a moment or two longer, then more insistently repeated, "I say you won't need to go near the stable. Everything's fed and watered, and I'll see that there's plenty of wood in. That will be all right, won't it?"

"Yes—of course—I heard you—" It was a curiously cold voice now, as if the words were chilled by their contact with the frosted pane. "Plenty to eat—plenty of wood to keep me warm—what more could a woman ask for?"

"But he's an old man—living there all alone. What is it, Ann? You're not like yourself this morning."

She shook her head without turning. "Pay no attention to me. Seven years a farmer's wife—it's time I was used to staying alone."

Slowly the clear place on the glass enlarged: oval, then round, then oval again. The sun was risen above the frost mists now, so keen and hard a glitter on the snow that instead of warmth its rays seemed shedding cold. One of the two-year-old colts that had cantered away when John turned the horses out for water stood covered with rime[1] at the stable door again, head down and body hunched, each breath a little plume of steam against the frosty air. She shivered, but did not turn. In the clear, bitter light the long white miles of prairie landscape seemed a region alien to life. Even the distant farmsteads she could see served only to intensify a sense of isolation. Scattered across the face of so vast and bleak a wilderness it was difficult to conceive them as a testimony of human hardihood and endurance. Rather they seemed futile, lost, to cower before the implacibility of snow-swept earth and clear pale sun-chilled sky.

And when at last she turned from the window there was a brooding stillness in her face as if she had recognized this mastery of snow and cold. It troubled John. "If you're really afraid," he yielded, "I

1. Frost.

won't go today. Lately it's been so cold, that's all. I just wanted to make sure he's all right in case we do have a storm."

"I know—I'm not really afraid." She was putting in a fire now, and he could no longer see her face. "Pay no attention. It's ten miles there and back, so you'd better get started."

"You ought to know by now I wouldn't stay away," he tried to brighten her. "No matter how it stormed. Before we were married—remember? Twice a week I never missed and we had some bad blizzards that winter too."

He was a slow, unambitious man, content with his farm and cattle, naïvely proud of Ann. He had been bewildered by it once, her caring for a dull-witted fellow like him; then assured at last of her affection he had relaxed against it gratefully, unsuspecting it might ever be less constant than his own. Even now, listening to the restless brooding in her voice, he felt only a quick, unformulated kind of pride that after seven years his absence for a day should still concern her. While she, his trust and earnestness controlling her again:

"I know. It's just that sometimes when you're away I get lonely. . . . There's a long cold tramp in front of you. You'll let me fix a scarf around your face."

He nodded. "And on my way I'll drop in at Steven's place. Maybe he'll come over tonight for a game of cards. You haven't seen anybody but me for the last two weeks."

She glanced up sharply, then busied herself clearing the table. "It will mean another two miles if you do. You're going to be cold and tired enough as it is. When you're gone I think I'll paint the kitchen woodwork. White this time—you remember we got the paint last fall. It's going to make the room a lot lighter. I'll be too busy to find the day long."

"I will though," he insisted, "and if a storm gets up you'll feel safer, knowing that he's coming. That's what you need, maybe— someone to talk to besides me."

She stood at the stove motionless a moment, then turned to him uneasily. "Will you shave then, John—now—before you go?"

He glanced at her questioningly, and avoiding his eyes she tried to explain, "I mean—he may be here before you're back—and you won't have a chance then."

"But it's only Steven—we're not going anywhere."

"He'll be shaved, though—that's what I mean—and I'd like you too to spend a little time on yourself."

He stood up, stroking the heavy stubble on his chin. "Maybe I should—only it softens up the skin too much. Especially when I've got to face the wind."

She nodded and began to help him dress, bringing heavy socks and a big woollen sweater from the bedroom, wrapping a scarf around his face and forehead. "I'll tell Steven to come early," he said, as he went out. "In time for supper. Likely there'll be chores for me to do, so if I'm not back by six don't wait."

From the bedroom window she watched him nearly a mile along the road. The fire had gone down when at last she turned away, and already through the house there was an encroaching chill. A blaze sprang up again when the draughts were opened, but as she went on clearing the table her movements were furtive and constrained. It was the silence weighing upon her—the frozen silence of the bitter fields and sun-chilled sky—lurking outside as if alive, relentlessly in wait, mile-deep between her now and John. She listened to it, suddenly tense, motionless. The fire crackled and the clock ticked. Always it was there. "I'm a fool," she whispered, rattling the dishes in defiance, going back to the stove to put in another fire. "Warm and safe—I'm a fool. It's a good chance when he's away to paint. The day will go quickly. I won't have time to brood."

Since November now the paint had been waiting warmer weather. The frost in the walls on a day like this would crack and peel it as it dried, but she needed something to keep her hands occupied, something to stave off the gathering cold and loneliness. "First of all," she said aloud, opening the paint and mixing it with a little turpentine, "I must get the house warmer. Fill up the stove and open the oven door so that all the heat comes out. Wad something along the window sills to keep out the draughts. Then I'll feel brighter. It's the cold that depresses."

She moved briskly, performing each little task with careful and exaggerated absorption, binding her thoughts to it, making it a screen between herself and the surrounding snow and silence. But when the stove was filled and the windows sealed it was more difficult again. Above the quiet, steady swishing of her brush against the bedroom door the clock began to tick. Suddenly her movements became precise, deliberate, her posture self-conscious, as if someone had entered the room and were watching her. It was the silence again, aggressive, hovering. The fire spit and crackled at it. Still it was there. "I'm a fool," she repeated. "All farmers' wives have to stay alone. I mustn't give in this way. I mustn't brood. A few hours now and they'll be here."

The sound of her voice reassured her. She went on: "I'll get them a good supper—and for coffee after cards bake some of the little cakes with raisins that he likes. . . . Just three of us, so I'll watch, and let John play. It's better with four, but at least we can talk. That's all I need—someone to talk to. John never talks. He's stronger—doesn't need to. But he likes Steven—no matter what the neighbours say. Maybe he'll have him come again, and some other young people too. It's what we need, both of us, to help keep young ourselves. . . . And then before we know it we'll be into March. It's cold still in March sometimes, but you never mind the same. At least you're beginning to think about spring."

She began to think about it now. Thoughts that outstripped her words, that left her alone again with herself and the ever-lurking silence. Eager and hopeful first, then clenched, rebellious, lonely. Windows open, sun and thawing earth again, the urge of growing, living things. Then the days that began in the morning at half-past four and lasted till ten at night; the meals at which John gulped his food and scarcely spoke a word; the brute-tired stupid eyes he turned on her if ever she mentioned town or visiting.

For spring was drudgery again. John never hired a man to help him. He wanted a mortgage-free farm; then a new house and pretty clothes for her. Sometimes, because with the best of crops it was going to take so long to pay off anyway, she wondered whether they mightn't better let the mortgage wait a little. Before they were worn out, before their best years were gone. It was something of life she wanted, not just a house and furniture; something of John, not pretty clothes when she would be too old to wear them. But John of course couldn't understand. To him it seemed only right that she should have the clothes—only right that he, fit for nothing else, should slave away fifteen hours a day to give them to her. There was in his devotion a baffling, insurmountable humility that made him feel the need of sacrifice. And when his muscles ached, when his feet dragged stolidly with weariness, then it seemed that in some measure at least he was making amends for his big hulking body and simple mind. Year after year their lives went on in the same little groove. He drove his horses in the field; she milked the cows and hoed potatoes. By dint of his drudgery he saved a few months' wages, added a few dollars more each fall to his payments on the mortgage; but the only real difference that it all made was to deprive her of his companionship, to make him a little duller, older, uglier than he might otherwise have been. He never saw their lives objectively. To him it was not what he actually accomplished by means of the sacrifice that mattered, but the sacrifice itself, the gesture—something done for her sake.

And she, understanding, kept her silence. In such a gesture, however futile, there was a graciousness not to be shattered lightly. "John," she would begin sometimes, "you're doing too much. Get a man to help you—just for a month—" but smiling down at her he would answer simply, "I don't mind. Look at the hands on me. They're made for work." While in his voice there would be a stalwart ring to tell her that by her thoughtfulness she had made him only the more resolved to serve her, to prove his devotion and fidelity.

They were useless, such thoughts. She knew. It was his very devotion that made them useless, that forbade her to rebel. Yet over and over, sometimes hunched still before their bleakness, sometimes her brush making swift sharp strokes to pace the chafe and rancour that they brought, she persisted in them.

This now, the winter, was their slack season. She could sleep sometimes till eight, and John till seven. They could linger over their meals a little, read, play cards, go visiting the neighbours. It was the time to relax, to indulge and enjoy themselves; but instead, fretful and impatient, they kept on waiting for the spring. They were compelled now, not by labour, but by the spirit of labour. A spirit that pervaded their lives and brought with idleness a sense of guilt. Sometimes they did sleep late, sometimes they did play cards, but always uneasily, always reproached by the thought of more important things that might be done. When John got up at five to attend to the fire he wanted to stay up and go out to the stable. When he sat down to a meal he hurried his food and pushed his chair away again, from habit, from sheer work-instinct, even though it was only to put more wood in the stove, or go down cellar to cut up beets and turnips for the cows.

And anyway, sometimes she asked herself, why sit trying to talk with a man who never talked? Why talk when there was nothing to talk about but crops and cattle, the weather and the neighbours? The neighbours, too—why go visiting them when still it was the same—crops and cattle, the weather and the other neighbours? Why go to the dances in the schoolhouse to sit among the older women, one of them now, married seven years, or to waltz with the work-bent, tired old farmers to a squeaky fiddle tune? Once she had danced with Steven six or seven times in the evening, and they had talked about it for as many months. It was easier to stay at home. John never danced or enjoyed himself. He was always uncomfortable in his good suit and shoes. He didn't like shaving in the cold weather oftener than once or twice a week. It was easier to stay at home, to stand at the window staring out across the bitter fields, to count the days and look forward to another spring.

But now, alone with herself in the winter silence, she saw the spring for what it really was. This spring—next spring—all the springs and summers still to come. While they grew old, while their bodies warped, while their minds kept shrivelling dry and empty like their lives. "I mustn't," she said aloud again. "I married him—and he's a good man. I mustn't keep on this way. It will be noon before long, and then time to think about supper. . . . Maybe he'll come early—and as soon as John is finished at the stable we can all play cards."

It was getting cold again, and she left her painting to put in more wood. But this time the warmth spread slowly. She pushed a mat up to the outside door, and went back to the window to pat down the woollen shirt that was wadded along the sill. Then she paced a few times round the room, then poked the fire and rattled the stove lids, then paced again. The fire crackled, the clock ticked. The silence now seemed more intense than ever, seemed to have reached a pitch where it faintly moaned. She began to pace on tiptoe, listening, her shoulders drawn together, not realising for a while that it was the wind she heard, thin-strained and whimpering through the eaves.

Then she wheeled to the window, and with quick short breaths

thawed the frost to see again. The glitter was gone. Across the drifts
sped swift and snakelike little tongues of snow. She could not follow
them, where they sprang from, or where they disappeared. It was as
if all across the yard the snow were shivering awake—roused by the
warnings of the wind to hold itself in readiness for the impending
storm. The sky had become a sombre, whitish grey. It, too, as if
in readiness, had shifted and lay close to earth. Before her as she
watched a mane of powdery snow reared up breast-high against the
darker background of the stable, tossed for a moment angrily, and
then subsided again as if whipped down to obedience and restraint.
But another followed, more reckless and impatient than the first.
Another reeled and dashed itself against the window where she
watched. Then ominously for a while there were only the angry little snakes of snow. The wind rose, creaking the troughs that were
wired beneath the eaves. In the distance, sky and prairie now were
merged into one another linelessly. All round her it was gathering;
already in its press and whimpering there strummed a boding of
eventual fury. Again she saw a mane of snow spring up, so dense
and high this time that all the sheds and stables were obscured.
Then others followed, whirling fiercely out of hand; and, when at
last they cleared, the stables seemed in dimmer outline than before.
It was the snow beginning, long lancet shafts of it, straight from the
north, borne almost level by the straining wind. "He'll be there
soon," she whispered, "and coming home it will be in his back.
He'll leave again right away. He saw the double wheel—he knows
the kind of storm there'll be."

She went back to her painting. For a while it was easier, all her
thoughts half-anxious ones of John in the blizzard, struggling his
way across the hills; but petulantly again she soon began, "I knew
we were going to have a storm—I told him so—but it doesn't matter what I say. Big stubborn fool—he goes his own way anyway. It
doesn't matter what becomes of me. In a storm like this he'll never
get home. He won't even try. And while he sits keeping his father
company I can look after his stable for him, go ploughing through
snowdrifts up to my knees—nearly frozen—"

Not that she meant or believed her words. It was just an effort to
convince herself that she did have a grievance, to justify her rebellious thoughts, to prove John responsible for her unhappiness. She

was young still, eager for excitement and distractions; and John's steadfastness rebuked her vanity, made her complaints seem weak and trivial. She went on, fretfully, "If he'd listen to me sometimes and not be so stubborn we wouldn't still be living in a house like this. Seven years in two rooms—seven years and never a new stick of furniture. . . . There—as if another coat of paint could make it different anyway."

She cleaned her brush, filled up the stove again, and went back to the window. There was a void white moment that she thought must be frost formed on the window pane; then, like a fitful shadow through the whirling snow, she recognized the stable roof. It was incredible. The sudden, maniac raging of the storm struck from her face all its pettishness. Her eyes glazed with fear a little; her lips blanched. "If he starts for home now," she whispered silently—"But he won't—he knows I'm safe—he knows Steven's coming. Across the hills he would never dare."

She turned to the stove, holding out her hands to the warmth. Around her now there seemed a constant sway and tremor, as if the air were vibrating with the shudderings of the walls. She stood quite still, listening. Sometimes the wind struck with sharp, savage blows. Sometimes it bore down in a sustained, minute-long blast, silent with effort and intensity; then with a foiled shriek of threat wheeled away to gather and assault again. Always the eave-troughs creaked and sawed. She stared towards the window again, then detecting the morbid trend of her thoughts, prepared fresh coffee and forced herself to drink a few mouthfuls. "He would never dare," she whispered again. "He wouldn't leave the old man anyway in such a storm. Safe in here—there's nothing for me to keep worrying about. It's after one already. I'll do my baking now, and then it will be time to get supper ready for Steven."

Soon, however, she began to doubt whether Steven would come. In such a storm even a mile was enough to make a man hesitate. Especially Steven, who was hardly the one to face a blizzard for the sake of someone else's chores. He had a stable of his own to look after anyway. It would be only natural for him to think that when the storm blew up John had turned again for home. Another man would have—would have put his wife first.

But she felt little dread or uneasiness at the prospect of spending the night alone. It was the first time she had been left like this on her own resources, and her reaction, now that she could face and appraise her situation calmly, was gradually to feel it a kind of adventure and responsibility. It stimulated her. Before nightfall she must go to the stable and feed everything. Wrap up in some of John's clothes—take a ball of string in her hand, one end tied to the door, so that no matter how blinding the storm she could at least find her way back to the house. She had heard of people having to do that. It appealed to her now because suddenly it made life dramatic. She had not felt the storm yet, only watched it for a minute through the window.

It took nearly an hour to find enough string, to choose the right socks and sweaters. Long before it was time to start out she tried on John's clothes, changing and rechanging, striding around the room to make sure there would be play enough for pitching hay and struggling over snowdrifts; then she took them off again, and for a while busied herself baking the little cakes with raisins that he liked.

Night came early. Just for a moment on the doorstep she shrank back, uncertain. The slow dimming of the light clutched her with an illogical sense of abandonment. It was like the covert withdrawal of an ally, leaving the alien miles unleashed and unrestrained. Watching the hurricane of writhing snow rage past the little house she forced herself, "They'll never stand the night unless I get them fed. It's nearly dark already, and I've work to last an hour."

Timidly, unwinding a little of the string, she crept out from the shelter of the doorway. A gust of wind spun her forward a few yards, then plunged her headlong against a drift that in the dense white whirl lay invisible across her path. For nearly a minute she huddled still, breathless and dazed. The snow was in her mouth and nostrils, inside her scarf and up her sleeves. As she tried to straighten a smothering scud flung itself against her face, cutting off her breath a second time. The wind struck from all sides, blustering and furious. It was as if the storm had discovered her, as if all its forces were concentrated upon her extinction. Seized with panic suddenly she threshed out a moment with her arms, then stumbled back and sprawled her length across the drift.

But this time she regained her feet quickly, roused by the whip and batter of the storm to retaliative anger. For a moment her impulse was to face the wind and strike back blow for blow; then, as suddenly as it had come, her frantic strength gave way to limpness and exhaustion. Suddenly, a comprehension so clear and terrifying that it struck all thoughts of the stable from her mind, she realized in such a storm her puniness. And the realization gave her new strength, stilled this time to a desperate persistence. Just for a moment the wind held her, numb and swaying in its vise; then slowly, buckled far forward, she groped her way again towards the house.

Inside, leaning against the door, she stood tense and still a while. It was almost dark now. The top of the stove glowed a deep, dull red. Heedless of the storm, self-absorbed and self-satisfied, the clock ticked on like a glib little idiot. "He shouldn't have gone," she whispered silently. "He saw the double wheel—he knew. He shouldn't have left me here alone."

For so fierce now, so insane and dominant did the blizzard seem, that she could not credit the safety of the house. The warmth and lull around her was not real yet, not to be relied upon. She was still at the mercy of the storm. Only her body pressing hard like this against the door was staving it off. She didn't dare move. She didn't dare ease the ache and strain. "He shouldn't have gone," she repeated, thinking of the stable again, reproached by her helplessness. "They'll freeze in their stalls—and I can't reach them. He'll say it's all my fault. He won't believe I tried."

Then Steven came. Quickly, startled to quietness and control, she let him in and lit the lamp. He stared at her a moment, then flinging off his cap crossed to where she stood by the table and seized her arms. "You're so white—what's wrong? Look at me—" It was like him in such little situations to be masterful. "You should have known better—for a while I thought I wasn't going to make it here myself—"

"I was afraid you wouldn't come—John left early, and there was the stable—"

But the storm had unnerved her, and suddenly at the assurance of his touch and voice the fear that had been gripping her gave way to an hysteria of relief. Scarcely aware of herself she seized his arm and sobbed against it. He remained still a moment unyielding, then slipped his other arm around her shoulder. It was comforting and she relaxed against it, hushed by a sudden sense of lull and safety.

Her shoulders trembled with the easing of the strain, then fell limp and still. "You're shivering,"—he drew her gently towards the stove. "It's all right—nothing to be afraid of. I'm going to see to the stable."

It was a quiet, sympathetic voice, yet with an undertone of insolence, a kind of mockery even, that made her draw away quickly and busy herself putting in a fire. With his lips drawn in a little smile he watched her till she looked at him again. The smile too was insolent, but at the same time companionable; Steven's smile, and therefore difficult to reprove. It lit up his lean, still-boyish face with a peculiar kind of arrogance: features and smile that were different from John's, from other men's—wilful and derisive, yet naïvely so— as if it were less the difference itself he was conscious of, than the long-accustomed privilege that thereby fell his due. He was erect, tall, square-shouldered. His hair was dark and trim, his lips curved soft and full. While John, she made the comparison swiftly, was thickset, heavy-jowled, and stooped. He always stood before her helpless, a kind of humility and wonderment in his attitude. And Steven now smiled on her appraisingly with the worldly-wise assurance of one for whom a woman holds neither mystery nor illusion.

"It was good of you to come, Steven," she responded, the words running into a sudden, empty laugh. "Such a storm to face—I suppose I should feel flattered."

For his presumption, his misunderstanding of what had been only a momentary weakness, instead of angering quickened her, roused from latency and long disuse all the instincts and resources of her femininity. She felt eager, challenged. Something was at hand that hitherto had always eluded her, even in the early days with John, something vital, beckoning, meaningful. She didn't understand, but she knew. The texture of the moment was satisfyingly dreamlike: an incredibility perceived as such, yet acquiesced in. She was John's wife—she knew—but also she knew that Steven standing here was different from John. There was no thought or motive, no understanding of herself as the knowledge persisted. Wary and poised round a sudden little core of blind excitement she evaded him, "But it's nearly dark—hadn't you better hurry if you're going to do the chores? Don't trouble—I can get them off myself—"

An hour later when he returned from the stable she was in another dress, hair rearranged, a little flush of colour in her face. Pouring warm water for him from the kettle into the basin she said evenly, "By the time you're washed supper will be ready. John said we weren't to wait for him."

He looked at her a moment, "You don't mean you're expecting John tonight? The way it's blowing—"

"Of course." As she spoke she could feel the colour deepening in her face. "We're going to play cards. He was the one that suggested it."

He went on washing, and then as they took their places at the table, resumed, "So John's coming. When are you expecting him?"

"He said it might be seven o'clock—or a little later." Conversation with Steven at other times had always been brisk and natural, but now all at once she found it strained. "He may have work to do for his father. That's what he said when he left. Why do you ask, Steven?"

"I was just wondering—it's a rough night."

"You don't know John. It would take more than a storm to stop him."

She glanced up again and he was smiling at her. The same insolence, the same little twist of mockery and appraisal. It made her flinch, and ask herself why she was pretending to expect John—why there should be this instinct of defence to force her. This time, instead of poise and excitement, it brought a reminder that she had changed her dress and rearranged her hair. It crushed in a sudden silence, through which she heard the whistling wind again, and the creaking saw of the eaves. Neither spoke now. There was something strange, almost frightening, about this Steven and his quiet, unrelenting smile; but strangest of all was the familiarity: the Steven she had never seen or encountered, and yet had always known, always expected, always waited for. It was less Steven himself that she felt than his inevitability. Just as she had felt the snow, the silence and the storm. She kept her eyes lowered, on the window past his shoulder, on the stove, but his smile now seemed to exist apart from him, to merge and hover with the silence. She clinked a cup—listened to the whistle of the storm—always it was there. He began to speak, but her mind missed the meaning of his words. Swiftly she was making comparisons again; his face so different to John's, so handsome and young and clean-shaven. Swiftly, helplessly, feeling the imperceptible and relentless ascendancy that thereby he was gaining over her, sensing sudden menace in this new, more vital life, even as she felt drawn towards it.

The lamp between them flickered as an onslaught of the storm sent shudderings through the room. She rose to build up the fire again and he followed her. For a long time they stood close to the stove, their arms almost touching. Once as the blizzard creaked the house she spun around sharply, fancying it was John at the door; but quietly he intercepted her. "Not tonight—you might as well make up your mind to it. Across the hills in a storm like this—it would be suicide to try."

Her lips trembled suddenly in an effort to answer, to parry the certainty in his voice, then set thin and bloodless. She was afraid now. Afraid of his face so different from John's—of his smile, of her own helplessness to rebuke it. Afraid of the storm, isolating her here alone with him. They tried to play cards, but she kept starting up at every creak and shiver of the walls. "It's too rough a night," he repeated. "Even for John. Just relax a few minutes—stop worrying and pay a little attention to me."

But in his tone there was a contradiction to his words. For it implied that she was not worrying—that her only concern was lest it really might be John at the door.

And the implication persisted. He filled up the stove for her, shuffled the cards—won—shuffled—still it was there. She tried to respond to his conversation, to think of the game, but helplessly into her cards instead she began to ask, Was he right? Was that why he smiled? Why he seemed to wait, expectant and assured?

The clock ticked, the fire crackled. Always it was there. Furtively for a moment she watched him as he deliberated over his hand. John, even in the days before they were married, had never looked like that. Only this morning she had asked him to shave. Because Steven was coming—because she had been afraid to see them side by side—because deep within herself she had known even then. The same knowledge, furtive and forbidden, that was flaunted now in Steven's smile. "You look cold," he said at last, dropping his cards and rising from the table. "We're not playing, anyway. Come over to the stove for a few minutes and get warm."

"But first I think we'll hang blankets over the door. When there's a blizzard like this we always do." It seemed that in sane, commonplace activity there might be release, a moment or two in which to recover herself. "John has nails to put them on. They keep out a little of the draught."

He stood on a chair for her, and hung the blankets that she carried from the bedroom. Then for a moment they stood silent, watching the blankets sway and tremble before the blade of wind that spurted around the jamb. "I forgot," she said at last, "that I painted the bedroom door. At the top there, see—I've smeared the blankets."

He glanced at her curiously, and went back to the stove. She followed him, trying to imagine the hills in such a storm, wondering whether John would come. "A man couldn't live in it," suddenly he answered her thoughts, lowering the oven door and drawing up their chairs one on each side of it. "He knows you're safe. It isn't likely that he'd leave his father, anyway."

"The wind will be in his back," she persisted. "The winter before we were married—all the blizzards that we had that year—and he never missed—"

"Blizzards like this one? Up in the hills he wouldn't be able to keep his direction for a hundred yards. Listen to it a minute and ask yourself."

His voice seemed softer, kindlier now. She met his smile a moment, its assured little twist of appraisal, then for a long time sat silent, tense, careful again to avoid his eyes.

Everything now seemed to depend on this. It was the same as a few hours ago when she braced the door against the storm. He was watching her, smiling. She dared not move, unclench her hands, or raise her eyes. The flames crackled, the clock ticked. The storm wrenched the walls as if to make them buckle in. So rigid and desperate were all her muscles set, withstanding, that the room around her seemed to swim and reel. So rigid and strained that for relief at last, despite herself, she raised her head and met his eyes again.

Intending that it should be for only an instant, just to breathe again, to ease the tension that had grown unbearable—but in his smile now, instead of the insolent appraisal that she feared, there seemed a kind of warmth and sympathy. An understanding that quickened and encouraged her—that made her wonder why but a moment ago she had been afraid. It was as if the storm had lulled, as if she had suddenly found calm and shelter.

Or perhaps, the thought seized her, perhaps instead of his smile it was she who had changed. She who, in the long, wind-creaked silence, had emerged from the increment of codes and loyalties to her real, unfettered self. She who now felt his air of appraisal as nothing more than an understanding of the unfulfilled woman that until this moment had lain within her brooding and unadmitted, reproved out of consciousness by the insistence of an outgrown, routine fidelity.

For there had always been Steven. She understood now. Seven years—almost as long as John—ever since the night they first danced together.

The lamp was burning dry, and through the dimming light, isolated in the fastness of silence and storm, they watched each other. Her face was white and struggling still. His was handsome, clean-shaven, young. Her eyes were fanatic, believing desperately, fixed upon him as if to exclude all else, as if to find justification. His were cool, bland, drooped a little with expectancy. The light kept dimming, gathering the shadows round them, hushed, conspiratorial. He was smiling still. Her hands again were clenched up white and hard.

"But he always came," she persisted. "The wildest, coldest nights—even such a night as this. There was never a storm—"

"Never a storm like this one." There was a quietness in his smile now, a kind of simplicity almost, as if to reassure her. "You were out in it yourself for a few minutes. He'd have it for five miles, across the hills. . . . I'd think twice myself, on such a night before risking even one."

Long after he was asleep she lay listening to the storm. As a check on the draught up the chimney they had left one of the stovelids partly off, and through the open bedroom door she could see the flickerings of flame and shadow on the kitchen wall. They leaped and sank fantastically. The longer she watched the more alive they seemed to be. There was one great shadow that struggled towards her threateningly, massive and black and engulfing all the room.

Again and again it advanced, about to spring, but each time a little whip of light subdued it to its place among the others on the wall. Yet though it never reached her still she cowered, feeling that gathered there was all the frozen wilderness, its heart of terror and invincibility.

Then she dozed a while, and the shadow was John. Interminably he advanced. The whips of light still flickered and coiled, but now suddenly they were the swift little snakes that this afternoon she had watched twist and shiver across the snow. And they too were advancing. They writhed and vanished and came again. She lay still, paralysed. He was over her now, so close that she could have touched him. Already it seemed that a deadly tightening hand was on her throat. She tried to scream but her lips were locked. Steven beside her slept on heedlessly.

Until suddenly as she lay staring up at him a gleam of light revealed his face. And in it was not a trace of threat or anger—only calm, and stonelike hopelessness.

That was like John. He began to withdraw, and frantically she tried to call him back. "It isn't true—not really true—listen, John—" but the words clung frozen to her lips. Already there was only the shriek of wind again, the sawing eaves, the leap and twist of shadow on the wall.

She sat up, startled now and awake. And so real had he seemed there, standing close to her, so vivid the sudden age and sorrow in his face, that at first she could not make herself understand she had been only dreaming. Against the conviction of his presence in the room it was necessary to insist over and over that he must still be with his father on the other side of the hills. Watching the shadows she had fallen asleep. It was only her mind, her imagination, distorted to a nightmare by the illogical and unadmitted dread of his return. But he wouldn't come. Steven was right. In such a storm he would never try. They were safe, alone. No one would ever know. It was only fear, morbid and irrational; only the sense of guilt that even her new-found and challenged womanhood could not entirely quell.

She knew now. She had not let herself understand or acknowledge it as guilt before, but gradually through the wind-torn silence of the night his face compelled her. The face that had watched her from the darkness with its stonelike sorrow—the face that was really John—John more than his features of mere flesh and bone could ever be.

She wept silently. The fitful gleam of light began to sink. On the ceiling and wall at last there was only a faint dull flickering glow. The little house shuddered and quailed, and a chill crept in again. Without wakening Steven she slipped out to build up the fire. It was burned to a few spent embers now, and the wood she put on seemed a long time catching light. The wind swirled through the blankets they had hung around the door, and then, hollow and moaning, roared up the chimney again, as if against its will drawn back to serve still longer with the onrush of the storm.

For a long time she crouched over the stove, listening. Earlier in the evening, with the lamp lit and the fire crackling, the house had seemed a stand against the wilderness, a refuge of feeble walls wherein persisted the elements of human meaning and survival. Now, in the cold, creaking darkness, it was strangely extinct, looted by the storm and abandoned again. She lifted the stove lid and fanned the embers till at last a swift little tongue of flame began to lick around the wood. Then she replaced the lid, extended her hands, and as if frozen in that attitude stood waiting.

It was not long now. After a few minutes she closed the draughts, and as the flames whirled back upon each other, beating against the top of the stove and sending out flickers of light again, a warmth surged up to relax her stiffened limbs. But shivering and numb it had been easier. The bodily well-being that the warmth induced gave play again to an ever more insistent mental suffering. She remembered the shadow that was John. She saw him bent towards her, then retreating, his features pale and overcast with unaccusing grief. She re-lived their seven years together and, in retrospect, found them to be years of worth and dignity. Until crushed by it all at last, seized by a sudden need to suffer and atone, she crossed to where the draught was bitter, and for a long time stood unflinching on the icy floor.

The storm was close here. Even through the blankets she could feel a sift of snow against her face. The eaves sawed, the walls creaked, and the wind was like a wolf in howling flight.

And yet, suddenly she asked herself, hadn't there been other storms, other blizzards? And through the worst of them hadn't he always reached her?

Clutched by the thought she stood rooted a minute. It was hard now to understand how she could have so deceived herself—how a moment of passion could have quieted within her not only conscience, but reason and discretion too. John always came. There could never be a storm to stop him. He was strong, inured to the cold. He had crossed the hills since his boyhood, knew every creekbed and gully. It was madness to go on like this—to wait. While there was still time she must waken Steven, and hurry him away.

But in the bedroom again, standing at Steven's side, she hesitated. In his detachment from it all, in his quiet, even breathing, there was such sanity, such realism. For him nothing had happened; nothing would. If she wakened him he would only laugh and tell her to listen to the storm. Already it was long past midnight; either John had lost his way or not set out at all. And she knew that in his devotion there was nothing foolhardy. He would never risk a storm beyond his endurance, never permit himself a sacrifice likely to endanger her lot or future. They were both safe. No one would ever know. She must control herself—be sane like Steven.

For comfort she let her hand rest a while on Steven's shoulder. It would be easier were he awake now, with her, sharing her guilt; but gradually as she watched his handsome face in the glimmering light she came to understand that for him no guilt existed. Just as there had been no passion, no conflict. Nothing but the sane appraisal of their situation, nothing but the expectant little smile, and the arrogance of features that were different from John's. She winced deeply, remembering how she had fixed her eyes on those features, how she had tried to believe that so handsome and young, so different from John's, they must in themselves be her justification.

In the flickering light they were still young, still handsome. No longer her justification—she knew now—John was the man—but wistfully still, wondering sharply at their power and tyranny, she touched them a moment with her fingertips again.

She could not blame him. There had been no passion, no guilt; therefore there could be no responsibility. Looking down at him as he slept, half-smiling still, his lips relaxed in the conscienceless complacency of his achievement, she understood that thus he was revealed in his entirety—all there ever was or ever could be. John was the man. With him lay all the future. For tonight, slowly and contritely through the day and years to come, she would try to make amends.

Then she stole back to the kitchen, and without thought, impelled by overwhelming need again, returned to the door where the draught was bitter still. Gradually towards morning the storm began to spend itself. Its terror blast became a feeble, worn-out moan. The leap of light and shadow sank, and a chill crept in again. Always the eaves creaked, tortured with wordless prophecy. Heedless of it all the clock ticked on in idiot content.

They found him the next day, less than a mile from home. Drifting with the storm he had run against his own pasture fence and overcome had frozen there, erect still, both hands clasping fast the wire.

"He was south of here," they said wonderingly when she told them how he had come across the hills. "Straight south—you'd wonder how he could have missed the buildings. It was the wind last night, coming every way at once. He shouldn't have tried. There was a double wheel around the moon."

She looked past them a moment, then as if to herself said simply, "If you knew him, though—John would try."

It was later, when they had left her a while to be alone with him, that she knelt and touched his hand. Her eyes dimmed, it was still such a strong and patient hand; then, transfixed, they suddenly grew wide and clear. On the palm, white even against its frozen whiteness, was a little smear of paint.

1939, 1968

Diane Schoemperlen
b. 1954

A native of Thunder Bay, in Northern Ontario, Schoemperlen graduated from Lakehead University before moving to Alberta, where she lived for several years. She then moved to Kingston, On-

tario, on the St. Lawrence River, to the old city that was supposed
to be the capital of Canada. It has a thriving community of artists
and writers, as well as the greystone Queen's University. It suits
Schoemperlen, who has published several volumes of short fiction,
including Double Exposures *(1984),* Forms of Devotion *(1998)*
winner of the Governor General's Award for fiction, and The Man
of My Dreams *(1990) from which this piece comes.*

Schoemperlen has created her own unique short fiction form,
made up of what might be called short short stories. It all looks de-
ceptively simple to compose. Each piece is like a story cycle, made up
of these small stories, which are linked by voice and theme. They
cover considerable time, ideas, images, characters. Schoemperlen
grounds her writing in specific details of ordinary people's lives,
which give this fiction immediacy, a strong sense of autobiography,
and a documentary tone, but Schoemperlen's work is always
strongly narrative.

Schoemperlen expects a participating reader, one who notices
patterns and repetitions, who enjoys making connections, who recognizes situations familiar from the story or from twentieth-century
life in Canada. As in the following story, Schoemperlen often points
beyond her piece, to another art form or book, in this case Canadian painter Alex Colville's well-known Horse and Train.

This story raises questions about whether or not there are underlying, possibly meaningful threads running through most people's
lives, like trains or horses or blankets or a nickname. It reminds us
that coming of age might be simple—for someone.

Railroading, or: Twelve Small Stories
with the Word "Train" in the Title

Love Train

For a long time after Lesley and Cliff broke up, Cliff was al-
ways sending her things.
　　Flowers.
Red roses by the dramatic dozen.
Delicate frilly carnations dyed turquoise at the edges (which re-

minded Lesley of a tradition they'd observed at her elementary school on Mother's Day when each child had to wear a carnation, red if your mother was alive, white if she was dead—there were only two kids in the whole school whose mothers were dead—and what then, she wondered, was turquoise meant to signify?)

A single white orchid nestled in tissue paper in a gold box, as if they had a big date for a formal dance.

Cards. Funny cards:

"I thought you'd like to know that I've decided to start dating seals again, and . . . oh yes, my umbilical cord has grown back!"

Sentimental cards:

"I love wearing the smile . . . you put on my face!"

Funny sentimental cards:

"You You You You You You You You You You You You . . . These are a few of my favourite things!"

Apology cards:

"Please forgive me . . . my mouth is bigger than my brain!"

and:

"I'm sorry, I was wrong . . . Well, not as wrong as you, but sorrier!"

Pretty picture cards to say:

"Happy Thanksgiving!"
"Happy Hallowe'en!"
"I'm just thinking of you!"
"I'm always thinking of you!"
"I'm still thinking of you!"

Letters. Mostly letters.

Often Cliff would call during the day and leave a message on Lesley's answering machine, apologizing for having bothered her with another card or letter when she'd already told him, in no uncertain terms, that she needed some space. Then he would call right back and leave another message to apologize for having left the first one when she'd already told him to leave her alone.

He did not send the letters through the mail in the conventional way, but delivered them by hand in the middle of the night. Lesley never did catch him in the act, but she could just picture him parking his car halfway down the block, sneaking up her driveway in the dark or the rain, depositing another white envelope in her black mailbox. Where she would find it first thing in the morning.

At first it gave Lesley the creeps to think of Cliff tippy-toeing around out there while she was inside sleeping, but then she got used to hearing from him in this way. She took to checking the mailbox every morning before she put the coffee on. Waiting in her housecoat and slippers for the toast to pop and the eggs to poach, she would study the envelope first. Sometimes he put her full name on it, first and last; sometimes her first name only; once, just her initials.

Inside, the letters were always neatly typewritten on expensive bond paper. They began with phrases like "Well no . . ." or "And yes . . ." or "But maybe . . .", as if Cliff were picking up a conversation (one-sided though it might be) right in the middle where they'd left off, or as if he still thought he could still read her mind.

One of the first letters was dense with scholarly historical quotes on the nature of war. Cliff had set these erudite excerpts carefully off from the rest of the text, single-spaced and indented:

In quarrels between countries, as well as those between individuals, when they have risen to a certain height, the first cause of dissension is no longer remembered, the minds of the parties being wholly engaged in recollecting and resenting the mutual expressions of their dislike. When feuds have reached that fatal point, all considerations of reason and equity vanish; a blind fury governs, or rather, confounds all things. A people no longer regards their interest, but rather the gratification of their wrath. (John Dickson).

And later in the letter he wrote:

> The strange thing about this crisis of August 1939 was that the object between Germany and Poland was not clearly defined, and could not therefore be expressed as a concrete demand. It was a part of Hitler's nature to avoid putting things in a concrete form; to him, differences of opinion were questions of power, and tests of one's nerves and strength. (Ernst von Weizäcker).

Lesley could not imagine that Cliff actually had a repertoire of such pedantic passages floating around inside his head, just waiting for an opportunity to be called up. But she couldn't imagine that he had really gone to the library and looked them up in order to quote them at her either.

Still, this letter made her mad enough to call him. When she said on the phone, "I don't take kindly to being compared to Hitler, thank you very much," Cliff said, "Don't be ridiculous. That's not what I meant. You just don't understand."

And she said, "Well no . . . I guess not."

He apologized for making her mad, which was exactly the opposite, he said, of what he was intending to do. But the more he apologized, the madder she got. The more he assured her that he loved her even though she was crabby, cantankerous, strangled and worried, hard, cynical and detached, mercenary, unsympathetic, callous, and sarcastic—the more he assured her that he loved her in spite of her *self*—the madder she got. Until finally she hung up on him and all day she was still mad, also feeling guilty, sorry, sad, simple-minded, and defeated. She promised herself that she would send the next letter back unopened, but of course there was little real chance of that. She tried several times that afternoon to compose a letter in answer to his repeated requests for one. But she got no further than saying:

> What it all comes down to is this: in the process of getting to know you, I realized that you were not the right person for me.

It should have been simple.

In the next letter, two mornings later, Cliff turned around and blamed himself for everything, saying:

At least understand that all of this was only the result of my relentless devotion to you.

Lesley took a bath after breakfast and contemplated the incongruous conjunction of these two words.

Relentless.

Devotion.

After she'd dried her hair and cleaned the tub, she looked up "relentless" in the thesaurus. Much as she'd suspected, it was not an adjective that should be allowed to have much to do with love:

> **relentless**, *adj.* unyielding, unrelenting, implacable, unsparing; inexorable, remorseless, unflagging, dogged; undeviating, unswerving, persistent, persevering, undaunted; rigid, stern, strict, harsh, grim, austere; merciless, ruthless, unmerciful, pitiless, unpitying, unforgiving; unmitigable, inflexible, unbending, resisting, grudging; hard, imperious, obdurate, adamant, intransigent; uncompassionate, unfeeling, unsympathetic, intolerant.

The next letter was delivered on a windy Saturday night when Lesley was out on a date with somebody else. It was sitting there in the mailbox when she got home at midnight. The weather had turned cold and her driveway was filling up suddenly with crispy yellow leaves. When she opened the back door, dozens of them swirled around her ankles and slipped inside. She imagined Cliff crunching through them on his way to the mailbox, worrying about the noise, which was amplified by the hour and the wind, then noticing that her car wasn't in the garage, and then worrying about that too.

In this letter, Cliff said:

I love you like ten thousand freight trains.

Lesley thought she rather liked this one, but then she wasn't sure. She thought she'd better think about it. She hung up her coat, poured herself a glass of white wine, and sat down in the dark kitchen to think. The oval of her face reflected in the window was distorted by the glass, so that her skin was pale, her eyes were holes, and her cheeks were sunken. She did not feel pale, hollow, or sunken. She felt just fine.

I love you like ten thousand freight trains.

This was like saying:

I love you to little bits.

Who wants to be loved to *little bits*?

This was like saying:

I love you to death.

Who wants to be loved to *death*?

I love you like ten thousand freight trains.

Who wants to be loved like or by *a freight train*?

The more she thought about it, the more she realized that she knew a thing or two about trains; railroading; relentlessness.

Dream Train

As a young girl growing up in Winnipeg, Lesley lived in an Insul-brick bungalow three doors down from the train tracks, a spur line leading to Genstar Feeds. Trains travelled the spur line so seldom that when one passed in the night, it would usually wake her up with its switching and shunting, its steel wheels squealing on the frozen rails. She would lie awake listening in her little trundle bed (it wasn't really a trundle bed, it was just an ordinary twin bed, but every night at eight o'clock her mother, Amelia, would say, "Come on, little one, time to tuck you into your little trundle bed.").

Lesley liked to imagine that the train outside was not a freight train but a *real* train, a passenger train: the Super Continental, carrying dignified wealthy people as carefully as if they were eggs clear across the country in its plush coaches, the conductors in their serious uniforms graciously bringing around drinks, pillows, and magazines. She imagined the silver coaches cruising slowly past, all lit up, the people inside riding backwards, eating, sleeping, playing cards with just their heads showing, laughing as if this were the most natural thing in the world. She imagined that the Super Continental could go all the way from Vancouver to St. John's (never mind the Gulf of St. Lawrence—there must be a way around it) without stopping once.

If the train on the spur line did not actually wake Lesley up, then it slid instead into her dreams, disguised as a shaggy behemoth with red eyes and silver hooves, shaking the snow from its curly brown fur as it pawed the rails and snorted steam.

Train Tracks

As a teenager, Lesley walked along the train tracks every morning to Glengarry Heights High School. On the way, she usually met up with a boy named Eric Henderson, who was two grades older and dressed all year round in faded blue jeans, a T-shirt, and a black leather jacket with studs. Occasionally he condescended to the cold weather by wearing a pair of black gloves.

After a couple of weeks, Eric took to waiting for Lesley on the tracks where they crossed her street. He would be leaning against the signal lights smoking when she came out her front door. They never walked home together at four o'clock because, even though Lesley sometimes loitered at her locker hoping, Eric was never around at that time, having, she assumed, other more interesting, more grown-up, things to do after school.

Every morning Lesley and Eric practised balancing on the rails with their arms outstretched, and they complained about the way the tar-coated ties were never spaced quite right for walking on. Lesley kept her ears open, looking over her shoulder every few minutes, just in case. Her mother, Amelia, had often warned her, "Don't get too close to a moving train or you'll get *sucked under*."

Sometimes Eric would line up bright pennies on the silver rails so the train would come and flatten them. Lesley would watch for the pennies on her way home from school, would gather them up and save them, thin as tinfoil, in a cigar box she kept under the bed. She never put pennies on the tracks herself because she was secretly afraid that they would cause a derailment and the train would come toppling off the tracks, exploding as it rolled down the embankment, demolishing her house and her neighbours' houses and everything in them. It was okay though when Eric did it, because somehow he could be both dangerous and charmed at the same time.

Every morning Eric told Lesley about what he'd done the night before. Lesley was not expected to reciprocate, which was just as well, since all she ever did in the evening was homework and dishes and talk on the phone.

One Monday morning Eric said he'd gone to the Gardens on Saturday night to see the Ike and Tina Turner Revue. He said Tina Turner was the sexiest woman in the world and the way she sang was like making love to the microphone right there on stage. He said he thought he'd die just watching her, and all the other guys went crazy too.

On the phone every night after supper, Lesley told her new best friend, Audrey, every little thing Eric had said to her that morning, especially the way he'd said, "I like your new haircut a lot," and then the way he'd winked at her in the hall between History and French.

"Do you think he likes me?" she asked Audrey over and over again.

"Of course he likes you, silly! He *adores* you!"

This went on all fall, all winter, all spring, until the raging crush which Lesley had on Eric Henderson could be nothing, it seemed, but true true love.

The week before final exams, Eric asked Audrey to the last school dance.

Lesley spent the night of the dance barricaded in her bedroom, lying on the floor with the record player blasting Tina Turner at top volume. She propped a chair against the door and would not let her parents in. She was mad at them too: at her father, Edward, because he'd laughed and said, "You'll get over it, pumpkin!"; and at her mother, Amelia, because she was old and married, probably happy, probably didn't even remember what love was *really* like, probably hadn't explained things properly in the first place, should have warned her about more than freight trains.

She would, Lesley promised herself savagely, spend the entire summer in her room, learning all the lyrics to Tina Turner's songs, and reading fat Russian novels which were all so satisfyingly melancholy, so clotted with complications and despair, and the characters had so many different, difficult names. Especially she would reread *Anna Karenina* and memorize the signal passage where Anna decides to take her own life:

. . . And all at once she thought of the man crushed by the train the day she had first met Vronsky, and she knew what she had to do. . . .

". . . And I will punish him and escape from everyone and from myself. . . ."

. . . And exactly at the moment when the space between the wheels came opposite her, she dropped the red bag, and drawing her head back into her shoulders, fell on her hands under the carriage, and lightly, as though she would rise again at once, dropped on to her knees. . . .

. . . She tried to get up, to drop backwards: but something huge and merciless struck her on the head and rolled her on her back. . . .

. . . And the light by which she had read the book filled with troubles, falsehoods, sorrow, and evil, flared up more brightly than ever before, lighted up for her all that had been in darkness, flickered, began to grow dim, and was quenched forever.

And she would probably carve Eric Henderson's initials into her thigh with a ballpoint pen, and she would probably not eat any-thing either, except maybe unsalted soda crackers, and she would not wash her hair more than once a week, and she would stay in her pyjamas all day long. Yes she would. She would LANGUISH. And for sure she would never ever ever ever fall in love or have a best friend ever again so long as she lived, so help her.

Night Train

When Lesley moved away from home at the age of twenty-one, she took the train because there was an air strike that summer. Her par-ents put her on the train in Winnipeg with a brown paper bag full of tuna sandwiches and chocolate-chip cookies, with the three-piece luggage set they'd bought her as a going-away present, and a book of crossword puzzles to do on the way. They were all weeping lightly, the three of them: her parents, Lesley assumed, out of a simple sad-ness, and herself, out of an intoxicating combination of excitement and anticipation, of new-found freedom, and, with it, fear. She was, she felt, on the brink of everything important. She was moving west to Alberta, which was booming.

Seated across the aisle of Coach Number 3003 (a good omen, Lesley thought, as she had long ago decided that three was her lucky number) was, by sheer coincidence, a young man named Arthur Hoop who'd given a lecture at the university in Winnipeg the night before. His topic was nuclear disarmament and Lesley had attended because peace was one of her most enduring interests.

After an hour or so, Lesley worked up enough courage to cross over to the empty seat beside him and say, "I really loved your lecture." Arthur Hoop seemed genuinely pleased and invited her to join him for lunch in the club car. Lesley stashed the brown-bag lunch under the seat in front of hers and followed Arthur, swaying and bobbing and grinning, down the whole length of the train.

Arthur Hoop, up close, was interesting, amiable, and affectionate, and his eyes were two different colours, the left one blue and the right one brown. Arthur was on his way back to Vancouver, where he lived with a woman named Laura who was sleeping with his best friend and he, Arthur, didn't know what he was going to do next. Whenever the train stopped at a station for more than five minutes, Arthur would get off and phone ahead to Vancouver, where Laura, on the other end, would either cry, yell, or hang up on him.

By the time the train pulled into Regina, Lesley and Arthur were holding hands, hugging, and having another beer in the club car, where the waiter said, "You two look so happy, you must be on your honeymoon!"

Lesley and Arthur giggled and giggled, and then, like fools or like children playing house, they shyly agreed. The next thing they knew, there was a red rose in a silver vase on their table and everyone in the car was buying them drinks and calling out, "Congratulations!" over the clicking of the train. Arthur kept hugging Lesley against him and winking, first with the brown eye, then with the blue.

They spent the dark hours back in Arthur's coach seat, snuggling under a scratchy grey blanket, kissing and touching and curling around each other like cats. Lesley was so wrapped up in her fantasy of how Arthur would get off the train with her in Calgary or how she would stay on the train with him all the way to Vancouver, and how, either way, her real life was about to begin, that she hardly noticed how brazen they were being until Arthur actually put it in, shuddered, and clutched her to him.

Lesley wept when she got off the train in Calgary and Arthur Hoop wept too, but he stayed on.

From her hotel room, Lesley wrote Arthur long sad letters and ordered up hamburgers and Chinese food from room service at odd hours of the day and night. On the fourth night, she called her mother collect in Winnipeg and cried into the phone because she felt afraid of everything and she wanted to come home. Her mother, wise Amelia, said, "Give it two weeks before you decide. You know we'll always take you back, pumpkin."

By the end of the two weeks, Lesley had a basement apartment in a small town called Ventura, just outside the city. She also had two job interviews, a kitten named Calypso, and a whole new outlook on life. She never did hear from Arthur Hoop and she wondered for a while what it was about trains, about men, the hypnotic rhythm of them, relentless, unremitting, and irresistible, the way they would go straight to your head, and when would she ever learn?

It wasn't long before she was laughing to herself over what Arthur must have told the other passengers when she left him flat like that, on their honeymoon no less.

Train Ticket

All the way home to Winnipeg to spend Christmas with her parents, Lesley drank lukewarm coffee out of Styrofoam cups, ate expensive dried-out pressed-chicken sandwiches, and tried to get comfortable in her maroon-upholstered seat with her purse as a pillow and her parka as a blanket. She tried to read but could not concentrate for long, could not keep herself from staring out the window at the passing scenery, which was as distracting as a flickering television set at the far end of the room. All the way across Saskatchewan, the train seemed to be miraculously ploughing its way through one endless snowbank, throwing up walls of white on either side of the tracks.

She didn't feel like talking to anyone and closed her eyes whenever the handsome young man across the rocking aisle looked her way hopefully. She had just started dating a man named Bruce back in Ventura and she did not like leaving him for Christmas. But this was her first Christmas since she'd moved away from home and the trip back for the holidays had been planned months ago. Once set in motion, the trip, it seemed, like the train once she had boarded it, could not be deflected. She was travelling now with a sorrowful but self-righteous sense of daughterly obligation that carried her inexorably eastward. For a time she'd believed that moving away from her parents' home would turn her instantly into a free, adult woman. But of course she was wrong.

She kept reaching into her purse, checking for her ticket. She memorized the messages printed on the back of it, as if they were a poem or a prayer:

RESERVATIONS: The enclosed ticket is of value. If your plans are altered, the ticket must be returned with the receipt coupon intact, for refund or credit. If you do not make the trip, please cancel your reservations.

ALCOHOLIC BEVERAGES: Alcoholic beverages purchased on board must be consumed in the premises where served. Provincial liquor laws prohibit the consumption of personal liquor on trains except in the confines of a bedroom or roomette.

BAGGAGE: Personal effects consisting of wearing apparel, toilet articles, and similar effects for the passenger's use, comfort, and convenience (except liquids and breakables) are accepted as baggage. Explosive, combustible, corrosive, and inflammable materials are prohibited by law.

The train trip took sixteen hours. The inside of Lesley's mouth, after 1300 kilometres, tasted like a toxic combination of diesel fuel and indoor-outdoor carpeting.

Her parents were there to meet her at the Winnipeg station, her father, Edward, smiling and smiling, his shy kiss landing somewhere near her left ear; her mother, Amelia, looking small in her big winter coat with a Christmas corsage of plastic mistletoe and tiny silver bells pinned to the lapel. The train pulled away effortlessly in a cloud of steam and snow.

Freight Train

They had a saying in Ventura—when Lesley was still living there with Bruce—a saying that was applied, with much laughter and lip-smacking, to people, usually women, who were less than attractive.

"She looks like she's been kissing freight trains," one of the boys in the bar would say, and the rest of them round the table would howl and nod and slap their knees. Lesley would laugh with them, even though she felt guilty for it, and sometimes, calling up within herself noble notions of sisterhood, sympathy, and such, she would sputter uselessly something in defence of the poor woman they were picking on.

But she would always laugh too in the end, because she knew she was pretty, she knew she was loved, she knew she was exempt from their disgust and the disfiguring, inexorable advent of trains.

Runaway Train

There was a story they told in Ventura—when Lesley was still living there with Bruce—about the time Old Jim Jacobs stole the train. It was back in the winter of 1972. Old Jim was a retired engineer who'd turned to drink in his later years. He sat in the Ventura Hotel day after day, night after night, ordering draft beer by the jug with two glasses, one for himself and one for his invisible friend. He would chat amiably for hours in an unintelligible language with the empty chair across from him, politely topping up the two glasses evenly and then drinking them both.

"At least he's never lonely," Bruce would always say.

On towards closing time, however, Old Jim or his invisible friend, or both, would start to get a little surly, and soon Old Jim would be jumping and cursing (in English), flinging himself around in the smoke-blue air of the bar.

"I hate you! I hate you!" he would cry.

"Let's step outside and settle this like men!" he would roar, hitching up his baggy pants and boxing in the air.

"So what then," Bruce would wonder, "is the point of having invisible friends, if you can't get along with them?"

Lesley knew Old Jim from when she worked in the grocery store and he'd be standing in the line-up in his old railway cap with a loaf of bread, a package of baloney, and some Kraft cheese slices. By the time he got to the cash register, he'd have made himself a sandwich and, wouldn't you know it, he must have left his wallet in his other pants—as if he even owned another pair of pants.

When he wasn't drinking or shopping, Old Jim was sitting in the long grass beside the CPR[1] main line, counting boxcars, and waving at the engineers.

At the time of the great train robbery, he'd been bingeing, so they said, for eight days straight (this number could be adjusted, at the story-teller's discretion, to up to as many as ten days but never down to less than six) in Hawkesville, a nearby town twelve miles west of Ventura. He'd been barred for two weeks from the Ventura Hotel for sleeping on the pool table, which explained why he was drinking in Hawkesville in the first place. So Old Jim was getting to be a little homesick after all that time away from his old stamping grounds, and on the Friday night he decided it was high time to get back, seeing as how his two weeks were up on Saturday. But he was flat broke after his binge, pension cheque long gone, no money for a cab, and it was too damn cold to hitch-hike. So he decided to take the train.

So he hopped right in, so they said, to the first engine he found in the yard, fired her up, and off he went, hauling forty-seven empty boxcars behind him (this number too could be adjusted, interminably up, it seemed, because, after all, who was counting?). He made it back to Ventura without mishap, parked her up on the siding behind the Ventura Hotel so he'd be good and ready when they opened in the morning and he knew they'd give him credit for a day or two. He curled up in the caboose and went to sleep. Which was where the railway police and the RCMP[2] found him when they surrounded the runaway train, guns drawn, sirens screaming, at 5:36 A.M. (the time of his legendary capture was unalterable, a part of the town's history which could not be tampered with).

"But what then," Bruce would wonder whenever he heard the

---

1. Canadian Pacific Railway.   2. Royal Canadian Mounted Police.

story again, "is the point of stealing a train, when you can never take it off the tracks, when you can only go back and forth, back and forth, back and forth, and you can never really get away?"

Express Train

One summer Lesley and Bruce took the train up to Edmonton where his brother was getting married. Halfway there, they were stopped on a siding in the middle of nowhere, waiting for a freight train to pass. Bruce was getting impatient, sighing huge conspicuous sighs as he fidgeted and fussed in his seat, while Lesley beside him read on peacefully.

Spotting a white horse from the window, he said, "Sometimes simple things glimpsed in the distance can bring great comfort."

Train Trip East

All the way back to Winnipeg for her Uncle Mel's funeral, Lesley drank beer out of cans and wrote postcards to Bruce in Ventura. She bought the cards at various train stations along the way and then she mailed them at the next stop. She suspected that Bruce was on the brink of having an affair with a French-Canadian woman named Analise who was spending the summer in Ventura with her sister. All of this suspicion, sticky and time-consuming as it was, had left Lesley feeling sick and tired, a little bit crazy too. On the back of a green lake, she wrote:

> I tried to take pictures from the train, of a tree and some water, some sky, but they wouldn't hold still long enough.

On the back of a red maple tree:

> I saw a coyote running from the train, also white horses, brown cows, black birds, and a little girl in Maple Creek wearing a pink sunsuit with polka dots, running. All of them running away from the train.

Black city spotted with blue and white lights:

> There was a station wagon stopped at a crossing. It was filled
> with suitcases, babies, and basketballs. For a minute, I wanted to
> scream: "Stop! Stop! There's a train coming! We'll all be killed!"
> Then I remembered that I was the train and I didn't have to
> stop for anything. Trains are so safe from the inside.

Yellow field of wheat:

> What else is there to do on a train any more but remember? I
> thought of a witchy woman who lived on the corner of Cross
> Street and Vine, in a wooden shack with pigeons on the roof
> and chickens in the porch. She watched me through the window
> when I walked by to Sunday School. The winter I was eight she
> got hit by a train. For a time I had nightmares . . .

Here she ran out of room on the card and finished up her message
on the next one. Purple mountain:

> . . . about arms and legs broken off like icicles, about a head
> rolling down a snowbank wearing a turquoise toque just like
> mine. Then I forgot all about her till now. I remember rocking
> my cousin, Gary, in his cradle, the way he couldn't hold his
> head up yet, and now he's the chef at a fancy French restaurant.

Sitting at her Aunt Helen's kitchen table in Winnipeg, surrounded by relatives, neighbours, warm casseroles, and frozen pound
cakes, she wrote on the back of a sympathy card:

> I've still got the sound of the train in my head. It makes it hard
> to think of anything but songs. Tomorrow.

War Train

In Lesley's parents' photo album, there was a picture of her mother
and her Aunt Helen seeing her father and her Uncle Mel off at the
train station. The women were waving and blowing kisses from the
platform, stylish in their broad-shouldered coats and little square

hats with veils. The men were grinning and walking away, handsome in their sleek uniforms and jaunty caps. They were all very young then, and splendid. The silver train was waiting behind them, its windows filled with the faces of many other young men. They went away to the war and then some of them came back again.

After her Uncle Mel's funeral, Lesley's father told her about the time he'd ridden the train all across France with Mel's head in his lap, Mel nearly dying of ptomaine poisoning from a Christmas turkey, but he didn't.

Train Trip West

All the way back to Ventura after her Uncle Mel's funeral, Lesley slept fitfully or looked out the train window and thought about how everything looks different when you are passing through it in the opposite direction. On this return journey, she was riding backwards, facing where she'd come from, as if she had eyes in the back of her head.

The train whistled through the backsides of a hundred anonymous towns, past old hotels of pink or beige stucco, past slaughterhouses, gas stations, trailer parks, and warehouses. Children and old men waved. Dogs barked, soundless, powerless, strangling themselves straining at their chains. White sheets tangled on backyard clotheslines and red tractors idled at unmarked crossings.

Lesley never knew where she was exactly: there are no mileage signs beside the train tracks the way there are on the highway. There is no way of knowing how far from, how far to. No way, on train time, of locating yourself accurately inside the continuum. You just have to keep on moving, forward and forward and forward, or back, trusting that wherever you are heading is still out there somewhere.

Horse and Train

One year for her birthday in Ventura (or could it have been Christmas . . . could it have been that same year when Lesley bought Bruce the guitar he'd been aching after, the Fender Stratocaster, and when she couldn't take the suspense a minute longer, she gave it to him on Christmas Eve instead of in the morning, just to see the look on his face, and then they stayed up all night playing music and singing, drinking eggnog till dawn . . . when Bruce took the guitar to bed with him and Lesley took a picture of him cuddling it under the puffy pink quilt her mother had sent, and then she kept him awake even longer, telling her theory that if men were the ones who had babies, then there would no more war . . . the best Christmas ever, it could have been then), Bruce gave Lesley a framed reproduction of the Alex Colville[3] painting *Horse and Train*.

In the painting, a purple-black horse on the right is running headlong down the tracks towards an oncoming train on the left. The landscape around them is gravel and brown prairie grass. The ears of the horse are flattened, its tail is extended, and the white smoke from the black train is drifting across the brown prairie sky at dusk.

Bruce hung the painting over the couch in the tiny living room of their basement apartment and Lesley admired it every time she walked into the room.

After Bruce left Lesley and moved to Montreal with Analise, Lesley took the painting off the wall and smashed it on the cement floor, so that she was vacuuming up glass for an hour afterwards, weeping.

When Lesley moved back to Winnipeg a few months later and rented the little stucco bungalow on Harris Street, she had the painting reframed with new glass and hung it on her bedroom wall. She liked to look at it before she went to sleep at night.

She looked at it when she was lying in bed with Cliff, who had his hands behind his head and the ashtray balanced on his bare chest, who was talking and smoking and talking, so happy to be spending the night. She looked at it as she tried to concentrate and follow Cliff's train of thought, but really she was thinking about how they'd been seeing each other for three months now and it wasn't working out.

But really she was thinking about an article she'd read in a women's magazine years ago, and the writer, a marriage counsellor, said that in every romantic relationship there was one person who loved less and one who loved more. The important question then, which a person must face was: which would you rather be: the one who loves less or the one who loves more?

3. Canadian magic realist painter (b. 1920).

When Lesley asked Cliff this question, she already knew what his answer would be.

Which would you rather be: the one who loves less or the one who loves more?

This was like saying:

Which would you rather be: the horse or the train?

It should have been simple.

1990

Stephen Scobie
b. 1943

A man of letters, Scobie was a founding member of Longspoon Press, as well as an editor for Books in Canada *and for* The Malahat Review. *He was elected to the Royal Society of Canada in 1995.*

Born in Scotland, Scobie immigrated to Canada in 1965, settling finally on Vancouver Island, where he is a faculty member at the University of Victoria. Beginning with Stone Poems *(1974), he has published more than twenty books of poems. He also writes biography (of Bob Dylan, Leonard Cohen, Sheila Watson) literary criticism, short stories, and essays. These pieces, from* Ghosts: A Glossary of the Intertext *(1990), fall somewhere among all these forms.*

Scobie has been an enthusiastic supporter of the gender- and genre-bending style which has marked late twentieth-century writing in Canada. He has a clear-eyed view of it, though, and is not above gently laughing at its post-post-literariness. His own writing is lyrical, always acutely aware of words. He likes the puns, the possibilities (the ghosts?) which hover around them. The clear voice of a strong personality is always present in Scobie's work.

Scobie is very aware of how one literary text builds on another—not often in topic but in response to words and their arranging. He also knows that a word like "love" is not to be used casually and that it can reach across great distances. Each of the following pieces seems written to someone. They all have the echoes of letter-writing about them, of the "post."

Intertext

Why is it that every time I sit down to read a book, my first impulse is to write something myself? That's what I just did, writing this: I'd got to the second sentence of a novel and I stopped, pulled the pad of yellow notepaper towards me, and started to write about why I was writing. After a paragraph or so, I will return to the novel, happily enough, and enter the space of its reading. One text has called to another, and this text, for the moment, has replied.

Love

It means nothing in tennis.

It occupies a curious location in space: you fall into it and then you fall out of it. Always falling, downwards; never climbing, never in control.

There is true love and there is abandoned love; there is courtly love and there is careless love. There is blind love and divine love. We ought to have as many different words for love as the Inuit have for snow.

But we don't. We have just the one, workmanlike word, which plods along with the weight of the world on its sloping shoulders. Love, love, love. There's even a shortage of decent rhymes: white snow dove, heaven above, hand in glove, dreaming of. (You can't do anything romantic with *shove*. No wonder poets have turned to free verse.)

And yet, of all words, it retains its power. I think you can hear it now, my love, even though I do not say it aloud, even though we are two thousand miles apart, I think you hear it as I write it now, I think your head turns, briefly, in the moment's breeze, wherever you are, whatever you are doing, you know—*I love you*—what I have just written down.

Post

What do you mean by angels? the interviewer asked me.

Messengers, I replied. Those who bring word from somewhere we don't know, to destinations that we cannot be sure of. You never know if the angels are talking to you; you can only eavesdrop on what they have to say. Regard them as celestial postmen. God's singing telegrams.

All this off the top of my head, where the headphones were, echoing my own voice back to me at one remove. I had crossed on the ferry, reading *La Carte Postale*;[1] it all came back to relays and switching stations. I sat in the studio like a guard at his post. The line was open to Toronto.

What is it, then, that comes back? What is it that can come after the post? Post-man, post-woman, after me the deluge. Postmodernist, post-structuralist, post-post. On the back of the card is an image of an angel.

I didn't know, said Maureen's mother, that Stephen believed in angels. If I were to write her a post card, I would say that I don't. But I believe in the post.

West

For Europeans, it was the direction of death. Sunset, the end of the day, the unknown limit of the flat earth. You sailed west until you dropped off the edge, into the great abyss. I.e., America.

So in America West was a shifting frontier, a line to be pushed across the map, against the direction of writing. America has never quite reconciled itself to the existence of the Pacific Ocean. It always wants new Wests, and none of them pacific.[2]

The Canadian West was never Wild; we take a perverse delight in

---

1. Book by Jacques Derrida (1980).   2. Peaceful.

insisting that the Mounties[3] got there first. Since we never had out-laws, we make do with politicians.

Then at the Coast we pause, in the moment of the margin. We watch the sun sink into the Far East, and we feel ourselves on edge. By the time they reach the West Coast, elections are decided, and New Years are old. Our tidal limit turns to the ebb, under the shadow of a raven's wing.

1990

Duncan Campbell Scott
1862–1947

Scott complained bitterly that it was hard to enjoy listening to Chopin when there was icy water leaking through his winter roof. He was part of a group referred to as the "Confederation Poets," all born around the time of Confederation (1867). They were the first poets to write Canada as they experienced it, resisting British styles, forms, and attitudes.

Born in Ottawa, Scott was in many ways the most sophisticated of the group. Often impatient with the push to hurriedly create a "Canadian literature," he thought it led to sloppy writing. "I declare," he said, "that I value form above all else."

Scott was primarily a poet, concerned about the destruction of European influences on native communities, but he also published two collections of short stories: In the Village of Viger *(1896) and* The Witching of Elspie *(1923). The first was a series of linked stories about a small town in Quebec. The second was harsher, set further north in territory Scott visited as the head of the Department of Indian Affairs. More "realist," it shows the influence of Modernism. Scott smuggled in a copy of James Joyce's (banned)* Ulysses, *because he was attracted to its literary experiments.*

This piece, part of Scott's first collection, has a complex combination of tastes and styles. The atmosphere is delicate, with soft colouring and hazes over the land, Romantic in its valuing of well-kept flower gardens and the gentle man. There is a strongly Gothic

---

3. Royal Canadian Mounted Police.

element in the maiden-in-distress and in the attics of her house. The theme is Victorian. Like many of his contemporaries, Scott worried about encroaching industrialization and urbanization, certain that it would destroy people's souls. In a foreshadowing of the late-twentieth-century fashion for the mystical or metaphysical, late-nineteenth-century writers often include people with supernatural abilities, like Paul Farlotte's.

Paul Farlotte

Near the outskirts of Viger, to the west, far away from the Blanche, but having a country outlook of their own, and a glimpse of a shadowy range of hills, stood two houses which would have attracted attention by their contrast, if for no other reason. One was a low cottage, surrounded by a garden, and covered with roses, which formed jalousies[1] for the encircling veranda. The garden was laid out with the care and completeness that told of a master hand. The cottage itself had the air of having been secured from the inroads of time as thoroughly as paint and a nail in the right place at the right time could effect that end. The other was a large gaunt-looking house, narrow and high, with many windows, some of which were boarded up, as if there was no further use for the chambers into which they had once admitted light. Standing on a rough piece of ground it seemed given over to the rudeness of decay. It appeared to have been the intention of its builder to veneer it with brick; but it stood there a wooden shell, discoloured by the weather, disjointed by the frost, and with the wind fluttering the rags of tar-paper which had been intended as a protection against the cold, but which now hung in patches and ribbons. But despite this dilapidation it had a sort of martial air about it, and seemed to watch over its embowered companion, warding off tempests and gradually falling to pieces on guard, like a faithful soldier who suffers at his post. In the road, just between the two, stood a beautiful Lombardy poplar. Its shadow fell upon the little cottage in the morning, and travelled across the garden, and in the evening

1. Shutters.

touched the corner of the tall house, and faded out with the sun, only to float there again in the moonlight, or to commence the journey next morning with the dawn. This shadow seemed, with its constant movement, to figure the connection that existed between the two houses.

The garden of the cottage was a marvel; there the finest roses in the parish grew, roses which people came miles to see, and parterres[2] of old-fashioned flowers, the seed of which came from France, and which in consequence seemed to blow with a rarer colour and more delicate perfume. This garden was a striking contrast to the stony ground about the neighbouring house, where only the commonest weeds grew unregarded; but its master had been born a gardener, just as another man is born a musician or a poet. There was a superstition in the village that all he had to do was to put anything, even a dry stick, into the ground, and it would grow. He was the village school-master, and Madame Laroque would remark spitefully enough that if Monsieur Paul Farlotte had been as successful in planting knowledge in the heads of his scholars as he was in planting roses in his garden Viger would have been celebrated the world over. But he was born a gardener, not a teacher; and he made the best of the fate which compelled him to depend for his living on something he disliked. He looked almost as dry as one of his own hyacinth bulbs; but like it he had life at his heart. He was a very small man, and frail, and looked older than he was. It was strange, but you rarely seemed to see his face; for he was bent with weeding and digging, and it seemed an effort for him to raise his head and look at you with the full glance of his eye. But when he did, you saw the eye was honest and full of light. He was not careful of his personal appearance, clinging to his old garments with a fondness which often laid him open to ridicule, which he was willing to bear for the sake of the comfort of an old pair of shoes, or a hat which had accommodated itself to the irregularities of his head. On the street he wore a curious skirt-coat that seemed to be made of some indestructible material, for he had worn it for years, and might be buried in it. It received an extra brush for Sundays and holidays, and always looked as good as new. He made a quaint picture, as he

2. Flat flower beds.

came down the road from the school. He had a hesitating walk, and constantly stopped and looked behind him; for he always fancied he heard a voice calling him by his name. He would be working in his flower-beds when he would hear it over his shoulder, "Paul"; or when he went to draw water from his well, "Paul"; or when he was reading by his fire, someone calling him softly, "Paul, Paul"; or in the dead of night, when nothing moved in his cottage he would hear it out of the dark, "Paul." So it came to be a sort of companionship for him, this haunting voice; and sometimes one could have seen him in his garden stretch out his hand and smile, as if he were welcoming an invisible guest. Sometimes the guest was not invisible, but took body and shape, and was a real presence; and often Paul was greeted with visions of things that had been, or that would be, and saw figures where, for other eyes, hung only the impalpable air.

He had one other passion besides his garden, and that was Montaigne.[3] He delved in one in the summer, in the other in the winter. With his feet on his stove he would become so absorbed with his author that he would burn his slippers and come to himself disturbed by the smell of the singed leather. He had only one great ambition, that was to return to France to see his mother before she died; and he had for years been trying to save enough money to take the journey. People who did not know him called him stingy, and said the saving for his journey was only a pretext to cover his miserly habits. It was strange, he had been saving for years, and yet he had not saved enough. Whenever anyone would ask him, "Well, Monsieur Farlotte, when do you go to France?" he would answer, "Next year—next year." So when he announced one spring that he was actually going, and when people saw that he was not making his garden with his accustomed care, it became the talk of the village: "Monsieur Farlotte is going to France"; "Monsieur Farlotte has saved enough money, true, true, he is going to France."

His proposed visit gave no one so much pleasure as it gave his neighbours in the gaunt, unkempt house which seemed to watch over his own; and no one would have imagined what a joy it was to Marie St. Denis, the tall girl who was mother to her orphan broth-

---

3. Michel de Montaigne (1533–1592), the French writer who created the personal essay.

ers and sisters, to hear Monsieur Farlotte say, "When I am in France"; for she knew what none of the villagers knew, that, if it had not been for her and her troubles, Monsieur Farlotte would have seen France many years before. How often she would recall the time when her father, who was in the employ of the great match factory near Viger, used to drive about collecting the little paper match-boxes which were made by hundreds of women in the village and the country around; how he had conceived the idea of making a machine in which a strip of paper would go in at one end, and the completed match-boxes would fall out at the other; how he had given up his situation and devoted his whole time and energy to the invention of this machine; how he had failed time and again, but continued with a perseverance which at last became a frantic passion; and how, to keep the family together, her mother, herself, and the children joined that army of workers which was making the match-boxes by hand. She would think of what would have happened to them then if Monsieur Farlotte had not been there with his help, or what would have happened when her mother died, worn out, and her father, overcome with disappointment, gave up his life and his task together, in despair. But whenever she would try to speak of these things Monsieur Farlotte would prevent her with a gesture, "Well, but what would you have me do—besides, I will go some day—now who knows, next year, perhaps." So here was the "next year," which she had so longed to see, and Monsieur Farlotte was giving her a daily lecture on how to treat the tulips after they had done flowering, preluding everything he had to say with, "When I am in France," for his heart was already there.

He had two places to visit, one was his old home, the other was the birthplace of his beloved Montaigne. He had often described to Marie the little cottage where he was born, with the vine arbours and the long garden walks, the lilac-bushes, with their cool dark-green leaves, the white eaves where the swallows nested, and the poplar, sentinel over all. "You see," he would say, "I have tried to make this little place like it; and my memory may have played me a trick, but I often fancy myself at home. That poplar and this long walk and the vines on the arbour—sometimes when I see the tulips by the border I fancy it is all in France."

Marie was going over his scant wardrobe, mending with her skilful fingers, putting a stitch in the trusty old coat, and securing its buttons. She was anxious that Monsieur Farlotte should get a new suit before he went on his journey; but he would not hear to it. "Not a bit of it," he would say, "if I made my appearance in a new suit, they would think I had been making money; and when they would find out that I had not enough to buy cabbage for the soup there would be a disappointment." She could not get him to write that he was coming. "No, no," he would say, "if I do that they will expect me." "Well, and why not—why not?" "Well, they would think about it—in ten days Paul comes home, then in five days Paul comes home, and then when I came they would set the dogs on me. No, I will just walk in—so—and when they are staring at my old coat I will just sit down in a corner, and my old mother will commence to cry. Oh, I have it all arranged."

So Marie let him have his own way; but she was fixed on having her way in some things. To save Monsieur Farlotte the heavier work, and allow him to keep his strength for the journey, she would make her brother Guy do the spading in the garden, much to his disgust, and that of Monsieur Farlotte, who would stand by and interfere, taking the spade into his own hands with infinite satisfaction. "See," he would say, "go deeper and turn it over so." And when Guy would dig in his own clumsy way, he would go off in despair, with the words, "God help us, nothing will grow there."

When Monsieur Farlotte insisted on taking his clothes in an old box covered with raw-hide, with his initials in brass tacks on the cover, Marie would not consent to it, and made Guy carry off the box without his knowledge and hide it. She had a good tin trunk which had belonged to her mother, which she knew where to find in the attic, and which would contain everything Monsieur Farlotte had to carry. Poor Marie never went into this attic without a shudder, for occupying most of the space was her father's work bench, and that complicated wheel, the model of his invention, which he had tried so hard to perfect, and which stood there like a monument of his failure. She had made Guy promise never to move it, fearing lest he might be tempted to finish what his father had begun—a fear that was almost an apprehension, so like him was he growing. He was tall and large-boned, with a dark restless eye, set under an overhanging forehead. He had long arms, out of proportion to his height, and he hung his head when he walked. His like-ness to his father made him seem a man before his time. He felt himself a man; for he had a good position in the match factory, and was like a father to his little brothers and sisters.

Although the model had always had a strange fascination for him, the lad had kept his promise to his sister, and had never touched the mechanism which had literally taken his father's life. Often when he went into the attic he would stand and gaze at the model and wonder why it had not succeeded, and recall his father bending over his work, with his compass and pencil. But he had a dread of it, too, and sometimes would hurry away, afraid lest its fas-cination would conquer him.

Monsieur Farlotte was to leave as soon as his school closed, but weeks before that he had everything ready, and could enjoy his roses in peace. After school hours he would walk in his garden, to and fro, to and fro, with his hands behind his back, and his eyes upon the ground, meditating; and once in a while he would pause and smile, or look over his shoulder when the haunting voice would call his name. His scholars had commenced to view him with additional interest, now that he was going to take such a prodigious journey; and two or three of them could always be seen peering through the palings, watching him as he walked up and down the path; and Marie would watch him, too, and wonder what he would say when he found that his trunk had disappeared. He missed it fully a month before he could expect to start; but he had resolved to pack that very evening.

"But there is plenty of time," remonstrated Marie.

"That's always the way," he answered. "Would you expect me to leave everything until the last moment?"

"But, Monsieur Farlotte, in ten minutes everything goes into the trunk."

"So, and in the same ten minutes something is left out of the trunk, and I am in France, and my shoes are in Viger, that will be the end of it."

So, to pacify him, she had to ask Guy to bring down the trunk from the attic. It was not yet dark there; the sunset threw a great colour into the room, touching all the familiar objects with transfig-uring light, and giving the shadows a rich depth. Guy saw the model glowing like some magic golden wheel, the metal points upon it gleaming like jewels in the light. As he passed he touched it, and with a musical click something dropped from it. He picked it up: it was one of the little paper match-boxes, but the defect that he remembered to have heard talked of was there. He held it in his hand and examined it; then he pulled it apart and spread it out. "Ah," he said to himself, "the fault was in the cutting." Then he turned the wheel, and one by one the imperfect boxes dropped out, until the strip of paper was exhausted. "But why,"—the question rose in his mind—"why could not that little difficulty be over-come?"

He took the trunk down to Marie, who at last persuaded Monsieur Farlotte to let her pack his clothes in it. He did so with a protestation, "Well, I know how it will be with a fine box like that, some fellow will whip it off when I am looking the other way, and that will be the end of it."

As soon as he could do so without attracting Marie's attention Guy returned to the attic with a lamp. When Marie had finished packing Monsieur Farlotte's wardrobe, she went home to put her children to bed; but when she saw that light in the attic window she nearly fainted from apprehension. When she pushed open the door of that room which she had entered so often with the scant meals she used to bring her father, she saw Guy bending over the model, examining every part of it. "Guy," she said, trying to command her voice, "you have broken your promise." He looked up quickly. "Marie, I am going to find it out—I can understand it—there is just one thing, if I can get that we will make a fortune out of it."

"Guy, don't delude yourself; those were father's words, and day after day I brought him his meals here, when he was too busy even to come downstairs; but nothing came of it, and while he was trying to make a machine for the boxes, we were making them with our fingers. O Guy," she cried, with her voice rising into a sob, "remember those days, remember what Monsieur Farlotte did for us, and what he would have to do again if you lost your place!"

"That's all nonsense, Marie. Two weeks will do it, and after that I could send Monsieur Farlotte home with a pocket full of gold."

"Guy, you are making a terrible mistake. That wheel was our curse, and it will follow us if you don't leave it alone. And think of

Monsieur Farlotte; if he finds out what you are working at he will not go to France—I know him; he will believe it his duty to stay here and help us, as he did when father was alive. Guy, Guy, listen to me!"

But Guy was bending over the model, absorbed in its labyrinths. In vain did Marie argue with him, try to persuade him, and threaten him; she attempted to lock the attic door and keep him out, but he twisted the lock off, and after that the door was always open. Then she resolved to break the wheel into a thousand pieces; but when she went upstairs, when Guy was away, she could not strike it with the axe she held. It seemed like a human thing that cried out with a hundred tongues against the murder she would do; and she could only sink down sobbing, and pray. Then failing everything else she simulated an interest in the thing, and tried to lead Guy to work at it moderately, and not to give up his whole time to it.

But he seemed to take up his father's passion where he had laid it down. Marie could do nothing with him; and the younger children, at first hanging around the attic door, as if he were their father come back again, gradually ventured into the room, and whispered together as they watched their rapt and unobservant brother working at his task. Marie's one thought was to devise a means of keeping the fact from Monsieur Farlotte; and she told him blankly that Guy had been sent away on business, and would not be back for six weeks. She hoped that by that time Monsieur Farlotte would be safely started on his journey. But night after night he saw a light in the attic window. In the past years it had been constant there, and he could only connect it with one cause. But he could get no answer from Marie when he asked her the reason; and the next night the distracted girl draped the window so that no ray of light could find its way out into the night. But Monsieur Farlotte was not satisfied; and a few evenings afterwards, as it was growing dusk, he went quietly into the house, and upstairs into the attic. There he saw Guy stretched along the work bench, his head in his hands, using the last light to ponder over a sketch he was making, and beside him, figured very clearly in the thick gold air of the sunset, the form of his father, bending over him, with the old eager, haggard look in his eyes. Monsieur Farlotte watched the two figures for a moment as they glowed in their rich atmosphere; then the apparition turned his head slowly, and warned him away with a motion of his hand.

All night long Monsieur Farlotte walked in his garden, patient and undisturbed, fixing his duty so that nothing could root it out. He found the comfort that comes to those who give up some exceeding deep desire of the heart, and when next morning the market-gardener from St. Valérie, driving by as the matin bell was clanging from St. Joseph's, and seeing the old teacher as if he were taking an early look at his growing roses, asked him, "Well, Monsieur Farlotte, when do you go to France?" he was able to answer cheerfully, "Next year—next year."

Marie could not unfix his determination. "No," he said, "they do not expect me. No one will be disappointed. I am too old to travel. I might be lost in the sea. Until Guy makes his invention we must not be apart."

At first the villagers thought that he was only joking, and that they would some morning wake up and find him gone; but when the holidays came, and when enough time had elapsed for him to make his journey twice over they began to think he was in earnest. When they knew that Guy St. Denis was chained to his father's invention, and when they saw that Marie and the children had commenced to make match-boxes again, they shook their heads. Some of them at least seemed to understand why Monsieur Farlotte had not gone to France.

But he never repined. He took up his garden again, was as contented as ever, and comforted himself with the wisdom of Montaigne. The people dropped the old question, "When are you going to France?" Only his companion voice called him more loudly, and more often he saw figures in the air that no one else could see.

Early one morning, as he was working in his garden around a growing pear-tree, he fell into a sort of stupor, and sinking down quietly on his knees he leaned against the slender stem for support. He saw a garden much like his own, flooded with the clear sunlight, in the shade of an arbour an old woman in a white cap was leaning back in a wheeled chair, her eyes were closed, she seemed asleep. A young woman was seated beside her holding her hand. Suddenly the old woman smiled, a childish smile, as if she were well pleased. "Paul," she murmured, "Paul, Paul." A moment later her companion started up with a cry; but she did not move, she was silent and tranquil. Then the young woman fell on her knees and wept, hiding her face. But the aged face was inexpressibly calm in the shadow, with the smile lingering upon it, fixed by the deeper sleep into which she had fallen.

Gradually the vision faded away, and Paul Farlotte found himself leaning against his pear-tree, which was almost too young as yet to support his weight. The bell was ringing from St. Joseph's, and had shaken the swallows from their nests in the steeple into the clear air. He heard their cries as they flew into his garden, and he heard the voices of his neighbour children as they played around the house.

Later in the day he told Marie that his mother had died that morning, and she wondered how he knew.

1896

David Suzuki
b. 1936

A respected geneticist, as well as a popular "scientific personality," Suzuki is the host of the Canadian Broadcasting Corporation's television show, "The Nature of Things." He has written many books, making science accessible to the general public. Since the 1960s, Suzuki has been drawing attention to various environmental issues. He founded and chairs the David Suzuki Foundation, in Vancouver, British Columbia, established to initiate and support projects working to solve environmental problems.

It seems astonishing that in less than 200 years we have moved from writing by explorers, like David Thompson, seeing a vast untamable wilderness, to work by scientists, like Suzuki, warning us about its destruction.

*Sadly, Suzuki says, he came to realize that there were always two opposing sides in environmental struggles: spotted owls **or** people; trees **or** jobs. As long as we saw these issues as adversarial, he suggests, we were getting nowhere. Suzuki reports that increasing contact with aboriginal people showed him that it is not necessary to cast the natural world as Other, apart from, or even opposed to peo-*

*ple and their interests. He has learned that people and the earth are
all made up of the same elements, so people all need the same things
the planet needs: earth, air, fire, and water. To that long-standing
list, Suzuki adds love and spirit, if we are to lead rich lives. He uses
this list as the organizing structure for his book,* The Sacred Balance *(1997, 2002).*

*This Introduction outlines how Suzuki arrived at this under-
standing. He provides a clear overview of these often complex topics, establishing the links among them. Seeing it all this way, he
says, gives him hope rather than the despair he was falling into. It
is all so basic, he says, and so interconnected. We cannot destroy
it all.*

Introduction to *The Sacred Balance*

Suppose that 200,000 years ago, biologists from another galaxy
searching for life forms in other parts of the universe had discovered Earth and parked their space vehicle above the Rift
Valley in Africa. They would have gazed upon vast grasslands filled
with plants and animals, including a newly evolved species, *Homo
sapiens*. It is highly unlikely that those extra-galactic exobiologists
would have concentrated their attention on this young upright ape
species in anticipation of its meteoric rise to preeminence a mere
two hundred millennia later. After all, those early humans lived in
small family groups that didn't rival the immense herds of wilde-
beest and antelope. In comparison with many other species, they
weren't especially large, fast or strong, or gifted with sensory acuity.
Those early humans possessed a survival trait that was invisible because it was locked within their skulls and only revealed through
their behaviour. Their immense and complex brains endowed them
with tremendous intelligence, conferring as well a vast capacity for
memory, an insatiable curiosity and an astonishing creativity, abilities that catapulted their descendants into a position of dominance
on the planet.

The eminent Nobel laureate François Jacob suggests that the human brain has an inbuilt need for order. Chaos is terrifying to us
because without an understanding of cause and effect, we have no

possibility of controlling the cosmic forces impinging on our lives. Early humans recognized that there are patterns in nature that are predictable—the diurnal cycle, the lunar cycle, the tides, the seasons, animal migration and plant succession. They were able to exploit these regularities for their own benefit and to avoid potential hazards. Over time, every human society evolved a culture that inculcated an understanding of its place on Earth and in the cosmos. The collective knowledge, beliefs, languages and songs of each society make up what anthropologists call a "world-view." In every world-view, there is an understanding that everything is connected to everything else, that nothing exists in isolation or alone. People have always understood that we are deeply embedded in and dependent upon the natural world.

In such a world of interconnectedness, it is understood that every action has consequences, and when we were part of that world, we had a responsibility to act properly to keep the world in order. Many of our rituals, songs, prayers and ceremonies were reaffirmations of our dependence on nature and our commitment to behave properly. That is how it has been for most of human existence all over the world.

From Naked Ape to Superspecies

But suddenly in the last century, *Homo sapiens* has undergone a radical transformation into a new kind of force that I call a "superspecies." For the first time in the 3.8 billion years that life has existed on Earth, one species—humanity—is altering the biological, physical and chemical features of the planet on a geological scale. That shift to superspecies has occurred with explosive speed through the conjunction of a number of factors. One is population. It took all of human existence to reach a billion people in the early nineteenth century. A hundred years later, when I was born, in 1936, there were two billion people on Earth. In my lifetime, that doubling time has shrunk to its current twelve to thirteen years while the population has tripled. Thus, by virtue of our numbers alone, our species' "ecological footprint" on the planet has enlarged explosively.

We are now the most numerous mammalian species on the planet but unlike all the others, our ecological impact has been greatly amplified by technology. Virtually all of modern technology has been developed within the past century, thereby escalating both the scale and the scope of our ability to exploit our surroundings. Resource exploitation is fuelled by an exploding consumer demand for products, and the fulfilment of that demand has become a critical component of economic growth. Hyperconsumption in the developed world serves as the model for people in developing countries now that globalization has rendered the entire world population a potential market. Taken together, human numbers, technology, consumption and a globalized economy have made us a new kind of force on the planet. Throughout our evolutionary past, we never had to worry about the collective impact of our entire species because our ecological footprint was so much lighter and nature was vast and endlessly self-renewing. Our new status of superspecies has been achieved so rapidly that we are only now becoming aware of a new level of collective responsibility, which reflects a dawning realization that taken all together, human activity is the main cause of the current decline in the biosphere's rich diversity and productivity that support all life on earth.

A Shattered World

As we have shifted status to a superspecies, our ancient understanding of the exquisite interconnectivity of all life has been shattered. We find it increasingly difficult to recognize the linkages that once gave us a sense of place and belonging. After all, we are flooded with food and goods that come from all parts of the world, so we scarcely notice that in the middle of winter we are still able to buy fresh strawberries and cherries. The constraints of locality and seasons are pushed aside by the global economy. Exacerbating the fragmentation of the world has been the stunning shift from predominant habitation in rural, village communities to population concentration in large cities. In big cities, it becomes easy to assume that we differ from all other species in that we create our own habitat and thereby escape the constraints of nature. Nature cleanses water, creates air, decomposes sewage, absorbs garbage, generates electricity and produces food, but in cities, these "ecosystem services" are assumed to be performed by the workings of the economy.

To make matters worse, as information both proliferates and shrinks to smaller and smaller bytes, the context, history and background needed to set new "facts" or events in place are lost and our world is broken up into disconnected bits and pieces. While we look to science to reveal the secrets of the cosmos, its primary methodology of reductionism focusses on parts of nature. And as the world around us is examined in pieces, the rhythms, patterns and cycles within which those pieces are integrated are lost and any insights we gain become illusions of understanding and mastery. Finally, as transnational corporations, politics and telecommunications move onto the global stage, the sense of the local is decimated.

This, then, is where we are at the beginning of the third millennium. With explosive speed, we have been transmogrified from a species like most others that live in balance with our surroundings into an unprecedented force, a superspecies. Like a foreign species that flourishes in a new environment, we have expanded beyond the capacity of our surroundings to support us. It is clear from the history of the past two centuries that the path we embarked on after the Industrial Revolution is leading us increasingly into conflict with the natural world. Despite forty years of experience in the environmental movement, we have not yet turned onto a different path.

The Growth of Environmentalism

Like millions of people around the world, I was galvanized in 1962 by Rachel Carson's eloquent call to action in her book *Silent Spring*. We were swept up in what was to become the "environmental movement." In British Columbia, that meant protesting such things as the American testing of nuclear weapons at Amchitka in the Aleutian Islands (a protest that gave birth to Greenpeace in Vancouver), clear-cut logging throughout the province, proposed offshore drilling for oil, the planned dam at Site C on the Peace River, and air and water pollution from pulp mills. In my mind, the problem was that we were taking too much from the environment and putting too much waste back into it. From that perspective, the solution was to set limits on how much and what could be removed from the biosphere for human use and how much and what could be put back into our surroundings, then make sure to enforce the regulations. So in addition to protesting, marching and blockading, many of us were lobbying politicians to set aside more parks, to enact Clean Water and Clean Air legislation, to pass Endangered Species Acts and to establish the agencies to enforce the regulations.

But Carson's book itself offered evidence of the need for a deeper analysis, and the more involved I became, the clearer it became to me that my rather simple-minded approach wouldn't work because we were too ignorant to anticipate the consequences of our activity and to set appropriate limits. Carson's book dealt with DDT.[1] In the 1930s when Paul Mueller, working for the chemical company Geigy in Switzerland, discovered that DDT killed insects, the economic benefits of a chemical pesticide were immediately obvious. Trumpeting the imminent scientific conquest of insect pests and their associated diseases, Geigy patented the discovery and went on to make millions, and Mueller was awarded the Nobel Prize in 1948. But years later, when bird watchers noted the decline of eagles and hawks, biologists investigated and discovered the hitherto unknown phenomenon of "biomagnification," whereby compounds become concentrated as they are ingested up the food chain. How could limits have been set on DDT in the early 1940s when we didn't even know about biomagnification as a biological process until birds began to disappear?

Similarly, CFCs[2] were hailed as a wonderful creation of chemistry. These complex molecules were chemically inert, so they didn't react with other compounds and thus made excellent fillers in aerosol cans to go along with substances such as deodorants. No one anticipated that because of their stability, CFCs would persist in the environment and drift into the upper atmosphere, where ultraviolet radiation would break off ozone-scavenging chlorine-free radicals. Most people had never heard of the ozone layer and certainly no one could have anticipated the long-term effects of CFCs, so how could the compounds have been regulated? I have absolutely no doubt that genetically modified organisms (GMOs) will also prove

1. Dichloro-Diphenyl-Trichloroethane, a powerful insecticide.

2. Chlorofluorocarbons, gases used in refrigeration and as propellants in spray cans.

to have unexpected consequences despite the benefits vaunted by biotech companies. But if we don't know enough to anticipate the long-term consequences of human technological innovation, how can its impact be managed? For me as a scientist, this posed a terrible conundrum.

A Way Out

I gained an important insight to free me from this quandary in the late 1970s. As host of the long-running television series *The Nature of Things*, I proposed that we do a program on the battle over clear-cut logging in the Queen Charlotte Islands, off the coast of British Columbia. For thousands of years, the islands have been home to the Haida, who refer to their lands as Haida Gwaii. The forestry giant MacMillan Bloedel had been clear-cut logging huge areas of the islands for years, an activity that had generated increasingly vocal opposition. I flew to Haida Gwaii to interview loggers, forestry officials, government bureaucrats, environmentalists and natives. One of the people I interviewed was a young Haida artist named Guujaaw who had led the opposition to logging for years.

Unemployment was very high in the Haida communities, and logging generated desperately needed jobs for the Haida. So I asked Guujaaw why he opposed the logging. He replied that of course after the trees were all gone, Haida people would still be there, but added, "Then we'll be like everyone else. We won't be Haida anymore." It was a simple statement whose implications escaped me at the time. But on reflection I realized that he had given me a glimpse into a profoundly different way of seeing the world. Guujaaw's statement suggested that for his people, the trees, the birds, the fish, the water, the wind are all parts of Haida identity. Haida history and culture and the very meaning of why Haida are on earth reside in the land. Ever since that interview, I have been a student learning from encounters with indigenous people in many parts of the world. From Japan to Australia, Papua New Guinea, Borneo, the Kalahari, the Amazon and the Arctic, aboriginal people express that vital need to be connected to the land. They refer to Earth as their Mother, who they say gives birth to us.

Changing our Perspective

In 1990, my wife, Tara Cullis, and I decided to establish an organi-
zation that would examine the root causes of ecological destruction
so that we could seek alternatives to our current practices. We decided to draft a document that would express the foundation's
world-view and perspective and could be offered to the Earth Sum-
mit in Rio de Janeiro in 1992. We called it a Declaration of Interde-
pendence. Tara and I formulated a rough draft and asked for input
from Guujaaw, ethnobiologist Wade Davis and the children's singer
Raffi. When I was working on the first draft, I tried writing "We
are made up of molecules from the air, water and soil," but this
sounded like a scientific treatise and didn't convey the simple truth
of our relationship with Earth in an emotional way. After spending
days pondering the lines, I suddenly thought, "We *are* the air, we
are the water, we *are* the earth, we *are* the Sun."

With this realization, I also saw that environmentalists like me
had been framing the issue improperly. There is no environment
"out there" that is separate from us. We can't manage our impact on
the environment if we *are* our surroundings. Indigenous people are
absolutely correct: we are born of the earth and constructed from
the four sacred elements of earth, air, fire and water. (Hindus list
these four and add a fifth element, space.)

Once I had finally understood the truth of these ancient wis-
doms, I also realized that we are intimately fused to our surroundings and the notion of separateness or isolation is an illusion.
Through reading I came to understand that science reaffirms the
profundity of these ancient truths over and over again. Looked at as
biological beings, we are no more removed from nature than any
other creature. Our animal nature dictates our essential needs: clean
air, clean water, clean soil, clean energy. This led me to another insight, that these four "sacred elements" are created, cleansed and re-
newed by the web of life itself. If there is to be a fifth sacred
element, it is biodiversity itself. And whatever we do to these elements, we do directly to ourselves.

As I read further, I discovered the famed psychologist Abraham
Maslow, who pointed out that we have a nested series of needs. At

the most basic level, we require the five sacred elements in order to live rich, full lives. But when those basic needs are met, a new set of necessities arises. We are social animals, and the most profound force shaping our humanity is love. And when that vital social need is fulfilled, then a new level of spiritual needs arises as an urgent priority. This is how I made the fundamental reexamination of our relationship with Earth that led to *The Sacred Balance*. In the five years since, I have yet to meet anyone who would dispute the reality and primacy of these fundamental needs. And everything in my reading and experiences since then has reaffirmed these basic needs. The challenge of this millennium is to recognize what we need to live rich, rewarding lives without undermining the very elements that ensure them.

1997

Audrey Thomas
b. 1935

Born in Binghamton, New York, and educated at Smith College, Thomas moved to Canada in 1959. She spent 1964–66 in Ghana and then returned to British Columbia, to Galiano Island, one of the beautiful Gulf Islands. She is a novelist and skilled short story writer. She has published six collections of short stories, beginning with Ten Green Bottles *(1967), and including* Goodbye Harold, Good Luck *(1986) from which this story comes.*

Thomas's fiction is often based in autobiography. Her early life, her years in Africa, and her experiences on Galiano Island recur in her stories and novels. She has sometimes re-worked stories to see what they would look like at different points in time. The stories often explore emotion, looking for ways to give voice to feeling, for which we have so few words. Thomas's fiction is always aware of itself as fiction, as an arranging of words and events, reaching toward freedom or understanding. It is not unusual to have a single character split into more than one, as different emotional states or moods play off one another.

In 1987 Thomas was awarded the Marian Engel Prize for the entire body of her work, which seems fitting, since in many ways, all her books connect to one another.

As Thomas and her narrators look at the world, they see it not through binoculars or through a microscope but through a kaleidoscope. Often, a single central event shifts and changes in the way of kaleidoscope patterns: the same pieces recur in different relation to one another.

Puns, allusions, and word play are always part of Thomas's writing. She is very aware of the slipperiness of words and their meanings. In this story the central "event" is a word which has happened by accident.

The Man with Clam Eyes

I came to the sea because my heart was broken. I rented a cabin from an old professor who stammered when he talked. He wanted to go far away and look at something. In the cabin there is a table, a chair, a bed, a woodstove, an aladdin lamp. Outside there is a well, a privy, rocks, trees and the sea.

(The lapping of waves, the scream of gulls.)

I came to this house because my heart was broken. I brought wine in green bottles and meaty soup bones. I set an iron pot on the back of the stove to simmer. I lit the lamp. It was no longer summer and the wind grieved around the door. Spiders and mice disapproved of my arrival. I could hear them clucking their tongues in corners.

(The sound of the waves and the wind.)

This house is spotless, shipshape. Except for the spiders. Except for the mice in corners, behind the walls. There are no clues. I have brought with me wine in green bottles, an eiderdown quilt, my brand-new *Bartlett's Familiar Quotations*. On the inside of the front jacket it says, "Who said: 1. In wildness is the preservation of the world. 2. All hell broke loose. 3. You are the sunshine of my life."

I want to add another. I want to add two more. Who said, "There is no nice way of saying this?" Who said, "Let's not go over it again?"   The wind grieves around the door. I stuff the cracks with rags torn from the bottom of my skirt. I am sad. Shall I leave here then? Shall I go and lie outside his door calling whoo—whoo—whoo like the wind?

(The sound of the waves and the wind.)

I drink all of the wine in one green bottle. I am like a glove. Not so much shapeless as empty, waiting to be filled up. I set my lamp in the window, I sleep to the sound of the wind's grieving.

(Quiet breathing, the wind still there, but soft, then gradually fading out. The passage of time, then seagulls, and then waves.)

How can I have slept when my heart is broken? I dreamt of a banquet table under green trees. I was a child and ate ripe figs with my fingers. Now I open the door—

(West-coast birds, the towhee with its strange cry, and the waves.)

The sea below is rumpled and wrinkled and the sun is shining. I can see islands and then more islands, as though my island had spawned islands in the night. The sun is shining. I have never felt so lonely in my life. I go back in. I want to write a message and throw it out to sea. I rinse my wine bottle from last night and set it above the stove to dry. I sit at the small table thinking. My message must be clear and yet compelling, like a lamp lit in a window on a dark night. There is a blue bowl on the table and a rough spoon carved from some sweet-smelling wood. I eat porridge with raisins while I think. The soup simmers on the back of the stove. The seagulls outside are riding the wind and crying ME ME ME. If this were a fairy tale, there would be someone here to help me, give me a ring, a cloak, a magic word. I bang on the table in my frustration. A small drawer pops open.

(Sound of the wind the waves lapping.)

Portents and signs mean something, point to something, otherwise—too cruel. The only thing in the drawer is part of a manuscript, perhaps some secret hobby of the far-off professor. It is a
story about a man on a train from Genoa to Rome. He has a gun in
his pocket and is going to Rome to kill his wife. After the conductor comes through, he goes along to the lavatory, locks the door,
takes out the gun, then stares at himself in the mirror. He is pleased
to note that his eyes are clear and clam.   *Clam?* Pleased to
note that his eyes are clear and clam?   I am not quick this
morning. It takes me a while before I see what has happened. And
then I laugh. How can I laugh when my heart is cracked like a
dropped plate? But I laugh at the man on the train to Rome, staring
at himself in the mirror—the man with clam eyes. I push aside the
porridge and open my *Bartlett's Familiar Quotations.* I imagine
Matthew Arnold—"The sea is clam tonight . . ." or Wordsworth—
"It is a beauteous evening, clam and free . . ." I know what to say in
my message.   The bottle is dry. I take the piece of paper and
push it in. Then the cork, which I seal with wax from a yellow can-
dle. I will wait just before dark.

(The waves, the lapping sea. The gulls, loud and then gradually
fading out. Time passes.)

Men came by in a boat with a pirate flag. They were diving for
sea urchins and when they saw me sitting on the rocks they gave me
one. They tell me to crack it open and eat the inside, here, they will
show me how. I cry No and No, I want to watch it for a while. They
shrug and swim away.   All afternoon I watched it in pleasant
idleness. I had corrected the typo of course—I am that sort of person—but the image of the man with clam eyes wouldn't leave me
and I went down on the rocks to think. That's when I saw the divers
with their pirate flag; that's when I was given the gift of the beautiful maroon sea urchin. The rocks were as grey and wrinkled as elephants, but warm, with enormous pores and pools licked out by the
wind and the sea. The sea urchin is a dark maroon, like the lips of
certain black men I have known. It moves constantly back/forth,
back/forth with all its spines turning. I take it up to the cabin. I let
it skate slowly back and forth across the table. I keep it wet with wa-

ter from my bucket. The soup smells good. This morning I add carrots, onions, potatoes, bay leaves and thyme. How can I be hungry
when my heart is broken? I cut bread with a long, sharp knife, holding the loaf against my breast. Before supper I put the urchin back
into the sea.

(Sound of the wind and the waves.)

My bottle is ready and there is a moon. I have eaten soup and
drunk wine and nibbled at my bread. I have read a lot of unfamiliar quotations. I have trimmed the wick and lit the lamp and
set it in the window. The sea is still tonight and the moon has left a
long trail of silver stretching almost to the rocks.

(Night sounds. A screech owl. No wind, but the waves lapping.)

I go down to the sea as far as I can go. I hold the corked bottle in
my right hand and fling it towards the stars. For a moment I think
that a hand has reached up and caught it as it fell back towards the
sea. I stand there. The moon and the stars light up my loneliness.
How will I fall asleep when my heart is broken?

(Waves, then fading out. The sound of the wild birds calling.)

I awoke with the first bird. I lay under my eiderdown and
watched my breath in the cold room. I wondered if the birds could
understand one another, if a chickadee could talk with a junco, for
example. I wondered whether, given the change in seasons and
birds, there was always the same first bird. I got up and lit the fire
and put a kettle on for washing.

(The iron stove is opened and wood lit.
It catches, snaps and crackles.
Water is poured into a large kettle.)

When I went outside to fling away the water, he was there, down
on the rocks below me, half-man, half-fish. His green scales glittered like sequins in the winter sunlight. He raised his arm and
beckoned to me.

(Sound of the distant gulls.)

We have been swimming. The water is cold, cold, cold. Now I sit on the rocks, combing out my hair. He tells me stories. My heart darts here and there like a frightened fish. The tracks of his fingers run silver along my leg. He told me that he is a drowned sailor, that he went overboard in a storm at sea. He speaks with a strong Spanish accent.

He has been with the traders who bought for a pittance the seaotters' pelts which trimmed the robes of Chinese mandarins. A dozen glass beads would be bartered with the Indians for six of the finest skins.

With Cook[1] he observed the transit of Venus in the cloudless skies of Tahiti.

With Drake[2] he had sailed on "The Golden Hind" for the Pacific Coast. They landed in a bay off California. His fingers leave silver tracks on my bare legs. I like to hear him say it—Cal-ee fórn-ya. The Indians there were friendly. The men were naked but the women wore petticoats of bulrushes.

Oh how I like it when he does that.

He was blown around the Cape of Good Hope with Diaz.[3] Only they called it the Cape of Storms. The King did not like the name and altered it.   Oh.   His cool tongue laps me. My breasts bloom in the moonlight. We dive—and rise out of the sea, gleaming. He decorates my hair with clamshells and stars, my body with sea-lettuce. I do not feel the cold. I laugh. He gives me a rope of giant kelp and I skip for him in the moonlight. He breaks open the shells of mussels and pulls out their sweet flesh with his long fingers. We tip the liquid into our throats; it tastes like tears.   He touches me with his explorer's hands.

(Waves, the sea—loud—louder. Fading out.)

---

1. Captain James Cook (1728–1779), English explorer of the Pacific and the southern hemisphere.
2. Sir Francis Drake (1540–1596), English navigator and privateer, the first Englishman to circumnavigate the globe.
3. Bartolomeu Diaz (1450?–1500), Portuguese navigator, first to sail around Africa to India.

I ask him to come with me, up to the professor's cabin. "It is im-póss-ee-ble," he says. He asks me to go with him. "It is impóss-ee-ble," I say. "Not at all."   I cannot breathe in the water. I will drown. I have no helpful sisters. I do not know a witch.

(Sea, waves, grow louder, fade, fading but not gone.)

He lifts me like a wave and carries me towards the water. I can feel the roll of the world. My legs dissolve at his touch and flow together. He shines like a green fish in the moonlight. "Is easy," he says, as my mouth fills up with tears. "Is nothing." The last portions of myself begin to shift and change.

I dive beneath the waves! He clasps me to him. We are going to swim to the edges of the world, he says, and I believe him.

I take one glance backwards and wave to the woman in the window. She has lit the lamp. She is eating soup and drinking wine. Her heart is broken. She is thinking about a man on a train who is going to kill his wife. The lamp lights up her loneliness. I wish her well.

1986

David Thompson
1770–1857

When Thompson was fourteen, he left his birthplace, the deeply historical city of London, England, on a ship of the Hudson's Bay Company bound for the wilds of North America. He was an apprentice, hired as a trader and a clerk, to help keep Company records.

Taken on as a writer, a recorder, Thompson complained that he was losing his skills through lack of practice and paper. Unable to write, he felt written upon, by cutting winds, by mosquitoes tattooing his skin. This was not a passive world, waiting to be described. It acted on him.

At the age of twenty, Thompson learned surveying and mapmaking. He joined the Northwest Company, which allowed him to travel into the unmapped interior and the northwest. He became one of Canada's best-known geographers.

Thompson's writing exemplifies the style of the eighteenth century, the age of rationalism, which valued clear, objective observation and recording. This was before the fashion of the nineteenth century's Romantic emotional response to nature, so clear in Susanna Moodie's writing. Thompson certainly observed closely. Who knew that a mosquito bite is a two-stage process?

For almost sixty years, Thompson kept daily journals as he explored and recorded the vast, surprising wilderness, well-known to its own native peoples but strangely wonderful to an Englishman's eyes. He covered about 80,000 miles on foot, in a canoe, or on horseback. In 1841, Thompson sat down with those journals to write the book of his travels, still unfinished when he died in Montreal. Writing in hindsight made it possible for him to comment on what he saw, so we hear a lively voice, with a sense of humour often directed at himself. This piece comes from David Thompson: Travels in Western North America, 1784–1812 *(1971), edited by Victor G. Hopwood.*

I Join the Hudson's Bay Company

In the month of May, 1784, at the Port of London, I embarked in the ship Prince Rupert belonging to the Hudson's Bay Company, as apprentice and clerk to the said company, bound for Churchill Factory on the west side of the Bay.

None of the officers or men had their stock of liquor on board from the high price of those articles. On the third morning at dawn of day, we perceived a Dutch lugger about half a mile from us. A boat was directly lowered, and the gunner, a tall handsome young man, stepped into her with four men; they were soon on board of the lugger; a case of gin was produced, a glass tasted and approved. The Dutchman was in a hurry, as he said a revenue cutter was cruising near at hand, and he must luff off; a guinea was paid, the case locked, put into the boat, and was soon placed in the steerage cabin of our ship.

The case was of half-inch boards tacked together and daubed red; on opening it there were nine square bottles of common glass; each was full, with the cork cut close to the neck of the bottle, except one with a long cork, the one which the gunner had tasted. It was taken out, a glass handed round and each praised it; but the carpenter, who was an old cruiser, wished to taste some of the other bottles; a cork was drawn, a glass filled; the colour had a fine look. It was tasted, spit out and declared to be sea water; all the others were found to be the same. The gunner who had thus paid a guinea for three half-pints of gin, the contents of the bottle, got into a fighting humour, but to no purpose; the Dutchman was luffing off in fine style.

The next morning about sunrise, the hills of Scotland lying blue in the western horizon, to the east of us about two miles, we saw a boat with six men coming from the deep-sea fishing. The wind was light, and they soon came alongside. They were fine manly hardy looking men; they were sitting up to their knees in fish, for the boat was full of the various kinds they had caught. Our captain bought some fine halibut and skate fish from them, for which they would not take money, but [only] old rope in exchange, to make fettels for their creels; these words I did not understand until the boatswain, who was a Scotchman, told me it was to make rope handles to their baskets and buckets.

Our captain, pleased with his bargain, told me to give them a hat full of biscuit. Umbrellas were not in those days, but our broad brimmed hats served for both purposes. Pleased with the ruddy looks of them, I filled my hat as full as it could hold, and had to carry it by the edges of the brim. As I passed by the captain I heard him give me a hearty curse, and saying "I'll never send him for biscuit again"; but the boat's crew were so pleased they told me to hand down a bucket, which they filled with fresh caught herrings, a great relief from salt meat.

On the sixth day about 9 pm, we anchored in the harbour of Stromness,[1] where the three ships bound for Hudson's Bay had to wait for final instructions and sailing orders. As there were no telegraphs in those [days] we were delayed three weeks.

Until this voyage I had passed my life near to Westminster Abbey, the last seven years in the Grey Coat School on royal foundation. This school was formerly something of a monastery and belonged to Westminster Abbey, from which it was taken at the

1. On the west coast of Scotland.

suppression of the monastic order, but not finally settled until the reign of Queen Anne.[2] It is still held from the Dean and Chapter of the Abbey on the tenure of paying a pepper corn to the said Dean and Chapter on a certain day, which the governors annually pay.

During the year our holidays at different times were about eighteen to twenty days, the greatest part of which I spent in this venerable abbey and its cloisters, reading the monumental inscriptions, and [as] often as possible [in the] Henry the Seventh Chapel. My strolls were to London Bridge, Chelsea, and Vauxhall and St. James's Park.

Books in those days were scarce and dear and most of the scholars got the loan of such books as his parents could lend him. Those which pleased us most were the Tales of the Genii, the Persian and Arabian Tales, with Robinson Crusoe and Gulliver's Travels; these gave us many subjects for discussion [on] how each would behave on various occasions. With such an account of the several regions of the earth and on such credible authority, I conceived myself to have knowledge to say something of any place I might come to, and the blue hills of Scotland were so distant as to leave imagination to paint them as she pleased. When I awoke in the morning and went upon deck, I could not help staring to see if [what] was before me was reality for I had never read of such a place. And at length [I] exclaimed, "I see no trees," to which a sailor answered, "No, no, people here do not spoil their clothes by climbing up trees."

One of the first objects that drew my attention were several kelp kilns for burning sea weed into a kind of potash. The sea weeds were collected by a number of men and women; their legs appeared red and swelled. The sea weeds were collected into baskets, the rope handles of which were passed round their breasts; each helped up the load for one another, and as they carried it over [the] rough rocky shore left by the ebb tide to the kilns, the sea water streamed down their backs.

The smoke of the fires of these kilns was as black as that of a coal fire. One day our captain had invited the other captains and some gentlemen from the island to dine with him; a little before the time, the wind changed, and the smoke of five of the kilns came direct on

2. Queen of England, Scotland, and Ireland from 1702 to 1714.

our ship turning day into night. The boatswain was ordered to go and make them put out their kilns, which they refused to do; upon which he threatened to send cannon balls among them to smash their kilns, but the sturdy fellows replied, "You may as well take our lives as our means, we will not put them out." Finding threats would not do, he enquired how much they gained a day; they said when the kilns burn well they gained tenpence; upon which he gave to each one shilling; the kilns were then soon put out, the smoke cleared away and we again saw daylight. I could not help comparing this hard wet labour for tenpence a day, where not even a whistle was heard, with the merry songs of the ploughboys in England.

This place to me was a new world; nothing reminded me of Westminster Abbey and my strolls to Vauxhall, Spring Gardens, and other places, where all was beauty to the eye and verdure for the feet. Here all was rock with very little soil, everywhere loose stones that hurt my feet, not a tree to be seen. I sadly missed the old oaks, under whose shade I sat and played. I could not conceive by what means the people lived; they appeared comfortable, and their low dark houses, with a peat fire, the smoke of which escaped by a small hole, contained all they required.

They carried on a considerable contraband trade with Holland, which, from the very high duties on liquors and other articles, gave them a profitable trade. None of the officers and crews of the three ships had provided themselves with liquors for the voyage, as they knew these things could be procured here cheaper and better than in London. One afternoon, taking a walk with one of the petty officers, we entered a low dark house. It was three or four minutes before we could perceive the gudeman, who in his homespun blue coat was sitting alone by his turf fire. My companion enquired how times went, and if he had an anker keg of comfort for a cold voyage; he said of late the revenue cutters had been very active, and stocks low, but he could accommodate him. The price was soon settled, and the gin found a place in the ship. And thus it will always be with high duties. . . .

We now held our course over the western ocean, and near the islands of America saw several icebergs, and Hudson's Straits were so full of ice as to require the time of near a month to pass them; this being effected, the three ships separated, one for Albany and Moose

Factories, another for York Factory, and the third for Churchill Factory, at which last place we arrived in the beginning of September, 1784.

Hudson's Bay, including James Bay, may be said to be an inland sea, connected to the Atlantic Ocean by Hudson's Straits; it is in the form of a horseshoe. . . . On its west side it receives the Seal, Churchill, Kisiskatchewan [Nelson], Hayes, Severn, Albany, and Moose Rivers. . . .

Churchill River, where it enters the sea, is a noble stream of about one and a half miles in width; on the south side it is bounded by a low point of rock and sand; on the north side by a low neck of sand with rock appearing through it, at the extremity of which the point is about an acre in width, on which was erected about the year 1745 a regular, well-constructed fort of granite, having about thirty cannon of six- to eighteen-pound shot. There was no approach to it but by the narrow isthmus of sand. The water was too shoal for three-fourths of a mile to the middle of the river for ships, and this was the only place a ship could come to. (It was at this fort that Mr Wales the astronomer observed the transit of Venus over the sun in 1769.)

In the war with the United States and with France, in the year 1782, the celebrated navigator de la Pérouse was sent from France, with one ship of seventy-four guns and two frigates, to take and destroy the forts of the Hudson's Bay Company. In the month of August these vessels anchored in the Bay, about four miles north of the fort, and the next day sent a boat well manned to sound the river.

At this time the fort was under the command of the well-known traveller Mr Samuel Hearne, who had been in the naval service. He allowed the French boat to sound the river to their satisfaction, without firing a single shot at them. From this conduct Admiral de la Pérouse judged what kind of a commander of the fort he had to contend with; accordingly next day, on the narrow isthmus of sand and rock of a full mile in length which leads to the fort, he landed four hundred men, who marched direct on the fort with only small arms. The men in the fort begged of Mr Hearne to allow them to mow down the French troops with the heavy guns loaded with grape shot, which he absolutely refused; and as they approached he ordered the gates to be opened, and went out to meet them, and surrendered at discretion.

All the goods, stores, with a large quantity of valuable furs fell into their hands. The fort was destroyed and burnt, but the stone walls of the fort were of such solid masonry the fire scarcely injured them. The French commander declared that had his sounding boat been fired at, he would not have thought of attacking such a strong fort so late in the season, when there was not time for a regular siege. Mr Hearne was received with cold politeness and looked upon with contempt by the French officers.

Mr Samuel Hearne was a handsome man of six feet in height, of a ruddy complexion and remarkably well made, enjoying good health; as soon as the Hudson's Bay Company could do without his services, they dismissed him for cowardice. Under him I served my first year. It was customary of a Sunday for a sermon to be read to the men, which was done in his room, the only comfortable one in the factory.[3] One Sunday after the service Mr Jefferson the reader and myself stayed a few minutes on orders; he then took Voltaire's dictionary, and said to us, "Here is my belief and I have no other." In the autumn of 1785 he returned to England, became a member of the Buck's Club and in two years was buried.

The present factory is about five miles above the fort, in a small bay formed by a ledge of rocks which closes on the river about five hundred yards below the factory, above which for seven miles is an extensive marsh to the lower rapids of the river. The factory is supplied once a year with goods and provisions by a ship which arrives on the last days of August or early in September, and in about ten days is ready for her homeward voyage, the severity of the climate requiring all possible dispatch.

A small room was allotted to me without the least article of furniture but a hard bed for the night. My fellow clerks were in the same situation. They were not comfortable but resigned, and I had to become so. In 10 days the cargo was loaded by means of a sloop of 70 tons and the long boat. They had only an hour before high water and an hour after to load the cargo; by this time the ebb tide had left the rocky ground to wait the next tide, such is the shoalness of these shores. While the ship remained at anchor, from my parent and friends [it] appeared only a few weeks' distance, but when the ship sailed and from the top of the rocks I lost sight of her, the dis-

3. Trading post.

tance became immeasurable, and I bid a long and sad farewell to my noble, my sacred country, an exile for ever, [This paragraph is from an early beginning of the *Travels*.][4]

The cold weather now came rapidly on, but as there was no thermometer, we could only judge of the intensity of the cold by our sensations, and its action on the land and water. On the fifteenth day of November this great and deep river was frozen over from side to side, and although the spring tides of new and full moon rose ten to twelve feet above the ordinary level, no impression was made on the ice; it kept firm and it was the middle of June the following year when the ice broke up and gave us the pleasant sight of water.

About the middle of October the marshes and swamps are frozen over, and the snow lies on the ground. For about two months the factory yard, enclosed by stockades of twelve feet in height, was kept clear of snow, but in the latter end of December a northeast snowstorm of three days' continuance drifted the snow to the height of the stockades and over them, and it filled the whole yard to the depth of six to ten feet, which could not be cleared, and through which avenues had to be cut and cleared of about four feet in width. And thus [it] remained till late in April, when a gradual thaw cleared the snow away.

From the end of October to the end of April every step we walk is in snowshoes. The natives walk with ease and activity, and also many of us, but some find them sad encumbrance; their feet become sore and their ankles sprained, with many a tumble in the snow from which it is sometimes difficult to rise. . . .

The country, soil, and climate in which we live have always a powerful effect upon the state of society, and the movements and comforts of every individual. He must conform himself to the circumstances under which he is placed, and as such we lived and conducted ourselves in this extreme cold climate. All our movements, more or less, were for self-preservation; all the wood that could be collected for fuel gave us only one fire in the morning and another in the evening. The rest of the day, if [there was] bad weather, we had to walk in the guard room with our heavy coats of dressed beaver, but when the weather was tolerable we passed the day in shooting grouse.

4. Note by Victor Hopwood, editor of Thompson's writings.

The interior of the walls of the house were covered with rime[5] to the thickness of four inches, pieces of which often broke off, to prevent which we wetted the whole extent, and made it a coat of ice, after which it remained firm and added to the warmth of the house. The cold is so intense that everything in a manner is shivered by it; continually the rocks are split with a sound like the report of a gun. . . .

After passing a long, gloomy, and most severe winter, it will naturally be thought with what delight we enjoy the spring and summer; of the former we know nothing but the melting of the snow, and the ice becoming dangerous. Summer, such as it is, comes at once, and with it myriads of tormenting mosquitoes; the air is thick with them; there is no cessation, day or night, of suffering from them. Smoke is no relief. They can stand more smoke than we can, and smoke cannot be carried about with us. The narrow windows were so crowded with them, they trod each other to death in such numbers, we had to sweep them out twice a day; a chance cold northeast gale of wind was a grateful relief, and [we] were thankful for the cold weather that put an end to our sufferings.

The mosquito bill, when viewed through a good microscope, is of a curious formation, composed of two distinct pieces; the upper is three-sided, of a black colour, and sharp-pointed, under which is a round white tube, like clear glass, the mouth inverted inwards. With the upper part the skin is perforated; it is then drawn back, and the clear tube applied to the wound and the blood sucked through it into the body till it is full. Thus their bite is two distinct operations but so quickly done as to feel as only one. Different persons feel them in a different manner; some are swelled, even bloated, with intolerable itching; others feel only the smart of minute wounds. Oil is the only remedy and that frequently applied; the natives rub themselves with sturgeon oil, which is found to be far more effective than any other oil. . . .

In September the sand fly and midgeuks are numerous; the latter insinuates itself all over the body; the skin becomes heated with itchings; these cease at sunset, but remain until the season becomes cold. October puts an end to all these plagues. It is a curious fact

5. Frost.

[that] the farther to the northward, the more and more numerous are all these flies, but their season is short.

While these insects are so numerous, they are a terror to every creature on dry lands, if swamps may be so called. The dogs howl, roll themselves on the ground, or hide themselves in the water; the fox seems always in a fighting humour; he barks, snaps on all sides, and however hungry and ready to go abirdsnesting, of which he is fond, is fairly driven to seek shelter in his hole. A sailor finding swearing of no use, tried what tar could do, and covered his face with it, but the mosquitoes stuck to it in such numbers as to blind him, and the tickling of their wings was worse than their bites. . . .

I was fortunate in passing my time in the company of three gentlemen, the officers of the factory: Mr Jefferson, the deputy governor; Mr Prince, the captain of the sloop that annually traded with the Esquimaux to the northward; and Mr Hodges, the surgeon. They had books which they freely lent to me; among them were several on history and on animated nature; these were what I paid most attention to, as the most instructive. Writing paper there was none but what was in the hands of the governor, and a few sheets among the officers. On my complaining that I should lose my writing for want of practice, Mr Hearne employed me a few days on his manuscript entitled "A Journey to the North," and at another time I copied an invoice.

It had been the custom for many years when the governors of the factory required a clerk, to send to the school in which I was educated to procure a scholar who had a mathematical education to send out as a clerk, and to save expenses, he was bound apprentice to them for seven years. To learn what? For all I had seen in their service neither writing nor reading was required, and my only business was to amuse myself, in winter growling at the cold, and in the open season shooting gulls, ducks, plover, and curlews, and quarrelling with mosquitoes and sand flies. . . .

Hudson's Bay is certainly a country that Sinbad the Sailor[6] never saw, as he makes no mention of mosquitoes.

1789, 1971

6. The wandering Baghdad merchant in *The Arabian Nights*.

Jane Urquhart
b. 1949

Urquhart began her publishing life with a book of poems, I Am Walking in the Garden of His Imaginary Palace *(1981). All her novels and short stories have the echo of poetry about them. They are highly imagist, and the language turns into unexpected places, with lovely nuances. In some ways, the title of that first book could be a title for all Urquhart's work. She does walk in the gardens of the world, in the fullest possible sense, noticing their details as she passes. She is intrigued by exotic places of the imagination and their palaces. Her female characters do have relationships with men who may want to put them into palaces—or their gardens.*

Through all Urquhart's writing—her many public appearances, her articles and her reviews—runs a conviction about the redemptive power of making art. Art matters.

Born in a small northern Ontario town, Urquhart grew up in Toronto. She grounds herself and her writing in the people and places of Ontario, but her work moves on an international stage. In 1996, for instance, she was named a Chevalier dans l'Ordre des Arts et des Lettres in France—a French knight.

Urquhart's prize-winning novels include The Whirlpool *(1986),* Changing Heaven *(1990),* Away *(1993),* The Underpainter *(1997), and* The Stone Carvers *(2001). This story comes from* Storm Glass *(1978). Echoes of that first poetry collection's title reverberate, as the young narrator comes to terms with having just been married. Typical of Urquhart's short fiction, it is suggestive and somewhat elusive, like a poem heard on the wind. The conventions of love and marriage, as well as the imaginary towers built around them, are familiar from fairy tale and from real life experiences.*

Dreams

As might be expected, her wedding-night dreams were both weird and eventful, taking her in and out of countries that she didn't even know existed. She would later attribute these flights of fancy to the after-effects of the food served at the reception. But that night the dreams gave her no time to ponder the reasons for their arrival. They just kept happening, one after another, until the one about the wheelchairs woke her up, shouting.

But not in fear, or at least not from any worry about her safety. She had felt, in fact, during the course of the dream, remarkably detached, as if she had been watching a play in which she had only one line; a line that was spoken from the wings. But when it came time for her to speak that line she was aware, even in the dream, that it came from some other, surer part of her brain, from those same heretofore-unrecognized countries.

"Don't forget your seatbelts! Don't forget your seatbelts!" she cried, waking both John and herself.

"Seatbelts!" he said. "What seatbelts?"

She confessed her dream. All the men she had known in her relatively short life had been presented to her in series, like credits at the end of a film. They were all in wheelchairs, but such wheelchairs! Suspended on thin strong ropes they gave their occupants the opportunity to swing back and forth against a clear blue sky. The men involved had looked to her like strange trapeze artists or happy preschool children on playground swings. They were having, it appeared, a wonderful time. Then for reasons unknown even to herself, the cautionary business of the seatbelts had grabbed her vocal cords.

Having no personal use for interpretation of any kind John pronounced the dream absurd and therefore boring. She agreed; they laughed and fell easily back to sleep.

The next morning they jogged two miles along the beach. She was always surprised by the response that the sight of a naked pair of male legs awoke in her. It was honest visual pleasure combined with admiration for a supple functioning form bereft of excess. Male excess was distributed elsewhere, in the face, around the middle, but rarely in the legs. They were holy territory, uninhabited by fat cells. They were perfectly fabricated systems designed, perhaps, to carry primitive hunters quietly and swiftly through some complicated forest. Now they carried John across the sand, through the wind, and along the frothy edges of the sea. Later, in the city, they would carry him through the labyrinth of street and subway to an office every weekday for the rest of his life. She watched the large muscle at the back of his thigh flex and relax with the rhythm of running.

Over lunch, which was served on the terrace of the hotel, they discussed the gifts they had received and divided them into three categories: lovely, passable, and impossible. Yellow was her favourite colour, so all of the yellow paraphernalia slipped easily into the "lovely" category. The steadily increasing profusion of yellow objects had been, in fact, a great comfort to her in the week or so preceding the wedding. She imagined the one-bedroom apartment they had chosen filling up with radiant sunlight like the gold-leaf backgrounds she had seen in old paintings. She pictured herself bent over a sewing machine stitching yellow gingham curtains while stew bubbled in the yellow enamel pot on the stove. There was also in this picture an image of John, threading his way through the subway system, coming home, on his long lithe legs, to her. At night, she imagined, they would rub themselves all over with the gift of giant yellow bath towels, just before they slipped between the gift of flowered yellow stay-press sheets.

She thought of John's legs rising without a ripple from the yellow bath mat at his feet.

In the category of "impossible" they placed such items as Blue Mountain pottery[1] and salt and pepper shakers with the words *salty* and *peppy* burned into them.

In "passable" they placed such items as electric frying pans and waffle irons.

This kind of classification game was one they played often. It had the twofold positive effect of supplying them with conversational material and providing them with a well-ordered private universe. Where categories were concerned they agreed on everything: from

1. Wilderness-themed ceramics formerly made in Collingwood, Ontario.

music to cocktails, from politics to comic strips, from airports to laundromats. Their value systems were as assured and as tidy as the Holiday Inn at which they were staying. It was all very comforting.

Games notwithstanding, they were neither of them children. He had practised law for a full five years and had, just recently, been offered a partnership in the firm. In his usual practical, deliberate way he had waited a week or so before saying yes to the proposition. It was the same week that she had handed in her resignation to the paper, giving marriage as her excuse. She felt little regret at the prospect of abandoning her career. Although it had been the job she wanted, the job she had studied for, it had quickly passed through a phase of novelty and into the hazy realm of habit—like most of her affairs. A few days before she left, the girls in the office held a small shower for her. A lot of the accumulated yellow objects were a result of this event.

A combination of the beer they had consumed with lunch and their first morning of strong sunshine had made them feel sleepy. They decided to return to the room for a rest. The desk clerk smiled benignly as they passed through the lobby, his face altering to the odd grimace of a man barely able to suppress a wink. He was aware of their honeymoon status. She remembered passing through similar lobbies of similar hotels with men she had not been married to. The desk clerks there had remained tactfully aloof, the situation being less easy to classify.

After they made love John rolled over and lit a cigarette. Some of the smoke became trapped in the few beams of sun that had managed to penetrate the heavy curtains.

"Why wheelchairs?" he asked. "Why were they in wheelchairs?"

"Who?" she replied drowsily from the other side of the bed.

"Your boyfriends, your boyfriends in the dream."

"Who knows?" she said, falling asleep. "Who ever knows in dreams?"

Later in the afternoon, when they awakened from their nap, John would decide to go for a swim. She would decide to sit on the balcony and write thank-you notes to her friends, the generous donors of "the lovely, the passable, and the impossible." "Dear Lillian," she would begin. Then something would capture her attention. It would be the sight of John walking down across the beach towards the water, walking on his beautiful spare legs. With his back turned he would be unaware that she was watching him. He would become smaller and smaller until, at last, he would collapse into the water. She would study the predictable repetitious motions of the waves surrounding him until, with a kind of slow horror, she would realize that the organized behaviour of the Atlantic was what the rest of her life would be, one week following another, expectations fulfilled in easy categories, and the hypnotic monotony of predictable responses. Oh, my God, she would think briefly—why does he seem to be having such a good time?

Then she would dismiss this and all other related thoughts from her mind forever and continue her thank-you note.

"Dear Lillian," she would write, "John and I just love Blue Mountain pottery."

1987

W. D. Valgardson
b. 1939

For many years a member of faculty at the University of Victoria, British Columbia, Valgardson was born in Winnipeg, but spent his childhood in Gimli, Manitoba, the centre of Canada's Icelandic community. That community was important to his writing, which often has the atmosphere of the Icelandic sagas. Those ancient story poems had a dark brooding sense of a hovering fate. They spoke of the archetypal themes of love, home, honour, betrayal, loyalty, feuds. Valgardson's four short story collections, beginning with Bloodflowers *(1973), have much in common with this tradition which persists in the literatures of northern countries.*

After writing all of his short stories out of that Icelandic view of the world, Valgardson was surprised to find himself turning to his mother's side of the family, to his Irish heritage. "I started letting the Irish out," he laughs. The results were somewhat surprising: a novel, The Girl with the Botticelli Face *(1992), and since then a series of prize-winning children's books.*

This story is part of Red Dust *(1978), Valgardson's third story collection. The wanderer often appears in an Icelandic saga, mov-*

*ing from place to place, gathering and re-telling stories. This trav-
eller, though, has decided that he wants a home and is willing to go
to considerable lengths for one and for a family. He is, himself, a
kind of walking "text," an interesting variant of the saga's wandering story-gatherer. His whole body carries story, in a way that gives
different meaning to ideas about story-telling, biography, or maybe
even autobiography.*

A Place of One's Own

The sound of the bell came all at once, as though the clapper
had been held and then suddenly released. The sharp, unexpected ringing startled Angela. She stopped picking strawberries, looked about the yard and, seeing neither her father nor
mother, rose to her feet and ran toward the road with a peculiar,
flat-footed shuffle.

When she reached the gate, she climbed the horizontal boards of
the white fence and leaned precariously forward. To her left, at the
bottom of a rutted gravel road that descended to a swamp, then rose
southward until it topped a gravel ridge thick with scrub brush, she
saw a black horse pulling a flatbed wagon. Set upon the wagon was
a high, narrow shed with a peaked roof. The outside of the shed had
been shingled. A small window had been set in the front wall. A
stove-pipe jutted like the tip of a finger toward heaven. The driver,
instead of riding, was walking beside the horse with the reins in his
left hand.

Angela watched for a minute, her short blond hair gleaming with
a reflected halo of light, then, cautiously setting one foot on the
ground, climbed down and hurried back to the strawberry patch.

She was kneeling on the path between two rows of plants when
her mother appeared at the corner of the house and called, "Who's
coming?"

"The pedlar," Angela replied without stopping work. She didn't
bother to look up.

Her mother, a heavy-set woman with a waxy pale face, stayed in
the shade cast by the eaves. She cupped a hand to her forehead. In
her other hand she held a ladle that dripped strawberry jam.

"What's going on?" Angela's father shouted from the doorway of the barn. Harry Fedorchuk was twenty years older than his wife. He was a swarthy man with a body so narrow that when he stood still he could easily be mistaken for the trunk of a maple tree. Although his eyesight was good enough for him to shoot pigeons from the barn roof, he claimed his hearing was so poor that he could only make out what was being said on television when the volume was turned to maximum. However, if anything was said that was private or interesting, he could hear it all the way across the yard.

"It's the pedlar," Sophie answered. "With the tattoos."

He cupped his hand to his ear and screwed up his face.

"What's wrong?" he called. His words, drawn out so that the vowels were multiplied three-fold, faded gradually, like the sound of a horn.

His wife, for all her sturdy appearance, suffered from emphysema and her voice was weak. Raising her voice exhausted her. A month before, she would have appealed to Angela to repeat the message or to run across the yard to answer her father's question but she knew it was no use. He no longer spoke to his daughter, refusing to acknowledge anything she said. When he had first realized what was wrong, he had beaten her with his razor strop, chasing her around the yard, into the house, in and out of rooms, her screaming with every blow and him threatening and demanding until, at last, she had crawled under her bed and curled into a corner. For the next week he had never quit questioning her, demanding the answer to one question over and over, even waking her in the middle of the night to try and catch her off guard.

At the end of seven days, when she still would not tell him what he wanted to know, he turned away from her, matching silence with silence. Since then, when she passed before him, his eyes looked through her and his lips set one against the other like the edges of a press used for crimping metal.

His daughter's condition was only the last of a series of blows. For three years in a row, there had been bad crops. One year, it had rained too much. The next year, it had snowed early. Now, the stunted grain was ripening with half-filled heads. Only two months before, his best cow had squeezed through the fence and been run down by a car. Because he was afraid of being sued, he had denied

that the cow was his and so did not even get to keep the meat. He
hadn't paid his taxes in two years.

He slopped across the yard in a pair of boots five sizes too big.
He loved bargains and regarded anything that was cheap as a bargain. Only after arriving home did he stop to consider the object's
appropriateness. His rubber boots had been on sale for a dollar because they were a size twelve. He took a size seven. However, rather
than admit that he had made a mistake, he fitted them with three
insoles and stuffed crumpled newspaper into the toes.

When Sophie told him the news, he went directly to the gate.
She followed him and stood, her arms crossed, her ladle firmly
clenched. The two of them looked as if they were preparing to repel
an attack.

The pedlar's wagon was so old that it had high wheels with
wooden spokes and iron rims. The upper section had been constructed with meticulous care so that, painted brown, the shingled
exterior looked like nothing so much as an old fishing shed. On the
sides, various large items hung from black hooks—galvanized tubs,
rakes, shovels, even some loops of electrical wire and small farm
equipment.

The pedlar walked with the steady, unhurried gait of someone
who has walked a long distance and still has a long distance to go.
He was tall and thin and he wore a hat with so wide a brim that it
seemed like a miniature umbrella. His long hair was tied back with
a shoelace. His beard was reddish brown and lay on his chest
in carefully combed waves. His face was narrow and the bones lay
close to the skin.

As the mare's head came even with the Fedorchuks, the pedlar
tightened the reins and the horse stopped.

"We got no money to buy nothing," Fedorchuk said, his gaze
passing the pedlar to run quickly over the goods hanging on the
caravan.

The pedlar remained motionless, not looking at them but to the
left of them as though someone else was there whom only he could
see. All at once, he looked directly into Fedorchuk's eyes and said,
"My horse needs watering. May I use your well?"

It was a request that could not be denied. There had been no rain
for weeks. The ditches were dry, their bottoms silvered with foxtail.

What water was to be found in the sloughs that lay between the Fedorchuks and the next farm was brown and stagnant and completely unfit for drinking.

"We don't need nothing," Fedorchuk said. Reluctantly, he lifted the latch and swung back the gate.

With a click of his tongue and a barely discernible flick of his wrist, the pedlar started the horse into the yard. The black mare stopped and nuzzled the pump. The pedlar took a pail from a hook and filled it with water. Fedorchuk followed right behind the pedlar.

"We didn't expect you back so soon," he said.

The horse began to drink noisily. The pedlar, instead of replying, held one hand over the spout and worked the handle until water flowed over the top of the casing. He knelt, put his lips against the spout and bent his palm so as to make an opening for the water. He drank greedily until there was no water left, then worked the handle and drank again. When he stood, he took a deep breath, clutched his beard and squeezed the water from it.

"It's a hot day," Fedorchuk said, eyeing a cream can he could make use of.

The pedlar nodded his agreement. He wore a plaid shirt, blue jeans and thick-soled boots that laced up past his ankles.

Sophie was standing three feet behind her husband, watching the pedlar so closely she might have been afraid he would, through some magical sleight of hand, steal the pump before their eyes.

"You needed thread the last time I was here," the pedlar said. "I've got lots of it this trip." As he spoke, he watched Angela out of the corner of his eye. She had her head bent so that her face was hidden. Her basin of strawberries gleamed white and red.

"Purple?"

"I think so. I'll have to look." In an attempt to be friendly, he added, "I'll give you a spool in exchange for the water."

Neither Fedorchuk nor his wife approved of people not brought up in the area. Of the pedlar, they were particularly contemptuous because he had no place of his own and, therefore, no trustworthy identity. Like all people who live on the very edge of having nothing, a place of one's own was very important to them. Divorced from the land, constantly travelling, appearing and disappearing without explanation, the pedlar was no better than a gypsy. Although he had come to their farm frequently during the past three years, he had never offered his name and they had never asked for it.

All through the Interlake,[1] there were rumours about him, many of which were contradictory. Some said he had been a criminal; others that he was a defrocked priest; still others that he had been involved in unsavoury politics. Some adhered to the theory that he was the cast-off son of a noble family. When he had first appeared in Eddyville, he worked as a day-laborer, going wherever he was needed, moving from farm to farm and camp to camp. He never talked about his past and, according to the postmaster, never received any mail.

It was while he was harvesting for a farmer south of town that someone saw him washing and discovered that his chest and back and arms were sprinkled with tattoos. That made him the object of intense curiosity for no-one in the district except a Ukrainian who had survived Auschwitz had a tattoo and his was only a number. People even went so far as to drive to where the pedlar was working and to ask him to take off his shirt. He had refused and his refusal had caused some resentment.

The pedlar, although at that time he was not yet called that, had made it a habit to stop at the parlour every Saturday night for a beer. Usually, he came in, ordered two draft and contented himself with sitting and nodding to the people he knew. It was during his second summer in the Eddyville area that a group of rowdies who had had too much to drink had surrounded his table and asked him to take off his shirt. He had shaken his head, then ignored them. When they insisted, he tried to leave. They had overpowered him and ripped his shirt into strips. All that was left were his cuffs. It was right after that that he disappeared. Everyone thought he had left the district until one day when he reappeared with his wagon and stock of goods.

Since then, he avoided crowds and towns, sticking to back roads, selling his goods at farms and camps. Sometimes, when there was a wedding or a funeral or even a bingo game, he would park his caravan on the road and watch from a distance but, if any notice was taken of him, he would drive off.

1. The area of Manitoba between Lake Winnipeg and Lake Manitoba.

"My horse," he said to Fedorchuk, "is favouring her right foot."
He bent down. Grasping the mare's leg, he gently raised it up.
Fedorchuk crouched to inspect the hoof but he kept his distance.
He had once been kicked by a horse and still bore the scar on his
chest. Gingerly, he reached out and grasped the shoe.

"That shoe's no good," he grunted. "It's a wonder she's not lame."

The pedlar poked and pulled at the shoe. "It needs a new one,"
he admitted. "I can do the work. Have you any equipment?"

Fedorchuk sucked on his teeth and said nothing.

"I'll give you that cream can for the use of your equipment," he
said. "I don't want anything for nothing."

Before, the pedlar had taken his time about answering. Now, it
was Fedorchuk's turn. He strolled to the pump. Even without socks,
his feet were sweltering. He took off one boot, held his left foot under the spout and pumped water over it. The pump clashed and
banged so much that there was no use trying to talk. When his foot
was cool, he took off the other boot and rinsed his right foot. His
ankles were thin and hairy and looked like two-inch planks with
knots. His feet were mottled purple and white.

"I'll need to see what I've got," he said at last.

With that settled, the pedlar turned to Sophie. "I'll get that spool
of thread," he offered. He disappeared into his caravan. When he
reappeared, he had an armload of boxes. "I'm not very well organized," he apologized. "I'll need to look until I find it."

Sophie didn't want her husband to think she might buy something so she didn't step forward but stretched her neck until she
appeared to be trying to see over some high obstruction. As the pedlar opened the first box, there was the acrid smell of stale smoke.
The box contained a tumbled assortment of narrow silk ties. He
dipped in his hand, raised the scarlets, indigoes and oranges to the
sunlight, then let them slide shimmering into the box.

"We got no use for neckties," Sophie said. "Harry's got one."

"There's no harm in looking," the pedlar replied. "It don't cost
nothing."

He set the box aside and opened another that contained a pile of
tiny handkerchiefs all marked with the initial M. Some of them
were charred around the edges but none were so badly burned that
they couldn't be used.

The pedlar's goods were constantly changing. No-one, not even the pedlar himself, knew from one trip to the next what he would be bringing. He purchased his stock not from a wholesaler but from a salvage company hidden among the slaughterhouses and factories that had sprung up on the edge of the city.

Sometimes, he managed to procure bankrupt stock but, more often, he bought fire-damaged goods. He gathered these on regular but infrequent trips to the city and stored them in an abandoned church, which he rented for $30 a month. His customers had long since grown accustomed to tea and sugar and chocolate that tasted as if they had been hung for a time over smouldering sawdust. They didn't complain. The pedlar's goods were cheap and they were delivered to the door.

One after another, the pedlar opened the boxes, spreading them over the rear of the wagon. When there was no room left, he began a second layer. There were items of every kind, the debris of ambition and greed and miscalculation and bad luck gathered indiscriminately together by misfortune—crocheted doilies, small mesh hats covered with velvet flowers only slightly crushed, white gloves, women's underthings (when he displayed these last items, he delicately looked away into the distance), needles, pins, cards filled with barrettes, brooches and earrings.

As he searched through his goods for the thread, he was silent. His face, what showed of it above his beard, was long and sad, the face of someone who has waited a long time for something and then been disappointed.

The door on one of the outbuildings banged. Fedorchuk strode across the yard on his mottled feet. His green workpants were rolled nearly to his knees. His pale legs were narrow as a goat's. He stopped near the tailgate, surveyed all the opened goods, twisted up the corner of his mouth in disapproval and said, "I got everything you need except coal."

The pedlar nodded gravely. "I guess," he said, "I could make it to the next farm."

Fedorchuk pretended to be looking at a box of toothbrushes but his eyes were fixed on the cream can. In his own mind, he already owned it and now that he was in danger of losing the can, he felt as though something was being stolen from him. To have it given to his neighbour who already had two cows and three pigs more than he had was nothing less than a personal injury.

"I can," he volunteered, swinging his eyes fiercely toward the pedlar as if to challenge him to combat, "get you some coal first thing in the morning."

At this offer, the pedlar gave a short, formal bow as though he had just been introduced to someone of consequence. The pedlar opened one more box. It was filled with spools of thread. He held it out so that Sophie could pick what she wanted.

The pedlar made his supper from sardines and bread and drank water from a small saucepan. When he had finished, he smoked his pipe for half an hour, then went to the back door of the house. Fedorchuk came to the landing and stood on the opposite side of the screen like a priest waiting to hear confession.

"Since I'm going to stay until tomorrow, I thought you and I might make a few dollars out of it."

At the mention of money, Fedorchuk turned his head to one side in the attitude of someone listening to the sound of distant thunder.

"You could phone your neighbours," the pedlar suggested, "and tell them I'm here. They can come and, whatever I sell, you get five percent."

Fedorchuk brushed his lips with his upraised index finger, looked over his shoulder into the kitchen to see if his wife had overheard the conversation, then let himself out. He caught the pedlar's arm and led him half-way across the yard. The sun sat above the barn, a circle slightly flattened at the top and bottom, so that it looked complacent like a fat banker who is resting after a profitable day.

When they were half-way between the house and the barn, Fedorchuk said, "They'll dig up my lawn with their cars." He pressed his small, monkey-like face close to the pedlar's.

The pedlar glanced at the hardpacked dirt that was dotted with islands of quack grass. "You could make a little extra," he suggested, "by serving food."

"Someone," Fedorchuk replied as his mind searched the nooks and crannies of profit, "might back into my fence. Anyways, how do I know I'll get anything out of it?"

"You've got to have faith. Other people have done okay."

"That," Fedorchuk answered, barely restraining a sneer, "was when things were more prosperous. Times have changed." All at once, his face, which had been full of anticipation, grew as still and cold as if he had seen a vision of his own death. "I don't want anyone coming around here," he declared. He swung his head back and forth like he was searching out a hidden enemy.

"Seven and a half percent," the pedlar countered. "You might make $20, $25 just off my sales."

Just then, the sun flared up, turning the horizon white, so that it seemed the sun was rising, not setting, but right after that, the light faded sharply.

"That would be a miracle," Fedorchuk said. He governed his life by the supposition that there was nothing that would not be worse shortly. "I've got trouble with my neighbors," he complained. His face worked with emotion, his muscles disturbing the skin like a turbulent current roiling the surface of a stream. He clamped his lips shut, drew his head into his shoulders and stared over the garden into a grove of stunted oak where shadows were rapidly gathering. "Someone," he said, at last, his words tightened to a whisper, "let his scrub bull in with my cows."

The pedlar stooped and dug a stone from the dirt. He rubbed it clean, then taking careful aim, threw it into the air. The stone rose in a high arc and looked, for a moment, as if it would follow the sun over the horizon. Instead, it dropped in a tangle of weeds. "Someone not coming might tell you something. Someone who comes and acts suspicious might tell you more. Maybe if you found out who it was, you could make a deal with him."

Fedorchuk did not appear to hear the suggestion. He gazed blankly toward the grove where his cattle moved through the shadows like great mythic beasts. It was as though he had turned back inside himself. His emotion was so great that his left arm jerked twice.

"I'll kill him," Fedorchuk whispered.

"Maybe," the pedlar began.

"It's a deal," Fedorchuk snapped. "Seven and a half."

"In that case, let's have a drink." The pedlar lifted two folding chairs from the roof of the caravan. Then he brought a gallon jug of homebrew and two glasses. They mixed the liquor with water from the well.

Without any discernible change, the grey of the sky became gradually darker until it was a deep, impenetrable black. A full moon of beaten brass rose with a stately, formal air, silvering the eastern sides of trees and buildings.

"You're very lucky," the pedlar said, his voice heavy with tiredness. When Fedorchuk looked up, a miniature moon was reflected in each eye. "To have a place of your own, I mean. To be able to stay in one place."

After this, he fell into a reverie that lasted until Fedorchuk said, "Riding on that seat must be pretty hard on your kidneys."

The pedlar refilled their glasses. The night air lay on their skins like warm water. Framed in the kitchen window, Angela might have been a delicately painted watercolour. Her skin glowed softly. Her face was enclosed by the curve of her yellow hair. The pedlar had set his chair at an angle so that by looking over Fedorchuk's shoulder, he could watch Angela without appearing to do so.

"Everyone," the pedlar sighed, "gets worn down after a while." They had both faded until all that was visible of them were their outlines. "I'm thinking of buying Grebon's store."

"It's a good business," Fedorchuk replied. Normally, he loved to gossip, gathering up scraps of information like a caretaker spearing gum wrappers on a pointed stick. It was a measure of his resentment and anger over his daughter's condition that he didn't try to draw out the pedlar. "I'll have to tell my wife!" he suddenly exclaimed. "She'll have lots of food to prepare."

When Fedorchuk woke at four, the sky had already begun to soften. He kept some money buried in a tobacco tin and his sleep had been haunted with images of someone digging up his yard. Still in his nightshirt, he crept outside and inspected the ground. Then, like a ghost, lifting his bare feet high so as not to stub his toes, he flitted from outbuilding to outbuilding, checking the padlocks. The pedlar's caravan he circled twice, as though to cast a spell upon it. Finally, he returned to the house, dressed, and sat in the window, brooding.

The morning sky was empty and vast. When the pedlar stepped down from his wagon, he glanced about and, seeing no-one, took off his shirt. Fedorchuk had already returned with the coal. He hid behind the shed door. Angela peeked from behind the blind of her bedroom window. The pedlar's body, from the edge of his pants to his neck and along his arms to his wrists, was solidly covered with tattoos. In the morning sun, his body glistened blue and red. There did not appear to be one piece of skin free of pictures.

All through the Interlake he was known as the pedlar. Although no-one called him that to his face, substituting *you* and *hey, there* for his name or avoiding calling him anything at all, once he had been called the pedlar, his first identity, that fragile endowment from parents whom no-one had ever met, whose existence and place in society no-one ever confirmed, was swept away. If anyone had come to town and had asked for him by name, no-one would have recognized who was wanted.

While many people spoke of him, it was seldom that they actually had anything to do with him. In any case, he was hard to find, for he never stayed long in any one place. Whatever his reason for coming to Eddyville, he had never settled. That robbed him of any chance of becoming respectable. In spite of the fact that most of the villagers were seasonal workers and regularly moved back and forth from town to fish camps or joined the freighting outfits for the winter season or disappeared into the bush to cut pulp, they all had a place of their own.

As soon as the pedlar had buttoned his shirt, Fedorchuk appeared, showed him the coal and the equipment and gave him some horseshoes that had been left from years before.

He watched the pedlar work, then asked in a disinterested fashion, as if it was of no consequence, "Have you ever thought of marrying?"

The pedlar was pumping a pair of hand bellows. He stopped as suddenly as if he'd touched a hot coal, then started again. His face had taken on the watchful look of a hunter hearing a piece of deadfall snap.

"I've thought of it," he admitted.

"Where do you come from?"

"East," he answered vaguely.

Fedorchuk lingered another minute or so but he asked no more questions.

When he entered the kitchen, his wife and daughter were making long rows of egg sandwiches.

"Spread the filling thinner," he ordered. He studied his daughter. All that revealed her pregnancy was the way she walked and that, he knew, would not mean much to an inexperienced man. "That pedlar," he said to neither of them in particular, "is not a bad fellow. He's buying a store for himself and settling down."

"He's got pictures all over himself," Sophie countered.

"His wife wouldn't need TV," he said. His eyes were fastened on his daughter's waistline. She was wearing a smock so he couldn't see if she had begun to thicken over her hips. "People do worse things to their bodies."

There was the sound of a hammer beating on steel.

"Tell her to take him some coffee," he ordered. "We're in business together."

With the doors open to the morning sun, the thick shadows of the shed had been forced back into the corners. The pedlar bent over the forge, his body enveloped by early-morning light. The air was pungent with the smell of steam and burning coal.

Angela appeared in the doorway with a white mug and hesitated on the threshold, pausing with the slender grace of a startled fawn. The pedlar, upon realizing who it was, stopped working and waited for her to approach. When she still held back, he went to her and accepted the cup. After drinking from it, he asked, "Will you dance tonight?"

"Dance?" she replied, uncertain of what he was asking.

"There'll be music."

Her eyes searched the corners of the shed as if seeking a shadowed place to hide and her face, which normally was smooth and fragile as the wild rose's that bloomed along the roadside, was drawn. Her cheeks were still pink, her nose still touched with a careless spray of freckles, but now the skin was pulled tightly at the corners of her eyes and mouth. Her eyes seemed deeper set and the flesh around them delicately bruised.

"There'll be lots to do," she said.

As she turned to go, he said, "I'm 32," but she made no sign that she had heard him. After she was gone, he remained where he was, watching the place where she had been.

When the horse was shod, he let it loose. He hated to see it tied and, if it began to stray, relied upon no more than a short, sharp whistle to bring it back. He leaned into his caravan and drew out a violin. The heat, as on the day before, lay over everything, silencing the fields. Here and there, a sparrow bathed in the dust. Occasionally, as if a child has released a spring, grasshoppers fluttered toward the sun then, before their leap had carried them more than a few feet, fell back.

Fedorchuk's house sat primly among a few scattered maples. It was white with blue trim and a blue roof. Although quite small, it looked a lot larger than it was because the front had been extended three feet on both sides. In the front yard, blue-and-white javex[2] bottles hung from the trees. They had been cut along the sides and the resulting flaps bent outward so that, in the slightest wind, they turned in constant circles. In the fall, when the wind was strong, the trees appeared ready to rise from the ground and shoot into the heavens.

An upended bathtub enclosing a plaster Mary and Joseph watching the Christ child faced the road. A sheet of glass had been set over the tub to protect the figures from the elements. At the moment, three dahlia bushes obscured the crèche; in the fall, however, they were cut back. On the twenty-first of December, in a yearly ritual he broke for no-one, Fedorchuk set out all the decorative figures he had collected over the years so that they staggered over the snowdrifts toward a star of Christmas set directly above the crèche—wise men leading a mixed parade of pink flamingoes, dwarves, deer, frogs, skunks and rabbits. Overhead, surrounding the star, he hung birds he had painstakingly carved and painted—robins, geese, bluebirds, jays, doves—and intermingled with these were a dozen handmade Messerschmitts and Spitfires.[3]

The pedlar tested the violin strings with his thumb. The sound of each string, as it was plucked, fell into the silence as precisely as a single drip of water striking the surface of an empty and resonant barrel. Satisfied, the pedlar began to play. He didn't play complete tunes but parts of many, some sad, some happy, some fast, some slow, as though he was remembering songs he had nearly forgotten.

---

2. Bleach.

3. German and British fighter planes of the Second World War (1939–1945).

Angela was sitting at the kitchen cupboard wrapping sandwiches in wax paper.

"Do you think many people will come?" she asked.

"The world is full of fools," her mother replied.

"I'll stay in my room if you want."

Her father was listening at the door. "She'll help serve," he said. "She's not there, people will talk. If they aren't already talking."

Angela's hands trembled so much that she was unable to fold the paper. "They don't know from me," she said, her voice husky with emotion.

Angered by the justice of her remark—in his first fury he had gone from house to house, drunk, seeking information—he spit out "Tell! Who needs to tell? That's been done for you. Do you think men keep secrets? He'll be bragging in the beer parlour every night." He beat his fist twice on the wall.

"She can't go out," Sophie said.

"She'll serve," he screamed. Rather than provoke him further, they both bowed their heads. He jerked around, stamped down the stairs and flung himself outside.

The pedlar's wagon sat directly before the window. It had large wheels, the spokes of which were the colour of weathered bone. The upper part sat well forward, so that there was about five feet of empty wagon bed at the back.

Sophie said, "He plays well."

"He's covered his body with pictures," Angela retorted.

After he had tried out various tunes for half an hour, the pedlar put away his violin. The plainness of his caravan was deceptive. He had, with the care and expertise of a master carpenter, constructed the caravan to perform a double duty. He unhooked the catches on the wall facing the house. As he swung the wall up, two long sticks unfolded in sections and these, he set into the sides of the wagon to form a canopy. He lifted up his bed and by setting it on its side with the bottom facing outward, he formed a counter. His goods he arranged in racks that pulled out from the walls.

Fedorchuk appeared, carrying a sawhorse under each arm. He put them down and went back for more. When he had six set out, he laid three sheets of plywood across them to make tables that were low enough for blocks of stove wood to be used as seats.

Angela arrived with an armload of newspaper, which she was to staple over the plywood. As she worked, the pedlar could not keep from glancing at her.

"Why did you come here?" she asked, without looking at him.

"I sell to all the farms," he replied. "My horse has a loose shoe so I had to stay."

She spread a layer of newspaper and tacked it in place. Her top, which fitted closely under her breasts and then flared outward, pulled up as she reached across the makeshift tables, baring a handspan of lightly tanned skin.

"Will you dance with me tonight?" he asked.

"I'm expecting someone," she answered confidently.

"I'm buying Grebon's store. I can pay half." He said it intensely as though it was of great importance.

"How come you've got pictures all over?"

He opened another box. "Would you like to see them?"

She stopped stapling and stood up. She had a spray of three anemones tucked behind her ear. While she watched, he undid his shirt and took it off. She came up close to study the crowded pictures.

"Why'd you do it?" she asked.

He put his shirt back on. "It's been a long time since I've shown those to anyone."

"You're like a picture-show," she said.

The pedlar chopped a block of wood into kindling. He crumpled some paper, set the wood around it, then hauled six cordwood sticks from Fedorchuk's pile. He laid these in a circle with one end of each log set on the kindling.

Fedorchuk came rushing over. "What're you doing?" he demanded.

"This is for the bonfire."

"What bonfire? You never said anything about a bonfire."

The pedlar clapped his hand to Fedorchuk's shoulder. "Leave this to me," he sighed. "I know what people like. A bonfire is good for another hundred dollars' worth of sales."

Just before six o'clock, the cars began to arrive. Fedorchuk had called every house within ten miles. He wanted to be certain that as many people as possible came. He was skeptical about their making any money but the pedlar's suggestion throbbed in his head. His determination not to have a grandson who was a bastard sat inside him like the tough, knotted root of an oak. A crowd quickly gathered around the caravan. The pedlar did a brisk trade.

"What you need," Fedorchuk said as the pedlar was frantically trying to make change and keep track of sales, "is a wife to help you."

As the pedlar had predicted, provided with food, liquor and company, nearly everyone stayed. Angela, under her father's watchful eye, wound her way through the crowd selling drinks and sandwiches. Over her white dress with its sprays of violets, she wore an apron with large pockets to hold her change. People were civil but the men held back, giving her no more than a nod or a curt hello. After she passed, their eyes followed her legs and buttocks speculatively. For her part, she kept her face as still as if it had been glazed with a fine layer of porcelain. Her eyes, however, never ceased to roam the edges of the crowd.

As darkness fell, the pedlar climbed down from his wagon and lit the bonfire. He wandered through the crowd, selling the last of his homebrew. Then, without anyone seeing him do so, he took up his violin and, standing well back in the shadows, began to play. To those lounging about the yard, the music seemed to rise from the ground. Then, slowly, as though he moved in a dream, the pedlar strolled into the light of the bonfire. He stood for a time, playing a high, wailing lament but then, before the last sounds had died, he broke into a wild, throbbing *kolamayka*.[4] From out of the darkness, a farmer, his face beaming, appeared with an accordion and, without waiting to be asked, joined in. Another farmer brought a guitar and still another rose from the table and, fitting two spoons between the fingers of each hand, began to beat out a steady rhythm.

The pedlar, turning this way and that as he played, was alternately exposed to the light of the bonfire and obscured by the shadows. His eyes glittered, then filled with pools of darkness and his teeth, even and white, flashed.

Gradually, the crowd formed a wide circle around the hub of fire.

4. A traditional Ukrainian circle dance tune, often played at weddings.

An open, grassy space lay between the crowd and the flames. There was only one break in this rim of bodies and that was where it met the caravan. The pedlar climbed onto the back of the wagon and stood above the crowd. The other musicians joined him. As the music grew louder and more insistent, a huge woman in a purple dress laughed out loud, grabbed a short, bald man standing beside her and whirled him into the cleared space.

Others followed until there was a solid mass of bodies moving around in an endless stream. The band, caught up in the excitement of its own music, didn't stop between numbers and, even when Fedorchuk urgently came forward to speak to the pedlar, the musicians went on.

"What's the matter?" the pedlar shouted above the noise.

"We're out of food. Have you got any?"

The pedlar shrugged and climbed into the caravan.

"That's it," he said when he returned. He handed over the better part of a case of canned sardines and kipper snacks and three loaves of bread.

When all the pedlar's food was sold, Angela came to sit on the steps of the caravan. The pedlar gave up his violin to a windburnt man in a white shirt and climbed down to join her. His face was flushed with exertion. Sweat ran down his face and disappeared into his beard. Angela didn't turn her head but sat staring straight ahead, her legs tucked back so she would not be stepped on.

"You don't dance," the pedlar observed.

Angela's face was pale and pinched and she looked as though she might cry. "There's time yet."

He nodded slowly and his face became heavy with sadness as though by his long isolation he knew exactly what she was feeling. He lifted his hand tentatively toward her cheek but lowered it without touching her.

The dancers whirled by, oblivious to everything but the music, their clothes creaking and rustling like sails in a high wind.

The dancing stopped at midnight. Within fifteen minutes the last car was gone, the yard silent. The fire had been reduced to embers. The pedlar moved about, picking up empty boxes and squares of wax paper and foam cups. From time to time, he dropped these onto the coals and, briefly, bright flames shot up, imitating the fire that had burned earlier. Angela had not moved from the end of the wagon. The dancing had been carried on without her and, now, she sat by herself.

When, at last, her father passed close to her, picking up papers, she said, in a plaintive, bewildered voice that made her sound like she was no more than twelve or thirteen, "No-one would dance with me."

"You fool," her father cried, grabbing her arm and flinging her toward the house so that she stumbled and looked, for a moment, like she might fall. "They'll ask you to dance, all right. But it won't be where anyone can see." He followed after her, making an obscene gesture by forming a circle with his thumb and finger and shoving his index finger through it. Savagely, he called, "Come here. Come here. Let's go to the car."

She fled to the house. The door slammed. Fedorchuk stood with his back to the fire, his body twitching and jerking. The pedlar stood at the corner of his caravan. He waited until Fedorchuk had composed himself, then carried an armload of paper to the fire. With his foot, he pushed the few remaining ends of wood onto the coals, then added the paper.

"Come and have a drink," he said. "I've kept a little. We can finish this in the morning."

He filled Fedorchuk's glass. Together, they squatted like savages around the fire, silent, brooding. The earlier gaiety pressed upon them like a heavy weight.

"We did well today," the pedlar said. "You must have made $200 gross and I've sold $400 worth of goods. That's $30 for you." He took some bills from his pocket. "It's $10 for the food I gave you." He counted out $20. "It's hard work," he said, holding out the money. "I'll be glad to be settled in one place."

Fedorchuk watched the pedlar with the corners of his eyes. He looked away into the darkness with the intensity of someone searching the sea for a sign of survivors.

"You'll need a wife," he said slyly. "You need two to keep a store open. You can't get no hired help that's any good today."

The pedlar shrugged his shoulders indifferently, but his face smoothed with expectation. "I've been careful with my money but if I'm to start a business. . . ." His voice trailed away. "She would have to be an asset."

Fedorchuk thought of the tobacco tin and the $500 he had secreted in it for emergencies. In other circumstances, the pedlar would have been unthinkable as a son-in-law. Now that no-one else would have his daughter, he was all that was available.

"You've been here a lot of times this year," he said.

"I pass this way when I go for supplies."

"No other reason?"

"I'm 32. I don't want to spend the rest of my life alone."

Fedorchuk tossed a wad of paper into the ashes. It smouldered, then burst into flame.

"I have a daughter," he said, "who's ready to marry."

"A wife's expensive."

"It takes two to run a store."

"Getting started . . ." the pedlar protested but there was no force in his voice.

Fedorchuk waited, letting the silence of the night settle between them. He had bought and sold a lot of cattle and he knew it wasn't wise to appear too eager. At last, when the only sound was the occasional tearing of grass as the black mare browsed invisibly beside them, he said, "I've got $300 put away. Instead of paying for a wedding, it could be a present."

The pedlar did not reply. Instead, he went to his caravan and lifted a pail from inside. The pump rasped and squealed and the water shot out like blood from a severed artery. He came to the grey patch of ashes and poured out a thin stream of water. Sparks and ashes flew up and the embers hissed and cracked and the air was filled with the bitter smell of drenched coals. When the fire was out, he said, "I'll tell you before I leave."

They concluded their agreement in the morning. The pedlar didn't speak to Angela. He and Fedorchuk shook hands and Fedorchuk gave him a hundred dollars. The pedlar returned directly to town, had a blood test, applied for a marriage licence and concluded the purchase of Grebon's store. He gave them an extra hundred dollars to be out in five days.

At nine o'clock in the morning, eight days later, Mr. and Mrs. Fedorchuk appeared with Angela seated between them. They parked in front of the Legion. A judge was in town to hear cases too serious for the local JP.[5] He took less than five minutes to perform the ceremony.

Afterward, Fedorchuk led them to the Sunset Café. They all sat in one booth and watched a group of boys try to cheat a pinball machine. Angela and the pedlar, whose name, on the licence, was John Crestyin, ordered hamburgers and french fries. Mr. and Mrs. Fedorchuk had chicken in a basket.

"People are talking about your buying Grebon's store," Fedorchuk said with a good deal of satisfaction. He had brought a mickey of homebrew in his jacket pocket and had added a little of it to their soft drinks.

"I'm going to put in a gas pump and go-karts," John replied.

Fedorchuk nodded his approval. "Kids got lots of money today."

When they were finished, they went to Fedorchuk's car and John transferred Angela's suitcase to the back of his truck. Fedorchuk handed him a white envelope covered with silver stickers in the shape of bells.

John waited until his in laws' car had disappeared, then gently touching Angela's arm, said, "Let's go home." He held the truck door open and helped her in.

Except for her responses when they were married, Angela had said nothing.

Instead of leaving, he sat and waited, working up enough courage to speak. In a few minutes, a Grey Goose bus pulled up beside them and the driver got off and went into the café.

"I came to your farm as often as I could," he said. "I never went to anybody else's as many times."

"I know," she murmured.

He opened the envelope Fedorchuk had given him and counted the money. There was $150. He took out his wallet and counted out the other hundred. He put the money on the seat so that it lay halfway between them.

"That's your wedding money," he said.

His store was five minutes from town. It sat on the corner of a crossroads facing the church where he stored his goods. On the other corner there was a community hall and an outdoor skating

5. Justice of the Peace, a local magistrate.

rink. The store was not large but it was large enough to make a living for a family. In the back there was a living space. In the small bedroom he had already set up a crib.

They lived together until the baby was born, then one day while he was behind the house feeding the black mare, his wife disappeared. The bus stopped for anyone who waved. He had heard it stop but had thought nothing of it, for passengers often stood on the corner. When he went inside, the store was empty, the child gone from its crib. His wife's suitcase and the wedding money, which she kept in a chocolate box on a closet shelf, were gone.

He stayed in the store for six months. Twice a day, when the bus went by, he stood at the window, watching to see if it would stop and, if it stopped, whether or not his wife would climb down. He kept the crib ready and left the house exactly as it had been when Angela left.

In the spring, he closed the store and went to the city for two weeks, wandering the streets all day and most of the night. When he returned to Eddyville, he sold the store at a loss to a retired farmer and disappeared for a second time. In a week, he reappeared, driving his caravan. There were only two differences: he no longer stopped at Fedorchuk's and on the lobe of each ear, he had a miniature daisy tattooed.

1978

Aritha van Herk
b. 1954

Born in Alberta, van Herk is a professor of literature and creative writing at the University of Calgary. She explores the roles of women in a sometimes aggressively male culture, especially in novels like Judith *(1978),* The Tent Peg *(1981), and* No Fixed Address *(1986), where women take on traditionally male roles, sometimes in disguise. These books are funny, sad, and defiant, challenging the spaces permitted to women. In works like* Places Far from Ellesmere *(1990) and* In Visible Ink *(1991), from which this piece is taken, van Herk plays with genre as well as ideas about language, criticism, and place. She balances parody with serious investigation of these topics..*

This non-fiction piece has elements of travel writing, personal essay, literary theory, story, and poem. In the frozen far north, van Herk finds herself outside words, outside a world of reading, writing, and speaking. Ironically, though, we read her doing all of those. She feels herself more written upon than writing in this unrelenting cold. Surveying a vast expanse, reminiscent of blank paper, she ponders writing. The not-so-empty text she finds herself in is written on by polar bears, seals, caribou, and foxes. In the absence of other writing, she reads their tracks.

The address to "The Reader" seems a leftover from a nineteenth-century novel, amusingly, deliberately, out of place in self-consciously Postmodern writing, where naming the north is best done in Inuktitut, not in English. As the writer jolts over broken ice, English becomes fragmented, only faintly intelligible in the face of a world which defeats it. There are readers in this arctic place, and writers. It is challenging to decide, though, which is which.

In Visible Ink

It is May. In the ordinary world, beyond these ridges of ice, beyond the edge of the Arctic Ocean, below the tree line, below the imaginary dashes of the Arctic Circle, it is spring: all the snow gone, the cold vanished in wait for next year's winter, and the sun a long light retiring into evening. This is the time of blackthorn winter, a metaphorical cold of the second week in May, unreal as this freezing surround is not.

It is the second week of May and I am sitting on the back of a komatik riding over the frozen Arctic Ocean. Everywhere that my eye reaches is dazzling snow, implacable ice, a white/blue/white/blue configuration of polar sea. The blue is not water but old, old ice, ice that has floed and shifted, that continually grinds against itself, that has never thawed, that will not melt for years. To the far edges of my seeing is frozen ocean, no skating smooth expanse but choppy with ridges, broken, a nordic goddess's tumbled cake pans.

I am travelling over this broken water, chopped and corrugated and firm as ground. The komatik I ride is not a comfortable mode of transportation. The traditional Inuit sledge, pulled by a snarlingly avid snowmobile, it bounces and bangs, rises precariously over icy ledges to slam down on the snow beyond. I am jarred to the very bone, the komatik creaking and groaning through this rutted and unpolished ice whose ironbound surface breaks and breaks.

And yet, in this distant, eerie world of ice, unwriting and unwritten, merely a cipher of human bone and blood, I am inexplicably, immeasurably happy: because I am finally free of words.

The Inuit make little distinction between land and water. In the extreme Arctic, living with an ocean that cracks open into water for only a few short months a year, they move from land to ice and ice to land with assurance of both's accessibility, opportunity for food and water and even shelter. For the Inuit, *the land* does not end where ocean begins: it only begins there. The ocean and its creatures are still the primary source of their survival. It is to the sea, its bountifulness, that the people of the north go. Inland is no preferred concept. There is ice and there is land. They are both, despite their fundamental difference, covered with snow. They are both consummate empagements, intagli[1] in the white of this endless folio.

May is relatively warm—between twenty and ten below[2]—and the Arctic sun keeps itself up for twenty-four hours, although it drops low on the horizon between ten at night and two in the morning. May is a good month for hunting seal, which come onto the ice to bask beside their holes. It is a good month to travel, before the ice breaks up. And I am travelling, by snowmobile and komatik, from Resolute Bay on Cornwallis Island to Grise Fiord (the most northerly of Canadian communities), on Ellesmere Island. Only Eureka and Alert lie farther north than Grise Fiord, and they are white man's stations (not settlements because no one lives there permanently), one a weather station and the other an army base.

You, reader, are entitled to wonder why I am doing this.

This journey's conditions are no more luxurious than riding in a komatik is comfortable. In order to stay warm, I wear five layers of clothing, I huddle beneath a caribou skin, and at night, I sleep on

---

1. Engravings.   2. On the Celsius scale. -20°C = 4°F.

that same caribou skin. The clothing I wear is of Inuit design, my kamiks warmer than any southern boot could imagine itself. Still, it is significantly below zero and wind intensifies the cold. Out on the open ice, the Arctic temperature prods every nerve, every bone. A reminder of where I am, and that who I am does not matter a writ in this cryptically enduring world.

I am not motivated by destination, although I appear to be enacting a journey: travelling between Resolute Bay and Grise Fiord. But departure and arrival are of no consequence. The six hundred odd kilometres we meander, the five days and nights we spend moving around Dungeness Point on Cornwallis Island, up Wellington Channel, across Devon Island, down Viks Fiord to Bear Bay, then across Jones Sound to South Cape on Ellesmere Island may offer the illusion of travel, but are essentially the measurements of measurement-obsessed man in the south. I know that when I return to my home in Calgary I will be bombarded with questions of measurement: how long did the trip take? how far did you go? how cold was it? Such determinations are meaningless here; they are completely effaced by the articulation of each moment's essense, this hereness, this nowness, and nothing else. I am suspended in an Arctic, not near Arctic or high Arctic but extreme Arctic, beyond all writing and its romance, beyond the intellectual comprehension or the geographical experience of most of those people calling themselves Canadians. I am simply here, reduced to *being*, breathing the ice-crystal air through my nose and into my lungs, stamping my feet against the granular snow to revive my circulation. I am at last beyond language, at last literately invisible.

Which is, reader, I confess, the state I ideally wish to attain. Finally, finally, in a life dominated by language, I am to some degree free of it, of having to speak and read and write. If you have read *Places Far From Ellesmere*,[3] you know that the time I spent at Lake Hazen in the northern part of Ellesmere Island taught me unreading, the act of dismantling a text past all its previous readings and writings. The landscape there, its delicious remoteness, calm unmeasurability, catalyzed my reading act into something beyond

3. van Herk, 1990. Its subtitle is *A geografictione: explorations on site.*

reading, enabling me to untie all the neatly laced up expectations of words and their printing, their arrangement on the page, the pages bound together into a directive narrative, that then refused to be static, but turned and began to read back, to read me, to unread my very reading and my personal geography. But reader, that was summer, however brief.

And yes, I always want to go farther, push back another boundary, cross another invisible line. Yes, reader, what I am about to confess is heresy, but I long, finally, to escape the page, to escape ink and my own implacable literacy, altogether.

Yes, I am anxious about reading, that I will always have something (enough) to read, that I will always have satisfying words for company, that I will never be stranded without a book, an addiction to reading the intimacies of language caressed by others. I am anxious about writing, that I will always find words to articulate my intellectual transgressions, the ideas I circle and circle, watching and writing. I force the two together, write about my reading, read my writing, refuse to function without one or the other implicated in some way, even if only silently, secretly, in my head. The conspiracies of bibliophilism.[4] I book my world, I word all possible collisions and encounters, I am enslaved to language, and I enslave my experience to language. Visible ink.

But reader, I am not complaining, not in distress. I do not dismiss language as primary and pivotal function, nor do I subscribe to the naive temptations of anti-intellectualism. Literacy is a powerful talisman; I do not decry its magic, and I hold it most precious skill of my life. My reading and writing sustain me beyond sustenance: they are both life and livelihood. Thus important enough for me to recognize that I should deprive—hardly even possible!—myself of them, even for a short time, to understand more completely their consequence in my life.

So reader, I have freed myself from words—at least, written and read words. For the first time since I learned to read at the age of five (and I am thirty-seven now) I am spending five days without reading a word, holding my breath. Although I took books with me to Resolute Bay, muttered and mumbled and weighed them in my

4. A love of books.

hand and turned them upside-down, I am now on the frozen reaches of the Arctic Ocean with no signs to signify for me, invisibled to print. And while the pedant will argue that there is always oral and mental language, that we carry our signs and their signifiers with us, that I am reading this Arctic I am suspended in; while you may be right that I struggle to find some corresponding signs to articulate my experience, ultimately this page of Arctic is not written or read by insignificant me. No, it (agent) reads and writes me. I am its text, impressionable, inscribable, desirous of contamination, a page open to its tattoo, marking.

How to describe or even begin to evoke this landscape? Reader, it occupies the realm of magic, a terrifying ecstasy. This world *is* beauty without adornment, beyond imagined possibility into almost hallucinatory beguilement. Here is a strange combination of mirage-like airiness and abiding perpetuity, a lapidification[5] of fluidity both physically daunting and terrifyingly lovely. So thin, so meager language seems in its capacity to re-cite this sublimity. Overwhelmed by this daunting and indifferent and resplendent Arctic, my paltry language is finally insufficient. I am merely filled with a wonder beyond wonder, invisibled by awe.

When we bump off Cornwallis Island and onto the ice, Resolute Bay quickly fades to a visual handful of coloured dust. No boundary crossed, a seemingly limitless surface tempting entrance, we are reduced to infinitesimal punctuation marks. The wind against my stinging face adjuratory breath, cold suffusing time.

Young seal sunning on the ice are still furry and gaze pure curiosity. Their open holes blue circles indiscernible in the blue snow around them, camouflaged as their black bodies are not. They slip into those apertures as slickly as their bodies' shape, phocine. The rough zigzagging of our path, ice blocks like chunks of cake thrust into blue and green pressure ridges. The komatik slams itself over a crease, then rises again and on a quick turn drives itself up against a huge block of ice, the runners stuck fast on either side. The snowmobile crescendoes fruitlessly, we climb out and back the komatik off, then push, heave it over the ridge. Right wooden runner cracked by the impact. Keep going, and at the next smooth spot we

5. Making into rock.

stop, Pijamini neatly saws a plywood piece to fit, nails from a tin, hammers the runner back to strength. Rough ice. Push more than we ride, climbing in and out of the komatik an ordeal wearing so many clothes, the cold cold, the sun hot. Bannock[6] dipped in hot tea. And again buckled ice, huge scrawling chunks that we inconceivably thread, intricate reading of passage a reminder that we are not travelling but static, finally arrested here, in the ice-landscape. And polar bear tracks, crossing before our tracks, lines of intersection conspicuous for their rarity (Wiebe, *Playing Dead* 50),[7] but here not rare, a veritable highway for the golden-white sovereign (*Thalarctus maritimus*) patrolling the broken ridges for absent-minded or sleeping seal. Stunningly huge, full-muscled and furred, moving effortlessly through the rough ice. Slows, walks, looks at us, scoops snow with his mouth, ambles away. Tracks, tracks, one bear days ago, a mother and two cubs a few hours ago, tracks, tracks, the creases of their padded feet clear as character, imprinted on the snow. Markings: claw marks on the ice side of an iceberg. And tracks, tracks, polar bear tracks followed by fox tracks, following the possibility of dozing seal, their flipper marks around ocean breathing holes. Our komatik tracks following themselves into tracklessness and invisibility. Writings of passage. Pressure ridges, lines where the ocean meets itself and forces its own force upwards. The tide under the ice, currents below solidity. Colophons.

I sleep on this cryptic and indifferent ocean. No hull between us, only solid solid ice, and the thin sail of a double-walled tent. Below me a down sleeping bag, then caribou skin, then foamy, then tent floor, then four inches of snow, then six feet of ice, then five hundred feet of freezing polar water cold as a fist; yet rich with fish, seal, whales, shrimp. They bump their noses against my sleeping skin, this sleep without dreams, without sign or reference, measureless and deep. Here or now invisible and unfathomable. Only sleeping. Written into sleep.

The komatik creaks and groans like an old ship battling high seas. Made of wood now (once bone and moss, skin and sinew and ice), but still lashed together only with rope, no nails. Pliable and

6. Flat, often unleavened bread, brought to Canada from Scotland.

7. Rudy Wiebe, 1989. A collection of essays about the Arctic.

resilient, it seems almost supple in its tracking of the snowmobile, giving into the jarring tilts and plunges of the fractured ice. And land no smoother in its dips and curves, banks under the runners, Devon Island wet and heavy with snow, even the cliffs jagged, and the sharp hooves of the elegant caribou, fleet as a sentence, a distant conjunction. Muskoxen lower their heads at us over a hill, then turn and drag their tracks away. Moss under the snow, and rock, screelings of gravel, emerging to stark cliffs as encarved as Egypt's Abu Simbel[8] and then ice again, a different phonation, ringing faintly under our runners.

There is hoarfrost on the snow, crystals of snow growing on snow, dazzling yellow and blue under the sun. Intricate, delicate rime of a cryological aesthetic, blades sometimes an inch long, and every frostflake exquisite construction. And patches of ice-fog, the contours of land and ice surreal disappearance, the komatik floating silently through silence, and I see grain elevators, caragana hedges, the parkland around the Battle River miraged onto this arctic. Reader, I have almost left myself behind, and in this ice-fog read my own erasure, written and engraved past, the language I am slave to made invisible. We drift eerily, and I cannot be sure if I sleep or wake, if we are suspended or moving. Still, when I lean over the komatik's side, the air rushes against my face, and I hear the steady hiss of the runners along the snow, another passing.

Sundogs[9] refract on either side of the glaring sun that my dark glasses cannot diminish. An omen surely, a reading of the snow and its polar perhelion, constituent activity. Warning or blessing, guide or direction? No sign. A polar body, coordinate, codeclination? Where am I? Vanished, effaced, unwritten. Invisibled.

Yes, reader, I have cited space and measurement, time and quotidian gesture, all in vain. I cannot read these reaches. I have no language for *arctic*, impossible to convey to you the sensation of stepping from a sleeping bag warm with night breath into an eagerly frigid weatherglass. I cannot measure polar bear tracks, or describe to you the habits of sunning seals. I am quite simply unable to write of or through this polar spell. Instead, it inscribes me, takes

---

8. Two elaborate temples: The temple of Ramses II and of Nefertari, near Aswan.

9. Bright spots on halos around the sun.

424 * ARITHA VAN HERK

over my cullible[1] imagination and its capacity for words: invents me for its own absent-minded pleasure. Effaces my referentiality, a transformation without continuity or chronology. I am re-invented by a great white page. Not *isolation* but complete invisibility, all causes and destinations blurred by causes other to causalities I believe I know.

And now know I do not know.

Even more extreme is the illusion of absence that is truly presence, tremendous presence, with no need to articulate itself narcissistically, being so much a *hereness*. This space, this landscape, this temperature, question all *document* and instead document me, without reference to an other; decipherable as glass I am, and fragile as any silenced voice, a tracement of arctic essence. No comparisons possible, no contrast available for measurement or ruler for diversity. This north is the gauge, and all else divergence. I am effaced, become an enunciative field, a page untouched by pen, no archive and no history. Happily.

Ah reader, what discourse is this? A snowmobile's diminished whine? The snowhiss of runners, the creak and groan of a labouring komatik, bouncing over what is not a smooth page of snow but a rough-toothed, jagged dimension, continually broken and interrupted by itself? As I am now, profoundly interrupted, disinherited of all that locates my literate self. Lost to text and language, become finally merely a text to be written. A flimsy alphabet. I could believe I have found the north in my own head (Wiebe, *Playing Dead* 113).

No, it has found me.

I wake in the morning to Pijamini's voice talking on the radio in the cooktent. He talks to Annie, whose husband he is, in Grise Fiord. The soft, throaty Inuktitut syllables bridge sleep and wakefulness, and signify morning—or is it afternoon, or evening? Time not measurable either, we seem to be getting up around two in the afternoon and travelling all night, but watches mean and matter nothing. Pijamini's voice speaks me into existence, creates my ears again. Huskily sibilant, his language in its rhythmic rise and fall delineates both where and who I am, unwritten here on the thick blue ice of the Arctic Ocean. Pijamini is short and solid, almost tiny, but

---

1. Sorting, arranging.

his strength is powerfully obvious, despite his age, sixty-four, he says with a grin. He is the leader, the most experienced person on this becalmed journey, and I ride in the komatik pulled by his snowmobile. How well he reads this invisible world, his body itself a signage, *polar* and *north* contained in his posture. He climbs icebergs to survey his north, then unerringly proceeds through the most impenetrable of ice fields.

He understands and speaks very simple (what does that mean, uncomplicated, uncluttered?) English, but he is at first shy, silent. Only after hours of pushing the komatik over rough ice, after I sight the first polar bear, does he say a word to me. I am ashamed that I use this rough, barbaric language, ashamed that I can speak to him only in the coldness of English, that I know no Inuktitut. I do not want to speak English with him, I want to talk to him in *his* language, the language of this overwhelming snowworld. I say nothing, smile only, push the komatik when it gets stuck. And then, in a sudden moment of desire, I ask him the Inuit word for sun. He tells me, poker-faced, a little curiously, and when I repeat it, he laughs. My epiglottal Dutch for once gives me some pronunciative advantage. "You speak good Inuktitut," he says. "Very good."

Reader, even invisibled to language, one makes what signs one can. I place my dwarfed foot in the foot-writing left by a polar bear. I circle every iceberg three times, on my right, reading myself a spell. And Pijamini names his world for me: cloud, sun, falling snow, snow on the ground, ice, bear, tracks, caribou, muskox, sundogs, iceberg, seal. He names his family to me, his seven children and their children. He names the points, the promontories, the edges of the islands as we pass. I repeat his namings, carefully shaping my mouth and tongue around their inflections and contours, and Pijamini laughs. "Very good, very good. You should come to Grise Fiord, study Inuktitut." He gives me *his* words, and thus names me, writes my invisible and unlanguaged self into his archaeology. I am written, finally, with that nomadic language.

Reader, reading you, I know you want me to put those words down here, reveal their magic incantation. Never. They are Pijamini's words, not mine, and if I was able to hear them and to mimic them, it was only through his agency. I will not raid them, or repeat them beyond the Arctic sea, beyond the secret worlds of ice.

They gave me a reading, read me in that space where I, trying to read anew, was finally written. Reader, this amulet of the first and most final of all crypto-frictions is that one can be disappeared and re-written in a language beyond one's own. Herein resides the ultimate illusion of text: you are not reading me but writing, not me but yourself; you are not reading writing but being read, a live text in a languaging world.

And yes, reader, in this cold May where I am finally freed from words, I am given a different text to carry south with me, to this oh so visible place full of words shouting everywhere, demanding to be read. In the silence after text dies, I will hear, somewhere in my buried polar ear, the soft Inuit voice of Pijamini naming the world in Inuktitut, and laughing.

1991

*

Glossary

actual reader the person who is reading a text, who may be like the implied reader—the one a writer might have been expecting—or very different because of differences in place, time, culture, or even language.

anecdote a sub-genre of fiction, telling a very brief, spare story about a particular event.

anthology a collection of works by different writers.

atmosphere the mood or feeling which hovers around fiction.

autobiography a text written about a person's own life, usually thought of as factual. A nonfiction sub-genre, autobiography may also make its way into fiction, implicity or explicitly.

bardic a bard was a poet in an oral society who constructed the stories of a people. This term is used for the voice of a writer who, similarly, speaks in a somewhat heightened language about a people, not primarily about his or her own individual experiences.

biography a factual account of a person's life other than one's own. Biography is one of the sub-genres of non-fiction.

character a person in a piece of fiction, usually a product of a writer's imagination, but often based on real people or at least on observations of real people.

character sketch   a presentation of a character as experienced by a reader, describing what sort of person this character seems to be. It does not examine or assess the methods a writer has used to create that character, but it often precedes such an exploration.

characterization   the process of presenting a character through dialogue, narrative description, actions, symbolism.

collage   literally, "glued" fragments which may not seem to connect but which have something in common: theme, form, imagery, language, character, or voice.

collection   a gathering of short pieces by the same author.

conte   a form used by French Canadian writers, similar to the oral fable, with a strong moral message and often with humanized animals as characters.

creative nonfiction   nonfiction which uses fictional elements like characterization and dialogue.

dialogue   conversation between two speakers.

diction   words chosen and the way of arranging them—formal, casual, slang.

discourse   the pattern of language use, including words, sentence structure, values, and attitudes.

documentary   realistic text that records what is seen or experienced, not imagined.

epilogue   a brief passage at the end of a work which may offer commentary on it.

essay   a sub-genre of nonfiction, which attempts to share an idea, an experience with a reader. The essay is characterized by a strong personal voice, close to the writer's, which may be subjective or objective. It is usually supported by specific observed details or by references to other writing.

fable   an ancient literary form, usually oral, told to teach a moral lesson. It often humanizes animals, plants, and natural objects.

feminist   an approach to writing or criticism which focuses on the portrayal of women in a text, the position of women in society, women's place in literary history, as well as women's lives, languages, or ways of writing.

flashback   a shift in chronology back to a time before the occurrence of the events being recounted.

flash forward   a shift in chronology to a time ahead of the occurrence of the events being recounted.

folktale   a short story which is retold orally, sometimes changing over time with different tellers, and becoming highly condensed, with strong focus on characters and plot.

formalist   an approach to literary criticism which focuses on internal aspects of the text, identifying them, and looking at their interactions or patterns, their contributions to the experience of reading, and their effects on a reader.

genre   from the French, meaning "kind" or "type." It refers to one of the literary forms, such as novel, short story, essay, or poem, implying that they have at least some characteristics in common.

gothic   a style of writing associated with the early nineteenth century, characterized by a brooding, ominous atmosphere of mystery, often in a neglected house which hides family secrets.

hypertext   a passage of writing for computer use, including links to other documents or Web sites.

imagery   the patterns of images in a text. Images create a picture in a reader's mind and appeal to the senses—sight, hearing, smell, taste, or touch—so their effects are sensual.

implied reader   the reader that a writer might have expected, visible in textual clues such as assumptions about knowledge, experience, and language.

intertextuality   references in one piece of writing to other pieces, usually well-known.

journal   a book of entries made regularly over a period of time, although not necessarily daily. Usually a journal includes reflections on what the writer is doing or thinking and so may be highly personal.

language   individual choices and patterns of word use which help to develop character or to set the tone of a piece of writing.

letter   a piece of writing addressed to a specific reader, usually a friend or acquaintance (although an "open letter" might be published in a newspaper, expecting a wide readership). A letter usually has a strong sense of the writer's voice and a clearly implied reader.

life-writing refers to what might earlier have been called autobiography. It includes any fiction or nonfiction piece which records a writer's life.

literary nonfiction a sub-genre of nonfiction, characterized by particular attention to the writing style, which may be more important than the actual content.

lyrical related to lyrical poetry (which in ancient Greece was accompanied by a lyre), characterized by musical language, melody, rhythm, and a personal voice.

magic realism a term applied to fiction and art of the 1960s and 1970s, especially in Latin America and Canada, where the real world is larger-than-life and seemingly magical events are not explained, but simply accepted.

metafiction fiction which is self-consciously fiction, explicit about the making of itself or fiction in general.

mock fable a sub-genre of fiction, which uses the characteristics of the traditional fable, but parodies or changes them in such a way that they remain recognizable.

Modernism the literary period from the early-to-mid twentieth century, characterized by a belief in art for art's sake, by an interest in psychology, in symbolism, in unity of form, in a distanced author.

monologue text spoken by a single voice.

narrative story-telling—a prime purpose of short fiction—which may show up as one of the techniques in nonfiction. It is usually seen as more vivid, more immediate, perhaps more memorable than expository writing.

narrator the storyteller, the identifying element of fiction. Writers enjoy playing with the creation of the narrator as with any other character in the story, placing the narrator in different **positions** in relation to the story told. A narrator may be **reliable** or **unreliable**, for any number of reasons. A **limited** narrator knows only some things about a story, because of some limitation of age, gender, bias, or awareness. An **omniscient** or all-knowing narrator knows all there is to know about the people or events in a text. A **first person** narrator speaks personally, using "I" or "we"; **a third person** narrator speaks of other people as "he," "she," "they." Often the events of a story and the reader's reaction to them are determined by the position of the narrator, which may shift or blur, moving closer or further away from a story. A narrator may be deliberately hiding—or may be looking back at events of an earlier time.

neo-Classical a term often applied to the writing of the eighteenth century, which valued wit, clarity, observation, recorded detail, and cleverness.

neo-historicism a school of literary criticism which investigates the social milieu of a piece of writing, the relationships between text and society, and connections with other time periods.

nonfiction writing which presents experiences, ideas, and attitudes directly through the writer's voice, without using the conventions of fiction such as plot, narrator, characterization, and dialogue.

parody a text that uses the style or form of another piece of writing and distorts it to some purpose of its own, mocking the original, extending it, or suggesting other ways of using it.

persona literally a "mask" from behind which someone speaks or writes; a created self or voice.

personal essay an essay that has a subjective tone or voice and presents the writer's views on a subject, as distinguished from a more formal essay, which reports information with little personal opinion.

poetic language or a form which uses some or all of the conventions of poetry: rhythm, rhyme, melody, and imagery.

plot a series of happenings arranged to create interest, suspense, surprise, and/or mystery.

plot line the pattern of incidents in a story.

Postmodernism a literary movement founded in the late twentieth century, which values fragmentation, collage, challenge to authority, inclusiveness, parody, ancient forms of literature, participation by a reader.

rationalism an attitude which emphasizes the importance of clear thinking, problem solving, observation, and clear objective reporting.

realism an approach to writing which emphasizes mirroring the real world.

Romantic   a term applied to writing of the first part of the nineteenth century, which values imagination, poetic language, and emotional or mystical response to setting or events.

saga   a sub-genre of fiction or poetry consisting of ancient northern long poems characterized by narrative, archetypal themes of death, love, revenge, loyalty, betrayal, family feuds, and a strong sense of a hovering and unpredictable fate.

setting   the place or time where something happens. It may be imaginary, realistic, interior, domestic, exterior, urban, small town, rural, wilderness.

short fiction   a term used to embrace all the sub-genres of short narrative, often used especially for contemporary pieces which may include several of those sub-genres, such as fable, saga, folktale or nonfiction genres such as journal, letter, and newspaper report.

short short story   very brief fiction, sometimes called postcard fiction, sudden fiction, or postscript fiction, which may focus on one of the elements of fiction such as character, event, voice, language, dialogue, or monologue.

short story   a sub-genre of fiction, developed in the nineteenth century. A narrative shaped to be read, with a traditional structure of an introduction, action rising to climax or insight, and action falling away to a conclusion.

short story cycle   a series of short stories linked by recurring voice, theme, setting, imagery, narrator, or language.

sketch   a short piece, usually nonfiction, focusing on one aspect of a character, situation, or event.

structure   the shape of a piece of writing, which may be linear, following a straight line of events or ideas; non-linear, circling around the main focus; collage, with fragments arranged according to some linking principle; serial, with a series of shorter fiction or nonfiction pieces.

sub-genre   in this collection, the main kinds or genres of writing are fiction and nonfiction. Within those overall categories, there are sub-types or sub-categories, referred to as sub-genres.

symbol   a concrete object which takes on an abstract meaning beyond itself. A symbol may have meaning within a piece of writing, a person's life, or a culture.

teaching tale a story, usually told orally, which has a strong message or moral, used to share knowledge or experience.

text a piece of writing, used to refer to writing in any genre or sub-genre.

theme the main idea explored in a text, which may be explicit (stated) or implicit (implied by events, characters, or the narrator). In nonfiction the theme is often central whereas in fiction it is more likely to be implicit. It may be supported or challenged by sub-themes.

travel writing writing which shares the experiences of a new (perhaps exotic) place. It is usually personal in tone, recording the writer's impressions.

trickster tale a story about the Trickster, a mythic artist figure who uses trickery and deception to achieve his purposes.

Victorian a term applied to the culture and writing of the second half of the nineteenth century, characterized by an interest in writing which offers social guidance, which provides a moral or a message, which is reticent about sexuality, and which often (perhaps unfairly) is seen as sentimental.

voice the "speaker" in a piece of writing, which is likely to be close to the writer's voice in nonfiction and which is the narrator's in fiction.

*

Permissions Acknowledgments

Claire Harris: "A Matter of Fact" from *Drawing Down a Daughter*. Copyright © Gooselane Press. Reprinted with the permission of the publisher.

Anne Hébert: "Québec: The Proud Province." Reprinted with the permission of Trust Banque Nationale.

Harold Horwood: "Of Frogs and Fairy Godmother" from *The Magic Ground*. Copyright © Harold Horwood. Reprinted with the permission of the author.

Isabel Huggan: "*Snow*" extracted from *Belonging: Home Away from Home* by Isabel Huggan. Copyright © 2003 Isabel Huggan. Reprinted by permission of Alfred A. Knopf Canada.

Linda Hutcheon: "The Particular Meets the Universal" from *Language in Her Eye*. Reprinted with the permission of the author, Linda Hutcheon.

J. B. Joe: "Cement Women" from *All My Relations*. Reprinted with the permission of the author.

Linda Kenyon: "Say for Me That I'm All Right" from *You Are Here*. Reprinted with the permission of the author.

Thomas King: "A Seat in the Garden" from *One Good Story, That One* by Thomas King. Published by HarperCollins Publishers Ltd. Copyright © 1993 by Thomas King. All rights reserved.

Annabel Lyon: "Song" from *Oxygen* by Annabel Lyon. Used by permission of McClelland & Stewart Ltd., *The Canadian Publishers*.

Alistair MacLeod: "To Every Thing There Is a Season" from *As Birds Bring Forth the Sun and Other Stories* by Alistair MacLeod. Used by permission of McClelland & Stewart Ltd., *The Canadian Publishers*.

Eric McCormack: from *Inspecting the Vaults*, copyright © Eric McCormack, 1987. Reprinted by permission of Penguin Group (Canada).

Rohinton Mistry: "Swimming Lessons" from *Tales from Firozsha Baag* (Penguin Books Canada, 1987, McClelland & Stewart, 1992, 1997). Copyright © 1987 Rohinton Mistry. With permission of the author.

Alice Munro: "Meneseteung" from *Friend of My Youth* by Alice Munro. Used by permission of McClelland & Stewart Ltd., *The Canadian Publishers*.

P. K. Page: "Usless the Eye Catch Fire" from *A Kind of Fiction* by P. K. Page. The Porcupine's Quill, Erin, Ontario, 2001.

Catherine Richards: "Excitable Tissues and Virtual Worlds: Art, Science and Techology." Reprinted with permission of the author, 2004.

Leon Rooke: "Art" from *Who Do You Love.* Copyright © Leon Rooke. Reprinted with the permission of the author.

Sinclair Ross: "The Painted Door" from *The Lamp at Noon & Other Stories* by Sinclair Ross. Used by permission of McClelland & Stewart Ltd., *The Canadian Publishers.*

Diane Schomperlen: from *Red Plaid Shirt: Stroies New and Selected* by Diane Schoemperlen. Published by HarperCollins Publishers Ltd. Copyright © 2002 by Diane Schoemperlen. All rights reserved.

Stephen Scobie: "Intertext, Love, Post, West" from *Ghosts: A Glossary of the Intertext.* Reprinted with the permission of the author.

David Suzuki: from *The Sacred Balance.* Copyright © 1997, 2002 David Suzuki, pages 1–8. Published by Greystone Books, a division of Douglas & McIntyre Ltd. Reprinted by permission of the publisher.

Audrey Thomas: from *Goodbye Harold, Good Luck.* Copyright © Audrey Thomas, 1986. Reprinted by permission of the Penguin Group (Canada).

Jane Urquhart: "Dreams" from *Storm Glass* by Jane Urquhart. Used by permission of McClelland & Stewart Ltd., *The Canadian Publishers.*

W. D. Valgardson: "A Place of One's Own" by W. D. Valgardson is reprinted from *Red Dust* by permission of Oberon Press.

Aritha van Heck: "In Visible Ink" from *In Visible Ink* (1991) by Aritha van Herk. Reprinted by permission of NeWest Publishers Ltd.

Every effort has been made to contact the copyright holders of each of the selections. Rights holders of any selections not credited should contact W. W. Norton & Company, Inc., 500 Fifth Avenue, New York, NY 10110, in order for a correction to be made in the next printing.